Law and Politics in the World Community

Law and Politics in the World Community

Essays on Hans Kelsen's
Pure Theory and Related Problems
in International Law
Compiled and Edited by
George A. Lipsky

1953
UNIVERSITY OF CALIFORNIA PRESS
Berkeley and Los Angeles

UNIVERSITY OF CALIFORNIA PRESS, BERKELEY AND LOS ANGELES, CALIFORNIA

CAMBRIDGE UNIVERSITY PRESS, LONDON, ENGLAND

LIBRARY OF CONGRESS CATALOG CARD NUMBER: 53-11241

Acknowledgments

THE EDITOR wishes to indicate his appreciation to those who in various ways have facilitated the preparation of the volume: to Professor Peter H. Odegard, for his original encouragement and approval of the project; to Regent Edward H. Heller, whose generosity made it possible; and to President Robert Gordon Sproul, whose support could always be relied upon. Thanks are also expressed to Mr. Horst Duhnke and Mr. Bohus Benes for assistance in translating contributions; to Dr. Helen Rosenberg, Mrs. Robert W. Tucker, Mrs. Georgia Eldridge, Mrs. Robert Stoker, and Mrs. Alvin Schulz for cheerfully accepting the drudgery connected with a work whose contributors are so widely scattered. I especially wish to indicate my appreciation of the invaluable contribution made to the quality of the volume by Mr. Maxwell E. Knight of the University of California Press; he was indefatigable in his efforts and applied to the editorial task a rare insight into the substantive and technical problems involved.

Acknowledgment with thanks is made to the following publishers and copyright holders for permission to use quoted material: American Institute of Pacific Relations, New York City; Cambridge University Press, New York City; Editions Domat, Paris; Harcourt, Brace and Company, New York City; Harvard University Press; Librairie Générale de Droit et de Jurisprudence, Paris; Librairie du Recueil Sirey, Paris; Little, Brown & Company, Boston; The Macmillan Company, New York City; Martinus Nijhoff, The Hague; Oxford University Press, New York City; Frederick A. Praeger, New York City; Springer-Verlag, Vienna; Stevens & Sons, London; The University of Chicago Press; The University of North Carolina Press; Professor Josef Dobretsberger, Graz, Austria; Professor Alf Ross, Lyngby, Denmark. G. A. L.

Contents

Part One: General Problems

Claims Commission, Mexico City, 1939–1940; later attached to the U.S. Maritime Commission and served as Captain in the Judge Advocate General's Office, U.S. Army; represented the United States at numerous international conferences as Assistant Legal Adviser of the U.S. Department of State; taught law at Ohio State University, 1947–1949; appointed United States Member, Inter-American Juridical Committee, by the President, and also served as Alternate Delegate of the United States to the First Meeting of the Inter-American Council of Jurists at Rio de Janeiro, 1950. U.S. Agent, Jones Claim against Norway. Author of *The International Responsibility of States for Denial of Justice* (1938), and of numerous contributions to legal periodicals in the United States and abroad.

The Geneva Conventions of August 12, 1949 279

By JOSEF L. KUNZ, Dr. Jur.

Professor of Law, University of Toledo, College of Law. Juridical Director, Austrian League of Nations Union, Vienna, 1920–1932; Assistant Professor of International Law, University of Vienna, 1927–1932; Professor, Académie de Droit International, The Hague, 1929–1932; between 1948 and 1953 Visiting Professor, National University of Mexico Law School, the Inter-American Academy of Comparative and International Law, Havana, University of California, Berkeley, Southern Methodist University School of Law, Dallas. Member, American Society of International Law, Foreign Law Association, Société de Législation Comparée of the Institute Argentino de Filosofia Jurídica y Social; honorary member, Mexican Bar Association; corresponding member, Hellenic Society of International Law; member, Board of Editors, *American Journal of International Law* and the *XXth Century Legal Philosophies Series* of the Association of American Law Schools. Author of *Die völkerrechtliche Option* (1925–1928); *Gaskrieg und Völkerrecht* (1927); *Die Anerkennung von Staaten und Regierungen im Völkerrecht* (1928); *Die Staatenverbindungen* (1929); *L'Option de Nationalité* (1930); *Die intrasystematische Stellung des Art. IX des Völkerbundpaktes* (1931); *L'Article XI du Pacte de la Société des Nations* (1932); *Die Revision der Pariser Friedensverträge* (1932); *Kriegsrecht und Neutralitätsrecht* (1935); *La Teoria Pura del Derecho* (1948); *Latin-American Philosophy of Law in the XXth Century* (1950); Editor of *Latin-American Legal Philosophy*.

Introduction

THIS VOLUME presents some central problems of international law and offers supplementary material for use in the study of cases. The contributors are among the foremost teachers and publicists in international law. The editor and the authors have aimed to produce a book that will, in addition to its general usefulness, highlight the teachings of Professor Hans Kelsen in the fields of international law, public law, and legal philosophy.

This introductory essay is intended as a survey of the system which Hans Kelsen has been teaching for fifty years, and of the context in which his work is to be understood; and to present the relevance of Kelsen's theory to the problem of international relations.

Professor Kelsen has been called by Dean Roscoe Pound "the leading jurist of the time." But Kelsen moves in a wider sphere. An extraordinary teacher with a powerful personality he has turned a host of students into disciples. Distinguished teachers speak of having "sat at his feet." Such language reveals a strong emotional attachment to a teacher with the capacity for great friendship. But that alone would be insufficient to explain the power of attraction of the original Vienna School of Law, founded by Kelsen. This school is the source of the Pure Theory of Law, surely the most significant and persuasive development in legal philosophy in the twentieth century.

In considering Kelsen's contribution, it is important to distinguish his methodology from his views reflecting his values. To illustrate this distinction: The Pure Theory of Law provides a method of determining the content of positive international law, of testing its validity, and of identifying the area of its operation. The Pure Theory of Law is—as Kelsen repeatedly affirms—a theory of positive law, not a speculation about the just law.

This separation of a theory of positive law from a philosophy of justice has been rejected by some of Kelsen's students. But even when his students have gone on to found careers of their own and in so doing have produced significant points of divergence from his doctrine, they have continued almost unanimously to acknowledge their indebtedness to his method. The greatest tribute in this respect is offered by those who are advocates of an objective natural law or who in some manner reject Kelsen's postulate to eliminate the problem of a natural law from the field of science of law—his view that a doctrine of natural law is a metaphysics of, not a science of, law. The present volume cantains contributions from such persons. Their willingness or desire to be included testifies to the fact that for them the highest form of intellectual life is beyond rancor.

The power of the Pure Theory of Law is revealed in the number of its adherents—and in the vigor of its opponents. It has offered to those concerned with its problems a magnificent structure to build upon, a tool to modify and to refine. Kelsen has never insisted upon rigid adherence to his formulations of doctrines. With humility he has invited those whom he has influenced to be creative, to scrutinize the basic theory, and not to be satisfied with its present formulation.

The essence of genius is often simplicity, the capacity to reach the heart of the matter and to reveal it in relatively elementary terms. Kelsen's thought appears often engagingly simple and is therefore highly compelling. In politics—where we can never dispense with the artist who formulates and selects the values which he recognizes intuitively as the community consensus—the analytical economy of Kelsen often reduces complexity to an unexpected simplicity. The Pure Theory of Law has, as William Ebenstein points out, the core function of determining what the law is or what its possible interpretations are. The Theory produces a key to understanding—a key that permits a proper distinction between science of law as prescription and law as description. It permits, in other words, a division between a normative order, on the one hand, and the total of psychological and other environmental factors conditioning the content of law, on the other. Kelsen asserts that confusion of these two spheres is the main weakness of sociological conceptions of the law.

The use of Kelsen's key to understanding is often denied men of smaller stature. Those who accept it as the opener of all doors sometimes betray an unfortunate rigidity of mind and reject refining argument. They resent subsequent jarring of their convictions; they are unreceptive to continuing influence. This surely has been Hans Kelsen's experience with some of his followers at an inadequate level of maturity. These have refused to proceed with their own evaluations, and in consequence their own product falls short of comprehension of the teacher. The latter must be as thoroughly protected against the ministrations of disciples as against the onslaught of enemies.

Kelsen's system is so complete, so strong is its appeal, that it has evoked the strongest attachments and the most ardent opposition. Proposing to be explicit as a science, it offers the occasion for close inspection and consequent definite acceptance or rejection. Such a situation provides a test of the adequacy of discipleship and the effectiveness of opposition. In the Anglo-American world, where the drive to resolve conflicts among first principles has not been strongly felt, the ambition to fulfill wishes by giving values more appeal through dressing them in a garb of scholarship may take the form of attacks upon those who disturb the disguise or the illusion. This happened to Kelsen. He has never hesitated to tear off disguises or shake illusions. Thus he endured not only the disadvantages of inadequate discipleship but the attacks of those who resent the shattering of their calm.

The desire to capture in a few words the essence of Hans Kelsen is hard to fulfill. A beginning might be made by stating that he brings to the study of law a rigorously logical analytical technique whose main purpose is to separate the law from other factors. Kelsen propounds a science of law as distinct from a sociology of law. Thus Kelsen stands as the principal expositor of one of the two major theories of law of the present day—the normative in contradistinction to the sociological theory.

The latter theory has for its object the actual behavior of human beings, making, applying, and obeying and disobeying the law. The specific science of law, according to Kelsen, has for its object the law as a system of norms, prescribing how men ought to behave. These norms are characterized by the fact that they try to bring about the desired behavior of men by prescribing coercive acts as sanctions, that is to say, as consequence of the contrary behavior. In this sense law is a coercive order; and in this sense the science of law is a normative science—a science the object of which are norms. It does not describe how men actually do behave, but how men—in accordance with the existing law—ought to behave.

From this point of view Kelsen presents in a new light the relationship between law and state. Since the state, too, is a normative order—and by its very nature a coercive order—law and state are not, as the traditional doctrine assumes, two different entities, according to Kelsen. The state is law or, more precisely formulated, the state is a legal order. This is that part of Kelsen's theory which has aroused perhaps the most passionate objections. However, it has not been shaken by logical arguments.

Kelsen as a man is extraordinary in many respects—in his work schedule that has produced one of the most extensive bibliographies of modern times presenting scientific expositions on legal and general philosophy and international law; in his capacity so to order study and preparation that his career could be launched in teaching and research at a very early age; in his ability to go directly to the heart of the matter, clearly distinguishing science and politics; and in his faculty to encompass vast systems of data and to expound them in a meaningful theory.

How were these qualities of mind and scholarship produced that make Kelsen great? Some may reply that Kelsen is the product of the end of his epoch—the nineteenth-century period of the apotheosis of science—and has persisted into an era that cannot understand him fully. But what Kelsen represents in the forward movement toward the necessary distinctions, on the whole front of intellectual inspection, between the normative area of freedom and the area of casual determinacy, can never be considered a part of a past epoch. To hold otherwise would be to hold that the triumphal march of man from transcendental or secular orthodoxy toward courageous awareness of his true predicament will be halted. In this age of hideous conformity, Kelsen himself may regret the departure of the spirit of the older century and reject the implications of the new. But the truth of his insights will remain true as long as there are intelligences to implant a pattern upon the cognitive object. No theory concerning the sociology of knowledge, confusing special knowledge with a theory of knowledge, can be successful in establishing a vulgar relativism that will overthrow the truths of Kelsen's contributions to a theory of knowledge.

Kelsen's most recent major work, *The Law of the United Nations,* is a book that has not overly endeared him to foreign offices. The controversy that it has occasioned is typical of the controversies that have divided Kelsen and his Pure Theory from those who define law as the basic norm "plus factors" (accident, contradiction, confused thinking, generalizations from inadequate data, and so forth). *The Law of the United Nations* charges that the United Nations Charter should have been composed with as much scientific exactitude as possible in order to clarify and reduce the number of possible alternative interpretations. Kelsen does not assume that conflicts of interpretation can ever be entirely removed. It remains the function of politics to select the interpretation to be used. To assume, as the sociological school does, that the law of the United States is only a "process"—never to be comprehended in a moment of time as "structure"—is to perpetuate the confusion between the function of legal science and the function of politics, the confusion between the legal norms of the Charter and the factors that condition them. If Kelsen's approach to the composition of the Charter had been followed, the strength of the concept of an international superior law would have been increased; also increased would probably have been the force of a legal dynamism in the international sphere that would have provided some greater opportunity for political compromise. Instead, the contrary approach of not seeking precision of legal statement was followed on the egregious assumption that for a normative order to function as a "process" or grow as a "political instrument" it must eschew precision. For Kelsen, the latter approach merely perpetuated undiluted international power politics.

The final result of drafting the Charter as a "process" is to bring it into disrepute as it ever more obviously becomes the instrument of the particular power or group of powers able to insist upon the decision that serves their interests among the welter of possibilities. No one can realistically suppose that the time has come when power politics can be removed from the international sphere; it would be fatuous to suggest that power politics have been removed even from the national scene in the United States. Politics will always remain to individualize norms, and the power component of the various interests will be forever present.

The wise decision for mankind, seeking security and consensus, is to construct an exact international legal order. The remarkable view that a legal instrument has greater validity because of its contradictions is certainly questionable. A legal instrument in the form of a constitution cannot contain all the individual norms that will be applied in particular cases; the instrument should develop as precedents multiply. But it is difficult to see how it can be expected to develop on the basis of contradictions—especially if it is also recognized that real growth can come only through international coöperation.

Kelsen's preference is for the conception that there exists an international law to which primacy should be assigned. To be sure, this conception is as much based on a value as is the view that assigns primacy to national law. Kelsen is quite aware of this fact. He emphasizes that the choice between the two views can not be determined by the science of law. What the science of law can do, and necessarily must do, with respect to the question of the relation between international and national law, is only this: to insist upon the unity of a system comprising both. This conception constitutes the so-called monistic view. Kelsen dismisses as logically impossible the pluralistic (or dualistic) conception that national legal orders are unrelated to international law. But Kelsen believes that, within a monistic view, it is possible to assume either the primacy of national law on the basis of which international law would have validity, or the primacy of international law, on the basis of which national law would have validity. It is not possible, says Kelsen, to assume the validity of the two types of legal orders as unrelated systems.

The nations of the world may continue to refuse to assign primacy to international law and to insist on those traditional devices of international relations that have produced catastrophe in the past and may produce extinction in the future. Kelsen is fundamentally an optimist. At least he realizes that operating on the assumption that the nations will forever adhere to their atavistic devices guarantees that the fears of the pessimists will come true. Kelsen's opponents may not all be pessimists, yet they counsel courses reflecting the pessimistic view that there are no new ways out of the chaos of international affairs.

Kelsen's interpretation of the law of the United Nations is an organic product of his legal philosophy. His distinction between science and politics results in a suggested course of action that might, if politically feasible, resolve some of the chaos of international affairs. Against this suggestion the sociological school of so-called "political realism" can only give the barren counsel to recognize an untransformable reality.

Kelsen's system is politically significant because it is a scientific system. In the nineteenth century and after, many thinkers have claimed to be "scientific." Among these, two different types may be distinguished: Those who believe that the present is so completely known that vast explaining generalizations can be safely made; and those for whom science is a call to humility and realization of the limitations of the human mind. Of the first type, Marx is the outstanding example, whereas Kelsen is typical of the second. Marxism claims to propound scientific socialism but, from Kelsen's standpoint, fails to establish its pretensions because it confuses the reality of history understood in a pattern of long-range prophecy with the subjective values preferred by socialists. Marxism forever turns its back upon the process of knowing what the function of science can be. Hans Kelsen stresses the objectivity of science, that is to say the separation of the rational description and interpretation of an object from the value judgments of the interpreter; even if the object of science is values, as e.g. in legal or political science.

In the area with which Kelsen is especially concerned, law and legal philosophy, science is limited to the inspection of what science can know and thus to the building of a Pure Theory of Law—unwarped by conceptions of what law should be.

A basic factor in Kelsen's thought is, as mentioned, the whole nineteenth-century revolution in science with its trend toward secularism: Kelsen represents a materialist position. Another factor in Kelsen's system, related to the first, is the great influence of Immanuel Kant, especially the latter's distinction between the "is" and the "ought." Kelsen, like Kant, makes this distinction. As Kant assumes *a priori* laws, so Kelsen assumes a *Grundnorm,* a basically presupposed norm system, in the law. It is a system which can be stated in a structure of words, a structure from which the validity of all subordinate normative system finally stems. Kelsen denies, however, that *Grundnorm* amounts to any objectification in external reality of any so-called "values" in terms of which right and wrong, good or bad may be judged. The scientist is given the opportunity to inspect the law as it is found in a structure of descending levels from, say, a national constitution to a village ordinance. Validity will turn upon the question of whether men do act ordinarily in conformity with the "ought" presupposed by the norm and whether those having the obligation to apply the norm do so ordinarily.

In view of Kelsen's training in Continental jurisprudence it is natural that he approached legal philosophy from the standpoint of theoretical and conceptual analysis. The law on the Continent is regularly conceived as given or existing. It does not follow that the rigorous analysis that Kelsen brings to bear upon the law in emphasizing the law as existing can deal only with the formal reality of a general norm and of necessity must neglect the individualization of the norm in particular cases. Anglo-American jurisprudence, acquainted with the apparent actuality of the law as always only "becoming" or, perhaps, as existing only in the individual case, stresses the importance of the factors conditioning the process. The strongly analytical approach is important; it is also important to be aware of the conditioning factors. The former is certainly more related to a science of law as law.

Hans Kelsen has expressed the wish that he might have chosen the fields of mathematics and physics. He might thus have been spared, in some degree, the harassment of doctrinal conflict in the social science—conflict he never attempted to evade. Unquestionably his mind is peculiarly suited to the exercise of speculation in mathematics and physics. But, of course, there is equal need for such qualities of mind in the fields which he has chosen—fields sufficiently studied by those with aesthetic or intuitional capacities. Where there is an aesthetic temperament wedded to a scientific drive, the combination is bound to approach perfection.

The fraternity of scholars may be thankful that Kelsen's interests are what they are. Billions of dollars were spent to release nuclear energy and fashion the atom bomb. No such investments were made in the fields chosen by Kelsen in which his intellectual contributions have been invaluable. It is to be hoped that those scholars who have been inspired by him will continue with some of his energy to inspect similar problems with the determination that he has shown.

July, 1953 George A. Lipsky

Part One: General Problems

QUINCY WRIGHT

Law and Politics in the World Community

THE DISTURBED STATE of the world in the middle of the twentieth century may be explained in many ways. Some emphasize the uncoöperativeness, if not aggressiveness, of the Soviet Union; some the inadequate coördination of the democracies; some the failure to stabilize the balance of power; some the imperfect organization of the United Nations; some the exaggerations of the concept of national sovereignty; some the rapid shrinking of the world through technological invention; and some the lagging development of a sense of world citizenship throughout the globe. Others would place major weight upon the destruction and impoverishment resulting from the world wars. Many other explanations have been given, each with a measure of truth and each suggesting remedies which might be applied. In this article, however, I present as one explanation the unbalanced relation between international law and international politics in the world community.

Law and Politics

No society can exist without both a system of law and a system of politics. The stability of the society depends upon the relationship between these two elements. Effective law gives reliability to social institutions and permits men to calculate many aspects of the future, but if not continually modified by a suitable system of politics, it tends to perpetuate a *status quo* which will presently prove unadapted to the conditions of a changing world.[1]

Politics gives flexibility to society and permits adaptation of institutions to changes in the centers of power, in the potentialities of technical progress, and in the ideals and aspirations of men, but if not regulated by law, it fills men with anxiety, discourages planning because of the unpredictability of the future, and tends to degenerate into warfare so destructive as to jeopardize civilization.[2]

Law is the process and the art by which a society compels its members and the sub-groups within it to observe those purposes, principles, and standards considered essential by the society or by its government.[3] Observance of law is never absolute. Jural law differs from scientific law in that violation of its rules is not only possible but is occasionally to be expected. Jural law is not a mere generalized description of how the society and its members behave, but a generalized description of how the society thinks, with such conviction that it provides means of enforcement, that they ought to behave. Jural law anticipates that there is such uniformity of culture and opinion in the society where it operates and that its rules so conform to prevailing customs and beliefs that most of the members of the society will conform voluntarily. Yet with the considerable variability of human personality and the cultural differences to be expected in large and progressive societies, occasional nonconformity is to be expected. If the nonconformers are not numerous and their departures from, and violations of, law are suppressed and remedied, the law is vindicated, and the society exists and is stable in the sense that the important aspects of its future can be predicted with reasonable reliability at least for a considerable period of time. The law constitutes a valid description, not only of the society's ideals and values, but also of the actual behavior of its members. In a satisfactory functioning system of law "ought" and "is" are united.[4]

Politics is the process and the art by which a group, whether a nation, a party, a faction, or an association, seeks to realize its purposes, principles, and standards against the opposition of other groups.[5] Politics tends to degenerate into war, and war into absolute war. Groups tend to become so convinced of the value of their goals that they will utilize any means to achieve them, even the total annihilation of opposing groups. If the powers of the opposing groups are about equal, the intensity of the conflict increases. This tendency, however, may be moderated by physical necessity, by respect for moral standards, or by the combination of the two which is called law.

A political system may develop such a balance of power that any opposition group attempting to destroy the system will be faced by an insuperable combination. Such a power combination tends to be formed when many groups fear that the conquest of one of their number will so augment the power of the conqueror that he will threaten their own future security. The community of nations has at times enjoyed stability under the balance of power, but in a world tending to divide into two camps, each equipped with weapons which give great advantage to the offensive, it is difficult to see how much stability can develop by such a balance-of-power system. There are not enough powers to form insuperable combinations. The power which thinks that time is running against it is tempted to initiate hostilities while it still has a chance of winning.[6]

Moral standards shared by all groups in political contention may limit the violence of the methods which any will resort to. The standards of custom usually impose such limitations on primitive societies, as did the standards of religion on medieval society in Europe. But in the contemporary world community there is no universally accepted body of custom or of religion, and there are few philosophical or ethical ideas shared by all peoples. The experience of the two world wars and of the cold war which has followed give little hope that moral standards will limit the methods which politics will employ in the relations of sovereign states.[7]

Is it possible that certain precise rules limiting the methods of politics can be backed by such organized force that prudence will counsel observance of the rules by governments, even if moral sense does not? Can law be developed to regulate politics among the members of the community of nations as it does within the nations?

Law has two aspects—essentialness and effectiveness. Law consists of those rules which a society believes are so essential that they ought to be enforced, and which at the same time are so effectively enforced that they can be relied upon. These two aspects may not be equally evident in a particular legal system. The law-making authority may pronounce rules to be law because the society considers them essential, but may fail to provide effective means of enforcement. Or the law-administering authority may enforce rules or decrees which do not seem essential, or even tolerable, to the members of the society.

Law in practice varies between the two extremes of ineffective advice on the one hand and intolerable tyranny on the other.[8]

The latter condition tends to prevail where the society has no important subgroups with political objectives, and consequently the force at the disposal of the central organs of the society to enforce its law is almost infinite in comparison with that of any group likely to oppose it. In such circumstances, the government is likely to make and enforce decrees to maintain its power with little regard for the public opinion of the society.[9]

The former condition tends to prevail where the society has within it political subgroups which rival it in power. In such circumstances the force at the disposal of the central organs to enforce law is frequently faced by oppositions which cannot be dealt with by normal methods of law enforcement such as police action, judicial administration, and execution of judgments.[10]

This is the situation of the community of nations. In theory this community has a law which substantially all states have solemnly agreed is essential for civilization and should be enforced. Yet, in fact, its power is so little superior to that of certain of its members that it is often obliged to deal with opposition to the law by political rather than by legal procedures. Under such conditions, law cannot effectively limit political methods. Balance in the relation of groups, subgroups, and supergroups is the condition most favorable to political stability and to law which is both just and enforced.[11]

The Law of the World Community

Let us consider some of the principles of law generally accepted by the community of nations and the problems which have arisen in connection with their enforcement. I will assume that there is not only a community of nations, but also a universal, although undeveloped, society of mankind. This assumption is controversial,[12] but I think the history of the world, since the age of discoveries in the fifteenth and sixteenth centuries brought all sections of mankind into permanent contact with one another, gives sufficient evidence of the existence of such a society. Men in all sections of the world have been trading and communicating with one another with increasing abundance. From these contacts common standards and common interests have emerged, and have been to an increasing extent formally stated in a network of bilateral and general treaties. These principles have been applied in numerous international adjudications and arbitrations and have been maintained and formulated into a system by the activities of diplomacy, by juristic writing, and by international organization. The United Nations Charter asserts certain universal principles concerning the rights, not only of states, but of individuals. It has organized procedures to promote and maintain these rights and to enforce some of them, not only against its members, but also against all states, against other groups, and even against individuals. However inadequate these procedures may be, it cannot easily be denied that there is a universal society organized by formal law as well as by systems of communication and coöperation.[13]

Among the principles of this law are the following:

1. Sovereign states are free to govern within their territories and to formulate and pursue foreign policies except where international law imposes limitations. The so-called "domestic jurisdiction" of states is the residual sphere of free action remaining to states outside of the limitations which continually developing international law imposes by establishing general principles, special rules, and the competence of international agencies.[14]

2. Among these limitations are the rights of other states defined by general international law. All states are entitled to equal territorial integrity and political independence; to freedom of navigation upon the high seas; and to respect for diplomatic and other official representatives and, in lesser degree, for their nationals abroad. All states are obliged to observe treaties to which they are parties, and to acquiesce in the exercise of powers given to national or international agencies by such treaties. The definition of these limitations constitutes the body of traditional international law.[15]

3. Another limitation prohibits aggression or the use of armed force as an instrument of national policy. This limitation has its roots in the distinction between just and unjust war emphasized in the writings of medieval and early modern jurists.[16] It was largely neglected in the practice and theory, of eighteenth- and nineteenth-century international law, but has developed since the Hague Conference of 1899. The first convention accepted at this conference asserted that war was a matter of concern to all states and that nonparticipants in a controversy should attempt to prevent war by the tender of good offices and mediation. Many treaties were made during the period before World War I which required states to abstain from hostilities under certain circumstances or during a period of time in which pacific modes of settlement would be attempted.[17]

These ideas were given greater emphasis in the League of Nations Covenant which forbade resort to war during a period of nine months while the League organs attempted peaceful settlement; which forbade aggression against the territorial integrity and political independence of another member; and which vested League organs with continuing authority to employ peaceful methods in order to prevent or stop hostilities. The practice of the League developed these principles and sought to establish effective procedures to maintain them, even declaring that resort to aggressive war was a crime.[18]

By the Kellogg-Briand pact of 1928, all states of the world, except three Latin American republics which, however, bound themselves to the same principles in the Argentine anti-war treaty of 1934, condemned war, renounced it as an instrument of national policy, and agreed never to seek the settlement of any controversy or dispute except by peaceful means. This treaty was the culmination of the movement to "outlaw war" which originated in the United States.[19] The profound effect it had on legal thought and on state action was illustrated in subsequent history. The Kellogg-Briand pact was invoked on the Soviet invasion of Manchuria in 1929 and Soviet forces were withdrawn. Its invocation in the Japanese invasion of Manchuria in 1931 led to participation by the United States in efforts of the League of Nations to stop this aggression and to acceptance by the United States and the League powers of the Stimson Doctrine asserting that no party to the pact should recognize as legal any title to territory acquired by an aggressor. The pact was again invoked on Mussolini's invasion of Ethiopia in 1935. Although the Stimson Doctrine was reasserted, many countries did eventually recognize the changed situation brought about by this aggression, but only after the League of Nations had by formal resolution permitted them to do so.[20] After World War II, the United Nations restored both Ethiopia and Manchuria to the status they had before these aggressions.

The pact was again invoked on Hitler's invasions of Austria, Czechoslovakia, Poland, the Low Countries, and Norway. France and Great Britain engaged in active hostilities to resist these aggressions. The United States and the Latin American countries recognized these acts as violations of international law as embodied in the Kellogg-Briand pact and assumed that the normal neutral obligations of impartiality among belligerents did not apply.[21] As a result the United States, before entering the war, gave assistance to the countries resisting aggression especially through giving fifty destroyers to Great Britain in exchange for naval bases in the summer of 1940; through passing and implementing the Lend-Lease Act in the spring of 1941 and the joint declaration with Great Britain known as the Atlantic Charter in August of that year.[22]

After the United States became involved in direct hostilities following the Japanese attack at Pearl Harbor in December, 1941, and the declaration of war by Hitler which shortly followed, it took the initiative in gaining general consent to the Declaration of the United Nations of January 1, 1942. By this instrument the parties accepted the Atlantic Charter and agreed to continue hostilities until the aggressors were defeated. Declarations at the conferences at Casablanca (1943), Moscow (1943), Teheran (1943), Cairo (1943), Quebec (1943, 1944), and

Yalta (1945) reasserted these principles making it clear that in the view of the United Nations the hositilities being waged throughout the world were not war in the old sense of a legitimate duel between states, in which each was equally entitled to use armed force limited only by the rules of war, but was on one side unlawful aggression and on the other lawful defense or police action.

The conception of "unconditional surrender" declared at Casablanca in 1943 accorded with this theory. The police do not negotiate with the law breaker but arrest him and subject him to judicial process. The legal consequences of the "outlawry of war" were further elaborated in the arguments of the prosecution and the opinion of the tribunal at the Nuremberg trial. This opinion held that a party to the Kellogg-Briand pact was legally forbidden to engage in armed hostilities except in the enforcement of its domestic law, in pursuance of a treaty or agreement binding the state within whose territory force was employed, in necessary self-defense against aggression, or in "collective self-defense" to suppress aggression against some other state. A detailed examination indicated that none of these exceptions justified the hostilities initiated by Hitler and that consequently they constituted unlawful aggression. The tribunal also held that individuals who engaged in, or authorized, armed hostilities without legal authority were engaging in acts of criminal aggression. The prosecution identified these acts with piracy and brigandage which had always been recognized as offenses against the law of nations.[23] If the individual believed that his state had legal authority to engage in the hostilities and if he acted under definite orders of a superior national authority, as would often apply to ordinary soldiers, criminal intent might not exist and the acts of hostility by such persons might not be treated as crimes. The tribunal decided after examining the acts and intentions of the high political, military, and naval officers before them that certain of them had initiated, prepared, planned, or waged aggressive war without any of these mitigating circumstances and were therefore guilty of a crime against peace. Others of the accused were found guilty of violation of the traditional law of war or of offenses against humanity. Three of the accused in the original Nuremberg trial were acquitted altogether.[24]

The same deductions from the "outlawry of war" by the Kellogg-Briand pact were made by the Tokyo tribunal and by subsequent tribunals at Nuremberg.[25] It is to be especially noted that criminal liability in these cases was not based only upon the Nuremberg charter or the other acts establishing the tribunals. These instruments were considered declaratory of the customary international law applied by courts for centuries, which made breaches of the law of war and other acts of violence committed outside the legal authority of any state crimes against the law of nations. They were also considered declaratory of the law accepted by the Kellogg-Briand pact, which in making aggressive war illegal put acts in pursuance of such a war outside the lawful authority of the state and thus eliminated the defense, recognized in international law, that acts of violence in pursuance of lawful war and not contrary to the law of war are permissible. Consequently in the opinion of the tribunal, there was no application of *ex post facto* law. The tribunal said:

> The [Nuremberg] Charter . . . is the expression of international law existing at the time of its creation. . . . The prohibition of aggressive war demanded by the conscience of the world, finds its expression in the series of pacts and treaties [since 1923] to which the Tribunal has . . . referred. . . . They [defendants] must have known that they were acting in defiance of all international law when in complete deliberation they carried out their designs of invasion and aggression. . . . The solemn renunciation of war as an instrument of national policy necessarily involves the proposition that such a war is illegal in international law; and that those who plan and wage such a war, with its inevitable and terrible consequences, are committing a crime in so doing. . . . For many years past, . . . military tribunals have tried and punished individuals guilty of violating the rules of land warfare laid down by this [Hague] Convention. . . . Those who wage aggressive war are doing that which is equally illegal, and of much greater moment than a breach of one of the rules of the Hague Convention. . . . Crimes against international law are committed by men, not by abstract entities and only by punishing individuals who commit such crimes can the provisions of international law be enforced. . . . The principle of international law which under certain circumstances, protects the representatives of a state, cannot be applied to acts which are condemned as criminal by international law. . . . He who violates the laws of war cannot obtain immunity while acting in pursuance of the authority of the state, if the state in authorizing the action moves outside its competence under international law.[26]

This interpretation of the legal consequences of resort to aggressive war have now been explicitly recognized by resolutions of the General Assembly of the United Nations as well as by the terms of the treaties which provided for the trial of major war criminals.[27]

4. In addition to the principles of customary international law and the agreements outlawing war, international law extends certain protections to individuals in the enjoyment of universal human rights and imposes certain liabilities upon them for offenses against the law of nations. As a result international law limits the sovereignty of states in dealing with their own nationals in their own territories. This limitation was recognized by the early writers on international law as a consequence of "natural law" which was believed to define certain individual rights

which all states must respect, and certain individual crimes which all must punish. In the nineteenth century a number of general treaties sought to protect African aborigines against reduction to slavery and other abuses. Subsequent agreements under the League of Nations extended these protections and added to them certain fundamental rights of labor and of national minorities. Customary international law has defined certain international crimes, such as piracy, brigandage, filibustering, counterfeiting, breach of the law of war, and attacks on diplomatic officers; and general conventions have defined others such as slave trading, privateering, traffic in dangerous drugs, damage to submarine cables, and political terrorism.[28]

Hitler's policy of denying all rights to Jews and other minorities, and of exterminating them in large numbers, gave a renewed emphasis to the necessity of providing international protection for human rights and for punishing offenses which shock the conscience of mankind. President Roosevelt insisted upon the Four Freedoms (freedom of speech and of religion, freedom from fear and from want) in his address of January, 1941. Statements concerning human rights in the Atlantic Charter (1941) and in the Declaration of the United Nations (1942) led to the incorporation of provisions on the subject in the United Nations Charter. These provisions imposed upon the General Assembly, the Economic and Social Council, and the Human Rights Commission, responsibility to promote universal respect for, and observance of, human rights and fundamental freedoms for all without distinction as to race, sex, language, or religion. The Charter even went beyond this and required the members to take joint and separate action in coöperation with the organization to achieve this purpose. Judicial decisions in Canada and the United States have refused to give effect to racially restrictive covenants and to racially discriminatory legislation found to be contrary to these provisions of the Charter.[29]

The United Nations General Assembly has defined these human rights in a resolution known as the Universal Declaration of Human Rights accepted without dissenting vote in 1948. Efforts have continued to negotiate a covenant providing procedures for giving effect to particular human rights. In a controversy concerning the denial of human rights to Cardinal Mindszenty and others, the International Court of Justice held that Hungary, Rumania, and Bulgaria were legally obliged to observe the procedural arrangement in the peace treaties to which they were parties, designed to implement provisions protecting certain human rights.[30] Allied declarations at London in 1942 and at Moscow in 1943 call for the punishment of war criminals, and agreements were negotiated in 1945 for the Nuremberg trial of major war criminals. The General Assembly has passed resolutions approving the Nuremberg principles, approving a convention defining the crime of genocide and requesting the International Law Commission to formulate the Nuremberg principles, to draft a code on other "offenses against the peace and security of mankind," and to recommend with reference to the establishment of an international criminal court to try such offenses. The General Assembly in 1950 authorized a special committee in Geneva in August, 1951, to prepare a draft convention on the latter topic. These draft codes have been formulated.[31]

Effectiveness of World Law

The preceding section has indicated the principles of law which have developed to define and maintain the competence of states flowing from their independence, the responsibility of states flowing from their interdependence, the outlawry of war, and the rights and duties of individuals. The United Nations is committed to the further development and the better maintenance of these principles.[32] Some of the steps which it has taken in pursuance of this commitment have been mentioned. Note should also be taken of its action in stopping invasions and hostilities in Iran, Greece, Indonesia, Palestine, and Kashmir; its contribution to ending the Berlin blockade;[33] and its action in Korea begun in June, 1950.[34] The successful enforcement of law in certain cases, however, should not blind us to the failure to enforce it in other cases.

The League of Nations found the Soviet Union guilty of aggression against Finland in 1939 and expelled that country from the League, but no action was taken to try or punish the leaders of the Soviet Union responsible for that aggression, nor have alleged Soviet aggressions against the Baltic states, Hungary, Rumania, Bulgaria, Czechoslovakia, and China been thoroughly considered by the United Nations.

Although eventually the aggressions of Japan, Italy, and Germany from 1931 to 1941 were ended by collective action of the United Nations and many of those responsible punished, this was only after many years of hostilities which in the material sense had the character of war rather than of police action. The solution was in fact more political than legal, was long delayed, and was excessively expensive.

After the United Nations had been functioning for five years, human rights and fundamental freedoms continue to be flagrantly violated by the Soviet Union and its satellites and to be imperfectly observed elsewhere. Many international crimes had gone unpunished and one of the Soviet satellites had invaded and occupied much of the territory of the Korean Republic. The world was arming because of the fear of other aggressions. Efforts to control and regulate atomic weapons and conventional armaments had failed.[35]

It is only too obvious that the conditions for effective maintenance of the principles of universal law which have been referred to do not exist. The power of the United Nations in comparison with that of certain of its members is not sufficient to assure the maintenance of law by orderly and effective procedures. The action of the United Nations has, therefore, been in large measure political rather than legal with the consequence that the society of nations is unstable, unpredictable, and unreliable. Mankind cannot move forward in its search for prosperity, freedom, and progress in confidence that these basic principles of law will be observed and that political controversy will be conducted subject to their limitations.[36]

The Balancing of Law and Politics

In this situation some people advocate a more intensive organization of the world. They urge the establishment of a world federation or a world government which will be able so to control all individuals in the world that the great nations cannot successfully defy it. Others fear that so centralized a power might become tyrannical and even more oppressive than the worst of the states. They believe that international relations must be controlled primarily by the flexible methods of politics, and that law can only regulate minor relations, not the major controversies concerning relative power and fundamental policies.[37]

Neither of these points of view seems satisfactory. A regime of law which compels subjection of the nations to the dominant opinion of the world in a large range of matters is not likely to be realized in any foreseeable future, would, in any case, prove oppressive to many in a world of various cultures, and would leave too little opportunity for change and progress through the competition of cultural, social, economic, and political experiments. A regime of politics which may rapidly degenerate into world war waged with air-borne atomic bombs is too dangerous for mankind to contemplate with equanimity. It might destroy all civilization.

Clearly what is needed is a balance between politics and law in the world. Law must be corrected and kept up to date by politics and politics must be regulated by law. Such a balance might permit a wide field for political adjustment in relations of nations with one another and with international organizations, and it might prevent the methods of politics from going beyond certain limits in the use of violence, fraud, and oppression. The United Nations seeks to achieve and maintain such a balance.[38] Its capacity to do so will be increased in proportion as its officials provide current and accurate information indicating changes in national anxieties, tensions, and opinions about significant symbols especially so far as such changes threaten disturbance to the world political equilibrium and law violation; as its principle organs understand the requirements of stability and recommend or enjoin suitable regulatory action founded on such information; and as governments recognize stability as a national interest and appreciate the improbability of achieving it except through common action in accord with United Nations recommendations and respect for law.[39]

Neither the United Nations nor national agencies, however, are likely to function effectively in this way unless the people of the world understand the nature of the problem and are prepared to support the United Nations whenever its law outlawing war and protecting the fundamental rights of nations and of individuals is threatened or violated. As the currency and intensity of that public opinion increases, the United Nations will increase in power and its law may effectively limit the methods of international politics.[40]

The iron curtain which prevents free communication between large sections of the human race is the most serious obstacle to the development of an effective world public opinion behind the basic law of the United Nations. Such a public opinion must accept the indefinite continuance of many diverse cultures, religions, polities, economies, and ideologies in the world; and must, therefore, place high in the scale of values a spirit of tolerance, ready to postpone achievement of any policy or ideal which excites important opposition until it can be accomplished by means which the law permits.[41]

Without free communication it is difficult to believe that the intolerant ideologies which now afflict large sections of the world can be ameliorated. Yet, since those ideologies could not survive if their adherents were permitted to observe the differances between the world they are taught to assume and the world as it is, the regimes which support them will not willingly permit free communication.[42]

The next generation will probably continue to live in a world of uncertainty and danger. We can hope, however, that the experience of two world wars, with the prospect that a third would be even more destructive, will have taught peoples and governments that aggression does not pay, that nations are valuable, and that individual personality should be respected as an end in itself. If these simple principles become accepted widely and with conviction, the machinery of the United Nations may be developed to maintain a balance between law and politics, permitting both stability and progress in the world community.

PAUL GUGGENHEIM

What Is Positive International Law?

THE ESSENCE and possible content of international law has been the object of passionate discussions in legal science and political theory ever since the beginning of international relations. The question remains unsolved to this day as to whether international law—as maintained by the doctrine of natural international law—realizes, just as any legal order, an absolute legal value—whether it be at all worth while to explore a possible content of the legal order beyond the individual norm of the not yet executed judgment.[1] Both the natural law doctrine and the sociological theory of international law leave in the last analysis no room for the existence of positive law. According to the first doctrine, the legal norm created in the procedure determined by international law derived its validity from its agreement with the presupposed norm of natural law. According to the other theory it is not possible, in view of the fact that the general norm is not recognized, to present in a scientific system those typical elements, which are characteristic of positive law. Hence the doctrine of positive law must completely overcome the objections which arise from this double front against it.

I

1. Let us first look at the position of natural law. It does not confront positive international law in that clear-cut combat position, corresponding to the basic view of natural law, which has for its goal always the realization of an absolute legal value, in spite of the differences in conception among its adherents.[2] In our time it fights only in a more disguised form the claim to total validity of positive international law. It sets out to prove that a large number of rules of international law appears incomprehensible without a natural-law basis and that they must therefore be considered component parts of natural inter-

national law. Furthermore, this position seeks to prove that the coercive order of positive law must be complemented by moral, natural-legal principles of law, and that only with natural-law support could the execution of the general norms of general international law be secured, the latter not being based on any national system of sanctions.[3] If this is the case, positive law loses its autonomy and independence.

2. The doctrine that positive international law is unable, without the support of natural law, to secure its own legal sphere, i.e., the creation and execution of the actually valid and effective legal rules, is expressed in various statements. They all limit themeselves to a proof that certain legal norms were not originally created as norms of positive international law but have only become part of the positive international legal order by reception. They often do not deny that the incorporation of such metapositive legal norms leads by necessity to their dissolution as nonpositive legal rules. However, they are not concerned with this objection, as it is not their intention to doubt the juridico-logical totality claim of positive law but rather to prove the original validity of positive legal norms as nonpositive legal norms.[4]

Some examples may further clarify this contention. The case is relatively simple when international tribunals admit legal rules from other spheres (municipal law, Roman law, feudal law), which until their admittance are not considered as part of the content of positive international law. International law concerning international delicts moves the international tribunals and courts to such an attitude, particularly in the settlement of reparation claims, because the latter are not stipulated in autonomous international legal norms.[5] Thus for instance, Federal President Lachenal, in his arbitration between France and Venezuela (in the Fabiani case) employed certain principles of the Roman law of liability for the establishment of direct and indirect damages.[6] When the invasion of German troops into the neutral Portuguese colonies of Mozambique and Angola during World War I was judged by National Councilor de Meuron and Federal Judges Guex and Fazy, the question, among others, of the causal relationship between the damaging act and the incurred damage had to be investigated.[7] The principle of adequate causation, as it has been developed by the Swiss Federal (Supreme) Court in the law of liability, was applied.[8] This doctrine has now also been taken over by the International Court in its legal opinion "Reparation des domages subis au service des Nations Unies."[9]

These arbitral decisions contain, despite contrary opinion in the literature, no admission of doctrines of natural law. The reason for validity of the legal norm concerned is, formally, not a rule of natural law. The basis for decision is the discretion awarded to the arbiter by the arbitral compromise to apply that norm which to him appears suitable. The Roman law of liability or that norm corresponding to the judicial decisions of the federal courts does not, therefore, have its reason for validity in natural law but in the law creating power of the international arbiter and judge, which is recognized within certain limits. Moreover, the question in the judicial deliberations is not one of the admission of a legal norm corresponding to an absolute legal value, but one of juridico-political principles which have already found their expression in various municipal laws. In no case can they claim, to a higher degree than other positive legal norms, to embody *the* idea of law, *the* absolute value of law, *the* legal ethic, *the* idea of justice.

3. The international judge often applies positive international law principally independent of an arbitral compromise. Thus is the case for instance, according to Article 38, paragraph 1 of the Hague court statute. The judge here carries out the general substantive norms *(Sachnormen)* relative to the facts of the case. It is possible that he applies a rule of law which until that date cannot be shown to be either a substantive norm of international law or of national law. This is how the Permanent Court of International Justice proceeded in its famous opinion on Mosul *(Series B, No. 12),* when it had to answer the question as to whether the votes of the disputants in the League Council should be counted in order to determine if this area should be alloted to Iraq or Turkey. It stated that the votes of the disputants could not be considered for the reason that nobody could be judge in his own case. This answer took note of the fact that the League Covenant had not regulated the problem of the "arbitral" activity of the League Council. It was therefore the task of the judge to fill in the gap.

Is it possible to consider the discretion accorded to the judge to fill in gaps as the application of natural law? This would indeed be the case if the judge arrived at his decision on the basis of an absolute legal value. In the Mosul opinion he executed only a juridico-political postulate established in municipal law. Only in this way could he avoid a *non-liquet* decision prohibited to him. If he had recognized the material right of the disputants to participate in the decision of the League Council he would have recognized a veto right and thus prevented a valid decision that might have disposed of the dispute. Therefore, the Permanent Court of International Justice had no other course than to apply the principle that no one can be judge in his own case. This decision of course presupposes that it had recognized the arbitral function of the Council of the League. But the opinion in the Mosul dispute has as little to do with natural law as the decision in the Fabiani case.

The same applies to the filling in of gaps in other cases. Thus, for instance, Article 21, paragraph 2, of the statute of the International Court of Justice contains no detailed provisions for the election of the registrar. It says nothing about the election procedure or the required majority for his election. But the court which is filling in this gap does not apply a rule of natural law but acts simply within the discretion accorded to it by positive law when it abolishes the intentional or unintentional vagueness of the general norm. The action is of course not limited to one that attempts to come to individual decision based exclusively on the content of the general norm. As usual in the interpretation of rules of law, we have here a juridico-political problem. The judge or arbiter, however, lacking one of those rare, clear rules of law from which only one single possibility of individualization can be derived, manages with the usual principles concerning recourse to previous decisions or the presumed intention of the party.[10]

4. The arbitral compromise may however *expressly* refer, with respect to the law to be applied, to norms which are not based on positive law; that is to say, the judge or arbiter may be authorized to apply a norm not having the character of positive law. Thus for instance Article 5, paragraph 2, of the Swiss-German Arbitration and Conciliation Treaty of December 3, 1921, following Article 1 of the Swiss Civil Law Code, provides as follows: "If in a particular case the legal bases mentioned above (treaties, custom, general principles of law) are inadequate, the Tribunal shall give an award in accordance with the principles of law which, in its opinion, should govern international law. For this purpose it shall be guided by decisions sanctioned by legal authorities and by jurisprudence." This rule of law has to this date not been applied. On the other hand, the not identical but largely corresponding Article 72 of the April 9, 1941, resolution of the Federal Council on navigation on the high seas under the flag of Switzerland was applied by the Federal Court. According to this resolution the generally recognized principles of maritime law apply if no rules for the decision of a civil-law case can be obtained from the Federal laws and international agreements. If such principles are lacking, the court shall decide the case according to that rule which it would make as a legislator, whereby it has to take account of legislation, custom, science, and the practice of the courts.

In the only known case in which the Federal Court has made use of its power as legislator, the principle of analogy was applied. The

Federal Court states in volume 73, part iii, that Swiss law contains a gap with respect to the procedure to be followed in case of attachment of foreign ships. Therefore, in applying Article 72, the court shall take into consideration the provisions of the Swiss navigation registration law on the distraint of ships registered in Switzerland. The reference to a norm of positive law excludes the application of natural law. Rather, a procedure of finding the law is applied, which corresponds to the traditional doctrine of the interpretation of positive law. This view coincides with that of the Federal Court, which has made the following statement: "It is not up to the court to complement the agreement or to seek solutions for non-regulated problems. Rather, it has to limit itself to the statement that the agreement provides no regulation for this case. . . ." (Decisions of the Federal Court, vol. 62, part i, p. 98).

5. Apart from the norms of contractual and customary law, international law recognizes three other kinds of norms from which judicial and arbitral decisions may be derived: first, those general principles, recognized by civilized nations (Article 38, section 1, paragraph 3 of the statute of the International Court of Justice), second, the clause permitting states to ask the International Court to decide *"ex aequo et bono,"* (Article 38, paragraph 2, of the Hague court statute) and, finally, those numerous arbitral compromises that, particularly in the nineteenth century but also in more recent times, direct the arbiter to decide on the basis of justice and equity.[11] Even a summary investigation will permit the statement that the arbitral tribunals and courts are far from deviating too much from positive law, even within the foregoing discretion.

a. Particularly Article 38, paragraph 2, of the court statute has been applied very cautiously by the Hague court. Thus it stated, for instance, in the dispute between Switzerland and France concerning freezones, as is well known, that the judge could not—even if the disputants so desired—award a settlement between them which would have been contrary to the judgment made in the same case.[12] No further attempts have so far been made to carry out Article 38, paragraph 2. But the new revision of the court statute, made after the International Court of Justice was placed under the United Nations, has attempted further to limit the *ex aequo et bono* rule of Article 38, paragraph 2. It is now stipulated expressly in Article 38, paragraph 1, of the court statute that it is the task of the court to decide disputes submitted to it "in accordance with international law." This new norm makes it easier for the court to reject the decision of disputes where the bases of decision lie outside the norms of international law, without formally excluding a settlement based on equity.[13]

b. Also, the general principles of law, mentioned in Article 38, paragraph 1*c*, of the Hague court statute, which lead to a significant extension of the sources of law in international law, do not have as their purpose—as is often maintained[14]—a reference to natural law. The principles of law recognized by civilized nations are applied in the practice of the International Court of Justice and other courts and tribunals first of all in cases where the norms of international law fail, and also in cases where the International Court—if it should not consider them—would come to the unsatisfactory result that there is in international law no obligation imposed upon the delinquent.[15] The Administrative Court of the League of Nations could—referring to the general principles of law—apply the *condictio indebiti*.[16]

c. Even a perusal of the older practice of arbitral tribunals, authorized by the arbitral compromise to judge on the basis of "justice and equity," reveals no new aspects of the problem we are discussing. The tribunals either limited themselves to the pronouncing of judgment according to positive international law, or they tried to impose upon the parties an obligatory proposal of conciliation by which the conflict was settled, not according to the requirement of the law, but according to the interest.[17]

6. Finally, there is the possibility that the tribunal or court is being charged with the task of giving a *law-creating judgment (Gestaltungsurteil)*, independent of the ascertainment of a delict, and of the awarding of reparation to the party which has been damaged. Such a function has a legislative character. It is a judicial function in the specific sense of the term; for in the judicial process one party appears as having done a wrong, the other as having suffered a wrong. In the practice of states, international courts and tribunals are authorized to render judgments of a legislative character, especially for the settlement of territorial disputes, e.g., the Permanent Court of Justice in the Jaworzina case and the Council of the League of Nations in the already mentioned Mosul case. The Swiss-Italian arbitration decision of 1874 concerning the Alp Cravairola may also be mentioned in this connection.

But the decision is not always within the free discretion of the law-making judge or arbiter. It is, of course, also permissible to achieve a solution of the dispute on the basis of general norms of positive law, as, for instance, by recognizing the theory of contiguity,[18] or by applying older treaties. The judgment, not creating but only ascertaining existing law, as rendered by Professor Max Huber concerning the allotment of the island of Palmas in 1927, appears as a typical example. The values motivating the judging authority can not, or only incompletely, be derived from positive law so far as the deciding organ expresses partly or exclusively a politically willed decision. Such were, for example, the decisions of the conference of ambassadors on the partition of Upper Silesia in 1922 and that of the Council of the League of Nations concerning the allotment of Mosul to Iraq in 1925. Giving reasons for the judgment, reference was made to the nationality principle, the religious affinity with the inhabitants of the claimed territory, the economic connection, the strategic necessity, and the so-called "historical right." Without denying the significance of such law-creating factors, none of them possesses such a general conviction of right as to have an exclusively motivating force. If one of them did, then the principle recognized as binding would belong to the inventory of positive international law. The report of the Commission of Jurists of the League of Nations on the allotment of the Åland Islands expressed its opinion correctly in this way.[19]

7. The preceding survey of the creation of law in international law is limited to those cases bringing up the problem of natural law in which the international judge and law giver is not in a position to derive the concretization of the individual legal norm from the content of the conditioning general norm of the higher level. But the result of our investigation shows that even in these cases the general legal norm applied in the concrete case does not rest on natural law or absolute legal values. If the international law giver and judge were not in a position to create international law exclusively by way of positive law, if he were bound to a natural legal order, a consequence would be the rending null and void of those of his decisions not in conformity with natural law.[20] Such a claim must be rejected, not because the question as to the existence of a "natural" law seems unjustified, but because the principle "natural law abrogates positive law," does not or cannot correspond in any way to the systematic connection of norms within the positive legal order.[21]

8. The fight of the adherents of the natural-law doctrine against those adhering to the doctrine of legal positivism is, however, not exhausted in the attempt to reduce the content of the general norm conditioning the act creating the individual legal norm to absolute prepositive values. They have recently also attacked the fundamental position of legal positivism. The latter, as is known, considers the law as a normative coercive order. That means that a legal order is valid under the condition that the delict, i.e., the violation of a norm created in

conformity with the legal order, is made the condition of a coercive act or a sanction. If, for instance, a state does not fulfill its obligation in a treaty of settlement, the state which obtained a right in this treaty may proceed with sanctions. Reprisals may be taken in the case of reparations demanded but not granted. To this it is objected that legal positivism overlooks the fact that not all legal norms possess this structure.[22] It is said that in all legal systems the norms of the highest level, to be executed by the highest organs, are not sanctioned. The illegal administration of a constitution by a legislative organ for instance—so far as this legislative act is not subjected to the revision of a constitutional court—has no sanction as a consequence. The same is said to be true with respect to the "illegal" decisions of the highest courts. The application of the rules of law through the highest organs, the so-called *Grenzorgane*—in international law, for instance, the application of rules of international law through the state organs, as far as the legality of the acts of these organ cannot be examined by courts or arbitral tribunals—is therefore not guaranteed by the threat of coercion. Hence an appeal to the conscience of these organs, an appeal or moral character, is necessary. It is directed at the organ concerned with the request for administration of the rule of law to the best of its judgment. Then the organ is thought to apply the rule of law, which is not sanctioned, and only "because of respect for the norm."

9. This view is the expression of the primitive juristic theory which erroneously assumes that the sanction is simply attached to the delicts. It proceeds from the incorrect opinion that there are "facts in themselves." The individualization of a general rule of law could be qualified as either legal or illegal, independent of a decision by an organ. It is, however, overlooked here that all facts of legal significance are established in a legal *procedure*. The execution of the general norm—whether by a higher or by a lower authority—is always done by an organ applying the general norm, by an organ which in its individualization realizes the values recognized by it. To the extent that the decision has the force of law *(Rechtskraft)* it appears as the authentic interpretation of the general rule of law by the law giver and cannot be shaken by any revision. It is therefore quite incorrect to think that an organ, when it individualizes the general rule of law by an act which assumes the force of law, can violate the law—that an act having the force of law can be incorrect, illegal.

This view corresponds also with the prevalent doctrine on acts of state organs. This doctrine refuses to interpret them as delicts because their content is to be considered as part of the legal order even if it is denied that they conform with the content of the general norm, which they are presumed to individualize.[23] Therefore, the norms contained in a general rule of law cannot be designated as the content of the positive law. The positive legal norm is created only when there is an authentic interpretation of the general rule in a decision of the organ carrying out the general rule by an act having the force of law. The law published in the law gazette in municipal law, therefore, is not considered the *final* expression of positive law; the latter appears only in the interpretation given by a judicial or administrative organ when administrating the norm by an act having the force of law. There is an irrefutable assumption of the legality of this act in view of the impossibility of annulling it.

10. In municipal law, an effective guarantee is given for an individualization of the general norm corresponding to the feeling of justice and the prevalent political ideas through the introduction of controlling authorities. But in positive international law there is no such guarantee because of the primitive character of this legal order. The individualization of the general legal norms, due to the nonexistence of the principle of division of labor, is being performed by the same subjects of law that participated in their creation. The subject of law is therefore at the same time a law-creating, a judicial, and an administrative organ.[24] Therefore contradictory qualifications of the acts by which general norms are individualized are possible. State A may claim an action by state B to be a violation of neutrality, while state B sees in it an individualization corresponding completely to a general rule of law. Only the feeling of justice expressed in world public opinion, the view of third subjects of law not involved in the conflict, and the retroactive recognition of a violation of law by the violator point the way to the correct interpretation of the individualized rule of law.[25] With the exception of a retroactive recognition of a violation of the law by the violator, a judgment concerning the legality of a situation, whether the judgment is made in accordance with a general feeling of justice or by third states, not involved in the situation, has never the character of a legally binding decision.

11. The incorrect doctrine according to which highest organs cannot individualize the general norms of the highest level by acts having the force of law without moral reinforcement proceeds from the incorrect presupposition that the lower organs could not commit delicts because their acts are subject to control by higher organs, before assuming the force of law.[26] If they are illegal they are abolished and replaced by legal acts. This conception is incorrect because, as far as acts of lower

organs which do not assume the force of law are concerned, the question as to whether the individualization of a general norm is legal or illegal does not arise at all. In view of the possibility of their annulment in a legal procedure, it is not their legality or illegality, but validity or nullity which is in question.[27] Therefore no problem of the legal or illegal individualization of the general rule of law exists. Should, however, the act of the lower organ not be contested and should there be, therefore, no review of the act by which the general rule of law is individualized, the act is to be considered as if it were the act of the highest organ having the force of law. Its quality as an act of positive law cannot be denied. No legal system can establish any guarantee of an individualization corresponding to the general rule of law, outside of a procedure for the revision of a contested act. Even the application of natural law cannot change the imperfection of the legal apparatus which, in the last analysis, is connected with the impossibility of a complete objectivization and with the contradictory interests of the human being functioning as organs competent to execute the law.

12. One last statement seems necessary in this connection to avoid misunderstandings. Positive law is realized — as already explained — through the activity of the law-creating and law-applying organs. They individualize the general norms in the process of concretizing the legal order and at the very end take care of the administration of the individual norm at the lowest law-creating level. Thus, for instance, a double-taxation agreement, arrived at by two states on the basis of their competence to conclude international treaties, is "applied" by the finance administration of both states. They have to clarify the obligations imposed by this treaty upon individuals and juristic persons. Of course the interpretation of rules of law can for the most part not be undertaken apart from the values motivating the administration of the norm. The only exception is the rule of law designated by the Permanent Court of International Justice as a *clear* norm, because its content can be determined in such a way that no obstacles can come into the way of its immediate administration. The "clear" rule of law, therefore, needs no "interpretation," that is, no "addition."[28] All those metalegal values, which by no means accidentally fight for predominance in the doctrine of interpretation of the rule of law, come further to the foreground the larger the free discretion of the organ individualizing the general norm. They are, as metalegal motives of the law creator, by virtue of their content in no way parts of positive law. On the other hand, they cannot be called absolute values of law or natural law. They can only be explained within the frame of a very complex,

psychic and sociological process. To explore it is not the task of legal science in a more narrow sense. However, it would be incorrect to suppose that the organs which create and apply the law on the different levels realize the metalegal values in different ways, especially that the acts of the highest administrative and judicial organs, which cannot be repealed, are performed on the basis of principles of interpretation different from those that determine the annullable acts of the lower organs. The feeling of justice, which to a great extent is the same among civilized nations, insures to a considerable degree the uniformity of the metalegal aspect which are instrumental in the individualization of the general rules of law. In addition, the way in which the individuals functioning as law-creating and law-applying organs are selected and their education, at least among the western states, from the precondition for similar juristic working methods.[29] Political factors may, however, impair these methods, as for instance the terror exercized in totalitarian states against the judiciary.

II

1. While natural law is trying to realize an absolute legal value and thereby enters into an indissoluble conflict with the autonomy of the legal-positive method of creating law, the sociological conception of international law leads to a negation of the existence of general norms. This concept can be characterized in its different variants as seeing in law and consequently in international law an actual process going on in time and space, a fact to be perceived with the senses that can be casually explained and understood. No normative parallel phenomenon can be found with the extreme representatives of legal sociology.[30] Legal science is in this view not a science different from natural science, because the causal laws determining natural science are also being applied to law. According to it, a certain behavior not in conformity with the will of those possessing power in a certain society leads to a coercive act against the persons or group of persons concerned. Traditional legal science, in the sociological view, attributes to the will of those wielding power an objective value. This, however, is nothing but an ideological, even metaphysical, justification of political power. Legal sociology demands, for this reason, an analysis of the exclusively social-psychological phenomenon of the obligatory force of so-called legal norms.[31] Such a view is inclined to consider only the individual legal act and the norm determining the judge's decision in a socio-psychological investigation and to recognize it as the "reality." Legal sociology sees the task of legal science in a narrow sense, often in the prediction of

the individual decisions the courts will render. Typical is Benjamin Cardozo's famous statement: "Psychologically law is a science of prediction par excellence." It is no accident that this statement was made by a jurist trained in the system of common law, who had at his disposition a system of obligatory court decisions, rendered for numerous individual cases; a system which therefore particularly in earlier times consciously neglected the general legal norms created by legislative acts—the statute law—as a source of law. It is true that in certain cases, on the basis of precedents, such a possibility of prediction is given also in international law.[32] But it appears still necessary to ask why the courts in a concrete case decide this way and not another.

If the problem is presented in this way, then the question as to the conformity or nonconformity of the individual legal norm with the general legal norm appears immediately and clearly, for it is not possible to make the prediction without taking into consideration the general legal norm. Also, if the possibility of prediction is not given then the law-creating organ does not have to individualize a preëxistent general legal norm, but has to create, as legislative organ, the general norm, or, as administrative organ, an individual norm within its free discretion, or as judge to decide a case *ex aequo et bono.*

2. The necessity of taking into consideration the normative meaning of law (or the law as a normative order) appears also in another way. The sociological jurisprudence reduces the meaning of a legal obligation—as already mentioned—to the statement that in the event of certain human behavior—contradictory to the will of those wielding power—the one or the other consequence will probably follow, for instance the administration of a punishment or another coercive measure. To disregard the qualification presented by the normative theory of such a behavior as an illegal act, leads necessarily to the identification of the validity of the law with the *efficacy* of the commands given by the ruler. In this way, however, the specific meaning of the law is abandoned. According to this view *every* command that can be executed is a valid command. The valid command does not have to be given within the frame of competence of the commanding organ, derived from a general norm. The fact that it can be enforced is the only criterion for its validity. In this way law and power are equated. Contrary to the normative theory of law no transformation of power into law takes place according to sociological jurisprudence. The normative theory sees the reason for validity of the legal order in the legally regulated, not arbitrarily exercized, power. Hence general norms have to be created to establish the criterion for the legality or illegality of human behavior,

unless every arbitrary act of rulers should lay claim to legal validity.

3. The answer to the question as to *why* human beings subjected to a power (in the normative doctrine of law: the persons subjected to the legal order) actually obey the commands of the rulers (in the normative doctrine of law: carry out the norms of the legal order) is neither a problem of the descriptive sociology of law nor of the normative doctrine of law. It is one of social psychology and ethics.[33] The scientifically useful results of these disciplines are rather scanty as far as they refer to the reason for the obligatory force of law.[34]

4. But this is not to deny the necessity for a functional investigation of the content of law. To explain the natural phenomena parallel to the content of the legal norms is of the greatest importance for political theory and the politics of law. The answer to the question, for instance, as to which were the motives for the United Nations intervention in the Korean conflict and its decisions directed against the delicts committed in this case is at least as important, if not more important, than the interpretation of the decisions of the General Assembly and the Security Council, including the investigation of their legality. But the first mentioned problem is as little of a juristic nature as the attempt to clarify the political effects of those decisions.

5. The sociology of law, to which belongs also the doctrine of international relations, presupposes a knowledge of the content of positive law. The starting point of sociological jurisprudence are legal phenomena as determined by normative jurisprudence, and not vice versa. It investigates the causes and effects of legally valid acts. It takes, therefore, its material from the positive legal order and works with the concepts of the normative theory of law. If it investigates, for instance, the effects of the exclusive jurisdiction of a state in the international organization, it employs the definition of *domaine réservé,* formed by the normative theory of law. It has also been observed in this connection that even in such essential concepts as "state" or "international organization," from which the sociological theory of law proceeds, the definition is not autonomously formed by it but adopted from the normative doctrine of positive national and international law. The concepts of the sociology of law have therefore a "secondary" character.[35]

III

1. After the autonomous character of positive law and its independence of natural law and the difference between the normative theory and the sociology of law have been shown, the structure of the law has to be

viewed more closely. Positive law is created by the real, imperfect human society and for this reason is a part of reality. Both its basic pillars, therefore, the claim to validity and efficacy, are directed toward the reality of social life. The process of individualizing the general norms of law, which is an expression of the hierarchical structure of the legal order, is terminated in the *effective* acts executing the law. The individual legal norms which are to be created on the basis of general norms and to be executed immediately in legal reality must therefore correspond to an effective normative idea. The rule which provides for peaceful passage through territorial waters of the merchant men and warships of the states living in peace with the littoral state is only then a valid norm when generally complied with by those to whom the norm is directed. If the efficacy falls below a minimum level, e.g., if the delicts—the violations of the norms—are neither annulled nor repaired, then not only the nonexecuted individual norm of the lowest level becomes obsolete, but the superior norm, from which it derives its validity, becomes also invalid. It ceases to be a valid legal norm. The treaty of the Holy Alliance of September 19 to 26, 1815, for example, which was never formally abolished, is invalid, because its claim to validity after a certain period of time proved to be ineffective when its individualization was attempted.

The inquiry directed toward the cognition of the norms of positive law must, therefore, first find out those violable rules of behavior which within a social group are usually complied with, but followed by a sanction if—by exception—violated. The compilation of the effective legal norms—that is, those which are effective so far as the sanctions provided are carried out—is therefore the first task of positive legal science. It must be ascertained, for instance, whether the obligation to free certain persons from taxation, stipulated in a double-taxation agreement, can be carried out, and if it is not carried out, whether it proves to be a norm providing for sanctions and whether these sanctions are actually applied. If this is so, the question enters into the scope of the inquiry directed toward cognition of the positive law: why can the effective norms of the lowest level of the legal order claim validity?

2. The effective, immediately executable norm is valid if it is created by an organ which is regarded competent to create it because authorized by a superior general rule of law. The validity of the general legal norm which institutes the organs for its individualization manifests itself in the fact that the individual norm created on the basis of the general norm is effective. It is, however, possible that the validity of the general legal norms—within the process of individualization—is disputed and

that this dispute is settled, in municipal law through control procedures, but such procedures take place only exceptionally in international law. It is therefore possible to annul created but not yet valid legal norms and the acts by which they are created. Positive law is, of course, only the norm which has the force of law and not a norm which can be abolished or annihilated through a process of seeking legal remedy. A court decision, not yet having the force of law but liable to be abolished by another court, can therefore not be qualified as a "positive legal norm." A law created through legal procedure on the basis of the constitution, however, can be so qualified, although it can only be carried out in legal reality by an ordinance issued on its basis.

3. It is not easy, particularly in international law, to make an inventory of the effective individual and superior general norms, in view of the often disputed claim of validity and efficacy of the norms. That is true above all for the rules of law not directly created by the states. These are the norms of customary international law created not through conscious purpose and in a decentralized way.[36] Their claim to validity and efficacy would be subject of justified controversies to a much lesser degree if an attempt to bring about agreement as to their validity and efficacy were successful. This is only possible through a universally recognized and obligatory adjudication. Such adjudication alone can overcome controversies in regard to the content of international law, which are due to contradictory interests, and thus prepare the codification of international law. Its premature codification, therefore—before the achievement of an all-inclusive adjudication, overcoming contrary interests—is doomed to fail. It can at this time only be successful in the form of so-called restatements, e.g., the attempt to formulate rules of positive law without obligatory force. The codification work of the Harvard Law School undertaken between the world wars is valuable. It deserves to be resumed on the basis of an extensive, systematic program.[37]

4. The scientific theory of positive law stands in a systematic, not polemic, opposition to the metaphysical doctrine of natural law and the pseudonatural scientific, sociological doctrine of law. It does not deny the possibility of natural law and the necessity of a sociological doctrine of law, but it maintains that the knowledge gained through these theories is without any real significance for a theory directed at the autonomous structure of the positive law. Its doctrine of interpretation permits the solution, within its own framework, of those problems which also occupy natural law doctrines and the sociology of law, but from different aspects and as another object of inquiry.

The recognition of the autonomy of positive law in no way leads to a dissolution of the concept of legal norms, but only to the statement that all creation and execution of legal norms is the work of human beings and hence imperfect; and that it appears impossible to comprehend the content of the positive legal order completely and without gaps. Norm creator and norm executor have the task, within a legally ordered power, to realize those values which the norm to be executed leaves to their creative freedom, in a constantly renewed process.[38] For the further development of international law the recognition of a juridico-political postulate arises, that only those rules of law can gain universal recognition whose content does not meet the resistance of special legal ideologies in individual legal civilizations, those which realize universally recognized values and interests. Positive international law is therefore by necessity secularized, religiously neutral law, in view of the manifold religious and ethical legal communities which constitute the society of nations.[39] All attempts to dissolve its secular character and to replace it with a legal order conforming to a *fixed* religious ideal are therefore directed against the stability of the valid and effective international legal order.

ROBERT W. TUCKER

The Principle of Effectiveness in International Law

An initial problem in any examination of the principle of effectiveness is the necessity for making clear that jurists, especially international jurists, have used the term "effectiveness" in two distinctly different senses. A clear reference to a rule of positive law may be implied when writers point to the acquisition of new territory by states as governed under international law by the rule of effectiveness. Quite different is the reference to the term effectiveness in connection with certain problems arising in legal theory; in examining, for example, the necessary conditions for the validity, that is, the specific existence, of law, the relationship between the validity of law and its effectiveness, or, as some prefer to state, the relationship between law and fact (power).

It is a commonplace that one of the characteristics of the law as a normative system is that the validity of the individual rules of this system cannot, in principle, be defined by statements concerning reality, that is statements concerning the effectiveness of legal rules. The reason for validity of a legal rule can only be found by reference to another rule according to which the former has been created. Law is the source of law; the reason for validity of law is, normally, law itself.

It is quite true that the search for the reason why the rules of a given legal order are valid must always lead to a point where validity can no longer be accounted for on the basis of positive law. It is evident that the reason why the historically first constitution of a state is valid cannot be given in terms of the positive law. And even if it is accepted that this latter question may be answered on the basis of international law we are still confronted with the problem of determining the basic reason for validity of the international legal order. Here it is clear that the question—as to why the rules of customary international law are valid—cannot be answered on the basis of positive law.

Still, if an answer is to be given to this question of the ultimate reason for validity of a legal order, and if this answer is to have any meaning in the sense that it accounts for the basis on which juristic statements concerning legal rules are at all possible, it must somehow render possible a normative interpretation of certain facts. More specifically it must make possible the normative interpretation of facts that constitute the creation and application of valid legal rules. And this is only to say that the content of the juristic presupposition, or hypothesis, which forms the basis for the normative interpretation of certain facts is determined not arbitrarily but by a consideration of reality.

If the question is then asked, under what condition(s) can a legal order be said to be valid, the answer appears to rest on the presupposition, made either consciously or unconsciously by jurists, that this order is on the whole effective. (Conversely a legal order is no longer valid under the condition that it is no longer by and large effective.) If one refers in this connection to a "principle of effectiveness," the reference is only to a juristic presupposition, not to a rule of positive law. The principle of effectiveness assists in clarifying the nature of the relationship between what normally appears to be two entirely separate spheres of cognition—that of normativity as distinguished from that of empirical reality. And the exceptional difficulty here lies in the fact that although a clear separation must normally be made between law and fact (power), validity and effectiveness, there is, nevertheless, an unavoidable relationship. The relationship simply consists in the recognition that the validity of a legal system, that is its specific existence as law, must in the last analysis depend upon a certain correspondence between its normative prescriptions and the actual behavior of men.

Despite the fact that the validity of a legal system depends upon whether this system is on the whole effective, it is the peculiar characteristic of every normative order, including law, that a certain tension exists between its normative prescriptions and social reality. In a sense a legal rule is established for the very contingency of its violation. A normative system would be almost meaningless, as Kelsen has so often insisted, if it prescribed that men ought to behave as they actually do behave. On the other hand, a legal system would possess little meaning if its prescriptions shared no correspondence with the way men do in fact behave. In short, while law is not to be identified with fact, there does exist a necessary relationship between the two allowing neither too great a discrepancy nor too complete an identification. The positivity of law consists in just this relationship between the prescriptions of a normative system presupposed as valid and the content of actual behavior.

The above remarks are intended to apply to the problem of determining the validity of a legal system as a whole, but not to the particular[1] rules of this system. Writers often exhibit a tendency to apply a principle of effectiveness in the sense defined above to the particular rules of a legal order. Thus it has been alleged on occasion that the criterion according to which the validity of the rules of international law can be ascertained is their effectiveness. According to this view a rule of international law is no longer valid when it is on the whole ineffective. This assertion may or may not be true; it is the purpose of this paper to examine just this question. Normally however the validity of a rule of law does not depend upon its effectiveness. For so long as it has not been invalidated in a manner provided by the positive law and belongs to a legal system on the whole effective, it must be considered as valid.[2]

The assertion then that the criterion for determining the validity of the particular rules of a legal system is that of effectiveness can only be accepted if it can be shown that this criterion—effectiveness—is a positive rule of the given order. A legal system may contain a rule whose content stipulates that if, after a certain period of time, a rule is by and large ineffective it is no longer to be considered as valid. The point must be emphasized, however, that here we are considering a "principle of effectiveness" in the strict sense of a rule of positive law.[3]

Once it has been ascertained that a legal system does contain a positive rule of effectiveness, there is the further problem of determining the specific content of this rule. For the content may be relatively restrictive, or, on the other hand, quite extensive in application. It may constitute the reason for validity for rules of a general, as well as of an individual, character. Although there seems to be little doubt as to the existence of a principle of effectiveness as a rule of positive international law, there is the greatest uncertainty among writers over the content of this principle. This latter question is of the greatest significance; because the more extensive the application of the rule of effectiveness the nearer does this system of international law approach an identification with power.

What then are some of the *possible* applications of this principle of effectiveness? It is to this question that attention must first be directed.

It might appear at first consideration that an application of the principle of effectiveness—as a principle of positive law—can be seen in creation of the rules of customary international law. Under international law custom, a long established practice of states which is accompanied by the conviction that such practice is obligatory or right, creates law. The rules of customary international law are not valid, however, because of a norm of positive law whose content stipulates that certain behavior must be considered as obligatory once this behavior is effectively established by a clear and continuous practice of states. It is quite true that the effectiveness of a practice is an essential criterion in the development of customary international law. But the reason why customary law is valid cannot be found in the positive law at all. It can be based only on a juristic presupposition, or hypothesis, that the validity of the rules of customary international law is to be found in their effectiveness as a long established practice.[4]

The application of a principle of effectiveness as a rule of positive law may be observed where the invalidation of legal rules by way of *desuetude* is allowed; and *desuetude* may be applied not only to customary law but to statutory law as well. Even within a highly developed legal system, in which statutory law has very largely taken the place of customary law, legal rules may lose their validity because over a certain period of time they are ineffective in the sense that they are neither obeyed nor applied. This occurrence within a highly developed legal system seemingly can be explained only on the basis of the fact that this system contains a rule of effectiveness—written or unwritten—allowing for the invalidation of rules of law in this manner.

The nearest approach to the rules of statutory law in the international legal system are those rules created by the express agreement of a large number of states, general rules of conventional international law. Are the general rules of conventional international law no longer valid once they are no longer effective? Whether the content of the rule of effectiveness—as a rule of customary international law—actually does allow for the invalidation of treaty law in this manner is a problem that can only be resolved on the basis of an actual analysis of the law.[5]

Still further, it is possible that the content of this same principle of effectiveness holds, in part, that certain situations, once effectively established, are to be considered as giving rise to individual norms creating rights and duties for definite subjects of the law, and this in spite of the fact that the situations may have originated in acts of an illegal nature. The acts in question may constitute violations of general rules of customary or conventional international law, yet the principle of effectiveness may confer upon these acts the further effect of creating new law. The point must be emphasized that we are not concerned here with the problem as to whether the general rules of conventional international law are no longer valid once they are no longer effective; for the acts referred to in this connection may violate general rules of law (whose validity is not in question) but nevertheless, by virtue of the rule of effectiveness, give rise to new law (individual norms). It is just this possible application of the principle of effectiveness that is at present most subject to controversy and consequently will be of principal concern in the following pages.

The evident effect of the incorporation into a legal system of a rule of effectiveness may well be the restriction of what is sometimes considered a fundamental principle of every legal order—*ex injuria jus non oritur.* It is true that the operation of effectiveness need not constitute a restriction of the principle *ex injuria jus non oritur.* A state's claim to territory on the basis of effective occupation involves no violation of international law if the act constitutes occupation of *terra nullius.* On the other hand the application of a rule of effectiveness may result in the considerable restriction of the principle that an illegal act cannot become a source of legal right. It is by no means impossible that theft may according to law give rise to ownership. Conquest, even in violation of treaty obligations, was long recognized almost without exception as a method of obtaining new territory under international law. Thus the contrary maxim *ex injuria jus oritur* is not excluded; its acceptance in a legal system, even though morally repugnant, at least involves no logical difficulty.[6]

The extent to which the operation of a rule of effectiveness may restrict the realization of *ex injuria jus non oritur* would appear to depend very largely upon the stage of procedural development reached in a legal system. Given a legal order in an advanced stage of procedural development (and procedural development implies essentially the effective centralization of the judicial, executive, and legislative functions) a principle of effectiveness, so far as this may imply the operation of *ex injuria jus oritur,* finds a very limited application. Here there is the near certainty that effective violations of the law will be precluded by the existence of centralized agencies competent to interpret and enforce the existing law. But a legal system still in a primitive stage of procedural development, with the consequent uncertainty that the law will be effectively applied and enforced, especially in the event of serious breaches, requires a very different consideration. There will be occasion later in this paper to show that these observations find special application in the still primitive international legal order.

Extensive application of a principle of effectiveness, and a corresponding restriction of *ex injuria jus non oritur,* is therefore a revelation that a legal system is relatively weak, especially in the enforcement of the law. But if we are to characterize a social order as law there are obviously limits below which its effectiveness may not fall. A so-called legal order which is on the whole ineffective in regulating the behavior of its subjects is, properly speaking, no law at all. And this objection cannot be overcome by invoking a general principle of effectiveness in every instance where the failure to restore a situation arising from a violation of law is apparent. To do so would come dangerously near the position of identifying law with fact (power). This identification however is untenable. For the law is not power although it cannot exist without power. Still, a primitive law may come very near to this identification of law and power. It is just this near identification existing in international law that marks it as primitive.

II

An essential function of international law is the determination of the respective spheres of competence of the various states which make up the international society. Professor Brierly writes that "if there is not to be a clash between their [states'] respective competences there must clearly be some principle to determine where the competence of one state ends and that of another begins."[7] A very important application of the rule of effectiveness may be seen in the manner by which international law determines the temporal and territorial spheres of competence of states.[8] The existence of the state in time as well as the determination of the state's territorial competence are both facts determined by the rule of effectiveness. Similarly these facts are, again according to the rule of effectiveness, "law creating" facts: This is only to say that the principle of effectiveness determines in these instances the conditions necessary for the operation of legal rights and duties normally attached to these conditions by the rules of general international law.

It is clear that to the extent effective change—territorial or otherwise, which is not in itself a violation of existing general rules of law—takes place, that change is according to the principle of effectiveness a condition of new legal rights and obligations.[9] The effective occupation of unclaimed territory, an act involving no violation of international law, increases the occupant state's territorial competence.[10] Other states are under the obligation to respect the validity of this new title.

Can it be said that change, once it is effective, gives rise according to the principle of effectiveness to the same legal consequences regardless of whether the particular change had its origin in a violation of law? There is an considerable group of writers who endorse the opinion of

Professor Lauterpacht that "facts, however undisputed, which are the result of conduct violative of international law cannot claim the same right to be incorporated automatically as part of the law of nations."[11] Disregarding for the present the qualifying term "automatically," the position that "facts" cannot claim a right to be incorporated as part of the law is most certainly correct. Facts as such, contrary to the opinion of some[12] are never a source of legal right. Not facts but norms are the source of legal right; hence only the validation of facts—though a principle of law which in effect considers these facts as law creating facts—can give rise to new legal rights and duties. It is precisely this latter function, the validation of facts, that forms part of the content of the rule of effectiveness. And in validating these facts the principle of effectiveness provides the condition for the application of rules of general international law and thus the creation of individual norms establishing rights and duties for definite subjects.

The assertion that acts having their origin in a violation of customary or conventional international law cannot produce the legal effects intended by the lawbreaker is based according to Professor Lauterpacht on two assumptions. "The first is that illegal acts cannot produce legal results beneficial to the wrongdoer. . . . The second assumption . . . is that it is competent for one state to pronounce judgment on the legality of the acts of another and to determine the validity of a new title acquired by such acts."[13]

It must be granted that a state is competent to pronounce judgment on the legality of the international acts of another state and to determine the validity of new titles acquired by such acts. This competence of states is indeed not unlimited. It must be performed according to established rules of international law and it must be restricted to those acts (here termed "international") whose content refers to an obligation imposed upon the state under international law. The contracting states to a treaty possess the competence to judge those acts performed by a contracting party in violation of treaty obligations, and such action as is appropriate may be taken to secure the performance of these obligations. The same competence may also extend to those acts alleged to be in violation of certain, not all, rules of customary international law—acts which are not only of potential injury to the rights of all other states but which it is in the legitimate interest of other states to prevent. A clear illustration of the latter would be the attempt by a state to apportion to itself a part of the open sea.[14]

The contrary opinion, that states do not possess the competence to judge the legality of the international acts of other states, is difficult to understand.[15] For if the position is maintained that states cannot pass judgment on the legality of the acts of other states then one result must be that no violation of international law can possibly occur. Few would accept this conclusion. Yet if we are to speak of states violating international law it is only by assuming that the decision as to a violation of law has been reached—in the absence of an agency competent to reach such decisions binding upon states—by the states themselves. It is needless to point out that this is not a satifactory condition. Still it is the only possible solution given the normal decentralization of international law.

The rule of customary international law that no state may exercise jurisdiction over another state may appear to be, but in fact is not, an exception to the above statement. That no state can exercise jurisdiction over another state means that the acts of a state are not subject to the jurisdiction of another state's, or other states', courts.[16] The actions of a state can be carried out only through those individuals acting on its behalf. To try a state's officials for acts which under international law are imputed to the state and for which the state is held responsible would be to exercise jurisdiction over the state itself; but this type of jurisdiction is normally denied under general international law. This rule is in a sense the direct result of the normal pattern of collective responsibility established under international law. The collective responsibility of the state for the acts of its organs or officials normally precludes the individual responsibility of the agents.

The state injured by the acts of another state may resort to war or reprisals—or take certain other measures—against the delinquent state. The fact that the injured state is not permitted to exercise jurisdiction in its courts over those individuals who performed the illegal acts of state does not imply though that the injured state exercises no act of jurisdiction. It obviously must exercise some sort of jurisdiction over the delinquent state if the coercive measures it takes are to be interpreted as sanctions. But the kind of jurisdiction exercised is of a special nature peculiar to the international legal system. For it is a jurisdiction exercised by that branch of government competent to act for the state under international law—the executive branch—and the consequence of this jurisdiction is not the personal responsibility of those individuals performing the acts of state but the collective responsibility of the state itself.

The position that illegal acts cannot produce results beneficial to the wrongdoer is based, however, not on the correct assumption that states are competent, under certain conditions, to determine the validity of those situations resulting from the unilateral action of a state, but rather on the highly questionable assumption that the principle *ex injuria jus non oritur* must, of necessity, be considered as a rule of positive international law. This particular assumption, as already noted,[17] is open to serious objection.

It is in fact not difficult to show that there are serious restrictions in international law to the principle *ex injuria jus non oritur.* In this connection the problem of determining the validity of treaties inconsistent with the obligations of previous treaties may be considered. There are writers who have maintained that since the conclusion of a later treaty by a state who is at the same time a contracting party to an earlier inconsistent treaty is an illegal act, the later treaty, consistent with the principle *ex injuria jus non oritur,* cannot have a legal effect. The later treaty must be considered null and void.[18]

But this view is here held to be unacceptable. The conclusion of a later treaty inconsistent with an earlier treaty may constitute an illegal act,[19] but this act is illegal only with respect to that state who is a party to the two inconsistent treaties. The state that is not obligated by the earlier treaty has not performed an illegal act.[20]

Most important is the question of the validity of treaties, bilateral or multilateral, whose contents are inconsistent with the obligations of an earlier treaty concluded by some—but not all—of the contracting parties to the later treaty. The extreme view is that the later treaty is null and void *ipso facto* by reason of the circumstances of its creation.[21] There is the opinion that the later treaty is simply voidable at the discretion of third states.[22] On the other hand the practice of states affords examples in which such treaties have been concluded and have been acted upon in spite of protests on the part of third states.[23] The correct view appears to be that although the creation of the later treaty is an illegal act on the part of the state (states), or party (parties) to the earlier treaty, the later treaty is nevertheless valid.[24] That the third state whose rights are injured by the later treaty protests and may refuse "to recognize" the later treaty cannot be interpreted to mean that the later treaty is not binding upon the contracting parties.

It has been suggested that it is "incompatible with the unity of the law to recognize and enforce mutually exclusive rules of conduct laid down in a contract in cases in which such inconsistency is known to both parties."[25] But there is no logical difficulty in maintaining that although two treaties are mutually inconsistent they are nevertheless valid. It is true, however, that the contracting party to the mutually incompatible treaties is in an unfortunate situation, since in fulfilling the one treaty it thereby performs an illegal act according to the terms of the other treaty.[26] The decisive point is that the act of a state in concluding a treaty may be illegal but the treaty itself must be considered valid, giving rise to new legal rights and obligations.

Writers are by no means in agreement with respect to the general problem of determining the validity of unilateral acts of states and the operation of *ex injuria jus non oritur.* Professor Quincy Wright has observed that "the exercise of clear legal powers may establish rights, even though these powers are exercised in breach of a legal duty."[27] Here the suggestion is made that a distinction should be drawn between legal powers that states normally possess, in the absence of treaty obligations to the contrary, and acts which under any conditions cannot be considered to constitute the exercise of legal powers, even if there is treaty which supports the exercise of such legal powers. Acts falling within the latter category are obviously those taken in violation of certain rules of customary international law, especially norms *juris cogentis.* Again, the rule providing for the freedom of the open sea provides an illustration. Any unilateral act by a state or treaty concluded between two states, attempting to restrict this freedom, must be considered null and void.

But the unilateral action of a state may constitute the exercise of what is normally a legal power, and hence be considered as valid even though in the particular instance the act has been taken in violation of treaty obligations. A state may by unilateral act grant certain advantages to another state with regard to its territory. The state granting the advantages has performed an illegal act in violating previous treaty obligations and may be liable to sanctions, but this does not affect the validity imputed under international law to the unilateral act.[28] It would appear that for the same reason many writers long maintained that the validity of the title to territory acquired by subjugation did not depend upon the acquiescence of third powers, even though subjugation took place in violation of treaty obligations.[29]

However correct the distinction drawn by Professor Wright may be with regard to the unilateral acts of states, it is clear that there are serious restrictions established by international law to the operation of *ex injuria jus non oritur.* And it is equally clear then that we are under no compulsion to accept the opinion of Professor Lauterpacht that "illegal acts cannot produce legal results beneficial to the wrongdoer."

III

It is one of the peculiarities of the principle of effectiveness that it is applied both in order to determine the legal existence of certain facts (situations), as well as to determine the legal consequences to be attached to these facts: two distinctly different, yet closely related, applications. It is customary to maintain that the legal consequences resulting from the existence of certain conditions (facts, acts) are questions of law, whereas the existence of conditions are questions of fact.[30] This, however, is not correct, because both questions are questions of law. There are no self-evident facts from the juristic point of view; there are only facts determined by a competent agency in a manner prescribed by law. To these facts—or conditions—once determined, the law will attach certain consequences; consequences as determined by the content of a particular rule of law.

Who is competent under international law to determine those facts to which the law will attach certain consequences? Due to the normal condition of decentralization prevailing in the international legal order the agencies endowed with this competence are the states themselves. And this function of determining legally relevant facts may be termed "recognition." Recognition then is that general procedure established under international law for the determination of facts which, once established, have specific legal consequences. Thus recognition determines the legal existence of such varied facts as state, belligerency, blockade, treaties, delicts, titles to territory, etc.; and to each of these facts international law attaches legal consequences.

It should be noted that recognition refers only to the general procedure according to which facts are determined. What the specific test, or criterion, is for the determination of a legal fact will of course depend upon the actual content of the rule of law relating to this fact. Thus the determination of the fact "treaty" can only be made on the basis of those rules of general international law regulating treaty procedure. The fact "belligerency" is determined according to the content of the general rule of law defining the status of belligerency. The fact "state" is determined according to that criterion established by a rule of general international law, the rule of effectiveness. Still further, the legal consequences resulting from these facts must then be considered separately. For legal consequences cannot be deduced simply from facts, but only from legal rules which confer upon the facts the further effect of creating new law.

This seemingly pedantic and rather obscure distinction is of considerable importance in reaching a clear understanding of the principle of effectiveness. The principle does provide the criterion for the determination of certain facts. Does this same principle determine the necessary conditions according to which these facts are to have their normal legal consequences, the latter in turn being determined by rules of general international law? This is obviously the case where these facts have not originated in a violation of law. In question is only whether the content of the principle of effectiveness confers this same law creating effect upon those facts which have resulted from the violation of general rules of customary or conventional international law.

In this light the meaning to be attached to the so-called doctrine of "nonrecognition" becomes clear. Nonrecognition does not usually imply, as so often assumed, the refusal to recognize certain facts. On the contrary so-called "nonrecognition" more often than not presupposes "recognition" in the sense that the latter term is here understood. The doctrine of nonrecognition would appear to mean that legally established facts—if having their origin in a violation of law—are not to be considered as law-creating facts; that the principle of effectiveness does not allow in these latter instances for the operation of the rules of general international law which would normally follow those facts if not originating in a violation of law. Hence facts illegal in origin cannot, according to this view, give rise to individual norms establishing new rights and obligations for certain states. But in the determination of these facts—the illegal annexation of territory for example—the latter are recognized, that is, are given a specific legal existence. To deny this would be to render a so-called policy of nonrecognition meaningless.[31] The nonrecognition of the annexation of one state by another in violation of international law, certainly does not mean that the "nonrecognition" states do not actually recognize that the annexed state (1) has ceased to exist, and (2) is under the effective control of the annexing state. This would truly be the giving to fictions a legal reality which they do not deserve. What nonrecognition does imply in this instance, if anything, is the denial of the existence of a general rule of international law that effective control of a territory by a government constitutes sovereignty over this territory (or as some writers prefer to say—does not result in a valid title), if this control has been established illegally.[32]

IV

The principal question raised by the so-called doctrine of "nonrecognition," so far as it relates to our examination of the principle of effectiveness, may now be examined. It is the question posed earlier in this paper: Can acts violative of international law be considered as giving rise to new rights and obligations (do these acts have the effect by virtue of the rule of effectiveness of creating new individual norms—concrete rights and duties of definite subjects), or, as some writers prefer to say, as producing those juridical effects conforming to the intentions of their authors?[33]

The answer to this question can be formulated as follows: The facts in question are, according to the principle of effectiveness, law-creating once they are no longer effectively contested by the interested states. Effectively to contest those effects brought about by the illegal acts of a state does not necessarily imply the use of force, but it must involve action which deprives the established situation of at least some of the important legal, not merely political, consequences the latter would normally bring about if its origin had not involved a violation of law and consequently had not been contested. A mere declaration alone by a state that it does not "recognize" that the change in question has given rise to new legal rights and obligations is, from the point of view presented here, of political but not legal significance. In short, the law-creating effect of facts illegal in origin will depend, presupposing the existence of a positive rule of effectiveness in the sense defined here, upon the effectiveness of the change; and the effectiveness of change depends upon the acquiescence, either express or implied, of other states directly concerned. Acquiescence may be determined by the absence of the attempt on the part of the injured states to prevent certain legal consequences which would result from a similar situation in law when there arose no question of the legality of the acts bringing about the change.[34]

This particular application of the rule of effectiveness forms one method by which a primitive and relatively weak legal system creates new law. It is interesting to note the practice of some publicists[35], in referring to the recognition by other states of situations illegal in origin as a "quasilegislative" measure, in order to distinguish this type of recognition from the recognition of situations involving no violation of law, the latter type of recognition being referred to as an "act of administration." But the objects of these "recognitions," are, in both instances, not facts but legal rules which attach to these facts certain legal consequences. And this so-called act of recognition is an administrative as well as a legislative act. It is an administrative act because the general rule of effectiveness is applied; it is a legislative act because new law is created by the act of validation.[36] The insistence on the "quasilegislative" character of the act only serves to obscure the fact that an application of the rule of effectiveness is always involved. The creation of law involves the application of law.[37]

A critical examination of the position of those who appear to deny the operation of a rule of effectiveness in the specific sense described above would appear to lead to the conclusion, either that their denial is only apparent, or that a political policy of "nonrecognition" has been confused with a legal policy. Professor Lauterpacht speaks of the "validation of illegality" by the operation of prescription, by the consent of the injured party, or by general recognition.[38] And although there are writers who deny that international law allows the operation of prescription[39] almost none denies that the effects of illegal acts may be validated by either the consent of the injured party or, at best, by general acquiescence of the states. There is no conflict between this view, if properly interpreted, and the operation of a principle of effectiveness as asserted here. The rule of effectiveness requires that the situation brought about by the illegal act or acts must be firmly established. This requirement is obviously not satisfied if the refusal of states to recognize the situation implies either that the illegal acts or the situation created by the acts is being seriously contested. Still further, the operation of the principle of effectiveness has never implied an immediate or automatic validation; a certain period of time is required before a situation originating in a violation of law can be considered as firmly established.[40] The admission, then, that states may, and do, "recognize" that illegal acts once effecting a firmly established situation give rise to new legal rights and duties is in reality nothing but the admission of *ex injuria jus oritur* in international law, and it is the principle of effectiveness that is applied.[41]

The extent to which international law allows, through the principle of effectiveness, for the creation of new legal rights and obligations brought about by illegal acts, obviously must depend upon the degree to which international society is prepared effectively to cope with violations of law. It can hardly be denied that in the absence of a multilateral treaty effectively organizing the states making up the international society and obligating states not to validate the consequences of an illegal act, that states are free to "recognize" those situations, effective in fact, produced by unlawful acts. It may be said that before World War I no such restriction was placed on the rule of effectiveness. This observation is brought out even more forcefully when it is recalled that the majority of writers before World War I did not draw a legal distinction between the lawful and unlawful use of force. A state whose rights were violated could resort to measures of self-help in order to contest the action of the lawbreaker. But once the unlawful act produced a situation effective in fact, international law, through the rule of effectiveness, conferred upon the fact the further effect of creating new law. The mere protest on the part of the injured state, or states, not followed by measures that effectively contested the new situation, were of little, if any, legal relevance in preventing the creation of a valid title.[42]

The above situation may be altered. A multilateral treaty adhered to by the majority of states may, for example, obligate the contracting parties to refrain from the use of force and permit force to be taken only against certain violations of the law. If the treaty through the lack of adequate centralization fails effectively to restore a situation upset by the illegal act of a state, it may at least obligate other states to refrain from conferring upon that act those legal consequences it would normally entail. The value of the latter obligation in the absence of an effective monopoly of force capable to restrain a lawbreaker is very problematic.[43] It cannot be denied that such an arrangement is possible, however. But the obligation to refrain from the illegal use of armed force, and to take sanctions against a state so resorting to force, cannot be taken as automatically implying the further obligation to refuse to "recognize" the consequences of a successful violation of law. And this conclusion would appear to carry added force in those situations where the treaty in question fails to provide for effective centralization, thus granting to each state the exclusive competence to decide whether an unlawful resort to armed force has occurred.

Both the Covenant of the League of Nations and the Kellogg-Briand pact forbade the resort to war under certain circumstances. Rendering a very liberal, though highly disputed, interpretation we may even admit that the effect of these two instruments was to forbid the resort to measures of armed force except in the case of individual or "collective" self-defense. Both instruments, however, provided for a completely decentralized operation. In each instance the decision as to the occurrence of an illegal resort to armed force was left solely to the competence of each of the contracting parties. Thus there was always the possibility that contradictory decisions would be reached. More important was the fact that neither under the Covenant nor under the Kellogg-Briand pact was there any obligation to resort to military sanctions, even after a state had reached the decision that an illegal resort to armed force had occurred. There was certainly no express provision in either instrument obligating states not "to recognize" the results of unlawful acts. It is difficult to see, therefore, how it can possibly be maintained that either the Covenant or the pact provided, even by implication, that states were obligated not to validate the results of a situation, effective in fact, however illegal in origin.[44]

It is not necessary here to review in detail the so-called policy of nonrecognition followed by certain states during the 1930's. But the implications of this policy so far as it affects the operation of the rule of effectiveness may be sketched in broad outline. The basis of the obligation of nonrecognition of territorial or other advantages acquired by force was asserted as resulting not only from the direct wording of the Covenant and the Kellogg-Briand pact but, as well, from the resolution adopted by the Assembly of the League on March 11, 1932, in which it was declared "that it is incumbent upon the members of the League of Nations not to recognize any situation, treaty, or agreement which may be brought about by means contrary to the Covenant of the League of Nations or to the Pact of Paris."[45] The opinion has already been expressed that it is extremely doubtful that any obligation of nonrecognition could be derived from the wording of the Covenant or pact. As to the Assembly resolution it may be pointed out the Covenant conferred no general authority on the Assembly to take such action that would have the effect of creating an obligation legally binding upon the members. The resolution was little more than a declaration of policy, with no binding effect, and at that only applicable to the case the Assembly was then considering.[46] It was never again expressly referred to in any official resolution taken by the Assembly, not even when Italy annexed Ethiopia.[47]

The chief difficulty in analyzing the nonrecognition policies of the 1930's lies in the failure on the part of writers to distinguish between a legal policy of nonrecognition properly so called and a policy which has hardly more than political implications.[48] It is almost meaningless to refer to a legal policy of nonrecognition unless it can be shown that some of the substantive consequences, which would normally result from a situation whose origin involved no violation of law, have been denied to the lawbreaker.[49] Simply to announce a policy of nonrecognition and then refuse to take those steps necessary to implement such a policy may prove of some political importance, and even this is debatable, but its legal significance is very problematic.[50] When the so-called policies of nonrecognition pursued in recent years are examined in this light it is difficult to avoid the conclusion that what we are dealing with is essentially a political, not a legal, problem.[51]

There are, in substance, two principal difficulties in the way of any attempt to restrict the rule of effectiveness so as to obligate states not to confer the normal legal consequences upon a situation (fact) illegal in origin. It is first of all evident that an "obligation" of nonrecognition, if such obligation is to have any substance, will inevitably result in a serious dispute between those states refusing to confer those legal consequences the act would otherwise entail, had its origin involved no illegality, and the state demanding such action. Nonrecognition in this sense implies a course of action which not only inflicts considerable hardship on the lawbreaker but very likely upon the nonrecognizing states as well.[52] It is a course of action which, if given substance, can easily lead to war.[53] But the anomaly here is that "nonrecognition" has almost always been the direct result of the failure to contest seriously illegal action when it originally occurred. Policies of nonrecognition have for this reason constituted for the most part a kind of soft option for states not desirious of fulfilling their international obligations by taking repressive measures against a lawbreaker. It is not without reason that commentaries on the legal importance of nonrecognition deal lightly with concrete legal consequences but speak at length concerning its moral, or symbolic, importance in furthering respect for the observance of law.[54]

A second major difficulty in implementing a legal obligation of nonrecognition is to be traced directly to the defects of the organization of international society. Nonrecognition as a legal obligation will only prove effective if carried out by all the states, and this can seemingly occur only under the condition that the decision to refrain from recognizing situations illegal in origin is reached in a concrete instance by a centralized organ competent to make such a judgment in a manner binding upon states. That prior to the Charter of the United Nations such an organization did not exist hardly requires discussion. It was for this reason that a situation effective in fact could be recognized by some states, not recognized by others, and recognized *de facto* but not *de jure* by third states.[55]

Whether the Charter of the United Nations will establish such an obligation for members cannot yet be foreseen with any degree of certainty. The Charter has provided for a high degree of centralization in the form of the Security Council. The effects of this centralization are largely nullified by the voting requirements necessary for Council action.[56] In the absence of decisive action on the part of the Security Council we are again confronted with the difficulties presented by a condition of decentralization.[57] A policy of nonrecognition under such circumstances will be subject then to the same considerations discussed above.

V

Does the principle of effectiveness operate to invalidate general rules of conventional international law? Can it be said that a general rule of conventional international law is no longer valid when it is no longer by and large effective in regulating the behavior of states? Although this would appear to be a question of considerable importance it has received little attention.

The main emphasis in this essay has been placed on an examination of the rule of effectiveness to the extent that this rule provides that certain acts, if giving rise to effective situations, are to be considered as law-creating acts. These acts, though violative of a general rule of international law, are not to be considered as thereby invalidating the rule itself. For the validity of a rule of law is not, in principle, affected by its violation on occasion. But is a consistently successful violation of a general rule of conventional international law sufficient cause for invalidation?[58]

It is difficult to answer this question with a degree of certainty. A clear illustration of the problem may be seen in the Covenant of the League of Nations. According to Article 16, paragraph 1, of the Covenant, a state was obliged to take economic sanctions once it had reached the decision that a "resort to war" in violation of the Covenant had taken place. What effect had the repeated failure of the members to apply this provision of Article 16? Was the obligatory character of the provision changed? There is strong support for the view that such a change had taken place.[59] The same question may be raised with regard to other provisions of the Covenant.[60] Again, the Kellogg-Briand pact raises a similar question. To what extent did the almost complete ineffectiveness of the pact in the decade following its conclusion serve to invalidate the obligations laid down upon signatories?

To repeat: No definite answer can be formulated with respect to this highly important question. Here it is only suggested that the view holding that a general rule of conventional international law is no longer valid when it is no longer, by and large, effective is relatively well founded, and this, especially in view of the primitive stage of procedural development of international law.[61]

VI

It is hardly an exaggeration to point out that it is just in an examination of the principle of effectiveness that we find the weaknesses of international law fully revealed. The rule is indicative of the plain fact that international law is a weak law; and its weakness is to be traced to the far reaching decentralization characteristic of this order.[62] Some may find the rule of effectiveness as developed in this paper little more than a somewhat strained attempt to justify a condition incompatible with the existence of legal order. The charge is not without reason. For the rule of effectiveness illustrates, at best, how closely international law approaches the identification of right with might.

GEORGES SCELLE

Some Reflections on Juridical Personality in International Law

THE PROBLEM of legal personality, in international law especially, the great dispute concerning the "physical personality" and the "moral personality," has been most often presented, it would seem, in equivocal terms.[1] It is fruitless to inquire, on the plane of sociology, whether the state, the province, the community, the association, the society, the family, the matrimonial community, and so forth, are or are not true "persons," comparable to physical persons and capable of serving as the foundations for juridical entities endowed with their own consciences distinct from those of the individuals who compose them; it would, besides, be fruitless to inquire whether these "persons" are irreducible to the sum of the individual consciences and capable, as such, of willing and acting juridically, that is to say, of producing legal effects and of engendering juridical situations. That inquiry would seem to be of a metaphysical order and to be relevant finally to a subjective view of the inquirer. My personal tendency is contrary to the positivist (or classical) conviction, not only because of repugnance toward the assimilative excesses of a Gierke (for example), but also because it appears that this search is useless. I am quite willing to declare that the conception or the juridical fiction of "moral personality" has played and plays an essential role in the juridical technique of the quasitotality of legal systems and that it has, consequently, a *raison d'être;* but it also has its disadvantages and should, in my opinion, be interpreted in a manner which would eliminate those disadvantages by destroying any anthropomorphic illusion.

I will content myself with presenting a brief and realistic outline of my conception of the problem of personality, exclusive of any distinction between the legal orders whatever they may be, and then I will suggest an application to interstate legal orders.

I

A juridical order, as Professor Hans Kelsen has established, ultimately coincides with personality. It is a set of norms valid for one or more physical persons or for groups. There are normative contractual, associational, local, regional, national, federative orders, and so forth. These normative wholes have their origin in phenomena of sociability, that is, as Dean Duguit would say, phenomena of "solidarity," or as Dean Hauriou thought, in *"idées d'oeuvre,"* that is, social aims. Originally, these aims appear extremely simple—the defense of the existence and security of the community and individual *(ubi societas ibi jus);* they are expressed by collective attitudes of unanimity. This original *unanimisme* and *simplisme* have become in our modern societies a numberless complexity. It matters little; the basic phenomena are always the same—the facts of sociability and the collective aims. These aims constitute the reality of the moral and juridical person, whatever may be the degree of their clear conscience. It is equally so when the proposed aim or interest considered seems individual—it has value only as long as it is recognized as social. The juridical, individual, contractual, collective norms have as a primary and essential meaning the *recognition* of their social value. They imply that the social organization sanctions them and demands their realization. Such is, in the interpretation here presented, the foundation of every juridical norm, of any rule of customary *(intuitive)* law or organic law, that is, legal, according to regulations, jurisprudential, and finally, conventional or contractual. The personality is but a technical means for the realization of social aims.

For the realization of this end, the legal norm ceasing to be implicitly an enunciator of the aim (declarative) becomes "constructive" (constitutive). It attributes means of action to individual legal agents. It orders or permits "attributions" and distributes "competences."

These *attributions of means* are established by individual appropriations or, on the contrary, by interdictions of appropriations with a view toward guaranteeing collective utilizations (the public domain, nationalizations, social patrimonies of all kind, endowments and trusteeships).

With respect to the *attributions of competences,* they are likewise governed by the idea of aim. Competence is a socially guaranteed power to will and to act. Therefore, it would only appertain to physical persons capable of understanding or of willing the norm and of conforming to it. Of course, it does not appertain to all, but only to those that the norm designates as such, because its authors consider them to be capable of willing and acting. The number of the legal agents endowed with competences may be extremely restricted *(patres familiae,* leaders of groups, adult males, etc.). The substance of the competence is, itself, extremely variable and oscillates between two poles of discretionary competence and obligatory or bound competence. The competences of functionaries are of the obligatory type; those of private persons, of the discretionary type, in the individualistic juridical systems. In any case, the power or the duty of acting and creating new situations or legal norms—such is the substance of the competence of any legal system. However, the rule of competences always remains dominated by the idea of social aim, in the sense that, even when the juridical agent exercises regularly the competence with which he is invested, the legal effect, that is, the social guarantee, disappears if the power to act is diverted from the social aim. That is the theory of the *"détournement de pouvoir"* so precisely applied by French administrative jurisprudence and already implicitly contained in Ihering's famous treaties *The Aim in Law.*

This recalling of elementary ideas, which are nothing but a statement of the constant facts of the general technique of law,[2] should permit us to sum up briefly the essential elements that are at the basis of the idea of legal personality. This technique is characterized by (a) a social aim the validity of which depends on the actual conception in force in the group; (b) the application of material means necessary for the pursuit and realization of that aim; (c) the normative determination of competences, obligatory or discretionary, which are necessary for that realization and are possessed by legal agents.

With this last term, legal agents, we assume that we are retaining the enigmatic word, or rather the word possessing the only certainty, useful in the domain of personality, that which allows getting rid of the insoluble problem of reality or fiction. In fact, it goes without saying that the creation of a norm or the realization of a legal situation can only result from the spontaneous or obligatory intervention, unilateral, bi- or multilateral, of one or more individuals endowed with intelligence and will, and whose manifestations are mutually conditioned. That these individuals act with regard to a personal interest or with regard to the interest of others or of a collectivity does not make any difference provided they possess the necessary competence. Thus the effects of their intervention will vary indefinitely in scope without the nature of this intervention being changed. The rule of competences may especially demand the intervention of all legal agents of a group (unanimity), or of the majority among them, or of certain of them previously designated as representatives. These are but modalities of operative technique. But the fact is that a considerable simplification results from the substitution of the representative act for collective or direct action, and that this action would be in many cases impossible either in private law (corporation) or in public law (state).

This question of technique does not change anything in legal reality. I have come to the point of saying and writing that I have never encountered in addition to the household of Mr. and Mrs. X their "legal community"—nor have I encountered the city of New York, the Italian state, or the Swiss confederation, any more than the Athenians encountered except in a dream Zeus or Aphrodite. That does not mean that the household X does not exist, nor that the city of New York may not be a living entity, nor that Italy may not be a state community materially definable. That means only that legal acts, the effects of which will interest the above-mentioned collectivities, are exclusively the acts of will of the competent legal agents—an administrator of a company, a mayor, a minister. I think that this is a statement of evidence and that the science of law does not need to be troubled with the unknowable.

It remains to draw conclusions from these statements in an international legal order.

II

I have referred to *an* international juridical order and not *the* international juridical order, for there exists a quantity of international legal orders superimposed, bilateral or multilateral, just as within a state there is an innumerable multiplicity of legal orders subordinated or coördinated.[3]

Classical international law seemed to repudiate this statement. It has subsisted a long time on that simple but false idea that international society was a global society formed solely of sixty to eighty legal persons alone endowed with personality, the states, and not admitting any physical person. This imaginary conception of the social phenomenon was unreal in fact and unique in law. There are no connections of sociability except basically among individuals and then among groups of individuals. Besides, there is no simple and homogeneous political society; it has probably never existed and the international society which unites and "tops" all others can only be the most complex of all. It has as a simple element, as any other, the individual, and as a final aim that of answering the need of sociability and security of individuals and of groups of individuals of which the state is no more than the best integrated and the most developed, because the most completely institutionalized. But the state is only the hinge between individuals and interstate societies, and finally the oecumenical, or human collectivity. The interstate social fact is just such a social fact as any other. It differs from it only by its contents and its extent, that is to say, quantitatively and not qualitatively. The frontiers, in the international domain as in the national domain, are only the delimiting lines of the competences of the agents. As for global international law, it is merely the last degree of superimposition of the normative interstate or federative systems.

The only interesting matters with respect to which an inquiry is important are the reasons for this conception, aberrant logically and today very shaken, namely the classical conception. I think that it is necessary to search for these foundations both in sociology and in political history.

In sociology, the actual political societies are still too near to their ancestral origins and to primitive exclusive *unanimisme*. The clan, the horde are still at the basis of our sentimental and impassioned conception of the nation. Moreover, we hardly distinguish the nation from the state even though the two notions are in essence very different. The essence of the nation is above all of a cultural, psychological and religious order; the essence of the state is of a material order. The state is a "mechanism" the wheels of which are the public services and which, chiefly in its imperial stage, includes most often a multiplicity of nationalities. Confusions between nation and state appear in an almost complete misunderstanding of the notion of the international society. This misunderstanding is still manifested in the opinions and works of writers, and leads to an often invincible resistance in rulers and the peoples to any realization of a federal goal, that is to say, to any superimposition of normative systems and to the so-called "relinquishment of sovereignty." This notion of sovereignty, the contents of which is absolute, corresponds neither with the reality of facts—for states and governments are unequal and interdependent—nor with a legal possibility—for sovereignty as an absolute excludes all multiplicity. If there were only two states, neither one of them would be sovereign without the other ceasing to be sovereign. But although there are eighty, the Charter of the United Nations again registers this absurdity: "The Organization is based on the principle of the sovereign equality of all its members" (Article 2, paragraph 1).

Besides this origin (of an emotional and racial character) of the classical conception of the state, there is another of a politico-historical order of a rather recent date. It has its origin in the medieval conception of political power known under the name of patrimonial sovereignty.

In the Middle Ages and up to our era, the possession of land served as the basis of political power. All feudal hierarchy was based on the hierarchy of tenures, and *Jean-sans-Terre* had no rights, that is, did not possess legal personality. There still exists a trace of this outdated conception in the opinion of those who make of territory an element of the person-state, a view which has no sense. Since feudal society preceded the society of states, there was a question of a "society of princes." It is still the same conception which was required under the monarchial regime. Louis XIV is reputed to have said, without any metaphysical, nor even metaphorical, mental reservation: "I am the state." From the viewpoint of the personification of the state he alone was, in fact, in possession of a juridical competence just as any other sovereign prince. The classical technique of the responsibility of states still derives from this conception and impregnates the complex theory of the protection of nationals abroad. This technique alone explains the theory's anomalies and the substitution of state damage for the real, that is, individual, damage. If the prince, at the end of his reign, feels remorse, thinking of the interests of his people, this is a sign of moral but by no means juridical responsibility. There was no King of the French until Louis Philippe. Until then the king as the owner of the land, of which he kept an eminent domain, was King of France, purely and simply.

The situation does not even change with the revolution or, rather, it becomes aggravated by a fiction. The nation considered as an abstract and immortal entity is substituted for the monarch through a kind of reclaiming miracle, and the legal technique, until then realistic, makes way before a mystic, and at the same time religious and democratic conception. The modern legal anthropomorphism joins the one of antiquity, and the gods of Olympus are changed into molochs.

Unfortunately, one often finds that this nebulous conception of the exclusivist state personality produces the reverse results of those desired. It has given a pseudojuridical justification to governmental absolutism in the international sphere, and it has made war a "discretionary competence" of the governments, the touchstone of sovereignty. The state, like the prince, becoming the sole subject of law, monopolizes the norm-creating activity. The fiction, at this extreme point, immunizes the act of the state, makes the real legal agents, that is to say rulers, disappear behind a screen of theories and correlatively suppresses the personal responsibility of these rulers by letting only that of the fictitious person of the state subsist, which, by the fact itself, that it is fictitious, escapes the penal consequences of that responsibility. It has been necessary to await the verdicts of Nuremberg to push aside those fictions, but yet in such a hesitant and at the same time brusque manner that one could wonder if there really is a question of a juridical revolution or rather of a victorious resentment.

The legal truth, which corresponds with the simple observation of facts, seems, however, simple enough. Under the term of state personality, there is nothing else but recognition by the international juridical order of the legitimacy of the aims and organicism of the state, when it is historically proved by its results. It is the accumulation of centuries of history which, by molding social activities, creates these political entities which we call states, and the new law attempts to eliminate from this continuous creation the processes of violence, of threat, and of fraud which result in sacrificing the aspirations of individuals and groups to combinations of power. It is on the basis of self-determination of individuals (nationalities) and of communities (law of the peoples) that modern international normativity seeks the legitimacy of aims, the attribution of material means, and the constitutional determination of international competences. Thus the priority of international law is the result of a kind of unification of the value of the social aim which it carried out. The same technique which makes of the legal order of a state a normative order superior to all internal orders, is roughly hewn in the international oecumenical society and by a series of federative stages, of successive normative stratifications results in a supreme normative order to which alone one would think of applying the qualification of sovereignty. It is within this general frame that the legal agents endowed with the necessary competences form, as if they were cells fitting one into the other, the legal orders corresponding with the innumerable phenomena of solidarity which appear therein, develop there and are transformed. These legal agents there as elsewhere are not able to be and never are anything but human individuals endowed with intelligence and will, and provided, through the norms that constitute their personality, with competences or means of action necessary for achieving socially recognized aims. The legal technique is *one* in the indefinite *pluralism* of collectivities.

For, juridical relations being social relations, they are not and never have been, in their materiality, anything but interindividual. These are the relations of exchange of all kinds: intellectual, of services, of objects, of powers; voluntary or compulsory, based on equality or hierarchical. Private international law, by formulating various solutions for conflicts of laws, and penal international law, by laying down the rules of territorial competence or of general competence for the crimes and delicts of international interest, have never done anything but sanction individual norms of conduct. Interstate public law by laying down the rules of attachment of nationals to such and such system of law, by working out treaties and conventions the result of which is always to delimit the competences of common private persons, of functionaries, or of rulers always regulates individual conduct. Arbiters, mixed commissions, international courts of justice in a more or less concealed manner and by more or less direct procedures settle disputes of a private order with more and more frequency; the universal declaration of human rights, the convention on genocide, the project of an international penal code of the Law Commission of the United Nations act directly on the competence of individuals, agents, rulers.

One should, however, pay attention, in public law and in matters of constitutional representative competences, to an aspect of the juridical technique too often neglected, even unsuspected. This technique I have elsewhere called "functional division."

The "functional division" is not peculiar to international law. One finds it in all legal systems of superimposition, that is to say, in fact, in all complexes of legal orders, each time that an institutional deficiency is likely to prevent the realization of a set of norms, determined by and responding to the phenomenon of necessary sociability.

Within the state, subordinate legal orders often exist without possessing organs of an administrative, judicial, executive, and sometimes even of a regulatory order, suitable for the realization of norms of which they consist. The community, the district, the county, the province, requiring an autonomous and exclusive order of customary, regulatory, or even legislative norms peculiar to themselves, are often deprived of organs necessary for their application. The governments of states, always centralizing and authoritative, and the competence of which is determined by a legal order of superimposition, require of the subordinate legal orders recourse to the state administrators, judges, or police, unless they prefer not to exercise tutelage over the local organs. Very often the same individuals or the same organs apply by their legal activity different systems of law; for instance, in France the prefect and the mayor are at the same time agents of the state and of either the *commune* or the *département;* for instance, again, judges are charged with applying at times the norms of state law and at times the norms of local law. This does not cause the legal orders to be confused, but the organ or the agent change roles and are sometimes local or regional, sometimes state agents—all depends on the contents of the norms and of legal situations which they are charged with realizing. The same situation exists in colonial matters and in the system of the protectorate where the "functional division" is applied to two different state orders. Several international situations have the same characteristics, such as military occupation, transfers of administration, and so forth. In the global international society, which is characterized precisely by the insolvency of its institutional organs superimposed on those of the states in order to assure the realization of the interstate legal order, the process of the functional division is generally presented in an aspect contrary to the one which it assumes in the framework of the state. In fact, it is necessary to borrow the organs charged with functional tasks from the legal orders which have instituted and perfected them. In the case in point it is the state legal orders which provide the necessary organs, in spite of their subordinated situation and the character of primacy of international law. This phenomenon has remained unapparent for a long time because it was veiled by the classical principle of state sovereignty according to which the state would be subject only to the rules of law to which it consented and would remain master of the settlement of the disputes in which it is interested without ever having to submit to a compulsory execution. Thus each government found itself invested with the competence necessary to assure the creation and the realization of the law of the international society to which it belonged. This idea is found more or less clearly expressed by the first classical internationalists, especially the Spanish theologians who considered the sovereign prince at the same time a ruler of a state and an international ruler charged with the realization of two juridical orders.

Of course, this nonhierarchical system of functional division, operating in a parallel fashion, resulted and does result in anarchy. The rulers whose task is thus found divided apply international law, of course, only as they conceive it and they conceive it only in the light of their particular interests.

However, the immanent force at the heart of the legal order, the necessity of international social life, has often resulted—certainly by way of custom—in the unification and the acceptance of a certain number of local, regional, and global international legal norms. It is thus, for instance, that the rule of conflict of laws or of jurisdictions, in that area of international law called "private"—while translating the conception which various state authorities make for themselves out of the optimal solution in the field of interindividual relations, and while determined to consider above all the calculated interest of each state collectively—have not failed to result, nevertheless, in general principles. These tend toward universality, such as *locus regit actum,* respect for acquired rights, respect for the local public order, personal statute in matters of state and capacity, real statute in matters of real property. Sometimes some persist in thinking that this is a question of solutions of *state* civil law. I believe, on the contrary, that here we are faced with supranational legal norms designed to be incorporated, for the sake of more precision, in conventional instruments. But this is a limited case. In public international law the functional division is constant. There are national parliaments which, by the procedure of authorized ratifications, coöperate in the international legislative activity of governments; there are national administrations which take upon themselves, within their respective territories, international public services, unless—and this happens more and more frequently—the international technical public services, such as the specialized agencies of the United Nations, substitute themselves and replace the technique of functional division by that of federalism through (public) services. And so forth.[4]

I would depart from the order of reflections to which this study is committed if I were to attempt to depict the progressive substitution of "institutional" federalism for "normative" federalism, which is nothing less than the constant law of the gradual superimposition of legal orders one upon another as the phenomena of solidarity and sociability become enlarged. I have not stressed the technique of functional division because it has seemed to me that it proved that, even in public law, the legal initiatives and realizations were never anything but the result of the initiative and the will of "legal agents" and that the fiction of collective or moral personality, itself, was only a technical process behind which is found again and always the agent, that is to say, the individual.

LEO GROSS

States as Organs of International Law and the Problem of Autointerpretation

INTRODUCTION

KELSEN's epochal contribution to the study of international relations consists in the theoretical conception of international law as the law above the states, as "law in the same sense as national law,"[1] and in the practical proposals for making this law a more effective instrument of social control than it had been in the unhappy past.[2] Thus, at the end of his fundamental study on sovereignty, written during and published almost immediately after World War I, he expressed the hope that the concept of state sovereignty will give way to the development of the present primitive society of nations toward a genuine *civitas maxima* in the substantive and political sense.[3] Indeed, in my view, Kelsen's theory of international law furnished the ideal foundation for the peace movement, that is, for all efforts directed at the substitution of international order for international anarchy and its instrument, imperialism.[4] Thus, many years later in discussing the theory of *bellum justum*, while claiming that the role of force, particularly of war, in international law and relations, admits of two interpretations equally possible from the scientific viewpoint, Kelsen declared that "it is not a scientific, but a political decision which gives preference to the *bellum justum* theory." He explained that his preference was justified "by the fact that only this interpretation conceives of the international order as law, although admittedly primitive law, the first step in an evolution which within the national community, the State, has led to a system of norms which is generally accepted as law. There can be little doubt that the international law of the present contains all the potentialities of such an evolution; it has shown a definite tendency in this direction. . . . We choose this interpretation (that is, *bellum justum*), hoping to have recognized the beginning of a development of the future and with the intention of strengthening as far as possible all the elements of present-day international law which tend to justify this interpretation and to promote the evolution we desire."[5]

Similarly, when discussing the alternatives of comprehending all legal phenomena as parts of a single system, namely the hypotheses of the primacy of national law and that of international law, Kelsen, while affirming that only a monistic construction is scientifically possible, denies that the science of law can impose the choice between those two equally possible epistemological hypotheses. The choice can be made, however, on ethical and political grounds.[6]

In appraising Kelsen's contribution to international law—outstanding in its theoretical as well as practical political aspects—it appears advisable to bear in mind his deep-seated desire to guide the development of international law toward a more centralized and therefore more effective legal order. Whenever scientifically two conceptions appear to him to be equally possible, he invariably declares his preference in favor of that likely to promote that objective. The intimate *rapport* between Kelsen's theoretical and political thinking is frequently overlooked by critics of the Vienna School who refer to it as "magnificently logical and barrenly abstract" and who believe that the "transfer of concepts and terms from the State environment, where they are native, to the profoundly different context of international relations," has thrown "legal theory into a confusion from which it can only emerge by violent distortions of the phenomena which it seeks to unify."[7] Kelsen has subjected traditional presentations of international law to a rigorous critique and has without question introduced into international law such concepts as monopoly of force, sanctions, delict, centralization, decentralization and, above all, a concept of law itself. It is proposed to examine in this paper some of these concepts in the hope of clarifying the issue of whether it is theory which is responsible for the "damaging repercussions on the practical plane,"[8] or whether these are rather due to the shortcomings of international law itself which Kelsen could certainly not be accused of glossing over. It may then be possible to determine whether it appears desirable to adjust somewhat the theory to the facts of international relations and what the necessary qualifications may be. It is commonly agreed that theory cannot be to any appreciable degree in advance of international law nor can it afford to lag behind. The inquiry will concentrate on one of Kelsen's principal theses, namely, that the international, like the national, society is characterized by a monopoly of force, that sanctions are applied by states as organs of the society, and consequently are to be constructed as the reaction of the society against the delict. This will lead to a brief analysis of one of the central problems of international law, that of autointerpretation. As the sanction is the key to Kelsen's concept of law, it may be useful to introduce the inquiry with a brief discussion of this concept and its application to international law.

Legal Rules and Validity of International Law

The starting point of Kelsen's theory of international law is the question whether international law is law in the same sense as national or municipal law, the prototype of all law. The basic unit of law is the legal rule or norm which Kelsen defines as a hypothetical judgment: "If A is, B ought to be" or, more specifically: "If someone steals, he ought to be punished."[9] The order of law being a coercive order, a sanction ought to take place when a delict occurs. The delict, far from being a negation of law, "is the fundamental condition for the application of the law, for the execution of the sanction established by law. . . . Only by the fact that a sanction is attached to certain conduct does this conduct become a delict in the juristic sense. . . . Delict and sanction are correlative ideas."[10] Law, by providing and socially organizing sanction, is distinguished from other normative orders such as religion and morality.[11] Kelsen distinguishes between primary and secondary norms. Thus the sentence "One shall not steal; if someone steals, he shall be punished" can be separated into the primary norm: if somebody steals, he shall be punished; and the secondary norm: one shall not steal. The secondary norm is contained in the primary norm, "which is the only genuine legal norm."[12] While the secondary norm addresses itself to the subjects and is "valid" for them, the primary norm addresses itself to the organ which ought to execute the sentence, and is "valid" for it. Consequently, "only the organ can, strictly speaking, 'obey' or 'disobey' the legal norm, by executing or not executing the stipulated sanction."[13] The efficacy of law can be subdivided into primary and secondary: primary efficacy refers to the application of the law by the organ; secondary efficacy refers to the subject's obedience to the law.[14] According to Kelsen, "law is efficacious if it is applied by the organ—if the organ executes the sentence. And the organ has to apply law precisely in the case where the subject 'disobeys' law: this is the case for which the sanction is stipulated. There is, however, a certain connection between factual obedience and the factual application of law. If a legal norm is permanently disobeyed by the subjects, it is probably no longer applied by the organ either. Therefore, though the efficacy of law is primarily its being applied by proper organs, secondarily its efficacy means its being obeyed by the subjects."[15]

There remains the question whether the organ is in duty bound to execute the sanction in case a subject disobeys the law, the norm in the secondary sense. In Kelsen's theory, the law-applying organ is

> legally obligated to execute the sanction . . . only if there is a further norm which attaches a further sanction to the nonexecution of the first sanction. . . . The organ of the second norm may in turn be obligated by a third norm to execute the sanction stipulated by the second norm, and so on and so forth. However, this series of norms cannot be extended indefinitely. There must be a last norm of the series such that the sanction which it stipulates is not a legal duty in the sense defined. If the meaning of this norm is also expressed by saying that under certain conditions a sanction 'ought to' be enacted, then the concept of 'ought' does not coincide with the concept of legal duty. An organ which 'ought' to enact a sanction may, or may not, be obligated to do so.[16]

It may be recalled here that Verdross, like Kelsen, also argued that in any legal order we arrive sooner or later at a "marginal" organ *(Grenzorgan)* which also ought to execute the law but whose failure to do so is not the condition of a legal sanction. Unlike Kelsen, however, Verdross derives from this phenomenon support for the view that the ultimate sanctions of law are moral in character—the marginal organ is in conscience morally bound to respect fully the law and to execute it to the best of its ability.[17] While Kelsen insists on a thorough separation of law and morality, Verdross on the contrary conceives the validity of law as dependent on morality, and far from being separated from other norms, law appears as interwoven with other categories of norms into a "normative carpet" *(normativer Teppich).*[18]

How is this general theory of law applied to international law? International law is law in the same sense as national law, says Kelsen, "if it is possible to describe the material which presents itself as international law in such a way that the employment of force by one state against another can be interpreted only either as delict or sanction."[19] As according to "a commonly accepted view . . . there exists in international law such a thing as a delict,"[20] it remains for Kelsen to show that there is also a sanction. It being generally agreed that reprisals namely, a "limited interference in the sphere of interests of one State by another" are "only admissible as a reaction against a wrong . . . there is nothing to prevent our calling a reprisal a sanction of international law."[21] However, in addition to the "limited" there is also the "unlimited" forcible interference in the spheres of interest of the states, which is known as war. The problem then arises whether it is "*possible* to interpret war . . . as either a delict or a reaction against a delict, a sanction."[22] This problem is fundamental because the characterization of international law as "true law" depends "upon whether it is *possible* to interpret international law in the sense of the theory of *bellum justum* or whether, in other words, it is possible to assume that, according to general international law, war is in principle forbidden being permitted only as a sanction, that is, as a reaction against a delict."[23] Kelsen's solution of this problem is well known. On the one hand, he admits that "the technical inadequacies of general international law do indeed to a certain extent justify the interpretation of the opponents of *bellum justum*." But, consistently, these opponents "must not regard international law as true law." On the other hand, the theory of *bellum justum* namely, "that war is in principle a delict and is permitted only as a sanction" is also possible. Scientifically, both theories are possible, and each will choose between them according to his political preference.[24]

The theory of *bellum justum* is intimately linked to the view of "general international law as an order turning the employment of force into a monopoly of the community." Whether or not the international community is endowed with or characterized by a monopoly of force will be discussed below. It may be useful at this point to examine briefly some of the other aspects of Kelsen's general theory of law as applied to international law. Assuming for the sake of argument that both reprisal and war are sanctions of international law, can the material traditionally known as international law be reduced to propositions of the type "if A is, then B ought to be"? This is not possible. In general international law, the "ought" must be replaced by "may."[25] International law authorizes but does not require states to execute sanctions against a wrong-doing state. The "organs" of international law or international community, the states, like the "organs" in primitive legal orders, are under "no legal duty . . . to execute the legal sanctions. . . . If the legal norm is expressed by saying that when certain conditions are fulfilled the organ ought to order and execute the sanction, then the word 'ought' only denotes the specific sense in which the sanction is 'stipulated,' 'provided,' 'determined,' in the norm."[26]

It will be recalled that, as stated above, an organ is under a duty to execute a sanction if its conduct is made the content of another superior norm, and that, finally, one arrives at a last norm, the sanction of which is not a legal duty of the "marginal organ." While municipal law, the prototype of "true law," is generally characterized by a hierarchy of organs, beginning with the "first" and ending with the "marginal" organ, general international law on the contrary is characterized by the coincidence between the first and the marginal organ: the "injured" state is generally the first and at the same time the marginal organ.[27] The organ of international law, however, has been said to be bound by the moral maxim of *bona fides*.[28]

The distinction between primary and secondary norms applies to international law (that is, states shall not break a treaty; if a state breaks a treaty, it shall be punished), provided it is borne in mind that the "ought" or "shall" in the primary norm of international law does not carry the meaning which, but for the marginal organ, it does carry in municipal law, namely, that of the legal duty. However, some difficulty is encountered in connection with what has been called above primary and secondary efficacy. The secondary norm is efficacious if it is obeyed by the subjects. The primary, what Kelsen calls the "genuine," norm, on the other hand, would be efficacious "if it is applied by the organ—if the organ executes the sanction; and the organ has to apply law precisely in the case where the subject 'disobeys' law: this is the case for which the sanction is stipulated."[29] Now, while it is commonly accepted that states by and large obey international law, that is, the secondary norms of which they are the addressees, the primary, genuine norm, that which provides for the application of the sanction, by the "organ" of the international community, is rarely applied. The cases of breaches of international law or, one ought to say more properly, perhaps, of alleged breaches of international law, which remain "unpunished" are many indeed. It is arguable, therefore, that the primary norms of international law are characterized by a lack of efficacy and that the international legal order on the whole is not efficacious. Whether a primitive legal order with which Kelsen frequently compares international law is or is not on the whole an efficacious order does not seem to be material in this context. It also appears unnecessary to examine here the question whether the international legal order may properly be called a primitive community or compared with primitive communities.[30]

The essential question is whether the international legal order is a valid one. Validity and effectiveness are sharply distinguished by Kelsen: "Validity of law means that the legal norms are valid, that men ought to behave as the legal norm prescribes; that men ought to obey and apply the legal norms. Efficacy of law means that men actually behave as, according to the legal norms, they ought to behave, that the norms are actually applied and obeyed."[31] Nevertheless, although conceptually validity is distinguished from efficacy and "the specific existence of a legal order, or of a system of norms, is not its efficacy but its validity," Kelsen admits an interdependence between validity and efficacy: "The efficacy of a legal order—the fact that its norms are really obeyed and applied—is of a certain importance for the validity of the legal order. Only a legal order the norms of which are generally obeyed and applied is considered valid. It is not necessary that all the norms of this order be always and without exception obeyed or applied; but it is necessary that it be on the whole efficacious."[32] It may be difficult to agree upon the meaning of the phrase "on the whole efficacious." If we continue to apply the distinction between primary and secondary norms, upon the efficacy of which of them does the validity depend? That international law is "on the whole" obeyed, that is, that the secondary norms are efficacious, is a proposition which has already been advanced. The norms of morality and religion, however, are also obeyed, perhaps even more consistently than those of international law. If validity depends also upon the efficacy of the primary, the "genuine" norms, that is, upon the execution of the sanction by the organ, then indeed it may be doubted whether international law is a valid order. The doubt is enhanced by the fact that owing to the decentralized character of international law, particularly with respect to the law-applying function, it may be debatable whether reprisals or war, when resorted to by one state against another, are actually used as a reaction against a wrong. If, furthermore, there is no certainty in particular cases whether an alleged rule is a rule of positive international law, and if there is no certainty whether in a given situation a state is not merely alleged to have violated it but has actually acted contrary to it, then obviously there is room for doubt whether the use of force should be construed as sanction or as delict. This chain of doubts, of which Kelsen is fully aware, has led some writers to deny that international law is positive or valid law in the same sense as national law.[33]

The Concept of the Monopoly of Force of the International Community

In order that there be a state of law, it is deemed necessary that there be a sphere of interests protected by law, which means that force be permitted only as a sanction against a delict and that moreover the sanction itself be conceived as "the reaction of the legal community against the delict."[34] This is the theoretical basis of Kelsen's concept of just war. If international law is to be described in the terms of the rule of law discussed above, then it must be possible to interpret the sanction — reprisal or war — as "a reaction of the international legal community."[35] In the primitive community, according to Kelsen,

> the man avenging the murder of his father upon one whom he considers to be the murderer is himself regarded not as a murderer but as an organ of the community. . . . The distinction between murder, as a delict, and homicide, as a fulfillment of a duty to avenge, is of the greatest importance for the primitive society. It means that killing is only permitted if the killer acts as an organ of his community, if his action is undertaken in execution of the legal order. The coercive action is reserved to the community and is, in consequence, a monopoly of this community.[36]

To be sure, a social order based on the principle of self-help

> leaves much to be desired. Nevertheless, it is possible to consider this state a legal state and this decentralized order a legal order. . . . History teaches that evolution everywhere proceeds from blood revenge toward the institution of courts and the development of a centralized executive power, that is toward steadily increasing centralization of the coercive social order. We are entirely justified in calling the still decentralized coercive order of primitive society 'law,' in spite of its rather crude techniques such as self-help; for this decentralized order constitutes the first step in an evolution which ultimately leads to the law of the State, to a centralized coercive order. As the embryo in the mother's womb is from the beginning a human being, so the decentralized coercive order of primitive self-help is already law, law *in statu nascendi.*[37]

The transition from a prestate community to the state, that is, from embryonic to full-fledged law is marked by the establishment of centralized judiciary.[38]

Is it possible to apply the concept of force monoply to the international community? Is it possible, in other words, to construe the materials known as international law in such a manner that the sanction appears as the reaction of the international community against a delict? From the point of view of the just war theory, this appears to be possible, whereas from the vantage point of those who reject it, it is not. According to a theory of *bellum justum,* war is forbidden in general international law and "is permitted only as a reaction against an illegal act, a delict, and only when directed against the State responsible for this delict."[39] Kelsen is, of course, fully aware of the objections against the *bellum justum* theory, such as the absence of any organ competent to determine whether a state and which state has violated "the sphere of interests of a State, normally protected by international law."[40] This question, given the absence of a tribunal in general international law, cannot be decided by the science of law but "only and exclusively" by the governments at variance. And they, as Kelsen notes, "may decide the question in different ways."[41] Similarly, as indicated above, science cannot decide that the *bellum justum* is the only possible theory but it can and does show that it is a possible one.[42] Having for political reasons opted in favor of the just war theory, Kelsen concludes that "the difference between national and international law is only a relative one; it consists, in the first place, in the degree of centralization or decentralization. National law is a relatively centralized legal order. . . . International law, compared with national law, is a more decentralized order. It represents the highest degree of decentralization occurring in positive law."[43] As a consequence of its decentralized character, general international law "leaves it to the parties to a controversy to ascertain whether one of them is responsible for a delict, as the other claims, and to decide upon, and execute, the sanction. General international law is in this respect, too, a primitive law. It has the technique of self-help. It is the state violated in its right, that is authorized to react against the violator by resorting to war or reprisals."[44]

The state that is thus authorized by international law to apply force "acts as an organ of the international community. Put in another way, it is the international legal community itself that reacts against the violator of the law through the medium of the State resorting to reprisal or waging a just war."[45] Admitting that from the sociotechnical point of view the difference in degree of centralization is important, Kelsen contends that the existence of a monopoly of force is even more important as "between an order that reserves to the community the use of force and one that does not, there exists a much greater difference than between two coercive orders both of which monopolize the use of force, but one of which is centralized and the other decentralized. If international law can be counted as an order which monopolizes the use of force—and such, as we have seen, is the case—then it is similar to national law in a decisive point."[46] Thus Kelsen has "answered the question whether so-called international law is law in the same sense as national law by saying that it is possible, though not necessary, to regard the material called international law as true law."[47]

Granted Kelsen's premise, then the statement that it is possible to regard international law as true law may be qualified to mean that international law like primitive law itself is an embryonic law, a law *in statu nascendi (werdendes Recht)*. Accordingly, the community constituted by such a law would appear as a prelegal order or as an embryonic community, just as the order constituted by primitive law was characterized by Kelsen as a "pre-statal legal order." And finally, if the concept of force monopoly is to be applied to the international community, then it would seem that in the present embryonic stage of the development of the international community, it is only imperfectly realized. The international community may be said to possess a force monopoly *in nuce*. Such qualifications should be acceptable to those who share Kelsen's estimate that international law even in the present state "contains all the potentialities" for an evolution which "within the national community, the State, has led to a system of norms which is generally accepted as law."[48]

The Sanction as a Reaction of the International Community Against a Delict

It appears from the foregoing that the starting point for Kelsen's argument is the concept of a force monopoly which characterizes national law. The concept of force monopoly means that all "forcible interference in the sphere of interests of one subject to the order must be regarded as either a delict or a sanction."[49] In opposition to this view, it has been pointed out that English law, for instance, "recognizes the use of force in several ways that are neither delict nor sanction," and that "in dictatorial States the sphere of 'extra-legal' force that is neither delict nor sanction is even greater."[50] The weight of Kelsen's theory, however, would seem to be not so much the concept of force monopoly, but its underlying idea that acts of force in a community must be construed as acts of force of the community. Such a presentation would have the virtue of avoiding the controversy as to whether or not, in fact, municipal law system—all of them or at least the majority of them—permit the use of force exclusively as a sanction against a delict. Thus, the question may be restated in this form: When a state resorts to reprisals or war, is it acting as an organ of the international community? Is it possible to regard reprisal or war as reaction of the international community against a delict? Without going into the controversy as to whether there exists a genuine international community, which is denied by some writers,[51] the answer to the question may be sought on the norm-logical plane or on the plane of positive international law. As the pure theory of law is also a theory of positive law and in this context of positive international law,[52] the latter approach seems to commend itself. Now, the materials considered as constituting international law scarcely support the contention that war or reprisals constitute a reaction of the international community against a delict. On the contrary, in a dispute between two states, one alleged to be the wrong-doing state and the state alleged to be the injured state, states not involved directly in the dispute are normally considered as strangers to the dispute; there is no obligation on the part of the states at variance to consult with, or seek the agreement, of third states before resorting to war or reprisals. Nor have, for that matter, strangers to the dispute normally the right to interfere or intervene in the dispute. This is precisely the reason why Articles 2 and 3 and Articles 27 and 48, respectively, of the Hague Conventions of 1899 and 1907 for the Pacific Settlement of International Disputes were considered as important innovations and improvements in international law and relations.[53] Under these provisions a modest measure of community interest in avoiding recourse to arms was affirmed. An important further step in developing community interests in preventing war is represented by Article 11 of the Covenant. Mr. Elihu Root, commenting on Colonel House's original draft covenant for a League of Nations, said with reference to the clause which later evolved into Article 11:

> The view now assumed and generally applied is that the use of force by one nation towards another is a matter in which only the two nations concerned are primarily interested, and if any other nation claims a right to be heard on the subject, it must show some specific interest of its own in the controversy. That burden of proof rests upon any other nation which seeks to take part if it will relieve itself of the charge of impertinent interference and avoid the resentment which always meets impertinent interference in the affairs of an independent sovereign State. . . . The requisite change is an abandonment of this view, and a universal formal and irrevocable acceptance and declaration of the view that an international breach of the peace is a matter which concerns every member of the Community of Nations—a matter in which every nation has a direct interest, and to which every nation has a right to object. . . . It is the gradual growth and substitution of this idea of community interest in preventing and punishing breaches of the peace which has done away with private wars among civilized peoples.[54]

Similarly, though independently, Lord Parker proposed, in the House of Lords on March 19, 1918, to introduce in international affairs the "hue and cry" and as a consequence to recognize that "war, from whatever cause, is a danger to our common civilization."[55] Professor Jessup pointed out, as did Mr. Root, that international law "resembles tort law rather than criminal law in the national legal system" and suggested that "the significance of this comparison is that under the traditional international legal system, a breach of international law is considered to be a matter which concerns only the States whose rights are directly infringed; and no other State, nor the community of states, is entitled to remonstrate or object or take action."[56] Although more could be said on this subject, it would seem unnecessary to labor the point.

Traditional international law normally does not consider reprisal or war resorted by one state against another as a reaction of the international community against a delict. To overcome this deficiency is precisely the *raison d'être* and the principal task of international organizations such as the League of Nations and the United Nations. Apart from special arrangements, international law furnishes no basis for the imputation of the sanctions to the international community.

States as Organs of the International Community

It is commonly agreed that the international community has no centralized and specialized organs for the creation, application and enforcement of law. Kelsen has consequently formulated two propositions: First, that the international community is a decentralized community, and, second, that states act as organs of this community. Along somewhat similar lines is Georges Scelle's concept of the *"dédoublement fonctionnel."* Starting, as does Kelsen, from the *"carence institutionnelle"* of international law, Scelle considers that organs created by the national states, such as heads of states, act in a dual capacity: as organs of the national as well as organs of the international community.[57] This he calls *dédoublement fonctionnel,* and the insight into this dual function of state organs has been said to be of the greatest importance for the understanding of international law.[58] The basic concept for Kelsen is the unity of national and international law, and "an aspect of this unity is the fact that the States as acting persons are organs of international law, or of the community constituted by it. The creation and execution of an order are the functions of its organs, and the international legal order is created and executed by States. It is especially the creation of international law by treaty that clearly reveals the States as organs of the international community."[59] By virtue of international law, "when two States conclude a treaty, they function as organs of international law. The representatives of the two contracting parties together form the composite organ that creates the contractual norm. . . . Of this composite order, the representatives of the contracting States are part organs. It is the international legal order which leaves it to each national order to determine the individual who, as a representative of the State, is competent to conclude treaties with the representative of another State. Hence, the representative of a contracting State is primarily a (partial) organ of the international community, and only secondarily an organ of his own State."[60]

For the following discussion of the role of states as organs for the application and enforcement of international law, it is important to bear in mind that it is not a single state but at least two states that constitute an organ for the creation of international law, this organ being conceived as a composite of which the participating states constitute part organs. However, this clear and, as I believe, correct interpretation of the process by which conventional international law is created is somewhat obscured by Kelsen's concluding words in the subchapter entitled: The State as Organ of the International Legal Order (The Creation of International Law): " 'The State as an organ of international law'—this is only a metaphorical expression of the fact that the legal order of each State, each national legal order, is organically connected with the international legal order and through this order with every other national order, so that all legal orders merge into one integrated legal system."[61] This indeed may be so if one speaks of one state as an organ of international law but then the metaphor becomes misleading, for few are the cases where one state, as single state, acts as an organ of general international law. Piracy may be used as a case in point. When a state captures and punishes a pirate, according to Kelsen's interpretation of piracy, that state may be said to act as an organ of the international community.[62] Here a single state acts as an organ of the international community. By stretching the point somewhat, one might also mention in this connection the prize courts. Belligerents that establish prize courts in case of maritime war may be regarded as organs of the international community, at least to the extent that they apply international and not the national law of the belligerents themselves.

Returning now to the application and enforcement of international law, the question arises whether one or the other state involved in a controversy may be considered as an "organ of the international legal order." As pointed out, Kelsen, in conformity with the decentralized character of international law, claims that it is the "injured State," that is "the State, violated in its right, which is authorized to react against the violator by resorting to war or reprisals."[63] The injured state thus is supposed to act as an organ of the international community. Kelsen, of course, is fully aware of the difficulties involved in his efforts to revive the *bellum justum* theory, of which the point here under consideration is an integral part. The medieval defenders of the theory of just war as well as its modern proponents face the difficulty: who determines what is a just cause of war? Which state is injured in its rights and therefore entitled to resort to war against a delinquent state? As long as emperor and pope enjoyed a position of preëminence in the family of nations, there may have been some support, however slight, for the doctrine of *bellum justum* in the actual conduct of international affairs. As soon as this preëminence vanished, there disappeared also the concrete basis for the *bellum justum* doctrine.[64] States which recognize no common superior may and, indeed, will use the doctrine of *bellum justum* as an ideology. History is replete with illustrations. Theories, however, die hard, and the theory of *bellum justum* continued to find proponents who developed subtle distinctions between "invincible ignorance," "excusable ignorance" and, presumably, downright bad faith. Who was to judge? Obviously, in the absence of a common superior, the state itself. And it has been said indeed that in place of the just-war doctrine there came "the idea that the Sovereign was to make war as an accuser and as a judge."[65] Now, if no self-evident criterion can be found for determining which state was just or wrong, the distinction might have conveniently been dropped, as was done by the positivists or it might be maintained in a diluted form, as was done by the eclectics including Vattel.

In the end result there would seem to be no basic difference between the view of the positivists that states may go to war for any reason or no reason, and the surviving view of the eclectics, shared by some positivists,[66] that states may go to war only if they are injured in their rights, but leave it to the states directly concerned to determine, in good faith, of course, whether they are injured, by which states, and what action to take. In either case states are considered to have the right to autodecision *(Recht der Selbstentscheidung)* and the right of autoenforcement *(Recht der Selbstdurchsetzung)*, and this view supposedly prevailed from the classic period of international law down to World War I.[67] The problematic character of this doctrine is by no means resolved by saying that states ought to exercise the right of autodecision and autoenforcement in good faith, because in the absence of a common superior the interested state will determine whether it acted in good faith or not.

Although Kelsen's theory avoids the obvious pitfalls of the theory of autodecision and autoenforcement, it has not been preserved from misunderstanding. Responsible for this may have been two aspects of Kelsen's writings.

On the one hand, Kelsen affirms that "general international law leaves it to the *parties* to the controversy to ascertain whether one of them is responsible for a delict, as the other claims, and to decide upon, and execute, the sanction."[68] It will be noted that here the parties are considered empowered by international law to determine the facts, the applicable law, and the sanction. True enough, in accordance with the principle or technique of self-help prevailing in international law the injured state is left with the choice of executing the sanction or refraining from it. In any case, the injured state, however, is that state which, in accordance with the foregoing, has been determined by the states at variance.

As Kelsen points out, on the other hand, in the absence of a tribunal competent to decide the questions whether a state has been injured, and by whom, this all-important question can only be decided by "mutual agreement between the parties. But this would be the exception inasmuch as a State would hardly admit having violated the rights of another State."[69] So far, there has been no deviation from the sound line of reasoning that in accordance with the decentralized character of international law the organ competent to decide the question of a violation is, like the organ competent to create conventional international law, a composite organ. The component parts of this organ are the states at variance, and perhaps other states, if they have a *locus standi* in the affair. Whether this composite organ can be established and will be in the position to reach a decision is, of course, open to question, although it may be noted in passing that cases where questions of alleged violations of international law have been decided by agreement between the parties are not so rare as might appear from Kelsen's statement. Cases of apologies and damages for injury done to other states as the result of mediation or arbitration are, in fact, quite frequent, though perhaps not as frequent as one would like them to be.

Had Kelsen left his analysis at this point, he would have remained within the framework of international law, but there would have been but scant basis for the *bellum justum* theory. To find that basis, Kelsen continued to argue that in the absence of an agreement between the parties at variance, no uniform solution can be reached, that the question of fact and law cannot be decided by the science of law or by jurists, and that "only and exclusively the Governments of the States in conflict are authorized to decide this question; and they may decide the question in different ways. . . . Thus, the distinction between war as a sanction and war as a delict would become highly problematic."[70] If Kelsen, in spite of the problematic nature of the distinction between just and unjust war which, to be sure, is "grounded primarily in the technical insufficiency of general international law,"[71] maintains the just-war doctrine and regards the "injured" state as an organ of the international community, then this is due to his desire to present international law as "true" law, as law in the same sense as national law.

This amounts to affirming a distinction between just and unjust war, and consequently the nature of international law as true law *in abstracto,* while *in concreto* it would appear from Kelsen's premise that neither the distinction nor the character of international law as true law can be maintained. This being so, is there any sound basis or any compelling reason for considering individual states as organs of international law? This question will be discussed presently.

AUTOINTERPRETATION IN INTERNATIONAL LAW

It will be readily appreciated that the phrase "the creation and execution of an order are a function of its organs and the international legal order is created and executed by States" and similar statements emphasizing the capacity of states as enforcement organs of international law as well as the doctrine of *bellum justum* itself lends itself easily to misunderstanding. Thus, it has been said that since there is no authority competent to determine alleged violations of international law a war is always "just" if the interested party pretends that an interest had been infringed; the state which determines the law and the delict is always the interested party.[72] Another writer believes that according to general international law and the theory of Kelsen in particular, each state has the exclusive right to determine the law, the fact, and the sanction; as each state has the same right there are two contradictory norms of international law opposed to each other and canceling each other out. The result then is that there is no international law above the states.[73] In the opinion of the same writer, a supranational legal order does not exist and is, in fact, logically impossible.[74] Instead of one supranational legal order, there are several state orders each having for its basic norm the rule that each state is the creator of law.[75] International law then may be regarded as positive morality or as the sum total of rules of a state order which attaches to certain facts the juridical consequence of war or of reprisals. The choice between these two views is regarded as a matter of personal preference or opinion.[76] If a state is the creator of law, domestic as well as international, then it may also freely change the rules, provided it has the power to guarantee their effectiveness.[77] A powerful state could even abolish the norm *pacta sunt servanda.*[78] A weak state, on the other hand, could not create international law because it lacks the power to enforce it by war or reprisals; but then in reality a weak state is not at all a state, only a "fictional" state.[79] This is the result, which may well be regarded as absurd, of an attempted *reductio ad absurdum* of Kelsen's theory of international law.

However, in fairness to the opinions mentioned above, it must be pointed out that they are by no means isolated. Efforts to explain the technical deficiency of international law by relying directly or indirectly on the prototype of law and organization, namely the law and organization of states, have paradoxically enough led sometimes to a denial of international law rather than to its vindication as law. It may be enough to recall Georg Jellinek's theory of autolimitation to show the legal character of international law, and his conclusion that in the absence of organization, international law is an "anarchical" law, and the international society has an anarchical character.[80] Similarly, Georges Scelle, in consequence of his theory of *dédoublement fonctionnel,* is moved to affirm that now as in the classic theory of international law, every government "possesses and possessed the competence to declare and enforce the law, and to act as an organ of international legal order. One should not fail to see the elements of anarchy inherent in this."[81] Professor Brierly contends that owing to the absence of a "central organ for the enforcement of international legal rights as such . . . each State remains free subject to the limitations on the use of force . . . to take such action as it thinks fit to enforce its own rights."[82] It stands to reason that if a state is free to enforce "its rights," it presumably has also the implied competence of determining what the applicable law is, and what its rights are under it.[83] This is substantially the same position which led Papaligouras to deny that there is such a thing as international law.

Of great interest is the work of Professor Buckhardt who also denies that international law is a valid order because it lacks organization. He criticizes the prevailing view that there is customary international law because taken by itself the application of rules by the subjects of the law cannot create binding customary law. Customary law must be declared as such by a competent organ, for instance, by a tribunal. In the international society, however, international tribunals have authority to declare the law only for the parties, and therefore do not create objective law.[84] In a polemic against Kelsen, Buckhardt argues that it is not enough to say that "in virtue of the law which is also his law, it is the State illegally violated in its rights which is called upon to enforce the law against the violator. And for this reason it acts as organ of the legal order."[85] For to say that the injured state is called upon to enforce its right is to anticipate the decision that the rights of this particular state were in fact violated, whereas it is the task of a legal order first to determine the injury before it can be known which state was injured.[86] Moreover, as abstract legal norms can be enforced only *in concreto,* it is incumbent upon the legal order to provide for an authoritative declaration whether a certain rule of law is still binding. In order to say that a certain conduct is legal or illegal, it is imperative to know not merely what the law may have been at any time, but what law is currently in force. It is the task of organization to perform this function.[87] A legal order cannot depend on the individual conviction or the good faith of every state; a legal order must be binding as it is, regardless of the conviction of the individual subject of law.[88]

To regard international law as a decentralized legal order or to affirm that international law lacks central organs for its creation, application, and execution is by no means tantamount to saying that each and every state acts as an organ of the international community. Whether states act as organs of international law is not a question which can be answered without reference to positive international law. It may also be well to remember that Kelsen uses the phrase "the State as an organ of international law" as a metaphorical expression for the unity of law, national as well as international. Kelsen, it is submitted, does not minimize the significance of the very real difference in the type or extent of organization prevailing in the national states and in the international society. While admitting the significance of this difference, as one of the contents of the national and international legal orders, he does not consider it essential from the point of view of the Pure Theory of Law insofar as its aim is to discover norm-logical relations.[89] Thus, absence of an organ empowered to determine objectively the violation of law as the condition of a sanction is seen as a serious practical and political shortcoming, and not as an obstacle to the theoretical construction of the lawful war as an international sanction.[90] But how far can a theory go in discounting practical difficulties and still remain a theory of positive international law? What modifications are necessary to restore harmony between theory and practice?

The technical organizational insufficiency of international law may, and in fact does, make it difficult to determine whether a state acts in accordance with, or contrary to, international law. It is one thing to admit the insufficiency and, I submit, quite another thing to exploit its existence to the point of contending that every state has a right of autodecision and autoenforcement. It is generally recognized that the root of the unsatisfactory situation in international law and relations is the absence of an authority generally competent to declare what the law is at any given time, how it applies to a given situation or dispute, and what the appropriate sanction may be. In the absence of such an authority, and failing agreement between the states at variance on these points, each state has a right to interpret the law, the right of autointerpretation, as it might be called. This interpretation, however, is not a "decision" and is neither final nor binding upon the other parties. In consequence of the technical insufficiency prevailing in general international law, we may never know, or, in some cases, we may not know for a time, which autointerpretation was correct. A controversy, in other words, may remain unsettled forever or for a long time. This is, for better or worse, the situation resulting from the organizational insufficiency of international law. Neither victory nor defeat in war are objective tests of the legal issues involved, if indeed the causes of war were differences of a legal and not of a political nature.

It can be shown, I believe, that states have the right of autointerpretation but not the right to decide questions of inernational law, that is, to make binding decisions for others. It may be well to remind ourselves that in general international law there is no duty for states to submit disputes to third-party decisions. Resort to all or any procedure for the settlement of disputes, be it a decisional or nondecisional procedure, is voluntary and not compulsory.[91] The decentralized character of international law in this matter manifests itself in the absence of a duty to submit disputes to any of the procedures and in the need for the parties to the dispute to collaborate in reaching an agreed solution as well as in the restriction of the solution reached to the parties concerned. The agreed interpretation of the rule of general international law resulting from negotiation or arbitration or adjudication, while binding upon the parties, is not authoritative for strangers to the dispute nor for any other tribunal which may be seized of the same or a substantially identical question. This explains the lack of uniformity in the jurisprudence of international tribunals on such subjects as the Calvo clause and others. It does not follow from the principle of voluntary submission to procedures for pacific settlement nor does it follow from the doctrine of sovereignty "that the State is in principle the sole judge of the existence of any individual rule of law, applicable to itself."[92] On the contrary, more than hundred years ago Chief Justice Marshall said that it was a consequence of the principle of "the perfect equality of nations . . . that no one can rightfully impose a rule on another. . . . As no nation can prescribe a rule for others, none can make a law of nations."[93] Equality and sovereignty are sometimes used as synonyms; even if this were not so, sovereignty in the sense indicated would obviously be incompatible with the sovereignty of any other state, and the state which claims to be "the sole judge of the existence of any individual rules of law" would thereby subject other states to its judgment. Regardless of the pretensions of writers and even of governments, "the well-known rule that no one can be judge in his own suit holds good."[94] Far from acting as disinterested organs of international law, let alone as objective judges, individual governments as subjects of international law are interested parties. Probably every arbitral proceeding would show that rather than act as the expounders of international law, they act as advocates for themselves. A few illustrations, it is hoped, will substantiate the point that attempts of governments to arrogate to themselves the right to decide questions of international law were emphatically rejected.

In its recent judgment in the Colombian-Peruvian asylum case, the International Court of Justice had occasion to pass on the right of a diplomatic representative to make a provisional qualification of an offense alleged to have been committed by the refugee seeking asylum and the right of the territorial state to contest the qualification. The court found that the Colombian government "has not claimed the right of qualification for the sole purpose of determining its own conduct," but "its claim must be understood in the sense that Columbia, as the State granting asylum, is competent to qualify the offense by a unilateral and definitive decision binding on Peru." The court held that "the principles of international law do not recognize any rule of unilateral and definitive qualification by the State granting asylum."[95] With reference to the facts, namely, whether or not on January 3-4, 1949, there existed in Peru a case of urgency within the meaning of Article 2, paragraph 2, of the Havana Convention on Asylum and the belief of the ambassador of Colombia in the existence of such urgency, the court declared: "But this subjective appreciation is not the relevant element in the decision which the Court is called upon to take concerning the validity of the asylum; the only important question to be considered here is the objective existence of the facts, and it is this which must determine the decision of the Court." And the court held that the grant of asylum was not made in conformity to the convention.[96] The judgment of the court clearly draws a line between the subjective appreciation of the facts made by the interested parties, and the objective appreciation made by the court. It also distinguishes sharply the right of a party to interpret international law and treaties "for the sole purpose of determining its own conduct," and the competence to decide the question of law with binding force for the other party. The right of autointerpretation is thus affirmed, as a limited right, and the right of autodecision is rejected.[97]

It may be useful to refer to some cases in which the resort to force against another state was put to the test of an arbitral or judicial decision. In the Naulilaa case between Germany and Portugal, the Mixed Arbitral Tribunal, in its award of July 31, 1928, found that the German aggression of October-December, 1914, against the frontier of Angola was not to be considered as licit reprisal in the absence of a proper cause, of a prior summons, and of a proportionality between the alleged offense and the reprisal.[98] Germany, having satisfied herself presumably that resort to reprisals was legitimate in the circumstance, acted at her own peril. She certainly did not act as an organ of the international community and her aggression could not be interpreted as the reaction of the international community against Portugal. More recently, in the Corfu Channel case, the International Court of Justice had occasion to consider resort to intervention and other methods of self-help. Following the explosions of October 22, 1946, in the Corfu Channel which caused damage to, and loss of human life on, British men-of-war passing through the channel, the United Kingdom government ordered a mine-sweeping operation in the channel ("Operation Retail") which took place without Albania's consent on November 12-13, 1946. Having rejected the British defense based on "the alleged right of intervention," the court, referring to the second justification of the United Kingdom, which "classified 'Operation Retail' among methods of self-protection or self-help," held:

> The Court cannot accept this defense either. Between independent States, respect for the territorial sovereignty is an essential foundation of international relations. The Court recognizes that the Albanian Government's complete failure to carry out its duties after the explosions and the dilatory nature of its diplomatic notes, are extenuating circumstances for the action of the United Kingdom Government. But to ensure respect for international law, of which it is the organ, the Court must declare that the action of the British Navy constituted a violation of Albanian sovereignty.[99]

Whether the court's decision should be understood "as a condemnation of all intervention involving the use or display of force, and as a rejection of the view that self-help . . . can ever be a legitimate means of redressing international wrongs" or as relating merely to the particular instance of self-help before the court, is of course a question which merits reflection and study.[100] What is immediately clear, however, is that put to the test of a judicial determination, the action of the United Kingdom government appeared not as a proper use of force, not as self-help resorted to as an organ of international law, nor as a reaction of the international community against a delict, but rather as an illegal act applied unilaterally by an interested party against another state, and without the latter's consent. Not the United Kingdom but the International Court of Justice, by agreement between the United Kingdom and Albania, fulfilled the functions of an organ of international law.

It will be recalled that before the signing of the Treaty for the Renunciation of War in Paris on August 27, 1928, the United States note of June 23, 1928 declared that the proposed treaty did not in any way restrict or impair the right of self-defense: "That right is inherent in every sovereign State, and is implicit in every treaty. Every nation is free at all times and regardless of treaty provisions to defend its territory from attack or invasion, and it alone is competent to decide whether circumstances require recourse to war in self-defense."[101] The United States may thus have conveyed the impression that the contracting parties have not merely the right of autointerpretation, but the right of autodecision as well. The International Military Tribunal, however, considering the question of whether the invasion of Denmark and Norway by Germany was an act of self-defense, declared: "It was further argued that Germany alone could decide, in accordance with the reservations made by many of the Signatory Powers, at the time of the conclusion of the Kellogg-Briand Pact, whether a preventive action was a necessity, and that in making her decision, her judgment was conclusive. But whether action taken under the claim of self-defense was in fact aggressive or defensive must ultimately be subject to investigation and adjudication if international law is ever to be enforced."[102] Thus what appeared to be a right of making a unilateral decision regarding the applicability of the inherent right of self-defense was found by the International Military Tribunal to be no more than the right of autointerpretation subject to objective investigation and conclusive adjudication.

It is interesting to note that Sir Hartley Shawcross, chief prosecutor for the United Kingdom, before the International Military Tribunal, when discussing the question of self-defense in connection with the Kellogg-Briand pact, had this to say:

> Neither the Pact of Paris nor any other treaty was intended to—or could—take away the right of self-defense. Nor did it deprive its signatories of the right to determine, in the first instance, whether there was danger in delaying and whether immediate action to defend themselves was imperative; and that only is the meaning of the express proviso that each State judges whether action in self-defense is necessary. But this does not mean that the State thus acting is the ultimate judge of the property and of the legality of its conduct. It acts at its peril. Just as the individual is answerable for the exercise of his common law right of defense, so the State is answerable if it abused its discretion, if it transforms 'self-defense' into an instrument of conquest and lawlessness, if it

twists the natural right of self-defense into a weapon of predatory aggrandizement and lust. The ultimate decision as to the lawfulness of action claimed to be taken in self-defense does not lie with the State concerned, and for that reason, the right of self-defense, whether expressly reserved or implied, does not impair the capacity of a treaty to create legal obligations against war.[103]

It may be noted in passing that the judgment of the International Military Tribunal followed the reasoning of Sir Hartley Shawcross and confirmed Professor Lauterpacht's interpretation of the Kellogg-Briand pact, namely that, although recourse to self-defense "must, in the first instance, be a matter for the judgment of the state concerned" and although the state has "the provisional right to act . . . the question of the right of recourse to war in self-defense is in itself capable of judicial decision."[104]

As international law in its conventional and customary form is not the product of the will of one state but emanates from the free will of two or more states, so is the competence of authentic or authoritative interpretation vested in the community of nations or in the states parties to the treaty. In the advisory opinion on the Jaworzina case, the Permanent Court of International Justice referred to the "established principle that the right of giving an authoritative interpretation of a legal rule belongs solely to the person or body who has the power to modify or suppress it."[105] This is so, it is submitted, because, as Kelsen pointed out, an "authentic interpretation . . . is a law-creating act."[106] An authentic interpretation, being binding, is within the competence of the norm-creating body. In a dispute regarding the interpretation of a bilateral treaty, the competent authority is the composite organ formed by the two contracting parties, or a tribunal instituted by the parties with the power to settle the dispute. To attribute to one party alone the capacity of an organ, that is, the right to decide the meaning of a treaty, would amount to conferring on it the right to create a norm binding on the other state, that is, juridically speaking, subordinate the other state to the jurisdiction of the former. If no other principle of international law then certainly the principle of equality militates against such an attribution. Obviously, autointerpretation has no binding character. In autodecision, such a character is implied, but without any justification in general international law. Thus, in the David J. Adams case, the Anglo-American arbitral tribunal declared: "The fundamental principle of the juridical equality of States is opposed to placing one State under the jurisdiction of another State. It is opposed to the subjection of one State to an interpretation of a Treaty asserted by another State. There is no reason why one more than the other should impose such a unilateral interpretation of a contract which is essentially bilateral."[107] It may be apposite to refer here to the note of September 19, 1949, from the United States to Rumania and the substantially identical notes to Bulgaria and Hungary in the dispute relating to the application of provisions regarding human rights under peace treaties entered into with those countries. In its note to Rumania, the United States stated:

> The United States Government considers that the Rumanian Government has no grounds for declaring unilaterally that a dispute over Rumania's execution of Article 3 of the Peace Treaty does not exist. Since the interpretation placed by the United States Government on the acts of the Rumanian Government with reference to the latter's treaty obligations respecting human rights and freedom does not correspond with the interpretation advanced by the Rumanian Government, the existence of a dispute is self-evident.[108]

It thus appears to be contrary to positive international law for one state to impose its interpretation of a treaty upon the other.

The same consideration applies in multilateral treaties. Each contracting party has a right of autointerpretation, but not of autodecision. The right of authentic interpretation is vested in the composite organ formed by all the contracting parties. Unless the treaty provides for an alternative procedure, an authoritative interpretation can result from negotiations leading to an agreement, or from arbitration or adjudication. The London Protocol of January 17, 1871, signed by the representatives of Great Britain, Austria-Hungary, France, Germany, Italy, Russia, and Turkey, expressly recognized "that it is an essential principle of the law of nations that no Power can liberate itself from the engagements of a treaty, nor modify the stipulations thereof, unless with the consent of the Contracting Powers, by means of an amicable arrangement."[109] This protocol is usually referred to in connection with the *clausula rebus sic stantibus* doctrine. However, the principle of the sanctity of treaties recognized by the great powers applies equally to modifications of treaties which may be brought about by interpretation. It is part of the principle of *pacta sunt servanda* that the right of authentic interpretation belongs to the composite organ which created the treaty and not to any of the states members of that organ. The prohibition is directed against unilateral interpretation amounting to modification of a multilateral treaty. The decentralized character of international law makes itself felt even here. For under general international law two state parties to a multilateral treaty may, to the extent that this does not prejudice the rights of others, make modifications derogating from the general treaty. Similarly, two or more states may submit a dispute concerning the interpretation of a multilateral treaty to arbitration or adjudication. The interpretation laid down by a tribunal or court is binding upon the parties and upon the parties to the proceedings alone. Article 59 of the statute of the International Court of Justice, in providing that "the decision of the Court has no binding force except between the parties and in respect of that particular case," constitutes an emphatic recognition of the decentralized character of international law.

The principle enunciated in the London Protocol rejecting unilateral interpretations which may be characterized as modifications of multilateral treaties lays down the procedure by dint of which a binding interpretation can be secured. That procedure is implied in the requirement of the consent of the contracting parties. A treaty, however, may establish, again with the consent of the contracting parties, alternative procedures for interpretation and formal modifications or amendments. Thus, the constitution of the International Labor Organization lays down in Article 36 the procedure for amendments, that is, for formal modifications, and in Article 37 a procedure for an interpretation by decision of the International Court of Justice.[110] The constitution of the International Civil Aviation Organization, in Article 94, provides for amendments, in Article 84, for interpretations by decision of the United Nations Council, from which an appeal may be taken to an *ad hoc* tribunal or to the International Court of Justice. The articles of agreement of the International Bank for Reconstruction and Development and of the International Monetary Fund, in Articles 8 and 17 respectively, provide for amendments and, in Articles 9 and 18 respectively, for binding decisions on questions of interpretation by the executive directors and for final decision by the board of governors. Such decisions are binding on all members. According to Article 75 of the constitution of the World Health Organization, disputes concerning application or interpretation may be settled by negotiation or by the Health Assembly or by the International Court of Justice, or another mode of settlement agreed to by the parties. There being no cut-and-dried difference between interpretation and modification, it would seem that in all cases in which a treaty provides for binding decisions on questions of interpretation by an organ of the organization, as well as for a formal amending procedure, there are in fact two possibilities or procedures for modifying the treaty—one through authoritative interpretation and another through amendment.

If a treaty fails to provide a procedure for settling questions of interpretation but includes provisions for amendment, the latter procedure or the agreement of all contracting parties is required to settle such questions. This situation exists in the United Nations. Any organ of the United Nations may interpret those parts of the Charter as are applicable to its particular function. In principle, such interpretations, however, are not authentic or authoritative, that is, they lack binding force. States at variance on the correct interpretation of the Charter may submit the dispute to the International Court of Justice, as in the case of any other treaty. The decision of the court, while binding upon the parties, would not *ipso facto* be binding upon the other members of the organization. In other words, so far as the other members are concerned, the interpretation of the court would not be authentic or authoritative. This was so understood by Committee IV/2 of the United Nations Conference on International Organization which declared: "If an interpretation made by any organ of the Organization or by a committee of jurists is not generally acceptable, it will be without binding force. In such circumstances, or in cases where it is desired to establish an authoritative interpretation as a precedent for the future, it may be necessary to embody the interpretation in an amendment to the Charter. This may always be accomplished by a recourse to the procedure provided for amendment."[111] The considerations set forth above seem to be entirely in harmony with the view adopted by the committee.

The principles applicable to the interpretation and modification of treaties are substantially identical with those governing the interpretation and modification of customary international law. If customary international law is considered as the product of the family of nations, then the family of nations alone is competent to interpret or modify rules of customary international law. There being no formal, institutionalized procedure to declare or formulate the will of the family of nations, its view may be ascertained through diplomatic channels or by means of a general conference leading to a resolution or treaty. In keeping with the decentralized character of the international society, any group of two or more states may agree on an authoritative or authentic interpretation with binding force for that group. Negotiation, conference, arbitration, or adjudication are among the procedures available for such purposes. The interpretation thus arrived at may find general acceptance by states not parties to the original proceedings.

Arbitration and adjudication appear to be among the classic methods for seeking and obtaining an authoritative interpretation on questions arising from the autonomous application and interpretation of international law. Usually, arbitration and adjudication are advocated as means to prevent war or as alternative to war, the "arbiter of nations."

This has been so particularly since the first Hague conference, and has become a stock in trade in the writings of the peace movement. This approach assumes that wars arise out of differences regarding the interpretation of international law. As a by-product of this line of thought there developed a controversy regarding the distinction between so-called justiciable and nonjusticiable disputes. The upshot of this controversy has been to clarify the issue to the extent of dispelling any doubt there may have been as to the suitability of arbitration and adjudication for deciding questions of international law, that is, questions concerning the interpretation and application of existing, positive international law. On the other hand, it brought into sharp focus the still prevailing reluctance, nay unwillingness, of states to submit such disputes to compulsory arbitration, that is, to a decisional procedure. Finally, and perhaps unwittingly, it revealed that many disputes ostensibly about questions of interpretation and application of international law are in fact controversies about claims for more or less far-reaching changes in the distribution of territories as elements in the struggle of power, or for other revisions of the existing treaty structure. Kelsen has been one of the most consistent opponents of the distinction between the so-called justiciable and nonjusticiable disputes, and an advocate of a comprehensive system of compulsory adjudication. These views were predicated on the ground that acceptance of compulsory adjudication and relinquishment of the untenable division of disputes into justiciable and nonjusticiable would materially contribute to a durable peace.[112] This no doubt is true, but only to the extent that disputes about international-law questions cause wars. Such a view, however, is perhaps an oversimplification of political realities. The legal arguments aired by governments on suitable occasions may in fact be legal cloaks for political ends. What causes war in such a situation is not the legal cloak but the clash of seemingly irreconcilable political ends. To expose the legal argument for what it is may serve a useful purpose, provided the governments concerned are willing to avoid or postpone the clash. Arbitration and adjudication are not particularly suitable for resolving political claims. Their role in the international society, like that of courts in national societies, is more modest. It is to settle disputes regarding interpretation and application of international law. Much would be gained if such disputes were regularly submitted to a decisional procedure. International law would gain greatly in stature and precision and many an international controversy would be reduced to size if submitted to arbitration. Theoretically as well as practically, the gain would consist in making autointerpretation not the final but, as it should be, the preliminary stage in disputes between states. Autointerpretation is easily presented, or rather misrepresented, as autodecision for want of a compulsory procedure leading to a heteronomous and binding decision. But appearances are misleading; they harden public opinion on one side or the other. States sometimes act as if they were organs of international law or as if they were authorized spokesmen for the international society, or as if they resorted to war in a just cause whereas in fact they are interested parties without any mandate or competence from the international society; and what is represented as a just cause of war or as a war in self-defense may, if put to the test of a judicial tribunal, turn out to have been nothing but an unjust war or war of aggression. Such is the lesson of the post-World War II trials. It cannot be the function of the theory of international law to lend color to the pretension that this or that state acts as an organ of the international society.

Moreover, the fact that in international relations recourse to a heteronomous procedure for the interpretation and application of international law is still the exception rather than the rule, and the further fact that negotiations often lead to deadlock rather than to an agreed solution render it extremely difficult to determine whether controversial rules of international law are still part of positive international law or have ceased to be so. The basic norm that states ought to behave as they have customarily behaved,[113] gives no indication concerning the content of positive international law. The empirical material which presents itself as international law contains inconsistencies and contradictions. States themselves have not followed and do not always follow the same line of conduct. The rule enunciated in the London Protocol which, it has been said, "was honored more in the breach than in the observance,"[114] is perhaps as good an example as any. Does it countenance the modification or termination of treaties by less than the agreement of the contracting parties? Is a modification contrary to that rule a violation of international law pure and simple, or a challenge to the basic norm, that is, an attempt at a revolutionary creation of international law?[115] If the revolution fails, the state which attempted the revolution is considered as a law breaker and, as the Nuremberg trial has shown, can be punished for defying the law. When, however, can it be said that a revolution, a challenge to the basic norm, has succeeded? Assuming that the post-war conduct of some states were put to the test of judicial determination, it is scarcely open to doubt that an uninstructed tribunal[116] would put that conduct to the test of traditional international law. As long, however, as allegation stands against allegation—and in international law and relations such allegations (autointerpretations) stand pitted against each other for long periods—it may be difficult to determine whether that conduct should be tested in the light of traditional international law or of the very principle on which it claims to be based. This problem is encountered in customary as well as in conventional international law. One may well ask whether the members of the United Nations, for instance, still adhere to the basic norm that they should behave in conformity with the Charter as adopted at San Francisco, or whether the basic norm is assumed to be that members should behave in conformity with the Charter as interpreted at any given moment by a two-thirds majority of the members. As the Charter of the United Nations, in contradistinction to the constitution of some of the specialized agencies mentioned above, does not confer upon the General Assembly the power to interpret the Charter authoritatively, the practice of the General Assembly amounts to an autointerpretation having the appearance and practical effect of an autodecision for as long as it is not submitted to the test of judicial investigation and determination. The conflict between East and West, to use the current and somewhat simplified formula, subjects customary as well as conventional international law to the strains and stresses characteristic of a period of transition in international law and relations.

Conclusion

Traditional international law, evolved gradually in the wake of the cataclysmic dismemberment of the hierarchical order of the Middle Ages, has been and still is characterized by a substantial degree of autonomy preserved by the states which form the international society. Autointerpretation is the result and principal manifestation of this autonomy. The establishment of an international tribunal with compulsory jurisdiction for all states and all disputes would inject into international law and relations a degree of heteronomy which would enhance the stature of international law as law. It was advocated by some as a guarantee against war. Others demanded it on the ground that without a modicum of organization it was premature to consider international law as true law, or as valid law, or as law at all. It was shown above that the practice of autointerpretation rooted in international law makes it difficult indeed to regard states as organs of international law and to maintain the *bellum justum* theory in any but a metaphorical sense. The absence of a modicum of institutionalized community interests is also an obstacle to the position that in its present stage the international society possesses a force monopoly.

Thus, for a variety of mutually complementary reasons, the development of institutions operating in the entire family of nations for a long time has been regarded as a desirable and indeed a feasible method to make international law an effective order without sacrificing its character as a law regulating the conduct of states on the basis of equality. This is, however, not necessarily the only method. World government or world federation are frequently praised and propagated as the more effective alternatives. Moreover, some observers claim to discern in the transitional period—the struggle between two agglomerations of states and power—the trend to a new hierarchial pattern within each of the two groups. This trend is characterized by the emergence of hegemonial or leading states. The effective establishment of the hegemony of one state or of a restricted concert of states might provide international law with the necessary degree of executive power, as, to some extent, it did in the nineteenth century. The present subordination of the states to the impersonal and unorganized authority of international law would be superseded by the subordination of the majority of states to the personal and organized authority of the leading state or states. This apparently has already happened in the group of states led and organized by the Soviet Union. For the "free world" it may not be too late to arrest the trend if it desires to remain free. States so far have been manifestly reluctant to subordinate themselves to collectively administered institutions for the creation, interpretation, and application of international law. The sacrifice in autonomy, particularly in the cherished right of autointerpretation involved in such an organization of the society of states, was deemed too great. The diminution inevitably involved in a hierarchical pattern may very likely be vastly greater. The choice seems no longer to be, as it has been in the past, between autonomy and heteronomy, but between different patterns of heteronomy.

H. LAUTERPACHT

Rules of Warfare in an Unlawful War

IT IS CONVENIENT to preface this essay by two observations of a general character. The first is that any consideration of the law of war must, if it is to avoid the justifiable reproach of being obsolete, take into account the fact that as the result of some general international treaties of a legislative character adopted after the two world wars the place of war in the system of international law has undergone a fundamental change. This is so because in consequence of the successive renunciation and prohibition of war in such instruments as the Covenant of the League of Nations, the Pact of Paris, and the Charter of the United Nations war has ceased to be a right which sovereign states are entitled to exercise at their unfettered discretion. War undertaken in violation of these enactments is an unlawful and criminal—not only an immoral—act. The true nature of that change has been obscured, in the popular estimation, by the repeated violations of these undertakings in the past and the widely felt danger of their being disregarded in the future. However, for the lawyer this circumstance—although relevant—cannot be decisive.

The second observation of a general character is that the results of that change in the position of war in the international legal system need not, in order to become legally cognizable and effective, be embodied in express international agreements incorporating the changes consequential upon the major development. *Cessante ratione cessat lex ipsa* is a maxim which is of general application. In the sphere of municipal law where the machinery of legislation is efficient and readily available, there is no frequent occasion to rely on that maxim for the purpose of drawing the necessary consequences from changes expressly enacted. The "consequential changes" are, as a rule, provided for in the very statute which has brought about the major reform. Skilled parliamentary draftsmen, well acquainted with the entire field of law, see to it that the consequential developments are not left to the hazards of advocacy or, for that matter, to judicial inventiveness and logic. In the realm of international legislation no such detailed provision for the resulting changes is feasible. The difficulties of securing agreement on the major enactment, as a rule, tax to the full the resources of the international conference and of the negotiators. To try to secure unanimous agreement on the multifarious and complicated alterations of the law resulting from the principal treaty might well wreck the contemplated principal change. And yet, once a treaty has been adopted which is of a fundamental and comprehensive character, it is difficult—and probably unscientific—to act on the view that it settles only that part of the law to which it expressly refers and nothing else. A treaty is not concluded in a legal vacuum. It is part of a legal system which, for that very reason, cannot contain rules which are contradictory.[1] Any such contradiction must be removed by a reasonable application of the principle that newly enacted law, if it is of a general and fundamental character, alters rules inconsistent with it. Admittedly, that indirect method of effecting—or ascertaining—changes in the law is unsatisfactory for various reasons. It introduces into the law an element of uncertainty and conjecture. It appears to make the law flow not from the express will of states, but from deductions made by judges or writers. As such it is open to objection that if governments really desire to change the law in any particular respect they ought to say so explicitly, and that unless they do so they must be deemed not to have desired the change in question.[2]

However, there is a limit beyond which we should not ascribe to governments the desire to will things which are incompatible and contradictory. That limit in turn must curb any excessive rigidity of the positivist method. Even if we assent to the dogma that the will of states is the only source of international law, that does not mean that their will must be express and specific in every detail. The manner in which some writers have denied that the undoubted illegality of aggressive war also implies its criminality—on the part both of the state as such and the individuals responsible for its conduct—has revealed the sterility of the approach which renders impossible the adaptation of specific rules and principles to major changes in the law expressly enacted.[3] Any such approach lends itself to criticism even more pertinent than that traditionally levied against what is described as the mere jurisprudence of concepts (*Begriffsjurisprudenz*). For the latter pays attention—in fact, that is the essence of its method—to extracting all possible logical effectiveness from notions and rules forming part of positive law. Its defect is due to an excessive concentration on that particular method of interpreting the law in disregard of wider considerations which may reasonably be considered to underlie the will of the legislator.

The above considerations apply directly to the question which forms the subject matter of this essay. How far has the change in the place of war in the international legal system, that is, its renunciation and prohibition as an instrument of national policy, affected the continued operation of the accepted rules of war and neutrality? Before the Covenant of the League of Nations, the general Treaty for the Renunciation of War, and the Charter of the United Nations it was generally believed that the question of the so-called justice or legality of the war was not in any way relevant to the question of the applicability of rules of warfare. In a distinct sense, that question did not arise at all. For under the law then in force every war was, legally, just; every war was legal. War was authorized not only as an instrument for enforcing existing rights. It was also permitted as a means for challenging the existing law—including the law as expressed in any particular treaty and limiting the right of a state to go to war as, for example, in a treaty of neutrality. However, the changes in international law as expressed in the abovementioned instruments have made it necessary to reconsider the relevance of the legality of war to the application of rules of warfare. There has been a tendency to maintain that these changes have not affected the validity of the view, previously held with virtual unanimity,[4] that the rules of war apply also in an illegal war.[5] That tendency has been represented with special emphasis by those who have uttered warnings against the neglect, in reliance upon the new developments, of the study and the formulation of rules of war.[6] Neither, as will be seen, have municipal courts shown any pronounced inclination to take into account the impact of that major change in the legal position of war. Undoubtedly the matter does not admit of a simple or drastic solution. However, this does not mean that we are entitled to leave out of account the legal consequences of the most important of all changes which have taken place in the international legal system.

The Operation of Rules of Warfare *Pendente Bello*

It would seem logical and fully consistent with principle that so far as war has ceased to be a right—or an exercise of power—authorized by international law, an illegal war—that is, a war resorted to contrary to the fundamental obligations accepted by a state and aiming at abolishing the institution of war as such—should no longer confer upon the guilty belligerent all the rights to which he was entitled under traditional international law. *Ex injuria jus non oritur* is a well-established principle of law. However, to state that principle in relation to an illegal war is to state only part of the problem. In a defective system of law—and international law is still a defective legal system in all the vital aspects of creation, ascertainment, and enforcement of the law—the maxim *ex injuria jus non oritur* often yields to the rival principle, *ex factis jus oritur.* Of this, the vicissitudes of the doctrine of nonrecognition—which is essentially an application of the principle *ex injuria jus non oritur*—provides an instructive example. In a different sphere the exercise, by municipal courts of some countries, of jurisdiction over persons and vessels brought before them in violation of international law affords yet another instance of the limitations, in the international sphere, of the rule *ex injuria jus non oritur.*

In relation to the applicability of rules of warfare to the belligerent engaging in an unlawful war rigid reliance on that principle would mean in practice that rules of war do not apply at all in a war of this nature. For, unless the aggressor has been defeated from the very outset (in which case *cadit quaestio*), it is impossible to visualize the conduct of hostilities in which one side would be bound by rules of warfare without benefiting from them and in which the other side would benefit from rules of warfare without being bound by them. Accordingly, any application to the actual conduct of war of the principle *ex injuria jus non oritur* would transform the contest into a struggle which is subject to no regulation at all. The result would be, in the first instance, the abandonment of that substantial part of rules of warfare which are of a humanitarian character. These rules have been generally observed in the past. It does not matter in this context that they have been so observed mainly for the reason that they did not seriously interfere with the achievement of the major purpose of the war. The decisive fact is that they have served to a considerable extent the purpose of preventing or diminishing human suffering, and that they would in fact cease to operate if their operation were made dependent upon the legality of the war on the part of one belligerent or group of belligerents. Unless hostilities are to degenerate into a savage contest of physical forces freed of all restraints of compassion, chivalry, and respect for the dignity of man, it is essential that the accepted rules of war in that—humanitarian—sphere should continue to be observed.

For these reasons the modern tendency, which has found expression, in particular, in the four Geneva conventions of 1949, has been to subject to the humanitarian rules of war also those contests which do not constitute war in the strictly legal sense of the word and to confer the status of lawful belligerents, bound by and entitled to the protection of rules of warfare, upon combatants who previously did not enjoy the protection of international law. Thus all four Geneva conventions of 1949 provide uniformly that in an armed conflict which is not of an international character occurring in the territory of one of the parties to the convention and which is party to the conflict the belligerents shall be bound to apply, as a minimum, certain fundamental provisions of a humanitarian nature.[7] The effect of these provisions is to subject the parties to the civil war—including the party which is not a recognized belligerent—to important restraints of the law of war.[8] In accordance with the same tendency, Article 4 of the convention on prisoners of war includes in the definition of prisoners of war "members of regular armed forces who profess allegiance to a government or an authority not recognized by the Detaining Power." Finally, the same convention marks a considerable advance upon the Hague regulations which apparently protected organized resistance movements only outside the area firmly occupied by the enemy. Article 4 of the convention lays down that members of militias and volunteer corps which do not form part of the regular armed forces as well as members "of organised resistance movements, belonging to a Party to the conflict and operating in or outside their own territory, even if this territory is occupied," are entitled to be treated as prisoners of war provided that they fulfill certain conditions.[9]

However, it is not only the abandonment of the humanitarian rules in the strict sense of the word which must necessarily deprive the conduct of hostilities of essential restraints. Most rules of warfare are, in a sense, of a humanitarian character inasmuch as their object is to safeguard, within the limits of the stern exigencies of war, human life and some other fundamental human rights and to make possible a measure of intercourse between enemies. These rules include those relating to the limitations of the use of force; flags of truce and, generally, intercourse between belligerents in the actual line of battle; protection of passengers and crews of merchant vessels; and, above all, the protection of the civilian population in occupied territory. The latter provides a persuasive illustration of the view—which, it is here submitted, is the correct and the only practicable view—that during the war all belligerents, including the aggressor, must be held to be under a duty to respect and are entitled to rely as among themselves on the observance of rules of warfare as generally recognized. The belligerent occupant, even if he is the aggressor, is entitled to exact from the civilian population the obedience—which is not necessarily synonymous with allegiance—due to him under international law. To say that the population is at liberty to differentiate between the "lawful" and "unlawful" occupant in the matter of obedience owed to him, is, in effect, to free the occupant of the obligation to treat the population, in such circumstances, in accordance with international law. He cannot be expected to treat as noncombatants inhabitants who claim the right to commit against him direct or indirect acts of hostility and who are not organized in a manner entitling them according to international law to be treated as lawful combatants.[10]

For these reasons the law of belligerent occupation in relation to inhabitants is a cogent example of the necessity of maintaining the operation of rules of war regardless of the illegality of the war undertaken by any of the belligerents. In the Hostages trial (the case of *U.S. v. Wilhelm List et al.*) the United States Military Tribunal at Nuremberg, in a judgment given in 1948, gave detailed reasons for rejecting the view that as the war was illegal on the part of Germany, the rules of warfare relating to belligerent occupation could not be invoked by her and that therefore the inhabitants were entitled to resist the German forces of occupation. It is convenient to quote this part of the judgment:

> The Prosecution advances the contention that since Germany's war against Yugoslavia and Greece were aggressive wars, the German occupation troops were there unlawfully and gained no rights whatever as an occupant. It is further asserted as a corollary, that the duties owed by the populace to an occupying power which are normally imposed under the rules of International Law, never became effective in the present case because of the criminal character of the invasion and occupation.
>
> For the purposes of this discussion, we accept the statement as true that the wars against Yugoslavia and Greece were in direct violation of the Kellogg-Briand Pact and were therefore criminal in character. But it does not follow that every act by the German occupation forces against person or property is a crime or that any and every act undertaken by the population of the occupied country against the German occupation forces thereby became legitimate defence. . . .
>
> At the outset, we desire to point out that International Law makes no distinction between a lawful and unlawful occupant in dealing with the respective duties of occupant and population in occupied territory. There is no reciprocal connection between the manner of the military occupation of territory and the rights and duties of the occupant and population to each other after the relationship has in fact been established. Whether the invasion was lawful or criminal is not an important factor in the consideration of this subject.[11]

The tribunal held, accordingly, that inhabitants who waged hostilities against Germany without complying with the provisions of Article 1 of the 4th Hague convention relating to lawful combatants, were liable to be treated as guerillas.

In the Zuhlke case the Netherlands Special Court of Cassation, in a judgment given in 1948, dissented from the decision of the lower court which held that as the war between Germany and the Netherlands was an "international crime" on the part of Germany "everything done by Germans as members of the occupying authorities, except that which occurred in the normal exercise of the law," was "illegitimate." The Special Court of Cassation held that it was "going too far to regard as war crimes all acts committed against the Netherlands or the Netherlanders by the German forces and other organs during the war, solely on the grounds of the illegal nature of the war, launched by the then German Reich."[12] At the same time the court expressed the view that as the war was an international crime on the part of Germany, Holland would have been entitled to answer the aggression with reprisals,[13] even with regard to the normal operation of the laws of war on land, sea, and in the air.[14] This latter qualification is, it is submitted, open to question inasmuch as, if admitted, it would amount to conceding to the victim of aggression the right to disregard, by way of reprisals, the laws of war as against the guilty belligerent.[15]

Other judgments given by Dutch courts, are to a similar effect. Thus, for instance, in the case of General Christiansen, who was commander of the German army of occupation in Holland—the Netherlands Special Court for War Criminals at Arnhem found the accused guilty of various acts of reprisals against the Dutch resistance movement. The tribunal held that "the rules of international law, insofar as they regulate the methods of warfare and the occupation of enemy territory make no distinction between wars which have been started legally and those which have been started illegally." Accordingly, the tribunal held that the occupant waging an illegal war was entitled, in principle, to punish members of the resistance movement except when such resistance was due to the unlawful acts of the occupant. On the other hand the court held that the resistance movement was lawful seeing that there was no rule of international law obliging the inhabitants to render obedience to the occupant—except that, as with respect to spies, international law permitted the belligerent to punish what was an otherwise legal act. The court found the accused guilty on the ground that the reprisals ordered by him against the civilian population exceeded the bounds permitted by international law.[16]

In the Grauser case the Supreme National Tribunal of Poland, without apparently drawing direct practical conclusions from its observations,[17] remarked that the hostilities which Germany launched in 1939 against Poland did not constitute a war according to international law, but a "criminal invasion" in violation of a pact of nonaggression. Accordingly, in view of the tribunal, the occupation of Polish territory by Germany was not an occupation in the true meaning of the word, but "an unlawful seizure of another's territory by force and compulsion."[18]

It is pertinent to refer to an extreme example of the consequence of the view that the guilty belligerent cannot rely on the laws of war. That view, when pushed to its rigid logical consequences, leads to the conclusion that the typical manifestation of belligerent action in war, namely, the killing of lawful combatants, is a criminal act of murder. That view seems occasionally to have been asserted.[19] Its corollary would seem to be that members of armed forces of the belligerent waging an unlawful war would be liable for murder if captured. Such consequences disclose the unsoundness of the major proposition from which it is derived. In fact they have been occasionally adduced as a warning against indiscriminate reliance on legal logic in this matter. Thus in the Altstötter case (the Justice trial) the United States Military Tribunal at Nuremberg, in a judgment given in 1947, declined to treat as relevant the fact of aggressive war in deciding whether the "Draconic laws" enacted in Germany for which the accused were responsible constituted crimes against humanity. It said: "If we should adopt the view that by reason of the fact that the war is a criminal war of aggression every act which would have been legal in a defensive war was illegal in this one, we would be forced to the conclusion that every soldier who marched under orders into occupied territory or who fought in the homeland was a criminal and a murderer. The rules of land warfare upon which the prosecution has relied would not be the measure of conduct and the pronouncement of guilt in any case would become a mere formality."[20]

Other tribunals have declined, in different spheres, to assent to the proposition that during the war the unlawful belligerent is not entitled to rely on rules of warfare. In the German High Command trial (the case of *U.S. v. Wilhelm Leeb et al.*), before the United States Military Tribunal at Nuremberg, it was contended by the prosecution, with respect to the charge of wanton destruction of property, that the accused could not properly plead military necessity: "The defence of military necessity can never be utilized to justify destruction in occupied territory by the perpetrator of an aggressive war. To allow such a defence to be interposed would result in a farcical paradox. It is perfectly apparent that the phrase "imperatively demanded by the necessities of war" was never intended to justify the commission of one criminal act in order to extricate the perpetrator from the consequences of another criminal act."[21] Referring to the presence of the accused in Russia, where he was "acting in furtherance of a criminal design," the prosecution added: "The only military necessity he can point to was caused by his being where it was a crime for him to be in the first place."[22] The tribunal did not adopt that reasoning. Without examining it directly, it answered it by implication by finding, with respect to most of the accused, that it had not been strictly proven that, in the circumstances, the devastation went beyond military necessity: "What constitutes devastation beyond military necessity in these situations requires detailed proof of an operational and tactical nature."[23]

However, courts have occasionally drawn consequences—although not of an extreme nature—from the proposition that the author of an unlawful war cannot avail himself during the war of all the rights of belligerency. Thus in the Rauter case, the Netherlands Special Court of Cassation, in a somewhat discursive judgment given in 1949, seems to have denied that Germany was entitled to have recourse to reprisals against Holland and the Dutch population. The court said:

> The appeal to this, in principle recognised, right of a belligerent State to take reprisals, provided they are of a permissible nature — eventually also against the population of occupied territory—cannot be of any avail to the defendant, as there was no previous international offence committed by the Netherlands against the German Reich, so that the Reich mentioned had absolutely no right to take genuine reprisals. It is indeed well known all over the world . . . and also convincingly established by the International Military Tribunal in Nuremberg . . . that the former German Reich unleashed against the Kingdom of the Netherlands, as it did against various other States in Europe, an unlawful war of aggression, and by so doing began on its part to violate International Law, an international offence for which in itself the Kingdom of the Netherlands was already justified in answering by taking reprisals against the aggressor.[24]

In its judgment given in 1949 in the Weizsaecker case the United States Military Tribunal at Nuremberg went far in the direction of drawing conclusions, some of which are controversial, from the Pact of Paris. From the proposition, which is unobjectionable, that "it implicitly authorized the other nations of the world to take such measures as they might deem proper or necessary to punish the transgressor" it concludes that "it [the Pact of Paris] placed the transgressor outside the society of nations." There is room for the opinion that the very act of punishing the transgressor recognizes, in a negative and specific sense, his place in society. What is of particular interest in the present discussion is the view of the tribunal that "he who initiates aggressive war loses the right to claim self-defense against those who seek to enforce the Treaty" and that that rule is merely "the embodiment, in international law, of a long established principle of criminal law."[25] The tribunal quoted here from Wharton: "There can be no self-defence against self-defence."[26]

In general, however, there is no judicial authority in support of the proposition that the aggressor is not entitled during the war to rely on those rules of warfare which bear on the actual conduct of hostilities, or that the members of his armed forces are, after the war, liable to punishment for acts committed during the war in conformity with rules of warfare.

The reasons which make it imperative to permit the full application, during the war and as between the belligerents, of the rules of war are especially cogent when we consider that in the present state of international organization there may be no means, so long as the war lasts, by which an authoritative judgment can be arrived at on the question as to which state is the aggressor. Thus nothing short of the unanimous concurrence of the permanent members of the Security Council, other than the guilty state itself, is sufficient for the determination that a particular state has resorted to war in violation of the principles of the Charter. The vote of the aggressor himself is essential when such finding is to be coupled with enforcement action. For the same reason it is impossible to accept the suggestion, which is occasionally made, that the state which is the victim of aggression should be entitled to resort to weapons the use of which may otherwise be illegal. Any such provision of the law presupposes the possibility of an authoritative determination of the question of aggression. As noted, there is no warrant for any such assumption. The plea of self-defense will be invoked alike by the author of aggression and its victim. In the din of battle the voice of the latter may be drowned by the strident and cynical protestations of the aggressor as a justification for resort, on his part, to the illegal weapons. Neither is there good reason for assuming that at the beginning of the hostilities prohibited weapons will not be available to the aggressor and that in that case, even if he does not go to the length of representing himself as the victim of aggression, he will tolerate passively the use of prohibited weapons against him.

Undoubtedly, the necessity of permitting the aggressor to avail himself of the protection of the law of war is, in a sense, illogical and expressive of a serious defect in the efficacy of international law. However, this is the necessary result of the fact that international law, although it may prohibit war, is not always able to prevent it. It may not be able to do so even if the international community acquires a higher degree of integration than it possesses at present—including the effective legal capacity of its organs to determine the fact of aggression and to enforce the peace collectively in pursuance of a decision of its members falling short, if necessary, of the unanimous vote of the great powers. For even then there will remain the necessity of regulating the conduct of the hostilities regardless of whether such collective enforcement is described as war or not—in the same way in which civil war within the state tends in the long run to be regulated by rules of war as established by international law.[27] It is possible that international society in the future will develop a body of appropriate rules and principles governing the collective use of force. However, unless the force at the disposal of the international community is so overwhelming as to approach rapid police action permitting of no organized resistance, it is doubtful whether such rules can differ appreciably from those governing the principal aspects of the relations of belligerents in an ordinary war. This is so although it is probably inaccurate and undesirable to describe such use of force as war. The dignity and the purpose of the collective enforcement of the rule of law in international society require that it should rank in a category different from war as traditionally understood in international law. During the hostilities arising out of the invasion, in 1950, of South Korea by North Korea there was no disposition on the part of the United Nations as a whole or of the individual states participating in the enforcement action under Chapter VII of the Charter to refer to the contest as war and to draw automatically the resulting consequences in the sphere of their municipal law.[28] No declaration of war was issued. At the same time neither side challenged the applicability of rules of warfare; both formally expressed their determination to abide by the provisions of the Geneva convention relating to prisoners of war.[29]

Consequences of the Illegality of the War Apart from Rules Relating to the Conduct of Hostilities

Reasons have been given in the preceding part of this article why, *so long as the hostilities last*, the fact of the illegality of the war undertaken by a party to the struggle in violation of its fundamental undertakings is irrelevant, *in the relations of the belligerents*, to the question of the applicability of rules of warfare in *matters relating to the conduct of hostilities in the strict sense of the word.* The italicized passages point to the qualifications of the view that the illegality of the war has no effect on the operation of the rules of war. In the first instance, that view can claim validity only during the war. Secondly, the illegality of the war has a bearing upon certain traditional rules of international law, which although not constituting rules of warfare proper, are directly connected with the institution of war. Thirdly, the rule which disregards the fact of the illegality of the war applies only to the laws of war in the strict sense of the word as distinguished from the law relating to acquisition of title over property. Fourthly, it does not apply to the relations of belligerents and neutrals, in particular after the war. These qualifications, however limited, of the view which contemplates the illegality of the war as irrelevant and which seems therefore obnoxious and illogical, will now be considered.

After the cessation of hostilities there is room for the application of the principle that in certain spheres no rights and benefits can accrue to the aggressor from his illegality. Some of these consequences of illegality may appear to be somewhat theoretical; others may be of immediate and practical application. Thus it follows from the principle *ex injuria jus non oritur* that a peace treaty imposed by the victorious aggressor has no legal validity. This is so notwithstanding the rule of orthodox international law which disregards the vitiating effect of duress in the conclusion of treaties. For that rule can reasonably be held to apply only to a war which the victor is entitled to wage. So long as international law authorized resort to war as an instrument of national policy and as an undisputed prerogative of national sovereignty, it was inevitable that it should countenance the validity of treaties imposed by the victor. That consideration does not apply, in relation to the guilty belligerent, in a system of international law in which war no longer occupies that position—although it is a consideration which continues to be valid in relation to the state which has been the victim of aggression.[30] However, that particular consequence of the illegality of war has, in fact, little relevance to the question of the application of rules of warfare. Also, although of considerable interest from the point of doctrine, that aspect of the matter is probably of little import in practice. It will cause no embarrassment to the aggressor who will either brush it aside with contempt or who will invoke in his aid that very rule by the simple device of describing himself as the object of the illegal war. To the actual victim of aggression it will afford little immediate comfort—though it may strengthen his position, morally and legally, when he is politically in the position to shake off some or all of the burdensome provisions of an imposed treaty of peace. It is also possible that neutral states and their courts, if they are politically in the position to do so, may draw the proper legal consequences from that particular qualification of the irrelevance of the illegality of the war.

Similar considerations apply to the question of the title which the aggressor purports to have acquired by conquest. So long as war was a permissible instrument of national policy, international law recognized title acquired by force—a mode of acquisition altogether alien to legal principle. The situation has altered as the result of the changes, indicated above, in the legal position of war.[31] However, the same reasons which limit, in practice, the consequences of the vitiating effect of duress in relation to treaties imposed by the aggressor, apply also to the invalidity of the title by conquest imposed in such circumstances—with the possible qualification that such conquest is open to the impact of the doctrine of nonrecognition of title illegally acquired.

Thirdly, while international law sets no limit to conditions of peace which the victor may exact from the defeated enemy, it has been customary not to compel him to pay compensation for damage arising out of operations connected with the lawful conduct of war. That custom must henceforth be deemed to lack a juridical basis in the case of a war unlawfully undertaken.[32] The Treaty of Versailles foreshadowed the adoption of that principle. In Article 231 Germany accepted the responsibility, for herself and her allies, "for causing all the loss and damage to which the Allied and Associated Governments and their nationals have been subjected as a consequence of the war imposed upon them by the aggression of Germany and her allies." In Article 232 she undertook to "make compensation for all damage done to the civilian population of the Allied and Associated Powers and to their property during the period of belligerency of and as an Allied or Associated Power against Germany, by such aggression by land, by sea, and in general by all damage as defined" in the treaty. At the time of the Treaty of Versailles—as well as in 1914 when Germany launched World War I—the fundamental changes in the position of war had not yet taken place and to that extent aggressive war had not yet become an illegal or criminal act. However, insofar as the victors rightly assumed that the war had been one of aggression on the part of Germany, these provisions of the Treaty of Versailles must be regarded as having paved the way for the adoption of what seems the correct principle on the subject. The peace treaties of 1947 concluded after World War II only partly illuminate the problem. For although all of them, in the respective preambles, charge the defeated states with having taken part in a war of aggression under the aegis of Germany, they adduce the mitigating circumstance of those states having abandoned the criminal alliance in the final stages of the war. However, there is in these treaties an element of differentiation in the treatment of the defeated aggressor states as well, as to some extent, an element of reparation. Thus in the treaty with Italy reparation is provided, in Article 74, in favor of Soviet Russia, though not of other allies. Moreover, although the treaty includes, in Article 76, an express renunciation by Italy of claims arising directly out of the war, there is no such express renunciation on the part of the Allied Powers. Also, the treaties provide for the right of the victor to seize, liquidate, and retain enemy property and to apply it for the satisfaction of the claims of the Allies and their nationals, including debts, under the peace treaties.[33] On the other hand, with regard to the property of the Allies and their nationals in enemy territory, the peace treaties of 1947 provide for the full restoration of "legal rights and interests" and for the return of other property. The differential treatment of the property of the victors and the defeated can properly be explained by the fact that, as stated in the preamble to these treaties, the defeated states bore the responsibility for taking part in the war of aggression.

The fact that this test—namely, participation in a war of aggression—has been applied after both world wars by the victors does not necessarily mean that it is a test altogether devoid of value. The test appears to be particularly valid, when the victors represent the overwhelming majority of states and when their action can thus be conceived as being in the nature of enforcement of international law. Undoubtedly, the actual application of this test—as of the other tests here examined—depends upon the success of the just cause and the defeat of aggression. That outcome, which is synonymous with the survival of international law, must be assumed. Without some such assumption any considerations of questions of international law is unreal. Once that assumption is granted, there is room for the adoption and application of principles which discourage lawlessness and penalize aggression. To what extent reparation—of a compensatory and penal nature—commensurate with the magnitude of the crime of aggressive war is economically feasible is outside the sphere of legal consideration. The fact that such reparation may not be fully practicable is not a sufficient reason for questioning the authority of the principle which underlies it.

The same considerations apply to yet another consequence of the illegality of aggressive war, namely, that the very act of initiating and waging war may, after the war, become the subject of a criminal charge and criminal responsibility. This, in fact, was one of the charges brought against the major war criminals in the trials at Nuremberg and in the Far East. That consequence of the illegality of aggressive war must, in the nature of things, be limited to persons who are in a position of political leadership and thus bear the responsibility for the major decision to embark upon the war of aggression. For that reason no attempt was made in the indictments in the above-mentioned trials to draw the full logical conclusion from the fact of the illegality of the war, for instance, by an allegation that, because of such illegality, acts otherwise lawful—such as orders to kill combatants or to perform requisitions in accordance with the Hague conventions—became criminal.[34] On the contrary, the indictments were limited (apart from the major charge of initiating and waging a war of aggression) to charges of war crimes proper, that is, of violations of the law of war and, in some cases, of crimes against humanity. That practice must be regarded as consistent with the principle that, during the war, the illegality of the war does not affect the continued operation of rules of warfare bearing directly upon the conduct of hostilities. That principle would become unreal to a large extent if after the war acts performed in accordance with rules of warfare were to be treated, retrospectively, as illegal and criminal. For reasons to be stated, these considerations do not fully apply to measures connected with the war and purporting to confer upon the unlawful belligerent title to property both during and after the war—a subject discussed in the next section.

There may be room, in yet another sphere, for the application—both before and during the war—of the principle that the aggressor cannot derive rights from his illegal conduct. Thus it has been suggested that that principle may properly be applied in relation to the rule that some treaties are abrogated as between belligerents as the result of the outbreak of war. Can the guilty belligerent and its nationals rely on that rule in order to render inoperative, as against them, the provisions of the treaty? It does not appear that courts have so far been prepared to consider—or that they have been invited by the parties to consider—that question from this point of view.[35]

Finally, reference may be made to the application of reprisals, during the war, against the guilty belligerent in matters not related directly to hostilities and bearing on the economic aspects of warfare. Thus in the retaliatory order in council issued by Great Britain in 1941 on the outbreak of the war with Japan, measures were announced for "restricting the commerce of Japan."[36] In its two opening recitals the order referred to the fact that "by reason of her unprovoked aggression His Majesty has been compelled to proclaim the existence of a state of war with Japan" and that "Japan has carried out attacks against British, United States and other territory without previous warning, either in the form of a declaration of war or an ultimatum with a conditional declaration of war, in flagrant violation of international law and particularly of Article 1 of the Third Hague Convention relative to the opening of hostilities." It is not clear why, if the intention of the order was to treat the illegality of the war on the part of Japan as a ground for the adoption of reprisals, no reference was made to the General Treaty for the Renunciation of War to which Japan was a party. Moreover, it appears from the other recitals of the order relating to Japan that by becoming an ally of Germany and Italy she automatically exposed herself to the impact of the retaliatory orders in the matter of maritime war previously issued against Germany and Italy. These latter orders were in fact recited in the order against Japan. But the order against Germany was based not on the illegality of the war undertaken by her, but on the fact of the violation by that belligerent of the laws of maritime war. Similarly, the order against Italy was based on the sole fact that she had become an ally of Germany against whom a retaliatory order had previously been issued. It would thus appear that there was, during World War II, no disposition to deny to the aggressor the benefit of the rules of war, in the sphere of maritime economic warfare, on account of the illegality of the war. It may be controversial to what extent such reprisals are open to the general objections outlined above which militate against the denial of belligerent rights to the aggressor.[37] While they do not bear directly upon hostilities proper, the vital importance of the economic weapon is such that reprisals of that nature may become the starting point for a more general abandonment, by both belligerents, of the restraints of the law of war not only at sea but also on land and in the air.

Acquisition by the Aggressor of Title Over Property in the Course of an Illegal War

As has been shown, compelling reasons of humanity and order lead to the adoption of the view that logic and principle must stop short of denying to the aggressor, during the war, the right to rely on accepted rules of warfare in matters relating directly to the conduct of hostilities. On the other hand these considerations do not require that the aggressor waging an unlawful war should be able to rely on rules of warfare for enriching himself by acquiring title and by validly transferring it in respect of acts which are otherwise lawful such as requisition, confiscation by way of penalty for ordinary criminal offences, other appropriation of public and private enemy property, and captures in prize. This aspect of the problem is of distinctly limited importance compared with the question of the operation of the laws of war proper. Moreover, as will be shown, the view which is here put forward—namely, that at least in this sphere the aggressor cannot benefit from the rules of warfare—has not yet secured judicial acceptance and cannot therefore be advanced as a rule of existing law. Yet, it is believed, this is the very minimum of principle that can be salvaged from a disturbing situation which otherwise compels us to ignore the factor of the illegality of war.

It is clear, in the first instance, that—except in relation to authorities which are subservient to him—the belligerent occupant, whether the war be lawful or not, does not acquire title in respect of acts which are contrary to the laws of war. Thus if he confiscates private property in violation of the law of war or, which amounts to the same, if he requisitions property without payment or effective substitute, he does not, in the contemplation of international law, acquire title. Those who take such property from him, whether for consideration or not, do it at their own peril. Any court, free to administer the law impartially, is entitled and bound to treat such purported title as invalid. The practice of municipal courts on the subject is well established.[38] There have been instances, both after World War I[39] and World War II[40], in which such acts on the part both of the agents of the occupant and his successors in title have been held to be not only null and void but also involving criminal responsibility. In World War II, confronted with a systematic policy of spoliation and plunder on the part of Germany in occupied territory, the Allied governments issued an express warning to that effect. In that warning which was declaratory of the correct legal position and which was addressed in particular to persons in neutral countries, the Allied governments announced that they intended to "do their utmost to defeat the methods of dispossession" practiced by Germany in occupied territory. They reserved their right to declare invalid, *inter alia,* transfers of property and interests situated in territories under enemy occupation.[41] That warning was subsequently acted upon by the courts of neutral countries—in particular of Switzerland.[42]

However, the question with which we are here primarily concerned is of a different nature. It is the question of the effect of measures which would be lawful but for the fact that they were taken by a belligerent waging an unlawful war. What is the position if such a belligerent purports to acquire title as the result of a requisition effected in full conformity with the Hague regulations? Does the person to whom the belligerent waging an unlawful war subsequently sells that property acquire title in it? Does the purchaser of a ship, lawfully condemned by such a belligerent, acquire title over her? What is the position with regard to booty and other public property of his adversary lawfully appropriated by the aggressor and transferred by him to a purchaser for value? It would appear—and this, it is submitted, is the answer most consistent with principle—that no enforceable right in any such property can be claimed by the guilty belligerent or his transferees or successors in title. In particular, persons who acquire it from him ought not to be in the position to assert successfully a title thus obtained before any courts independent of his power.

It is consistent with the legal principle which prompts the conclusion that during the war, in the relations of the belligerent, the fact of the illegality of war must be left out of account, that the aggressor should not be allowed to retain, after the war, any profit that may have accrued to him from his illegality. Nor should those retain profit who went out of their way to lend the aggressor support by acquiring from him property of which he had dispossessed the victim of aggression or his nationals. Undoubtedly, if he is defeated, the very fact of defeat and the decisions of the victor will in the majority of cases effectively deprive the aggressor or his successor in title of most of his gains. Any decision of the victor in that direction is not a mere assertion of victorious power. In those cases in which the question of the aggressor's title comes before courts, a judicial denial of title grounded in the initial illegality of the war seems both proper and imperative. These courts may be those of the victorious belligerent, of the defeated aggressor, or of neutral states. There is no reason why the judicial nullification of such acquisitions and title should be postponed till after the end of the war. The courts of the aggressor will naturally be unable to do so during the hostilities. They may do it after he has been defeated and conditions have been restored in his own country for an independent administration of the law, international and municipal, provided that these courts are willing to avail themselves of their regained independence and to dissociate themselves from the ideology of the regime which became guilty of a war of aggression.[43] Such denial of the validity of the title acquired or transferred by the aggressor would appear to be the very minimum of the consequences flowing from the illegality—and criminality—of his original action, because the operation of the rules of war, during an illegal war and in the mutual relations of the belligerents, does not follow from principle. It is contrary to principle. It follows from cogent reasons of humanity. When—and as soon as—these reasons cease to operate, the fact of the illegality of the war must be taken into account. As already suggested, the person who purchases property from the aggressor does so at his risk. There is no compulsion for him to do so. Undoubtedly, the inhabitants of the occupied territory must obey the orders of the aggressor; they have no alternative.[44] But they need not encourage him and, above all, strengthen his war effort by excess of coöperation such as buying goods requisitioned or otherwise appropriated by him. If they do so, they must take the consequences. The same can properly be expected of persons within neutral jurisdiction. It is inconsistent both with international law and international morality that neutral territory should become for the aggressor a convenient and profitable repository for the spoils of aggression.

While the principle here advanced—the principle of the invalidity of title acquired by the belligerent waging an unlawful war—seems consistent with and prompted by cogent legal considerations, it has not become part of the practice of courts. To that extent the reader must be warned that what is here represented as a correct principle of law is so, at present, substantially *de lege ferenda* only. In examining, after World War II, the validity of the title acquired or transferred by the aggressor, courts have done so only by reference to the question whether such title was acquired in conformity with the law of war. With minor exceptions they have not considered as relevant the fact that the war was an illegal war of aggression on the part of Germany and her allies. Moreover, it appears that in most of these cases the question was not raised by the interested party. An interesting case—*French State v. Etablissements Monmousseau*[45]—decided in 1948 by the Court of Orleans may be mentioned as an example. In this case the French state brought action to recover a number of metal wine vats, which before the war were the property of the French army and which, after having been seized by the German occupation authorities, were sold by them to the defendant company. The French state supported its claim on various grounds such as that the occupant, being only the usufructuary of the public property of the occupied state, whether moveable or immovable, could not acquire ownership in it; and, in particular, that the wine vats, being a permanent fixture attached to immovable property were, according to French law, to be regarded themselves as immovable property and as such governed in any case by the specific provision of Article 55 of the 4th Hague convention, according to which the occupant is only the administrator and usufructuary of the immovable property belonging to the occupied state. The court found against the French state. In particular, the court held that the conception of *immovables par destination* could not be applied to the interpretation of the Hague convention and that Germany had validly acquired title over moveable property belonging to France. The issue of the illegality of the war and of the propriety of a French subject acquiring, in a war of that description, property of which his state has been divested by the aggressor, was not raised. Neither was the question of the relevance of the illegality of the war raised in the cases in which the courts held that either the acquisition or the subsequent transfer of title by the occupant was invalid on the ground that the original taking was contrary to international law.[46] It may be said that as in these cases the courts were in the position to reach their conclusion by reference to the fact that the action of the occupant was in violation of the rules of warfare, it was unnecessary for them to raise the wider issue of the applicability of the laws of warfare. However, such argument is persuasive only on the assumption that the view here put forward as to the nullity, in this sphere, of the acts of aggression because of the initial inapplicability of rules of warfare is unfounded or at least controversial. Reasons have been given why that view ought to be regarded as an irreducible minimum of a proper judicial appreciation of the consequences of the illegality of war.

The same principle, it is submitted, ought to apply to title acquired or transferred by the aggressor as the result of valid captures and condemnations in prize proceedings. There would appear to be no adequate reason—such as prompt the full application of the law of war in other spheres—why the aggressor waging an illegal war should be deemed to have acquired a valid and permanent title in vessels and goods, whether enemy or neutral, condemned as a lawful prize in proceedings which are otherwise in accordance with international law. Neither is there any cogent reason why persons who acquire from him such vessels and goods and who thus aid him in his war effort should be deemed to have acquired an indefeasible—or initially valid—title. Yet, somewhat strangely, this seems to have been the view taken by the Allied governments in the peace treaties of 1947. The peace treaty with Italy—an aggressor state—merely provided for the revision of decisions and orders of Italian prize courts which were not in conformity with international law.[47] Essentially the same attitude seems to have been adopted with regard to appropriation of property, public and private, on land. The warning, referred to above and contained in the London declaration of 1943,[48] apparently was intended to cover only such acts of dispossession as were contrary to international law. It applied "whether such transfers or dealings have taken the form of open looting or plunder, or of transactions apparently legal in form, even when they purport to be voluntarily effected." There seems to have been no intention to declare such acquisitions and transfers to be illegal on account of the unlawfulness of the war waged by Germany and her allies. Thus the various authorities of the United Nations held on a number of occasions that booty and other property acquired by German forces validly transferred title to Germany—occasionally with the incidental result that such property subsequently captured by the United Nations from Germany in turn transferred title to the United Nations and that the title of the original owners was accordingly deemed to have been extinguished.[49] The alternative—and, it is believed, more satisfactory—solution would have been to hold that no transfer to Germany had originally taken place, that therefore neither Germany nor the United Nations had acquired the property in question, and that the latter must be restored to the original owners.

It may be noted that the view here put forward as to the invalidity of title acquired by the aggressor—even if acquired in accordance with the laws of war—was formulated in 1939 with some clarity, though without elaboration, in the Harvard Research Draft in Rights and Duties of States in Case of Aggression. That draft laid down, in Article 5, that subject to the continued application of humanitarian rules prescribed by customary and conventional international law, "an aggressor does not have any of the rights which it would have if it were a [lawful] belligerent" and that "titles to property are not affected by an aggressor's purported exercise of such rights." It is also possible that a measure of recognition of that principle may be found in those occasional pronouncements of neutral courts which have declined to give effect to decrees of the belligerent occupant on the ground that such occupation had not been recognized—apparently on the ground of the illegality of the war on the part of the occupant. Some such interpretation may be put on judgments of some courts of the United States during World War II at a time when the United States was neutral. Thus in *Amstelbank, N.V. v. Guaranty Trust Company of New York* the decision of the court was based on the fact that "the government of the United States has refused to recognize the German military control of Holland" and that "therefore any German decrees promulgated in the Netherlands should be given no force or effect whatever in the determination of questions involving property in this State."[50] Normally, the question of recognition of belligerent occupation does not arise, and the refusal to recognize it may perhaps be explained by reference to the illegality of the war undertaken by the aggressor. The same line of thought may be discerned indirectly in the criticism, by a high authority on the subject, of the judgment given by an English court in 1937 in *Bank of Ethiopia v. National Bank of Egypt and Liquori.*[51] Sir Arnold McNair, while questioning the decision of the court on the specific ground that it invested the Italian occupation of Abyssinia with a degree of power not warranted by the rules of international law in the matter of belligerent occupation, doubted its soundness also on the additional ground that it "puts a premium upon aggression by the recognition which it gives to the decrees of a successful invader."[52]

The Law of Neutrality

The present essay is concerned with the operation of rules of warfare as between the belligerents. It is therefore not proposed to discuss here in any detail the effects of the illegality of the war in the relations of the belligerents and neutrals. Yet it is probable that it is mainly in that sphere that, already during the war, there may be room—in law—for drawing the requisite consequences from the fact that the war is illegal on the part of one belligerent or set of belligerents. For there has now disappeared the principal explanation and justification of the modern law of neutrality conceived as an attitude of absolute impartiality. That explanation was that up to World War I the right to wage war constituted an unlimited prerogative right of sovereign states and that therefore no neutral state could arrogate for itself the right to pass judgment on the legality of the war and to shape its conduct accordingly. The question simply did not arise. In this respect the position has now undergone a fundamental change. The unlimited right of war is no longer a prerogative of the sovereign state. International law now recognizes that a state may act unlawfully by the very act of declaring or going to war. It recognizes the distinction between wars which are lawful and those which are not. To that extent it has reëstablished the historic foundation of qualified—discriminatory and discriminating—neutrality.

Moreover, insofar as the prohibition or limitation of the right of war has been combined with the establishment of a system of collective security and collective enforcement of peace—such as in the Covenant of the League of Nations or the Charter of the United Nations—the right of the neutral to discriminate against and to penalize the aggressor has been transformed into a duty. That duty may assume the complexion of the supreme obligation to abandon the neutral status itself. It may also be compatible with the retention of neutral status in all cases in which the system of collective security so permits and in which the aggressor does not elect to add to his original unlawful act the further illegality of treating as a belligerent the neutral state which discriminates against him. These contingencies need not be examined here.[53]

On the other hand there must be borne in mind that explanation of the principle of absolute neutrality which is partly legal and partly political and which has not been decisively affected by the new developments. That explanation is that the belligerent cannot be expected to submit, without retaliation, to discriminatory measures on the part of the neutral. The relation between the neutral and belligerent implies a reciprocity of rights and duties; it demands forbearance and limitation of freedom of action on both sides. It is clear therefore that the belligerent against whom discrimination is practiced and against whom the neutral state or states presume to exercise judgment will—so far as it lies in his power—oppose any such departure from an attitude of impartiality. In practice the solution will be determined by the relative strength of the belligerent and the neutral. A weak neutral whose territory neighbors on that of a powerful belligerent will hardly be able to afford practical adherence to principle—authorizing or enjoining him to discriminate against the aggressor—and the resulting danger of reprisals and invasion. A powerful neutral, especially if his territory is separated from that of the belligerent, will be in the position to draw the full consequences from his right and, in a system of collective security, his duty to exercise judgment in the matter of the legality of the war waged by the belligerents and to translate his judgment into practice. Of this possibility the second period of the neutrality of the United States before its entry into World War II provides a clear example. In pursuance both of what it conceived to be its vital national interest and its rights and obligations under international law the United States, in the year preceding its entry into the war, adopted against Germany a policy of discrimination which expressed itself in various forms of assistance, falling short of direct military participation in the war, to Great Britain and her allies. But it was only after a long succession of such acts of assistance and only in conjunction with the extraneous factor of the entry of Japan into the war that Germany declared war upon the United States. In relation to a less formidable neutral such pronounced departure from an attitude of impartiality would have been met by utmost resistance in the form of reprisals and war. However that may be, there is nothing—save, perhaps, the victory of the aggressor—to prevent the courts and other organs of neutral states from drawing after the war the appropriate consequences from the fact that the war was illegal on the part of one belligerent and could therefore confer no lasting rights upon him. The nature of these consequences, both with regard to acquisition of title over property and otherwise, has been indicated above.

Conclusions

The conclusions of this essay may be briefly stated as follows:

(1) It is incumbent upon courts and other organs of the state as well as upon the science of international law to draw, in relation to a war illegally undertaken by a state and within limits determined by considerations of humanity, the requisite consequences from the principle *ex injuria jus non oritur.*

(2) While in principle the aggressor—that is, the state which has embarked upon war in violation of its obligation—cannot invoke for its benefit the rules of warfare, that principle does not apply, *durante bello,* to the actual conduct of hostilities and, generally, to the mutual relations of belligerents.

(3) On the other hand, there is room in other spheres for giving full effect to the principle that a state cannot acquire rights from its wrongful acts. In particular, a state waging an unlawful war is not entitled, after the war, to invoke the rules of customary international law which disregard the vitiating effect of duress in the conclusion of treaties; which recognize title acquired by conquest; which absolve the belligerent from payment of reparations for damage caused by lawful acts of warfare; which give it the right to regard as dissolved treaties concluded before the outbreak of the war; and which render it—and the individuals responsible for its actions—immune from criminal responsibility for the initiation of a war of aggression.

(4) A state waging an unlawful war does not obtain or validly transmit title with respect to property acquired in connection with the conduct of war regardless of whether such title is acquired in accordance with the law of war or not. This applies in particular to title claimed to have been acquired by requisition, by other forms of appropriation of public and private enemy property, and by condemnations in prize.

(5) Both during and after the war it is open to and in proper cases incumbent upon neutral states, especially if bound by the obligations of a system of collective security, to discriminate against the state waging an unlawful war and to deny to it and its transferees title to property in accordance with (4) above.

These conclusions seem to be both inconclusive and unsatisfactory from the point of view of wider principle. On the crucial issue of the applicability of rules of warfare directly bearing on the conduct of hostilities they appear to leave totally out of account the fact of the illegality of the war. Insofar as these conclusions consider that factor relevant they bear on matters connected with the liquidation of the war rather than with its conduct. In the sphere of the invalidity of title acquired by the aggressor—a question of relatively minor compass—the conclusions here submitted have not yet been accepted by courts or acted upon by governments. Moreover when the rules here summarized are derived from the fact of the illegality of the war their efficacy is necessarily dependent upon the ultimate defeat of the aggressor. All this affords little cause for satisfaction. However, the phenomenon of war does not fully admit of treatment in accordance with canons of legal logic. Banished as a legal institution, it remains an event calling for legal regulation for the sake of humanity, of the dignity of man, and of safeguarding the possibility of some measure of reconciliation between the belligerents after the war. At the same time, these considerations are not inconsistent with giving effect, within a limited sphere, to the principle that an unlawful act ought not to become a source of benefit and title to the wrongdoer. The application of that principle within that limited sphere touches only the fringes of the problem. Yet that irreducible minimum of conformity with the fundamental change in the legal place of war in international society has wider implications and cannot be disregarded except as grave peril to the authority of international law and to the ultimate effectiveness of that fundamental change itself.

Undoubtedly, this dualism of considerations is baffling and confusing. It has baffled the science of international law from the very inception. Grotius hesitated inconclusively between disregarding, in deference to dictates of humanity, the fact of illegality of war on the part of the aggressor[54] and drawing far-reaching consequences from the distinction between *bellum justum* and *bellum injustum*.[55] Others have done so in the past and will continue to do so in the future.[56] But that very hesitation is a credit to the science of international law. There is no room for clear-cut solutions in a situation analogous to a revolution within the state. For in a system of international law in which war is prohibited, recourse to war is in the nature of a revolution against the basic law of the international community. The fact of revolution and of its suppression calls for some temporary adaptation of the apparent inexorabilities of the law to the dictates of humanity. While the contest is in progress legal logic must not be allowed to add to the cruelties and sufferings of battle. But, it has been shown, there is no compelling reason for going beyond that inescapable derogation from legal principle and for perpetuating the fruits of illegality for the benefit of the aggressor.

J. G. STARKE

Regionalism as a Problem of International Law

THE CONCEPT of regionalism is not new in international relations. Long before Articles 51-54 of the United Nations Charter were drawn up in 1945, standard text books[1] contained definitions of "particular" international law, meaning rules of conduct recognized as binding among a group of states only, which could accordingly apply exclusively in a particular region. Also it had been widely and generally recognized long before the specific acknowledgment of this by the International Court of Justice in the Haya de la Torre case (1950) that the Latin American communities followed rules of international law which were different in numerous and vital respects from those which commanded the general acceptance of states in the rest of the world.

The Locarno Treaty of Mutual Guarantee of 1925 was a special regional treaty relating to an area in western Europe. Before that, the Quadruple Pacific Treaty of 1921 among the United States, the British Empire, France, and Japan concerned only the *status quo* in the Pacific. Moreover, regional agencies, or at least regional organizations, existed before the conclusion of the United States Charter. The European Danube Commission had been created by the Treaty of Paris of 1856[2] to deal with an area of special importance, namely the estuary of the Danube; and of course the various inter-American agencies, which represented the earlier form of the present Organization of American States, were in existence before 1945.

Regional implications were latent in certain traditional concepts of international law and international practice, such as the institution of neutralization of a particular state or area by collective guarantee, and the notion of "spheres of influence" and of "spheres of interest." Special regional rules relating to the occupation of areas in Africa were laid down in Articles 34 and 35 of the General Act of the Berlin Congo Conference of 1885, and relating to fisheries and other matters in the North Sea by the North Sea Treaties of 1882 and 1887. Even the use of the word "regional" is not a novelty, in the United Nations Charter for Article 21 of the League of Nations Covenant had provided that the Covenant itself was not to affect "regional understandings like the Monroe doctrine."

What is new, however, is the widespread application that is being given to the concept of regionalism at the present time. First and foremost, this concept has now received general recognition among international lawyers, international administrators, and statesmen as a standard formula or device for solving particular problems, whether they relate to security, economics, or international labor questions. Thinking in terms of regionalism has become an established habit, and as a result practical examples of regional solutions have been multiplying during the period following World War II. Whether this is good or bad from the standpoint of international law needs to be considered. Without at this stage exploring the question in detail, I must admit an uneasy impression that the abounding enthusiasm for regional solutions is based less on a closely reasoned appreciation of the requirements of the situation, than on a tendency to follow the fashion of the moment. In my opinion, however, it is quite unnecessary to import regional solutions into every state of affairs in the international community calling for collective action. Regionalism can serve useful purposes without being overemployed.

The explanation of the current stress on regionalism is historical in character. The alleged deficiencies of the League of Nations and of the system of collective security in the interwar period were attributed to two facts in particular, both of which led thinkers on international affairs to advocate a greater use of regional arrangements and regional agencies. One fact was that certain countries stood outside the League of Nations system, whereas they might have participated in regional security and other arrangements confined to an area in which they were more directly interested. The other fact was the necessity for buttressing the League by coördinated security machinery operating in particular danger areas of the world, so as to ensure the direct collaboration of the states most interested in these areas. So it was that, in the period immediately preceding World War II, writers and publicists urged the need for the conclusion of regional arrangements and for the creation of regional agencies in respect to regions of particular importance. The outbreak of the war prevented such regional plans. Since then, however, inter-American conferences and the creation of inter-American agencies have provided an excellent model of regionalism practically at work, and in the United Nations Charter specific provision was made for regional arrangements and regional agencies. Since the signing of the Charter, a number of regional arrangements were concluded, including notably the North Atlantic Security Pact of April, 1949, and the Pacific Security Pact of September, 1951.

Thus, it is undeniable that regionalism, despite being merely a fashion to many, has responded to a practical need of the international community. With further refinement and specialization it should, indeed, make an even more notable contribution to international law and to diplomatic practice.

The object of the present study is to consider briefly the various directions in which international law has been influenced by regional developments, and the necessary limits of that influence.

Regional Customary International Law

Customary rules may develop among the different states in a particular region. These rules may not only be different from the rules of general international law of similar incidence and application, but they may be entirely new. To this extent, these customary rules of the region represent a special kind of customary international law of limited range. Historically, there were several examples of such a regionalized system of international law, for instance the so-called "intermunicipal" rules applicable among the city states of ancient Greece, and the customary rules that evolved from the welter of practice and usage governing the relations among the principalities of the Italy of the Middle Ages and of the Renaissance. A present-day illustration is the number of special customary rules recognized as binding among the states of Latin America.

This Latin American system of international law recently received consideration by the International Court of Justice in the abovementioned Haya de la Torre case (1950). The case itself revolved around the taking of refuge by an alleged Peruvian rebel in the Colombian embassy of Lima, the Peruvian capital. The Colombian ambassador to Peru had granted asylum and requested safe-conduct from the Peruvian government to enable the refugee to leave the country stating that he had been "qualified" as a "political" refugee. But the Peruvian government refused to accept this classification and rejected the request for safe-conduct. The case was submitted to the International Court of

Justice. In the course of the proceedings Colombia maintained that according to "American International Law" the state of refuge was entitled unilaterally to classify refugees taking asylum as "political" or otherwise, and that it was the duty of the territorial state to accept this classification.

The court held that there was too much contradiction and fluctuation in the evidence concerning the alleged practice of "American International Law" to discern in it a usage peculiar to Latin America and accepted as law. The court therefore found against the Colombian submission.

The case is none the less significant as showing that the Latin American communities, in principle, recognize a right of political asylum, which itself is not a part of universal or general international law, and that an international court must give effect to regional rules of international law, if duly proved.

Individual judges of the court made pertinent observations on the so-called "American International Law." Judge Alvarez said it was really "Latin-American International Law," and therefore more correctly a subdivision of "American International Law," and accordingly not binding upon the United States. Such a regional system of international law was in his opinion not subordinate to universal international law, but "correlated" to it. Judge Read also emphasized the "complementary" rather than the subordinate character of these regional rules by defining them as "... a body of conventional and customary law complementary to universal international law, and governing interstate relations in the Pan-American world."

There has for long been the feeling among the Latin American states that certain doctrines to which they subscribe should become more generalized as principles of universal international law. Undoubtedly, their practices and principles have had some influence in this direction, as witness the recent formulation by the United Nations International Law Commission of the Draft Declaration on the (Basic) Rights and Duties of States, founded on earlier enunciations in Latin America. This regional system of Latin-American international law is not necessarily or primarily of a heterodox character; as Judge Manley O. Hudson has pointed out:[3]

> This conception [of an "American international law"] is not merely a rationalization of a separatist tendency, nor is it necessarily an indication of hostility to European ideas; it had its origin in juristic writings in Latin America. which emphasized special doctrines not sufficiently appreciated in other parts of the world. The emergence of eighteen American Republics in the course of

the nineteenth century and their struggle to establish themselves in the society of nations tested many of the former precedents, and led to some formulations of old principles. In the attempted assimilation of the position of aliens to that of nationals, for example, doctrines have been enunciated which have had a considerable influence on the development of the international law with respect to State responsibility.[4]

There is a perceptible analogy between these regionalized customary rules of international law and the customary rules confined to a particular province or county which frequently have to be taken into account by municipal courts when applying municipal law.[5] In both spheres, it must be proved by adequate evidence that the alleged customary rules are regarded as binding; and even then it does not follow that these local customary rules are anything but complementary to general municipal law.

It may be queried whether the extreme development of regional international law would be healthy from the standpoint of general international law. If each region regarded itself as self-contained, and professed to follow only such rules of international law as the states belonging to that region recognized as binding, legal chaos would result. It would serve little purpose, then, for the United Nations International Law Commission to continue its studies on the codification and development of international law as each region would follow only such codified or developed rules as it decided to accept. Instead of a "state positivism," which is bad enough in itself, so far as international law is concerned, we would have something far worse—a "regional positivism." This would completely unbalance the existing system of international law.

At the present time, however, no such developments are likely. On the one hand, Latin American regionalism is of a limited character. Although extensive regional Latin American doctrines exist, they have been formulated because they were thought to embody ideals that should be adhered to generally by the international community, rather than because of their regional character and application. On the other hand, Soviet Russia and its Communist states have been urging doctrines which stress regionalism. Thus the governments of these states have during the past five years interpreted state sovereignty in a much broader way than is customary in the West. But neither in Latin America nor in the Soviet orbit has regionalism reached extremes which could threaten the foundations of general international law.

Regional Treaty Rules of International Law

The observations made above with respect to regional customary international law apply similarly to regional treaty rules of international law. Again, the best example of such a regional trend has been the Organization of American States, and as a component of it the group of Latin American States. The Organization of American States in no way threatens the general international legislative procedure now operating under the aegis of the United Nations and its specialized agencies. Although the number of treaty rules formulated by the American states, is considerable, many treaties have been purely declaratory of customary rules of international law; others have dealt with specific regional matters, for example the procedure of consultation between American states, questions of security, and the creation of regional agencies. European textbooks on international law have given increasing attention to these American or Latin American formulations of rules, sometimes merely to show differences in state practices, but mostly because these formulations were consistent with general international law. Moreover, many of these treaty rules gave expression to the wishes of the American states for a more democratic, more humanitarian system of international law, and, if these aspirations cannot for the moment be realized, a valuable service to international law has none the less been performed by recording them, and by indicating to the world that the American (or Latin American) grouping supports these rules. Therefore, again, to use Judge Read's description in the Haya de la Torre case, the American or Latin American regional system of treaty rules is "complementary" to, but neither subordinate to nor inconsistent with general international law.

Regional Security

Regionalism in international law is most evident in the field of security. Since the end of World War II, a number of important regional security pacts have been concluded. Sufficient material is now available for the analysis of the general trend of developments in this direction, and in the light of Articles 51-54 of the United Nations Charter. Articles 52-54, contained in Chapter VIII, were grouped under the chapter heading Regional Arrangements and specifically dealt with the subject; Article 51 is indirectly related to these regional arrangements, because it provided *inter alia* for a right of collective self-defense in the event of armed attack against a member of the United Nations.

The draftsmen of Articles 52-54 attempted to preserve a balance or, at best, a compromise between universalism and regionalism in the matter of security. One guiding notion was to maintain the overriding authority of the Security Council of the United Nations as a world pivotal body for the enforcement of peace; hence the limiting provisions that: (a) any regional security arrangements or agencies shall be consistent with the "purposes and principles" of the United Nations; (b) although the Security Council may utilize such arrangements or agencies for enforcement action, in general no enforcement action is to be taken without the authorization of the Security Council; (c) the Security Council is at all times to be kept fully informed of activities undertaken or in contemplation under such arrangements or by such agencies.

Under the last limitation the Security Council could, strictly speaking, require that it be informed of the results of secret staff talks or projected plans of self-defense by the states associated under the regional arrangement. Hence, there was a greater measure of independence preserved to states acting under regional arrangements according to Article 21 of the League of Nations Covenant—which provided in bare terms that nothing in the Covenant was to affect "regional understandings" such as the Monroe Doctrine—than to states acting under regional arrangements within the meaning of Articles 52-54 of the United Nations Charter.

It was, however, only if disputes could not be solved by regional machinery that they were to be referred to the Security Council (Article 52, paragraph 2), so that to this extent a sphere was reserved for regional action. But it could well be argued that this sphere was a limited one itself, relating only to the peaceful settlement of disputes, and not to enforcement action in defense of the integrity of the states regionally associated.

It is not surprising that these provisions in the United Nations Charter were regarded as somewhat of a hindrance to those twelve states which became grouped in the most momentous regional pact ever concluded—the North Atlantic Security Pact of April, 1949. Besides, there was the consideration that if a regional security arrangement became subordinated to the overriding authority of the Security Council of the United Nations, complete frustration might result through the operation of the veto, in decisions about the kind or even the necessity of enforcement action. That is why the draftsmen of the North Atlantic pact chose to rely rather upon the provisions in Article 51 of the Charter, relative to the collective right of self-defense against armed attack. It explains too, the disavowal by certain authoritative spokesmen[7] on behalf of the member powers in the North Atlantic Security Organization that the North Atlantic pact is a "regional arrangement" within the meaning of Articles 52-54 of the Charter.

Four important regional security pacts have been concluded since the signing of the United Nations Charter and its coming into force in 1945, namely: (1) The Inter-American Treaty of Reciprocal Assistance signed at Rio de Janeiro in September, 1947; (2) The Western Union Pact signed by Great Britain, France, and the Benelux countries at Brussels in March, 1948; (3) The North Atlantic Security Pact signed at Washington in April, 1949; (4) The Pacific Security Pact signed by the United States, Australia, and New Zealand at San Francisco in September, 1951. Each of these regional arrangements is primarily based on the collective self-defense provisions in Article 51 of the United Nations Charter, and in each of them it has been provided that collective self-defense measures may be taken against armed attack until the Security Council has taken the measures necessary to maintain international peace and security. It is undeniable, however, that the three later treaties show far less reliance on the all-seeing enforcement-action wisdom of the Security Council than does the first. For example, the Rio treaty contained in Article 5 the following very comprehensive provision designed to bring all regional security measures taken or contemplated within the purview of the Security Council:

> The High Contracting Parties shall immediately send to the Security Council of the United Nations, in conformity with Articles 51 and 54 of the Charter of the United Nations, complete information concerning the activities undertaken or in contemplation in the exercise of the right of self-defense or for the purpose of maintaining inter-American peace and security.

Nothing comparable appears in the three later treaties. For instance, the North Atlantic Security Pact is content baldly to provide in Article 5 that any armed attack, against which the Parties collectively defend themselves, "and all measures taken *as a result thereof*" (i.e., not prior thereto) shall be immediately reported to the Security Council, and it adds in Article 7 that the treaty is not to affect the rights and obligations under the United Nations Charter of states parties which are members of the United Nations or the primary responsibility of the Security Council for maintaining peace and security. But it nowhere specifically provides that the plenitude of all the activities of the North Atlantic Treaty Organization is to be fully reported to the Security Council.

It seems to follow that, notwithstanding the provisions in Articles 52-54 of the Charter, there has been a waning in the emphasis on universalism so far as security is concerned. For the same reasons which led writers and statesmen before the last war to advocate more closely knit regional security arrangements—namely to secure direct action by states interested in a particular area and to buttress the central collective security system (i.e., of the League of Nations)—there has been a strong current reaction in favor of regional security machinery, less subordinated to central control. This trend is reflected in the regional security treaties concluded in the years 1948-1951. As regards the most recent regional security pact, the Pacific pact of September, 1951, it is significant that notwithstanding the fact that "collective" enforcement action has been Nations since the middle of 1950, three powers so directly interested in the Pacific as the United States, Australia, and New Zealand should have chosen to pin their faith in a new regional pact similar in its general purport to the North Atlantic pact of April, 1949.

Regionalism and Neutrality

The number and importance of the existing regional security pacts, when taken in conjunction with the collective-security system of the United Nations, must have a certain impact on the law of neutrality. For they have limited the occasions and circumstances in which the most important states in the world and the more important middle and smaller powers can profess neutrality. Where an armed attack on one state member of a regional security grouping is considered an armed attack on all members of the groupings, and where there are obligations of mutual consultation, it becomes more and more difficult to envisage the possible situations in which any such state can remain a neutral. The traditional historical background which favored neutrality as an institution of international law in the nineteenth century had already been slipping away in the first half of the present century, and the question is whether recent regional developments have left very much more scope for this institution in the modern world. It may be claimed that there will still be room for neutrality because there will continue to be states such as Sweden, standing outside regional security arrangements. But would regional associations of states involved in a life-and-death struggle necessarily respect as traditional the alleged neutral rights of a nonbelligerent? Nor must it be forgotten that such states would be hardly likely to press their neutral rights, and would have very strong inducements to isolate and insulate themselves from all contacts which could possibly draw them into the war.

It may well be, therefore, that "absolute" neutrality is already declining into desuetude. "Qualified" neutrality may survive, so far as it is specifically provided for in the United Nations Charter[8] or in a regional security treaty. But in any event the vast majority of the traditional rules of neutrality, on which a nineteenth-century American secretary of state would have insisted firmly in any brush with a belligerent state, may have practically drifted into the domain of past history.

Regional International Organs

In addition to the category of regional security agencies, such as those set up under the regional security treaties mentioned above, regional international organs established in practice can be divided into three principal classes:

(a) Regional international administrative bodies, of a more or less autonomous character, whether advisory or technical, for coördinating certain matters of common concern in a particular region, for example, the South Pacific Commission.

(b) Organs established as regional agencies of existing international institutions with specialized functions, for example, the Economic Commission for Asia and the Far East (ECAFE) set up by the United Nations Economic and Social Council, and the various regional agencies created by the International Labor Organization for special purposes in special areas.

(c) Regional international consultative and deliberative organs with very generalized functions, for example, the Council of Europe.[9]

Generally speaking, these bodies are of more significance from the standpoint of international organization as a branch of political science than they are from the standpoint of international law, which is the aspect primarily under consideration in this study. However, there are certain respects in which these regional international organs are bound to have a direct impact on international law. First, regardless to which of the above-mentioned categories such organs belong, they must, in accordance with the recent advisory opinion of the International Court of Justice,[10] be deemed to be subjects of international law. Therefore the increasing number of such regional organs during the past six years has necessarily added and will continue to add to the range, diversity, and complexity of international law. Second, just as in the past customary rules evolved from the practices and usages of states in their mutual relations, so new customary rules of international law will naturally develop from: (a) the relations among states or territories, and such regional organs; (b) the relations among such regional organs and international institutions of a general character; (c) the relations among such regional organs themselves; and (d) the relations among such regional organs and individuals, so far as these come within the ambit of international law. One particular field, in which it is not difficult to envisage a growth of customary rules of this kind, is that of rules of international administrative law relating to the constitutional functioning of such regional organs.

The existence of regional organs will, besides, facilitate the working or operation of other international law institutions. A specific case in point is that of the United Nations trusteeship system and of the trust territories administered under that system. The majority of the trusteeship agreements[11] concluded make provision for associating trust territories wherever possible with regional advisory commissions, or regional technical organizations, so that the benefits of regional administration may not be lost to them. This contrasts forcibly with the administration of the mandates by the League of Nations. In certain respects, the League's methods of world-wide administration and supervision from Geneva were ill-adjusted to the special needs of the less advanced mandated territories,[12] as Duncan Hall has pointed out:[13]

> The general policy of the League was on the whole unfavourable to regionalism on the ground that the League must be universal and apply wherever possible universal solutions, and in its narrower sphere the Mandates Commission used its powers and influence against regional unions on the ground that they infringed the true theory of the mandate by implying that the mandatory possessed sovereignty.

This gap or defect is less extensive with respect to trust territories because of the postwar establishment of regional organs.

Other directions in which regional organs must necessarily function in aid of international law are in assisting the *application* of existing rules, particularly the rules laid down in complicated technical international conventions. The world-wide application of such conventions from an international center has always been difficult, but can be improved through coördinating the work and decentralizing it through regional agencies. The improved administration of international law means a stronger system of rules and more respect for its observance. Again, without regional organs in aid of general international organizations, international law could not so effectively spread its wings and embrace the wide variety of matters now calling for international regulation, such as questions of health, labor, economics, education, and transport, as to which each region has special problems that demand regional direction and supervision.

Regional International Tribunals

A similar need for decentralization has been stressed by those who claim that regional tribunals are needed in addition to general international tribunals such as the International Court of Justice. The creation of regional international courts of human rights has already been mooted in certain quarters for the reason that recourse to regional tribunals rather than to a general Court of Human Rights would be more expeditious and less costly, and thus facilitate the enforcement of human rights.

Past experiments in regional tribunals are not conclusive. The Central American Court of Justice, which functioned from 1908 to 1918, was scarcely a success, notwithstanding the bestowal upon it of a fairly wide jurisdiction, including the power to deal with disputes between states and private individuals. The average number of cases that came before it was one per year, and its contribution to the development of international law was meager in the extreme. Suggestions have repeatedly come from Latin America, nonetheless, for the further creation of regional tribunals, and before the last war, it was more than once suggested that the Permanent Court of International Justice should develop regional chambers. The statute of the International Court of Justice makes provision for special chambers in a way that would permit the creation *ad hoc* of a regional chamber (Article 26), and it further provides that such special chambers "may, with the consent of the parties, sit and exercise their functions elsewhere than at The Hague" (Article 28). The practical question is whether, assuming a regional chamber of the International Court were created or a special regional international tribunal were established, there would be sufficient work for it. A further point is whether the regionalization of international justice would impair the integrity and uniformity of international law as a system by permitting particularistic developments. Judge Manley O. Hudson has hinted at such a danger,[14] and warned: "In the field of adjudication . . . it is important to safeguard the primacy of general international law, to protect the universality of its application, and to assure uniformity in its administration."

But it may be asked whether municipal tribunals or international tribunals, applying international law, have ever deviated greatly from following general rather than particular rules; and, accordingly, whether the danger that regional tribunals will lean toward particularistic developments is not overestimated. Surely, the more practical purpose of creating a regional tribunal is to allow and encourage a freer and speedier access to an international court by states seeking international justice, and this is not inconsistent with the preservation of international law as a general and uniform system of legal rules to be applied by such tribunals.

Regional Solutions of International Law Problems

Finally, to close this study, the aspect of regional solutions for certain problems may be mentioned. Questions which are live issues today, such as the "continental shelf," use of the air space, freedom of navigation along international rivers, abuse of water rights, and the like, may be solved better by dealing with their special regional aspects on a regional basis than by demanding a solution in terms of a general world-wide formula. It is not suggested that every question of international law should be approached as if it needed dissection into its regional elements, but common sense and convenience will often point the way toward the most practical path. There have been precedents in the past for particular regional rules—for example, as mentioned earlier, the Articles 34 and 35 of the General Act of the Berlin Congo Conference of 1885 relating to the occupation of areas of territory in Africa. There is no reason why in carefully selected cases, regional solutions of this character might not be more appropriate than a general rule or body of rules which is apt to work injustice, because of unsuitability to local conditions.

To sum up, there is an undeniably good case for regionalism at the present stage of development on international law, provided it is not debased by becoming a fad, and provided that a stern sense of proportion is applied to keep it within practical bounds. So far, the balance of convenience has not been upset, and much still remains to be done in the direction of exploring the full scope of its applications in the field of international law.

Part Two: Contemporary Problems

CLYDE EAGLETON

The United Nations: A Legal Order?

IN MY YOUNGER DAYS, with the assistance of deeply moral parents and the influence of church and community, I had a very clear concept of law. It was, I thought, a set of rules laid down by an omniscient authority above, which could give a definite answer to any dispute and could properly punish any crime. Courts applied this law, and sometimes an ignorant or corrupt judge might apply it improperly; but that was not the fault of the law, which always provided a precise and certain answer. I might have wondered even then at the existence of numerous species of persons called lawyers, upon whom vast sums of money were spent in order to twist the law one way or the other. At any rate, international law, when I began to study it, did not seem to harmonize with this concept, and, in general, it began to appear that no law is precise and certain as I had idealized it to be.

Now I pick up Professor Kelsen's book on *The Law of the United Nations*,[1] and find in its Preface:

> The view, however, that the verbal expression of a legal norm has only one 'true' meaning which can be discerned by correct interpretation is a fiction, adopted to maintain the illusion of legal security, to make the law-seeking public believe that there is only one possible answer to the question of law in a concrete case. Unfortunately, the contrary is true.

Law is not certain, not perfect; but it exists, the ancient reliance and the future hope of mankind. In the sense of international law, there is perhaps more hope than reliance at the moment, but from all over the world comes the demand for an international legal order. There is a strange dichotomy here—it may be that schizophrenia is a more applicable term—because those persons who clamor for such an international legal order, among them especially professional lawyers, are inclined to scoff and ridicule international law. Doubtless all peoples, everywhere, think of law as the necessary solvent for clashes among states as they think of it between individuals; the pressure of increasing interdependence among peoples pushes the need upon them; yet, even while they yearn for it, they are unwilling to pay the price in national freedom of action which must be paid if they are to have law among nations.

Even so, there is an international law which, limited in scope as it may be, is entitled to respect on the basis of achievement recorded. Much work and study and support is needed for it, and it can only be widened and strengthened as needed through an international organization, such as the United Nations. Like all law, it is subject to interpretation, and doubtless there can be more debate as to the meaning of a rule of international law than would be for systems of law with many centuries of precedent building behind them. Interpretation and usage may indeed modify and develop law, but somewhere a line should be drawn so that the law is not interpreted out of existence. There is a difference between interpretation and development of the law, on the one hand, and disregard and neglect of the law, on the other hand.

Law in the Charter of the United Nations

The United Nations represents the latest aspiration of human beings to build a system of law which would establish peace and justice among nations.[2] One must doubt, however, whether those who made the Charter of the United Nations regarded law as the most important element in its making, and whether those who carry on the work of the United Nations do so with proper respect for law. The Dumbarton Oaks proposals contained the words "international law" in only one place—the clause concerning "domestic questions," which was itself a derogation from that law. Even from this spot the words were removed at San Francisco, and they would not have been in the Charter at all but for the insistence of the Chinese, who, backed by many smaller states, succeeded in having them interpolated in Articles 1 and 13.

In the minds of those primarily responsible for the Charter, the overriding preoccupation was to provide security against war, and it was thought that, for this purpose, there were more important means than law. The Report of the United States Delegation spoke of the

> effort to restrict the freedom of the Security Council by proposing that it be limited in its decisions by reference to the principles of international law and justice. These were opposed by the United States and other States on the ground that due observance of justice and of international law was assured by Articles 1 and 2, as revised, and that the Security Council should not be hampered by detailed direction of its activities.[3]

In only one other place does this report give favorable—though inconsistent—mention of international law, where it speaks of "a Charter which places justice and international law among its foundation stones."[4]

The text of the Charter offers further evidence of this lack of interest in law. It establishes no obligation upon members, even in legal questions, to refer their disputes to judicial settlement; the effort to give compulsory jurisdiction to the court was rejected by the great powers, though supported by a large number of other states. Consequently, under Article 36, paragraph 3, the Security Council can do no more than recommend to members that they refer their legal disputes to the International Court of Justice. No legislative power was given to any organ; the General Assembly, under Article 13, could only "initiate studies and make recommendations" for "encouraging the progressive development of international law and its codification." No sanctions were put behind law (except for the uncertain phrase in Article 94, which depends upon voluntary submission of the dispute); the only sanctions are against aggression, and these may be applied by the Security Council without regard to law. The words "international law" were removed from what is now Article 2, paragraph 7, thus leaving no judge and no criteria for determining whether a nation was thus removed from the domain of international law. Apparently, it was intended that each nation should be able to decide for itself whether its case was a domestic question.[5] Carried to an extreme, this would mean no law at all.

Whatever the Charter may have originally been intended to mean, that meaning has been greatly modified by practice, which has often disregarded or overridden the Charter, the constitutional law of the United Nations. Ample opportunity exists under the Charter to make use of arbitration or judicial settlement of legal disputes, but United Nations organs have shown little disposition to do so. The Security Council has in only one case recommended to the parties that they take their dispute to the International Court of Justice; this was done, as the president remarked, because "Council action was, shall I say, frustrated by" the veto.[6] Similarly, the General Assembly has referred to the court only such matters as it found itself unable to handle alone, and in which it hoped for reinforcement from the court. In the studies made by the Interim Committee concerning the pacific settlement of disputes, emphasis was laid upon methods of conciliation rather than upon legal settlement. In the course of debates delegates frequently argue upon the basis of the Charter in one situation, and take the opposite attitude in another situation; the organ itself makes no decision.

The primary purpose of a constitution is to set limitations upon the powers of the government which it creates, but in a number of cases an organ of the United Nations by majority vote strode past the restriction set in the Charter without looking at it, or without considering the strong argument that the vote was illegal. The right of each organ of the United Nations to interpret the Charter for itself is apparently established, but it must be observed that the organs do not in fact make such an interpretation; of this I shall say more later.

"Realism"

Let us interrupt this examination of United Nations practice to consider for a moment some related currents of thought. Today is the nadir of international law, so far as popular or national or United Nations support for it can be estimated. International law is impatiently pushed aside by those—on either side of a dispute—who seek action along desired lines. Leading lawyers oppose its development along even humanitarian lines, on the ground that proposed treaties might produce a change in domestic law. No financial support is available for organizations to do study and research with regard to badly needed new law. Not even the remarkably successful Harvard Research in International Law can obtain funds to continue its work; and the Carnegie Endowment for International Peace has withdrawn its support in this field and turned its attention to international politics and organization.

It is the day of "realism," a word which must be put into quotation marks because the doctrine of this school of thought can no longer—if ever—be regarded as realistic. "Realism" regards the power of a state as the only worthwhile consideration; it sets up the term "power politics" in opposition to the idea of international law and collective security. In a recent book,[7] Professor Hans Morgenthau states this viewpoint in bald terms. He devotes a page or so to "legalism," which he lists as one of the errors of American thinking; and another page to the United Nations, which is useful only as a meeting place where power politicians can work out their problems in terms of national interest. Nothing is higher than the desires of a nation—not law, not morality. A similar viewpoint is taken by George Kennan[8] and others; and statesmen seem to follow this thought.

With this, of course, Hitler and Mussolini and Tojo and others of earlier history would agree; it is simply anarchy among nations—and not even ideal anarchy. One may admire "wise statesmanship"—which is desirable in any system—but human beings have not been so wise that they could always avoid armed conflict by diplomacy alone. The ultimate solution of conflicts under this philosophy is of course war. It is somewhat surprising, after waves of public opinion have beaten against war, after a Pact of Paris and a Covenant and a Charter made in response to this public opinion, to find thinkers going back to a system recognized as inadequate, and now feared as too dangerous for humanity to accept. If war is the only answer, then human intelligence has failed; and this I am not ready to concede.

The "realistic" school of thought falls into error in several ways. They assume—as indeed does the less expert average person anywhere after centuries of habit forming—that the state is the best possible protector of the individual human being. If this were true, ever, it is certainly incorrect in these days of interdependence. No state can provide economic security for its own people; its prosperity depends upon what other nations do, or upon what happens to other nations. No state can give its people physical security, because any other state may plunge it into war; wars today become world-wide and engulf even those states which desperately try to keep out of them. If one follows the "realists" advice, the very means by which a state would ultimately protect its citizens—war—inevitably wrecks both prosperity and security for the citizen. This is not realism, but desperation.

The only way of handling conflicts between individuals which has been consistently approved by humanity is law and government; but the same individuals who believe in domestic law are reluctant to accept law as between nations. Their reluctance derives from a history in which organization of the community of nations had not appeared; it continues as part of the human nature which hesitates to take the risk of new things. This reliance upon—almost deification of—the state, leads to the destruction of individual liberties, for not only is there a tendency in thinking and loyalty to submit to whatever is willed by government, but modern war—even modern economic war—cannot be waged except through powerful governmental controls. The continuance of war as a solution for human differences pushes us inevitably toward totalitarianism. There is no realism in a system which destroys the liberties it is created to guard.

The mistake of the "realist" is not that he believes in power, but rather in his belief that power belongs to and can only be used by the sovereign state; that only in this fashion can a state defend the interests of its members. A state must therefore always waste the major proportion of its resources in preparation for war, rather than in advancing the welfare of humanity; when "wise statesmanship" fails against the hardheaded aggressor or against the fool, the cost of the war which is the "realistic" answer is greater by now than humanity can afford. Surely, human intelligence can find a better answer than that!

Of course, it has done so: that answer is law and legal order. Power is always with us, a dangerous element, like fire, when uncontrolled. It is the purpose of law and government to provide controls for political power; to channel this power for the good of man rather than for the destruction of man. There is no necessary conflict between power politics on the one hand and international law or the United Nations on the other. In any human organization there will be conflicts of power, just as there are within a state; the essential things are the controls which regulate, the rules under which the conflict must be waged.[9]

The Dispute Over Interpretation of the Charter

If, then, we are to progress in the direction that experience and intelligence—and theoretical acceptance—point out to us, the United Nations should be a legal order. It is not to be expected that power, so long unlicensed, can be brought at once under control for the service of mankind; many centuries were required to discover and apply the service of fire. Some principles have been laid down, through customary international law and treaties; the development of an adequate legal order among sovereign states long habituated to resist external controls will necessarily be gradual. The United Nations cannot yet claim to be an adequate legal order.

Nevertheless, it is a legal order, at least it operates under and is restricted by a fundamental law, the Charter. This instrument is a most unsatisfying one, attempting to combine conflicting views and noble ideals into vague verbiage. It did, however, lay down some principles, and some limitations, without which it would not have been accepted; like most constitutions, its primary purpose was to set controls upon the organism which it created. In fact, the Charter set too many controls, so many that the machinery which it created could not operate efficiently. A system which allows the accused to escape jurisdiction on the ground (Article 2, paragraph 7) that the illegal act was his own affair or which permits him to veto any action against himself or his friends (Article 27), cannot be regarded as an effective legal order; and any constitution which forbids its own amendment must face the danger which confronts any obstacle to change—it may be pushed out of the way.

The desire to move ahead in spite of Charter restrictions has led to strong division of opinion as to the interpretation of the Charter and its application in practice. Some states wished to adhere strictly to the letter of the law—and it must be recalled that they accepted the Charter on the condition that this law would apply; others were impatient with this legal hamstringing of the hopes which they had had and demanded a very liberal interpretation; indeed, some have been inclined to go ahead, beyond interpretation, and to move ahead in disregard of the Charter.

The magisterial treatise *The Law of the United Nations* by Professor Kelsen finds itself in the center of this controversy. This is a thousand-page commentary on the Charter, section by section, derived entirely from official documents, and written with the keenness of analysis and the clarity of expression which characterize this great international lawyer. To many who wish to see the United Nations go ahead and more rapidly accomplish its purpose, it is a disappointing book. Thus Mr. A. H. Feller, late General Counsel and Director of the Legal Department of the United Nations, doubted "whether on the whole these contributions are worth the damage done to the fundamental conception of the Charter as a living instrument to guide the conduct of international life." To Mr. Feller, the Charter was "a political document designed to embody statements of ideals, of principles, and of moral sentiment;" he questioned the use of "logical semantic analysis as the primary if not the sole tool" for application of a constitutional document.[10] Professor Louis B. Sohn, of the Harvard Law School, says that Kelsen "has chosen the path of irony and criticism rather than the road of helpful assistance."[11] Mr. Oscar Schachter, of the Legal Department of the United Nations, argues that "the Charter is surely not to be contrued like a lease of land or an insurance policy; it is a constitutional instrument whose broad phrases were designed to meet changing circumstances for an undefined future."[12] Others, such as Professor Goodrich of Columbia,[13] regard the limited purposes expressed by Kelsen in his Preface as reducing the usefulness of the book.

Professor Kelsen, however, is unconcerned in this book, with political factors; he regards his task as that of "finding, by critical analysis, the possible meaning of the legal norm undergoing interpretation; and then, to show their consequences,"[14] leaving it to the competent legal authorities to choose, for political reasons, the preferable interpretation. Thus he admits the possibility of more than one interpretation and rejects the position of the dogmatic interpreter who must find the one and only answer. He would, presumably, expect Mr. Feller to choose his own interpretation—or the General Assembly, or the International Court of Justice, or other any organ which may be regarded as competent. These authorities may make use of his scientific analysis as they wish.

There is no doubt that Kelsen is devastating in his criticism of the Charter, but in this there is nothing new; that instrument has been severely criticized by the best friends of the United Nations or of legal order. The analysis to which it is subjected should be of great value when, in 1955, the question of revision of the Charter automatically appears on the agenda of the tenth General Assembly; it should be useful in the drafting of all future constitutional documents. The book does not, as some reviewers have charged, confine itself to the words of the text; it goes deeply into the *travaux préparatoires,* and considers thoroughly the viewpoints there expressed.

Nevertheless, the effect of the analysis given is one which would restrict the desires of many delegates, and would prevent the United Nations from taking certain steps which now seem to be needed. How could it be otherwise when those who made the Charter intended it to be as restrictive as possible? The emphasis was laid upon "sovereign equality," not upon law; the authority to take effective action for carrying out the stated purposes and principles was intentionally limited. It should not be forgotten that it was the United States delegation, fearful of the Senate and of the American people, who took the lead in imposing these restrictions. Today, when circumstances have changed, these restrictions are regretted; tomorrow, when a majority may be against us, we may fall back heavily upon them. Here is the political element.

Disregard of the Charter

This political element, rather than respect for the Charter, has governed the votes of delegates and the decisions of organs. Such a pressure, if consistent, could lead properly enough into new constitutional interpretations and allow for desirable growth. The practice of the United Nations, however, has not been consistent in this fashion. Delegates have, for one situation, upheld the restrictions of the Charter and, for another situation, have denied or disregarded such restrictions. Aside from the International Court of Justice, in rare cases called upon, organs of the United Nations do not take decisions, even when challenged, as to the constitutional right to act as proposed.

The most famous questions of constitutionality have arisen under the "domestic questions" clause (Article 2, paragraph 7). When Mr. Manuilsky, on January 21, 1946, complained of the presence of British troops in Indonesia, Mr. Bevin (U.K.) said that the United Nations could not interfere in the domestic jurisdiction of The Netherlands;[15] two years later, when Chile asked for investigation of the *coup d'état* in Czechoslovakia, Mr. Gromyko (U.S.S.R.) argued that this would be illegal, and Sir Alexander Cadogan (U.K.) supported the investigation.[16] In the Indonesian case, Mr. van Kleffens argued many times that the Charter forbade intervention in such a domestic question, and asked that the question of constitutionality be referred to the International Court of Justice. No decision on this point was ever taken, and the political pressure of United Nations action lost Indonesia to The Netherlands.

The Security Council and the General Assembly both sought ways to take action against the Franco government in Spain. It was argued that the Spanish situation, if not a threat to or breach of the peace, at any rate threatened the maintenance of peace and security; but no decision was taken upon this point. Such a decision, had it been taken, might have been regarded as a decision that it was not a domestic question; not even this was done. Constitutionality was simply passed by, and condemnatory resolutions were adopted. The question also appeared in this case as to whether the General Assembly could recommend "action," or whether, under Article 11, paragraph 2, it must refer the matter to the Security Council. Actually, it did recommend action, including one of the nonmilitary enforcement measures under Article 41, without pausing to decide whether it had a right to do so.

With regard to the treatment of Indians in South Africa, the argument that this was certainly a domestic question and the appeal to submit to the International Court the right of the Assembly to act were simply overridden. The resolution did not make clear what were the grounds for assuming that it was not a domestic question. South Africa has, with some justification, been indignant at this treatment and recalcitrant in other matters.

An illustration outside the field of peace and security may be found in the debate concerning information to be transmitted under Article 73(e), during which France and Belgium stated that they would never have signed the Charter if they had understood that such requirements could be made. After the resolutions had been adopted, over these protests, Belgium, France, and the United Kingdom announced that they did not feel bound by these illegal resolutions.[17]

The trend to disregard law and Charter continues strongly, and as inconsistently as ever, in the consideration by the Security Council of the complaints made by the United Kingdom against Iran and Egypt. In the former case, England was able to bring the question before the International Court of Justice, since both states had accepted the optional clause; but Iran immediately rejected the jurisdiction of the court on the ground that the nationalization of oil was exclusively a domestic question. When the matter came before the Security Council, Sir Gladwyn Jebb (U.K.) asked that the opinion of the court be upheld, rather than flouted, and asserted: "The rule of law as opposed to that of force must entail willingness to submit disputes of a legal character to judicial decision and a willingness to abide by the results, or there is no rule of law."[18] In this statement he was quite correct, and the question was clearly one of international law; but the Council members, acting on political bases, took no stand in support of law.

On the other hand, in the case of the Egyptian blockade, Sir Gladwyn said: "These legal issues are no doubt debatable, but I still do not consider that it is necessary for the Security Council to go into them. It is at least questionable whether the Security Council is really qualified to undertake the detailed legal study and analysis which would certainly be required . . . the view which the Council takes on this question should depend, in our opinion, on the actual situation as it exists rather than on any legal technicalities." The representative of the United States did not mention law in the course of his discussion of the matter, though several other delegates did.[19]

On various occasions, delegates have expressed their impatience with "legalism" and refused to argue as to the meaning of the Charter and its obligations or restrictions. Thus General Romulo (Philippines), discussing the Uniting for Peace resolution, said:

> This authority springs from the broad powers of the General Assembly under the Charter, from the United Nations' inherent right of survival, and from the supreme responsibility to all the world's peoples to preserve peace. No legal technicality, no matter how brilliantly advanced, can prevail against the overriding force of this threefold principle.[20]

And the Peruvian delegate urged a dynamic and moral concept of the Charter. The result has been to deprive the Security Council of a solid basis for decision and action and to leave to it only the hope of political compromise, a hope which has culminated in the near impotence of the Council shown in the recent Iranian and Egyptian cases.[21]

This attitude on the part of delegates in United Nations organs is itself a weighty matter, deserving of consideration. How is it to be explained, in the light of a universal desire for a legal order among nations and in the face of the fact that the Charter creates legal obligations which should be respected?

A large part of the explanation is, doubtless, a praiseworthy desire to accomplish the purposes of the United Nations, and a resulting impatience with restrictions put into the Charter which embarrass or prevent such accomplishment. But it must be recalled, as it has been in several debates, that those who joined the organization did so on the condition that it should be barred from doing certain things. While they might by membership give up a few of their sovereign rights, all others they sought carefully to protect—and none more so than the United States of America. They have a right to complain when these legal rights are overridden by a majority vote; they may resist decisions or withdraw from the organization. It cannot be accepted that a subject of law can approve and support the law when it is on his side, but reject that law when it works against him.

A generous interpretation of the Charter is of course permissible. No law can be written in words rigid enough to meet all possible situations, all changes of circumstances. The more vague the statement of that law, the more room there is for interpretation; and this should leave much room as regards the Charter of the United Nations. It is a document so vague in its wording and meaning that liberal interpretation is needed even to enable it to move toward its own purposes. Furthermore, it may be urged that a larger generosity of interpretation should be admissible where no possibility of amendment exists.

A Possible Boundary Line

Granted all this, it must be recalled that we are talking of interpretation, and not of disregard, of the law. The line between a far-stretched interpretation and complete disregard may sometimes be difficult to draw; yet somewhere, in between the "realistic" rejection of law by Morgenthau and others and the rigid "semantic" interpretation by Kelsen, it should be possible to find a median course. We may agree with Mr. Schachter when he says: "Law in the United Nations does not consist in symbols that have a fixed and defined meaning as in pure mathematics. Its rules and concepts relate to political life, and grammar and logic alone will not enable one to understand their meaning." This, I take it, is true of all law. We may even follow him in saying that the Charter is "an expression of general purposes to achieve certain ends," and a grant of authority.[22] It seems to me, however, that he passes very lightly over the fact that a Constitution not only grants authority, it also sets limitations and restrictions upon that authority. The Charter of the United Nations does not confer an unlimited authority for its organs to do anything for which a political majority can be commanded at that moment. States which are denied the protection expected from the Charter may feel that they can do nothing but reject such action as illegal; several, in fact, have done so, though none yet have gone so far as to withdraw from the United Nations.

It would be best if all questions concerning the interpretation of the Charter could be turned over to the International Court of Justice for judicial rather than political interpretation; it would mean some progress toward observance of law if organs of the United Nations would at least call upon the court for an advisory opinion on legal questions which the organ is not qualified to handle. The attitudes of states apparently make this procedure unacceptable at present. At the least, however, the precedent could be established that, when a claim of unconstitutionality or illegality is raised, the organ concerned would first vote upon this preliminary question before it proceeds to vote on the question at issue. Though the Charter designates no authority to give interpretations of its meaning in practice, it is maintained that each organ may make its own interpretation.[23] In fact, however, the various organs do not make such interpretations, even when challenged; and I suggest that when an organ has proceeded, against claims that the action is illegal, to take an action desired by the majority, it has crossed the boundary line between respect for law and purely political decision.

It may be said that the decision would be the same in either case. This I doubt, for a state will hesitate to go on record, establishing a precedent which may later be used against it; it is much easier to cast a political vote untrammeled by the thought of what the Charter means. It is claimed, of course, that the taking of a decision, on whatever grounds, is sufficient evidence that the organ which takes it regards its action as in accordance with the Charter. This claim can be compared with the action of India in seizing Hyderabad, or of Iran in seizing the oil industry, and then asserting that the action was domestic and not subject to interference from the outside; it would be as if a robber should say, "I have stolen the goods; this proves that my action was legal." Perhaps the decision of a United Nations organ is not quite so bad as this; it would not be surprising if the people of The Netherlands should feel that such a comparison was justifiable in the case of Indonesia.

If the United Nations is to maintain any pretension of being a legal order, of seeking to carry out its purposes in terms of its fundamental law, it cannot do so by arriving at whatever decision the emotions of the moment demand and then asserting that the action taken was legal because it was taken. Nor is the situation improved by the assertion that a decision taken by law cannot be enforced, that it leaves rancor behind it, that conciliation is softer and more acceptable. One may ask, for example, why recommend to the parties in the Kashmir imbroglio, that they refer their dispute to arbitration or to the court? Would they follow the recommendation? And if a judicial decision were given, would this alter the attitude of either party? Would it be politically possible to carry out such a decision?

This is so-called "realism," hopeless and impotent. Has it been any more possible to reach a solution through haggling and long-drawn-out negotiation? Has "wise statesmanship" made any impression upon the parties? The answer to such questions is that a solution is possible when enough pressure is brought to bear by the community of nations, whether behind a judicial decision or a political one. Conciliation is of course desirable, and the proper procedure for the Security Council to follow in most cases—though in some, it should be apparent from the beginning that a judicial decision is needed. Where conciliation is tried and fails, it may be possible to find an answer by application of law; it is not necessary to abandon the effort in the belief that there is no other recourse than political agreement. On clearly legal questions, a legal answer offers a far more solid foundation: the parties hesitate to accept the opprobrium of lawless rejection; more moral support from other states is to be expected.

The refusal to resort to law on the ground that it will not be respected is absurd; how can one know that it will not be respected? How can one know that another procedure will be respected? Have other procedures in practice been any more successful? If the United Nations disregards law, then India is encouraged to refuse arbitration, and Iran and Egypt are encouraged to flout treaty obligations and court decisions, and we fall back into anarchy. Some problems call for political settlement, but even these should be handled in accordance with the obligations and restrictions laid down in the Charter; some call for judicial settlement, and the organs of the United Nations should in such cases encourage settlement by law.

The preliminary consideration of the question of constitutional competence which I have proposed is a minimum. I, like others, am dissatisfied with the limitative character of the Charter; I would prefer to see it a more flexible instrument, and would therefore support liberal interpretation of its words. The Security Council should have a wide freedom of action; it should use persuasion and conciliation; its decisions or recommendations must be largely political in character. But the Council, or the United Nations, should not push law aside entirely, as they now tend to do; the unwillingness to support legal principles in the current Iranian and Egyptian cases is shocking. There should be some rules for the political contest within the United Nations; if all decisions of the United Nations are to be made solely on political grounds—that is, through such compromise of national interests as can be obtained at a given moment—the United Nations becomes no more than a convenient meeting place for negotiation. Most people, I believe, want the United Nations to be more than this.

A boundary line can be drawn between strict application of the words of the Charter and irresponsible political decision by majority vote. In a more orderly world, that line could be drawn nearer to the Charter and be based more firmly upon judicial interpretation of the Charter. As things now stand, it must be drawn nearer to political action. The least that an organ of the United Nations can do to show its respect for its Charter is to consider, and determine for itself even if on political grounds, that the action which it takes is in harmony with the Charter.

HANS J. MORGENTHAU

Political Limitations of the United Nations

THE UNDERSTANDING of the functions which the United Nations can perform for the preservation of peace under present world conditions is hampered by one main obstacle. It is the tendency to look at the legal provisions of the Charter and the institutions derived from them as though they were self-sufficient entities which receive their political meaning and their ability to perform political functions from their own literal content without reference to the political environment within and with regard to which they are supposed to operate. Such a legalistic approach to legal rules is possible in municipal law, in the measure in which those legal rules are an organic outgrowth of the social situation and in which, therefore, the social functions they are supposed to perform are directly revealed in the literal text of the legal rule. Such areas where legal rule and social context correspond are relatively large in municipal law; they are not as large in international law. In municipal law there exist wide areas which are, at least temporarily, exempt from conflicts of interests—economic, social, or political—and where therefore the literal text of the legal rule represents a consensus as to the social function the legal rule is intended to fulfill. Conflicts concerning such legal rules, then, concern either questions of fact to be subsumed under the legal rule or its mere technical interpretation for the purpose of ascertaining its literal meaning.

In international law, such areas of convergence of legal rule and social function are always precarious because they exist only by virtue of a permanently precarious consensus among the interested nations. More particularly, the socially more important branches of international law are normally characterized by a thorough discrepancy between the literal meaning of their rules and their social environment. For the socially more important rules of international law are not the organic outgrowth of a social situation upon whose legal regulation a consensus has been established. They are either the result of an attempt to gloss over existing and, for the time being, irremediable dissension through agreement on a meaningless verbal formula which preserves the status quo with regard to the existing conflict. Or else they serve the purpose of creating procedural devices which may in the future be used to resolve the conflict either by both sides through compromise or by either side on its own terms.

It may be useful to apply these considerations to two aspects of the United Nations: Chapter I of the Charter, dealing with purposes and principles, and the general functions which the United Nations is able to perform for the preservation of peace.

I

The problem of ascertaining the meaning of Chapter I of the Charter can be approached in two different ways. One can try to ascertain the meaning of the words which are found in Chapter I of the Charter and elsewhere with regard to the purposes and principles of the organization. This is, indeed, the indispensable first step toward understanding what Chapter I of the Charter means. Yet the task is bound to remain incomplete, and the results of the first step may even be grossly misleading, if one does not put these results into the context of the over-all functions which the Charter and the institutions created by virtue of it are supposed to fulfill within the social context of the contemporary world.

What the purposes and principles of the United Nations are supposed to be is revealed not only in Chapter I of the Charter, containing Articles 1 and 2, but also in its Preamble. The differences in this respect between the Preamble and Chapter I are obvious. The Preamble makes a logical distinction between ends and means, while Chapter I, in a less logical fashion, distinguishes between purposes and principles. Article 1 formulates the four purposes of the United Nations, which cover both ends and means, and Article 2 defines the seven principles which are to guide the actions of the members of the organization. The logical relationship between Articles 1 and 2 seems to be that Article 1 defines ends and means, while Article 2 lays down the general standards of action to be observed with regard to those ends and means.

The first question one must ask oneself is whether the Preamble and Chapter I of the Charter are mere ideological embellishments, innocuous statements of good intentions and of ideal objectives, or whether they have a concrete legal and political meaning, in view of the functions which the United Nations is supposed and able to fulfill for international society. If the latter alternative is the correct one—and I think it is—then we must ask what meaning the Preamble and Chapter I have in view of these functions of the United Nations.

The existence of an organic connection between the Preamble and Chapter I, on the one hand, and the main body of the Charter, on the other, is indicated by the fact that in two places—Article 9, paragraph 1, and, more particularly, Article 24, paragraph 2—the Charter refers expressly to Chapter I. In Article 9 it is said that "The General Assembly may consider the general principles of cooperation in the maintenance of international peace and security . . . and may make recommendations with regard to such principles to the Members or to the Security Council or to both." More explicitly in Article 24, paragraph 2, it is said that "In discharging these duties, the Security Council is acting in accordance with the purposes and principles of the United Nations."

What, then, is the systematic connection of Chapter I with the main body of the Charter? If the provisions of Chapter I have an actual political and legal meaning so that the day-by-day operations of the United Nations will be guided by the purposes and principles laid down in Chapter I, then these purposes and principles must be integrated into the specific provisions of the Charter. It is interesting to note, and it sheds an illuminating light upon the functions which the United Nations was intended to perform from the outset, that some of the principles and purposes defined in Chapter I are elaborated in the main body of the Charter in considerable detail, while others are neither elaborated nor even referred to. The principle of the preservation of peace, for instance, is spelled out in the main body of the Charter (Articles 11, 12, 13, 14, 18, 23, 24, 26, 33 ff., 39 ff., 52 ff.). Similarly, the principle of universality is referred to in the main body of the Charter (Articles 4, 10, 11, 14, 34, 35). On the other hand, the references of Chapter I to the principles of justice and self-determination are not taken up by any other provision of the Charter. What the Charter elaborates are the procedural principles serving the objective of peace. What it does not elaborate are the substantive rules of justice, upon which the concrete decision of a concrete case depends.

In this respect, the United Nations differs significantly from both its predecessors, the Holy Alliance and the League of Nations. For the treaties forming the Holy Alliance were centered upon a substantive principle of justice, that is, the principle of legitimacy, which could provide a standard of action whenever a concrete case was to be decided.

What brought about the downfall of the Holy Alliance was not lack of a substantive principle of justice, but fundamental disagreement concerning the application of that principle to concrete cases.

The League of Nations, too, was based upon a substantive principle of justice which was able to provide guidance for its actions—the preservation of the territorial status quo of 1919. Supplementing it was the principle that changes in that status quo were to come about only in accordance with the wishes of the majority of the populations concerned, that is, the principle of national self-determination. The League of Nations distintegrated when, on the one hand, the nations opposed to the status quo of 1919 became strong enough to challenge openly the nations pledged to protect it, and when, on the other hand, the application of these principles to the cases of the Sudetenland and the Russian-Finnish War brought about politically and militarily absurd consequences.

That the purposes and principles laid down in Chapter I of the Charter perform either a mere procedural function for the United Nations or else no function at all becomes also obvious from an analysis of these principles and purposes themselves and their relations to each other and to the whole of the Charter. The Charter contains two different types of principles and purposes, both with regard to the mode of action as well as with regard to the kind of action to be performed.

As concerns the mode of action, the principle of collectivity stands against the principle of individual autonomy. The former principle permeates the main body of the Charter. The latter principle is expressed in Article 2, paragraph 1, to the effect that "The organization is based upon the principle of the sovereign equality of all its Members." As concerns the kind of action to be performed, supranational principles referring either to the humanitarian objectives of general welfare or peaceful change or collective security stand against the principle of national policies. The latter is again expressed in the concept of sovereign equality, as well as in the reservation of domestic jurisdiction, as stipulated in Article 2, paragraph 7, in the concepts of self-defense and regionalism of Articles 51ff., and in Articles 106 and 107 concerning traditional security agreements.

Which of these principles and purposes have a direct connection with the functions that the United Nations is at present able to perform? More particularly, what is the respective weight which, in view of these functions, must be attributed to the collective and supranational principles as over against the individualistic and national ones? A closer look at the Charter as a whole in view of its intended and possible functions shows the existence of three purposes and principles which are of the very essence of the United Nations, but which are mentioned neither in Chapter I nor anywhere else in the text of the Charter.

The first of these principles is that of traditional diplomacy as over against the principle of collective, pseudoparliamentary decision. The very essence of the Charter, so far as the preservation of peace through the application of sanctions and through a decision of concrete cases is concerned, lies in the unity of the great powers (Article 27). The Charter presupposes the existence of this unity, but it does not contain instrumentalities through which it can be established. Such unity is supposed to exist at the moment when the Charter comes into operation. It can then only have been established by the traditional means of diplomacy. The whole structure of the United Nations and its ability to perform functions within the given social environment rests upon the premise of successful diplomatic action which establishes and maintains the unity of the great powers.

The second principle implicit in the Charter is that of the sovereign equality of the great powers as over against what might be called paradoxically the "sovereign inequality" of the other member nations of the organization. The structure of the Security Council shows clearly that those nations which have permanent membership in that organ, because of their actual or alleged superiority in power, were intended to function, with the assistance of two nonpermanent members of the Security Council, as a kind of limited world government, to which not only the other member nations of the organization, but in a certain measure all nations would have been subject. This function envisaged implicitly in the Charter has never been realized; for the lack of unity among the great powers has made it impossible for the Security Council to function as intended in the Charter.

Finally, the Charter contains the principle of regionalism as opposed to that of universality. Articles 51 and 52 not only establish the principle of regionalism, but also, by implication and in spite of the wording of the legal text, the primacy of the regional principle over that of universality. According to Article 51, the right of individual or collective self-defense shall have precedence in fact over the functions assigned to the organs of the United Nations. Articles 51 and 52 establish what one might call the principle of regional collective security, aimed primarily, if not exclusively, against aggression from outside the region.[1]

If one takes the Preamble and Chapter I of the Charter at their literal meaning, divorced not only from the main body of the Charter, but also from the functions which the United Nations was supposed to perform and actually performs, one must conclude that the Charter establishes a definite preference of the supranational, collective principles over those of national sovereignty and national interest. In actuality, however, the scales are rather weighted the other way. The Charter of the United Nations, far from intending to replace or actually replacing the traditional methods of diplomacy, actually presupposes the continuous successful operation of these methods. This is particularly obvious from the recent organizational developments which have taken their start from Articles 51 and 52 of the Charter. These developments have been widely hailed as steps towards strengthening the United Nations, toward realizing the intentions of the Charter, and toward enhancing peace and security. In actuality, these developments run counter to the function envisaged by the Charter in view of the anticipated continuing unity of the great powers. They are the very negation of these functions. For they stem from the realization that the unity of the great powers, upon which the operation of the United Nations was predicated, is unattainable under present world conditions.

If the United Nations was to perform substantive political functions at all—in contrast to serving as a meeting place for diplomats and as a forum for propaganda—it could do so only by becoming the instrument, not of all great powers, but of those who are able to control in common at least part of the institutional machinery and of the functions of the United Nations. The United Nations was originally envisaged as the second story of an edifice, built upon the foundations of the continuing unity of the great powers to be maintained by the traditional methods of diplomacy. With that unity having crumbled, the United Nations, as intended by the Charter, has no foundation upon which to rest. The only foundation that is left is the unity of the Western alliance under the leadership of the United States, and what is—politically speaking—called the United Nations today is but a wing of the original structure resting on that foundation.

II

As concerns the general functions which the United Nations is able to perform for the preservation of peace, the problem which we must face is in its essence not different from the problem posed by the relationship between substantive goals and organizational form in general. The relationship between the substantive goal of a group of people and the institutional forms through which they endeavor to materialize that goal is essentially identical on all social levels. What is true in this respect of the family is also true of a trade or labor organization, a political party, an international organization. On all levels, except the international one, it would be obvious to everybody that organization as such cannot be a substitute for substantive policies. It is only on the international level that it has almost become a dogma that organization is not so much a means to an end as an end in itself.

Two examples of this misconception stand out in recent history. One concerns the League of Nations; the other, the United Nations. We are all familiar with the argument that one of the main causes of the breakdown of the League of Nations was its lack of universality, and, more particularly, the absence of the United States. This argument assumes that the success of an organization whose purpose it is to preserve international peace depends primarily upon an element of organization itself, that is, the comprehensiveness of its membership. It ought, however, to be obvious that the comprehensiveness of membership in its influence upon the success of the organization is distinctly subordinate to the substantive policies pursued by the most influential members of society inside and outside the organization.

What brought the international order of 1919 to its downfall was not the refusal of the United States to join the League of Nations, but the policies pursued by the great powers, the United States included, inside and outside the League of Nations. If the United States as a member of the League of Nations had pursued the same policies which it pursued outside it—a most likely contingency—the League of Nations would have failed in its objective to preserve international peace no less disastrously than it actually did. Had the United States, not being a member of the League of Nations, used its influence as the potentially most powerful nation on earth in support of policies conducive to the preservation of peace, peace might have been preserved regardless of what the League of Nations as an organization might have done. The argument, then, that the League of Nations failed because the United States did not join it, is tantamount to an alibi by which the burden of responsibility for failure is shifted from the substantive policies of the great powers, where it belongs, to a flaw in international organization.

The same misconception of regarding international organization as a substitute for substantive policies, is manifest in the expectations which have been associated with the United Nations, and in the policies concerning it. When Mr. Cordell Hull returned in 1943 from the Moscow conference, where the foundation of the United Nations had been laid, he declared that the new international organization would mean the end of power politics and usher in a new era of international collaboration. Three years later, Mr. Philip Noel-Baker, then British minister of state, echoed Mr. Hull by stating in the House of Commons that the British government was "determined to use the institutions of the United Nations to kill power politics in order that, by the methods of diplomacy, the will of the people shall prevail."

These and many other observers of the international scene start with the assumption that membership in, and support of, an international organization provides an alternative to the traditional methods and objectives of international politics, that, in other words, nations have a choice between membership in, and support of, an international organization, on the one hand, and traditional power politics, on the other. It would have been closer to the truth to assume that membership in, and support of, an international organization, such as the United Nations, provides a new medium for the traditional methods of international politics, and adds a new instrument for the pursuance of its traditional objectives. Not only has the United Nations not replaced power politics, but the new organizational forms and procedures of the United Nations have been put at the service of power politics.

To say, as has been said many times by spokesmen for American foreign policy, that the foreign policy of the United States is the United Nations policy, is no more meaningful and no less misleading than to say that the policy of the United States Steel Corporation is the policy of the National Association of Manufacturers, or that the policy of Macy's is the policy of the United States Chamber of Commerce. There is no such thing as the policy of an organization, international or domestic, apart from the policy of its most influential member or members. This is true of national organizations, and it is true to an even greater extent of international organizations. For here the disparity of influence between the most powerful members and the common run of the weak ones is much greater than on the national scene. The United States pursues its own foreign policies, conceived, if not defined, in the traditional terms of the national interest. It may pursue these policies within or without the United Nations. If it does the former, it will try to persuade the necessary majority of the members of the United Nations to identify themselves with the policies of the United States. If the United States succeeds in bringing this identification about, it has then succeeded in transforming its own foreign policies into policies of the United Nations. Such transformation is naturally advantageous from the point of view of the political interests of the United States. For the success of all political action depends to a considerable degree upon the ability of the actor to identify its own interest with the interest of the community.

At best, then, the attempt of statesmen to explain national policies in terms of United Nations' policies amounts to ideological rationalizations and justifications of national policies in terms of supranational ones. At worst, such attempts are a cloak for the absence of any positive national policy whatsoever. An example of the latter is provided by one of the arguments by which the United States has justified its refusal to follow the advice of Winston Churchill, Walter Lippmann, Arnold Toynbee, and others, to try to negotiate a settlement with the Soviet Union as long as there is still time. According to this argument, the United States cannot enter into bilateral negotiations with the Soviet Union, especially where the interests of third nations are at stake, and the United States will meet the Soviet Union only on the platform of the United Nations. Here again, we witness an attempt to substitute the nonexisting policies of an international organization for the policies of individual nations. As concerns world politics, the United Nations, as originally intended, is nothing but the United States plus the Soviet Union and their respective allies; and the policies of the United Nations, as originally envisaged, are nothing but the identical or parallel policies of the great powers. For a nation to say, then, that it cannot pursue a certain policy outside the United Nations is simply another way of saying that with regard to the matter under discussion it refuses to have a positive policy at all.

This criticism of the prevailing misconceptions of the relationship between international organization and foreign policy does, however, not imply that international organizations, such as the United Nations, have no positive functions to fulfill for the foreign policies of the individual nations and for the maintenance of international peace. However, these functions are both more modest than, and different from, the ones generally expected from an international organization. They are essentially twofold.

First of all and most importantly, an international organization, such as the United Nations, provides opportunities for the development of new techniques of diplomacy which, if used properly, can contribute much to the mitigation and the peaceful settlement of international conflicts. Especially under the conditions of the cold war, when diplomatic relations between East and West are reduced to a bare minimum, the different agencies of the United Nations make it inevitable that the representatives of the contending camps be in constant personal contact, which can be used unobtrusively for political purposes. The use of the United Nations for the discreet settlement of the Berlin blockade is a case in point.

Second, so far as national policies are channeled through the United Nations, they need the approval of whatever majority of members the Charter stipulates, in order to enable the United Nations to take action. National policies, then, must be presented in such a way as to gain the approval of other nations whose national interests and policies may differ from those submitted for approval. This requirement will always lead to the ideological justification and rationalization of national policies in terms of supranational ones. Yet it will sometimes also result in the blunting of the sharp edges of a national policy, its reformulation and adaptation in the light of the point of view of the most influential members whose support is needed. This influence of an international organization upon national policies is indeed a very subtle one, whose strength will depend primarily upon the distribution of power between the nation seeking support for its policies and the nations whose support is sought.

These influences are different both in quality and in importance from those which are generally supposed to exist between international organization and foreign policy. Yet they are no less real for being less tangible and less radical. They, too, point to the basic consideration that the United Nations, far from being a substitute for the traditional policies pursued by the great powers with traditional methods, can only be one of the instruments of these policies. If those policies converge or run on parallel lines, the United Nations can become an instrument for the policies which all the great powers have in common. As long as such political harmony is lacking, the United Nations will at best serve as an instrument for the policies of one group of powers against another group of powers, both members of the organization. The contribution it is able to make for the preservation of peace, as for the achievement of any other kind of political objective, can only be minor. Whatever functions it is able to fulfill in these respects will not depend primarily upon the legal provisions of the Charter or the institutions established in accordance with them, but upon the political policies pursued by the great powers through the medium of the traditional methods of diplomacy.

ALFRED VON VERDROSS

The Charter of the United Nations and General International Law

I

THE QUESTION here posed is one application of a problem repeatedly dealt with by Kelsen: the problem of the relationship between two normative orders. This investigation seems therefore particularly suited to be contained in a symposium honoring Kelsen.

As Kelsen has correctly pointed out, a threefold relationship is possible between two normative orders. Either normative order "A" is derived from (delegated by) normative order "B" or normative order "B" is derived from normative order "A," or both are based on a higher normative order.[1]

But this scheme is only rendered exhaustive if one assumes the simultaneous validity of different normative orders. If one does not assume this precondition, the displacement of one normative order by another would also come within the area of the problem here posed. If we apply this scheme to our problem, the question arises first whether the Charter of the United Nations has displaced general international law or whether it is valid on the basis of general international law.

The solution of this problem seems to be simple at first sight, because the Charter of the United Nations was agreed upon in the form of a state treaty concluded on the basis of general international law according to the norms of treaty procedure of this legal order. To this must be added that this agreement is not a world-wide treaty, having neither been concluded, nor later recognized, by all states. There seems no doubt, for these reasons, that general international law continues to be valid while the Charter of the United Nations forms only *particular* international law, binding on the basis and within the framework of general international law.

But this result is being subjected to doubts because the Charter of the United Nations according to Article 2, paragraph 6, extends its sphere of validity to nonmembers of the United Nations as well. One could however, claim against this clause that it is not binding for nonmembers, because a treaty is in principle only binding upon those states which have ratified it. But against this objection it can again be said that this principle knows exceptions.[2] Besides, it is obvious that this objection presupposes the continued validity of general international law. If the Charter of the United Nations should be considered to have abolished general international law, the principle that a treaty is only binding upon partners to it would also have been put out of force.

It could further be stated against the case for the abolition of general international law by the Charter of the United Nations that, according to the universal constitution of the community of states, a norm of general international law could only be changed by a universal norm of customary international law or a world treaty. But even this objection would not be decisive because it considers only the *constitutional* change of the norms of international law. Besides, a *revolutionary* change of norms can occur in international law just as in internal state law. I have referred to this for the first time in my *Einheit des rechtlichen Weltbildes auf Grund der Völkerrechtsverfassung.* The present constitution of the community of states, rooted in customary international law, could for example be abolished by the dictate of a world conqueror.

It would, therefore, have been possible for the founding nations of the United Nations to intend to abolish general international law in a revolutionary way. But such a fundamental change has not occurred for the following reasons: The above-mentioned clause of Article 2, paragraph 6, of the Charter is not intended to comprehend all international legal relations of nonmembers but only directs organs of the United Nations to see to it that nonmembers, as well as members, shall observe those principles of the Charter dealing with the maintenance of international peace and security. To this must be added the fact that even the relations between members of the United Nations have not been regulated exhaustively by the Charter. The Charter is intended rather to regulate only part of these relations. It therefore contains the presupposition of the continued validity of general international law. This can be seen at once in the fact that the Charter presupposes that its members are subject to international law as well as the obligatory force of the treaty embodying the Charter concluded by them. But the continued validity of general international law is expressed in the Charter itself. The preamble of the Charter demands the fulfillment of the obligations resulting from the treaty as well as of those which have been or will in future be based on other sources of international law. A more detailed explanation of this idea can be found in Article 38 of the statute of the International Court of Justice, forming according to Article 92 of the Charter an integral part of the Charter. This clause not only recognizes treaties but also customary international law and the general principles of law recognized by all civilized nations as sources of international law. To this must be added judicial decisions, according to Article 38, paragraph d, of the statute and the doctrine of international law, as auxiliary sources of law. This proves clearly that general international law continues to be valid.

But the question can be asked whether *single* norms of general international law have not perhaps been changed by the Charter. In this connection, it is appropriate to refer to the basic prohibition of the use of force in Article 2, paragraph 4, of the Charter, which seems to contradict general international law, since the latter recognizes war not only as a defensive measure but also as a means to enforce rights. Even the Kellogg pact prohibits war only "as a means of national policy" but not in terms of military reprisal. Yet the wording of Article 2, paragraph 4, of the Charter is not a change of general international law because international law does not prescribe forcible self-help but only permits states to use it *if they have not assumed conflicting treaty obligations.*

But the case is quite different in the clause of Article 2, paragraph 6 of the Charter. This clause permits the Security Council of the United Nations to take preventive and repressive enforcement action against that nonmember who has made use of self-help in a way undeniably permitted by general international law in order to enforce its legally founded claim.[4] This is in no way altered if one considers the Kellogg pact as part of international law, since the Security Council can order enforcement measures against a nonmember who has ratified the Kellogg pact if that nonmember has resorted to military reprisals. This, although the Kellogg pact—as already mentioned—prohibits war only as "a means of national policy" but not as a military reprisal. These two examples demonstrate the fact that the United Nations can also take measures against a nonmember who has stayed strictly within the framework of general international law and the Kellogg pact. But this means that, if sanctions are permitted according to the Charter against a nonmember who has not violated general international law, the Charter is an attempt to obligate nonmembers. This is true in spite of the fact that it does not directly impose obligations but only directs the United Nations to see to it that nonmembers also will respect the norms of the Charter on the maintenance of peace and international security.

But if the clause of Article 2, paragraph 6, of the Charter is viewed as a norm obligating nonmembers, although it imposes duties upon them without their consent, which they do not have on the basis of general international law, including the Kellogg pact, then it is clear that this clause was not established on the basis of general international law but in contradiction to it. It must then be a norm which can only have been created in a *revolutionary* way.[5]

It is also possible to refer to Article 103 of the Charter in support of the possibility that there has occurred a revolutionary change of law through individual clauses of the Charter. According to these clauses, the obligations of the Charter have priority not only over treaty obligations between members, but also over treaty obligations vis-a-vis nonmembers. But this norm has been formulated in such an ambiguous fashion that it need not necessarily be understood in the sense of an automatic cancellation of these obligations. It can also mean merely that there is a duty of member states to take all permissible steps in order to cancel treaty obligations conflicting with the Charter.[6]

It is not necessary, however, to go into a discussion of the *rights* which the Charter of the United Nations grants to nonmembers since it is undisputed that, even according to general international law, treaties *in favor* of third states are possible and valid.[7]

II

Up to this point, the investigation shows that, although the Charter of the United Nations presupposes the continued validity of general international law, it also creates—just as any other treaty—new rights and duties. The Charter of the United Nations constitutes therefore a *lex specialis* having priority over the dispensable norms *(jus dispositiorem)* of general international law but also abrogating its compelling norms *(jus cogens)*, if the possibility of revolutionary establishment of law is recognized.

But this abrogation is not final because the respective norms of general international law are only suspended by the Charter of the United Nations and will again be fully applied if the Charter is amended according to Article 108. But the single groups of norms under general international law which the Charter has abrogated can be revived even without amendment to the Charter. This situation may appear when the Security Council, in the case of an armed attack, is not able to take the measures necessary to restore the peace. The state attacked may not only exercise the right of self-defense in such a situation but the other states may come to the aid of that state[8] and support it with all forcible means until the Security Council has taken the measures necessary to restore the peace. If the Security Council arrives at such a decision, even if belated, all states are obliged according to Article 25 of the Charter to follow the directives of the Security Council. The Security Council can, of course, direct the states which have made use of the right to employ measures of collective self-defense according to Article 51 of the Charter to continue or cease these measures. But if the Security Council cannot reach a decision on the sanctions to be taken because the votes necessary for such a decision according to Article 27, paragraph 3, of the Charter are lacking, the individual and collective measures of self-help according to Article 51 of the Charter can be continued until the defeat of the attacker. They are admissable as long as the Security Council has not decided otherwise.

This proves that the measures of self-help are provisional when the Security Council functions properly, but final when the Security Council has been crippled for whatever reason.

In such a situation the measures of self-help according to Article 51 assume the character of a war limited only by the norms of *general* international law. This proves that general international law replaces individual norms of the Charter, if these cannot be applied because of the crippling of the Security Council.

The content of Article 51 is particularly significant when a permanent member of the Council is involved directly or indirectly in a conflict, because such members can prevent an intervention against the attacking power by the use of their so-called veto right. Sanctions of the Security Council are therefore practically excluded against them. They must be replaced by the subsidiary sanctions of Article 51. Otherwise the prohibition against the use of force according to Article 2, paragraph 4, would be merely *lex imperfecta* for the permanent members of the Council. If, in agreement with Kelsen, we do not consider norms without sanctions as legal norms, the prohibition of the use of force according to Article 2, paragraph 4, would have no legal basis at all unless the sanctions according to Article 51 are admitted as well.

But this legal situation seems to have changed since the fifth meeting of the General Assembly. It decided on November 3, 1950 (52 votes in favor, 5 against, and 2 abstentions) to empower the General Assembly itself to recommend to the members the taking of collective measures if the Security Council should be unable to act.[9] The question arises, however, what steps the General Assembly can take on the basis of the Charter, in order to achieve the restoration of the peace. The preamble of the Charter states, in the first place, that the peoples of the United Nations have decided "to unite [their] strength to maintain international peace and security."[10] Article 1, paragraph 1, states, therefore, as the first purpose of the United Nations that of maintaining "international peace and security, and to that end: [that of taking] *effective collective measures* for the prevention and removal of threats to the peace, and for the *suppression of acts of aggression* and other breaches of the peace,"[11] . . . Furthermore, according to Article 2, paragraph 5, "All members shall give the United Nations every assistance in *any action* it takes in accordance with the present Charter . . ."[12]

But Articles 39 ff. entrust only the Security Council with the taking of enforcement measures. In addition, the last sentence of Article 11, paragraph 2, provides that the General Assembly shall submit any question which it discusses "on which action is necessary" to the Security Council. What steps in this direction can the General Assembly therefore take *on the basis of the Charter?*

It should first be noted that the Security Council has according to Article 24 of the Charter the "primary responsibility," but not the exclusive responsibility, "for the maintenance of international peace and security." In addition, Article 10 of the Charter gives to the General Assembly general competence to discuss any question or matter within the scope of the purposes of the Charter or connected with the powers and functions of any organ provided for in the Charter. Beyond this it can make recommendations to the members of the United Nations or the Security Council or to both on any questions or matters. But this general competence of the General Assembly has an exception. This is the prescription in Article 12 to which Article 10 already refers. According to this exception, the General Assembly can make no recommendations on a question *while the Security Council is exercising functions in such a matter* conferred upon it by the Charter, unless the Security Council has invited the General Assembly to do so. Article 12, paragraph 2 of the Charter, therefore, orders the Secretary General to "notify the General Assembly at each session of any matters relative to the maintenance of international peace and security which are being dealt with by the Security Council . . ." and to "notify the General Assembly, or the Members of the United Nations if the General Assembly is not in session, *immediately the Security Council ceases* to deal with such matters."[13] The General Assembly has, therefore, the right to discuss the taking of enforcement measures and to make recommendations if in a concrete attack the Security Council exercises no function at all or when it has ceased to deal with it. The before-mentioned prescription in the last sentence of Article 11, paragraph 2, does not prevent the General Assembly from acting in this way. This clause is not one of the exceptions from the general competence of the General Assembly recognized in Article 10—the power to discuss any matter falling within the sphere of activity of the United Nations and to make recommendations thereon. There is, indeed, no exception concerning the content of these recommendations, but only concerning the time during which the recommendations may be made, stipulated in Article 12. The wording of Article 11, paragraph 2, does not exclude even this interpretation, although it only mentions that such a matter shall be referred to the Security Council "before or after discussion," since it is nowhere prohibited that the discussion can be concluded with a recommendation to the Security Council. The last sentence of Article 11, paragraph 2, can therefore not at all refer to the *recommendation* of enforcement measures but only to the ordering of enforcement measures which is conferred upon the Security Council alone. But the General Assembly can, according to Article 10, recommend to the Security Council the taking of such measures.[14] But the Security Council does not receive the competence to order and execute such measures through the recommendation of the General Assembly. It possesses it directly on the basis of Articles 39 ff. of the Charter. The recommendation of the General Assembly could not be executed by the Security Council if this jurisdiction of the Security Council did not exist, since the General Assembly cannot confer a jurisdiction upon the Security Council which it does not possess itself, *Nemo plus juris transferre potest quam ipse habet.* It is, therefore, not necessary to ask the question here whether a delegation of competence from the General Assembly to other organs is at all possible.

But is it possible, on the basis of the existing Charter, that the General Assembly can recommend to individual members the taking of enforcement measures against a state guilty of an armed attack?[15] It is not sufficient to refer to the general competence, already discussed, of the General Assembly according to Article 10 in order to answer this question in the affirmative. As already mentioned, the General Assembly, itself, possesses no jurisdiction to take enforcement measures and cannot, therefore, according to the existing Charter, confer the right to take such measures upon individual members. To this must be added the fact that Article 2, paragraph 4, of the Charter prohibits the use of force in principle. This can neither be abolished nor changed by a mere recommendation of the General Assembly. This proves that the General Assembly can only recommend to the individual members the taking of enforcement measures to the extent that they are authorized by the Charter to take such measures at all.

But the only regulation of this kind is the already discussed clause of Article 51 of the Charter. It recognizes not only the right of self-defense of the attacked state but also authorizes the other states to give the state attacked emergency aid as long as the Security Council has not issued differing orders.

The General Assembly can, therefore, *recommend* to individual members on the basis of the Charter that they make use of their right of collective self-defense granted to them by Article 51, if the Security Council takes no measures against the attacker in case of an armed attack. But on the basis of the existing Charter, the General Assembly can only recommend the taking of enforcement measures in case of an armed attack, which is the condition for measures of self-help according to Article 51. The Security Council, however, can recommend or take enforcement measures, if, according to Article 39, another breach of the peace or a mere threat of aggression exists.

But the entire competence of the Security Council is not transferred to the General Assembly, according to the Charter, if the Security Council is paralyzed. The General Assembly can only exercise jurisdiction to the extent that the Charter grants independent jurisdiction to it.

But the difference between the jurisdictions relating to the General Assembly and the Security Council is reduced by Article 43, paragraph 1, of the Charter which makes the *ordering* of military enforcement measures by the Security Council dependent upon the conclusion of special agreements. Since such agreements have not been concluded as yet, the Security Council also can at present only *recommend* to the members of the United Nations that they take such measures. Yet there remains an enormous difference between the discussed relative competence of the General Assembly and Security Council, since only the latter can take decisions, according to Articles 39 and 41 of the Charter, which all members are obliged to execute according to Article 25. But the recommendations of the General Assembly, just as those of the Security Council, have but a political and psychological and not a positive legal effect.[16]

Therefore the members of the United Nations have to decide for themselves whether and to what extent such recommendations should be executed. They are here—lacking differing regulations of the Charter—limited only by general international law. This again proves that general international law continues to be valid as far as it is not derogated by the Charter of the United Nations.

III

It must finally be mentioned that general international law participates also in the further evolution of the United Nations Charter, although Articles 108 and 109 contain separate provisions concerning the amendment of its norms. These, just like all treaty norms, can be amended, not only by the procedure provided for by the treaty itself, but also in the manner regulated by general international law.[17] Among these norms, however, can be found the principle that a treaty norm can be changed by *desuetudo*.[18]

This principle is also maintained by the Charter of the United Nations. Article 38 of the statute of the International Court of Justice expressly recognized customary law as a source of international law. The hotly contested regulation of Article 27, paragraph 3, of the Charter can for this reason be amended, not only according to the procedure of Article 108 of the Charter, but also by *desuetudo*. But the investigation of the question as to whether this has already been done by the previous practice[19] would go beyond the framework of this paper. Another provision of the Charter could also be amended by new customary law.

New customary law could therefore also expand the jurisdiction of the General Assembly beyond the competence granted to it in the Charter if the condition of Article 38, paragraph b, of the statute of the International Court of Justice—a usage recognized as law—is met.

Such a change of customary law cannot be prevented by any treaty since the treaty itself is only a source of law *on the basis* of general international law. The treaty can, therefore, as just stated, be amended, not only by a procedure which it has itself established, but also by a procedure provided by general international law.

The above discussion proves that general international law not only forms the basis of the Charter and completes its juridical-political gaps but also assists in the further evolution of the Charter.

ERICH HULA

International Law and the Protection of Human Rights

THE DIFFERENCE of subject matters regulated by national law on the one side and international law on the other, has been one of the principal arguments the proponents of the dualist doctrine have been employing in support of their position. National law, the dualists have been maintaining, is concerned with relations among individual persons and between the state and its subjects. The concern of international law are relations between states. The argument, no doubt, carried some weight as long as the actual contents of the typical rules of international law corresponded more or less closely to the theoretical assertion.

Even at the time when the weight of evidence seemed to be against him, Hans Kelsen refused to accept the dualist thesis. As his first treatise on the theory of international law proves, Kelsen realized from the very beginning the contingent character of the contents of nineteenth-century international law. Ever since then, he has been insisting that "there is no matter that cannot be regulated by a rule of customary or contractual international law." The potential transformation of any domestic matter into an international matter, by making it the subject of an international treaty, has been used by Kelsen as one of the main arguments in support of the unity of national and international law.[1]

The development of the law of nations in the twentieth century has been a full justification of Kelsen's theoretical position. An ever-growing number of relations within each single state, relations between the state and its subjects as well as among individuals, has in the last decades actually been made, or proposed as the subject matter of international treaties, particular and general. No less striking is the tendency to extend international law to domestic matters of highly political complexion, including those that are internally regulated by constitutional law. The most important manifestation of this tendency is the attempt of the United Nations to secure the protection of human rights by means of international law. Limitations on consitutional autonomy, formerly the mark of inferior rank in the community of nations, will, it is hoped, be accepted by all nations in the future.

The recent history of international law has thus been a telling refutation of the dualist thesis that the subject matters of the rules of national and international law are necessarily and always different, and has corroborated the monistic assertion of the unity of law.

However, it is one thing to maintain that an internal relation within states can be made the subject of international norms, and an entirely different matter to decide in a concrete case *de lege ferenda* whether it should be regulated by international law. The latter question is a problem of legal policy, and, as in any other question of policy, the answer to it involves a decision on ends and means, unrelated to legal theory proper.

Accordingly, international regulation of internal matters must, in each concrete case in which it is proposed, be justified first of all in terms of the objective which it is intended to serve. In view of the complexity of human affairs, however, it is not sufficient to weigh an objective in terms of its absolute merits alone. The question must therefore be asked how the adoption of a suggested scheme might affect other vital interests of international society, and, especially, whether it is likely to further or impair peaceful relations among its members. Moreover, extension of international law to domestic affairs means a change in the division of powers between the community of nations and the several states. Does the end to be attained by international regulation justify such limitations upon internal independence as are involved in the proposal?

Finally, it must be asked whether the objective of establishing uniformity is a feasible one considering the diverse conditions to which uniform regulation is recommended to be applied. Is agreement on uniform rules possible at all, and, if it is, how effective is it going to be? After all, international regulation of internal relations within states does not mean that those relations cease to be shaped and determined primarily by national factors, moral, political, economic, and social. Is it reasonable to expect that the latter can be made to yield to the force, persuasive rather than coercive, of international law? What influence is the structure of international society likely to have upon attempts to give effect to the uniform regulation? As a matter of fact, from a realistic point of view the question of the limits within which the purpose of international regulation of domestic policies stands a reasonable chance to be achieved is of decisive importance. For a rational policy will carefully avoid aiming at unattainable ends.

The attempt to secure the observance and protection of human rights and freedoms everywhere by an international covenant must therefore not be judged in terms of the worthiness of the objective alone. The latter can be granted, and at the same time the wisdom of the undertaking doubted. The question which comes first to mind when one tries to pass judgment on the efforts of the last five years to internationalize human rights is, of course, whether and to what extent it is a realistic scheme. The covenant on human rights is not intended to be *un text simplement dogmatique,* as the French Declaration of the Rights of Man and the Citizen of 1789 was.[2] It is planned to be a legal instrument which is not only to give additional protection to rights and freedoms already enjoyed by citizens of free countries, but to establish government by internationally guaranteed law where it does not exist. To extend the range of freedom and justice is the very *ratio legis,* but it is also the most ambitious part of the project.

The goal set—uniformity of constitutional relations between state and citizen throughout the world—is higher and to be attained on a wider scale than the objective of any other international instrument that has ever been contemplated or enacted. But the idea of subjecting domestic affairs to international control has been tried before, though for more modest purposes. The most important examples of devices for regulating internal relations by international treaties with a view to securing human rights and freedoms are the system of international labor conventions, the system of international minorities protection and the mandates system. An examination of the first and second instances, especially, might enlighten us on the legal and political problems involved in the internationalization of human rights. The one is significant by its intended world-wide scope, the other as an attempt at guaranteeing constitutional rights. We shall therefore do well to consult "that best oracle of wisdom, experience."

I

The most striking feature of the constitution of the International Labor Organization is the combination of far-reaching ultimate objectives with gradualism in attaining them.

By promoting international labor conventions the organization is not only to strengthen the legal guarantees of humane conditions of labor already gained by workers in advanced industrial communities, but to extend their benefits to the working people of economically and socially backward countries as well. In fact, the constitution states as the aim of the organization the general improvement of conditions beyond the standards already achieved in any one of the member states. However, this task is to be accomplished by stages. The constitution itself establishes the necessary machinery, but refrains from laying down any uniform rules immediately binding upon the members. The statement of general principles of labor legislation in the original constitution and especially in the Declaration of Philadelphia of 1944 anticipates, it is true, the catalogue of economic and social rights to be incorporated, according to present plans, in the future covenant on human rights. Those principles lack, however, as those of the economic and social rights proclaimed in the Universal Declaration of Human Rights of 1948, the force of positive law. They are common standards to be aimed at by future international and national action. The constitution recognizes expressly "that differences of climate, habits and customs, of economic opportunity and industrial tradition, make strict uniformity in the conditions of labor difficult of immediate attainment." It therefore provides for various gradual processes through which the general conference, the quasi-legislative agency of the organization, should try to arrive at the ultimate goal.

The conference is to proceed by consecutive acts. Each of them is to be limited to the regulation of a particular matter of clearly defined scope. If the circumstances are such that the subject, or an aspect of it, being dealt with by the conference is considered to be not yet suitable or appropriate for a convention legally binding upon ratifying states, the conference is to confine itself to a mere recommendation without obligatory force. It may adopt conventions embodying general principles rather than providing for specific obligations. It may limit itself to establishing minimum standards instead of decreeing maximum standards. Moreover, in framing a convention or recommendation of general application the conference shall have due regard for special national conditions and shall suggest the modifications, if any, which it considers may be required to meet the case of such members. Finally, the constitution rules out any attempt to effect by conventions a deviation from the domestic constitutional division of powers between central government and self-governing units, be they component parts of a federal state or nonmetropolitan territories.

Thus the system has been designed with a view to securing the widest acceptance of conference decisions at the risk of rendering them practically meaningless. For only general, more or less precise, rules, generally applicable and applied, can effect the improvement and the equalization of unequal conditions that form the very task of the organization.

The conference is composed not only of government delegates, but of representatives of industrial organizations of workers and employers as well. No doubt, it is in the history of international organization the closest approximation to a parliament of man. It would, however, be difficult to maintain that the conference has ever displayed a revolutionary mood. Nothing is more characteristic of its conservative attitude than its reluctance to regulate by conventions relations that traditionally belong to the province of domestic constitutional law. To assure freedom of association has from the beginning been one of the main objectives of the organization. In fact, the principle forms the very foundation of its tripartite structure. But the conference did not incorporate it in a convention earlier than 1948, and apparently then only in response to competitive efforts of the United Nations Commission on Human Rights.

All the same, the unsatisfactory number of ratifications of conventions indicates that the conference has, frequently under the pressure of organized public opinion, gone further than the realities of the situation have warranted. In discussing the prewar experience of the International Labor Organization, an official report of 1946 concedes "the very unequal extent to which the Conventions have been ratified by different Members of the Organization, and the large number of cases in which Conventions have not been ratified by Members the government representatives of which voted for their adoption."[3] Since World War II the record of ratifications has been poorer still.[4]

What is, however, more revealing than the inadequate number of ratifications, especially in the post-war period, are the reasons tentatively suggested in the report of the director-general of 1949. The explanation of the disappointing results is, according to the view of "experienced observers" "that certain conventions were drawn up in too much detail, or that the standards set are too high for the majority of States Members." The director-general confessed that the organization "would fail in one of its essential tasks," unless the basis could be laid for an ever wider acceptance of conference decisions.[5]

However, one may wonder whether the lessening of the practical social significance of conventions is not the only price for which a large number of ratifications can be bought. The reasons that seem to account mainly for the frequent failure of states to ratify conventions for which they voted at the conference cannot be remedied by mechanical devices, but suggest rather the unrealistic objectives and assumptions of what is called international legislation.

The labor conference borrows its procedures from national parliaments and adopts decisions that are by their subject matter measures of domestic legislation. All the same they are international treaties, so far as their legal validity depends upon the voluntary act of ratification. It is not the same thing to vote for a convention at Geneva, where purely tactical considerations of the international parliamentary game are allowed to sway the decision, and to give legal effect to it at Washington, Paris, or New Delhi where the stubborn facts of domestic politics are bound to be decisive. The convention being substantially, though not formally, internal legislation, any burden and risk to be assumed under its terms will be weighed most carefully with a view to the domestic political, economic, and social consequences of the measure proposed.

Moreover, labor conventions are not and cannot by their very nature be founded on that actual mutuality of interests which induces independent states to become voluntary partners in binding international treaties of the usual type, as, for example, treaties regarding the intercourse between states and among their nationals. This mutuality of interests is lacking especially whenever a labor convention is considerably more than a least-common denominator of standards, or than a statement of vague and flexible principles. Conventions setting high goals or formulating precise rules are by their very purpose bound to affect some countries more severely than others, be it with regard to the conditions of international competition or the state of domestic social legislation in general. What is for some states only formal confirmation of actual policies means for others the acceptance of the obligation to change their policies without receiving reciprocal benefits for the burdens and risks involved in ratifying conventions.

The inherent qualities of labor conventions account also for their unsatisfactory observance by states that have ratified them. In their annual reports to the organization on the application of ratified conventions, some governments state with disarming frankness that their national legislation and administration are not, or only partly, in harmony with the conventions accepted by them.[6] Time and again various agencies of the organization have found it necessary to emphasize "that the ratification of an international labor convention is as solemn and binding as the ratification of any other international treaty, and that ratification thereof imposes a definite obligation upon the ratifying Member States to give effect to the terms of the Convention completely and punctually."[7] The inadequate performance of labor conventions is the more noteworthy as the fathers of the organizations have taken very bold steps in trying to secure it by an elaborate system of implementation and enforcement procedures.

By mutually accepting limitations on their traditionally unlimited legislative authority over their own nationals, states parties to labor conventions acquire on the other hand the mutual right to interfere in the labor policies of the other parties, so far as those policies are regulated by the conventions. What formerly would have been intervention in domestic affairs is legally now a means of requesting performance of international treaties. Accordingly, under the constitution of the organization any one of the members may file a complaint with the International Labor Office "if it is not satisfied that any other Member is securing the effective observance of any Convention which both have ratified." In other words, this right is in no way dependent upon an actual interest of the complaining state in the observance of the convention by the party against which the complaint is directed.

Nor is the compliance with labor conventions the concern only of the particular states that have ratified them. By authorizing the delegates to the general conference to complain to the governing body about infractions of a convention, the constitution recognizes indirectly a right of third states and nongovernmental organizations as well to set in motion the machinery of implementation by issuing to their respective conference delegate the pertinent instructions. Nongovernmental organizations in addition are entitled to make to the governing body so-called "representations" that any of the member states has failed to give effect to a convention to which it is a party. Last, but not least, the governing body may also initiate implementation proceedings of its own motion.

The separation of the lawful concern in the performance of a treaty from the status of party is the legal expression of the idea that the observance of an international agreement is an interest of the community as a whole and of each of its members as much as of the parties to the agreement. The constitution of the International Labor Organization therefore establishes objective procedures of implemention and enforcement for protecting this interest. The preliminary decision whether a complaint should be investigated rests with the governing body. If the body decides in the affirmative, it shall appoint a Commission of Enquiry for establishing the facts relevant to the alleged nonperformance of a convention, and for making such recommendations as it may think proper as to the steps which should be taken by the defaulting government to meet the complaint. Each of the governments concerned in the complaint has the right to refer the complaint to the International Court of Justice, which has compulsory jurisdiction with regard to the interpretation of all labor conventions. Finally, if the defaulting member fails to carry out the recommendations of the commission or of the court, as the case may be, it may be subjected to collective enforcement measures, possibly economic, aiming at securing its compliance with the recommendations.

The implementation and enforcement provisions of the constitution have suffered a strange fate. Their practical effect has been to deter the members of the organization from ratifying labor conventions rather than to induce them to give effect to conventions they have ratified. What is stranger still, in spite of the inadequate performance of labor conventions, officially attested, the history of the organization records only one case of a complaint and three cases of representation.[8] The lesson we receive from this history is highly instructive all the same.

The conference of 1945 appointed a delegation on constitutional questions with a comprehensive mandate to review all outstanding questions relating to the constitution and constitutional practice of the International Labor Organization. The suggestions made by this delegation were adopted by the conference of 1946 with a view to amending the original constitution of 1919.

Needless to say, the delegation has not failed to examine the possibility of supplementing "the procedures of representation and complaint already provided for in the Constitution, by further measures of international supervision designed to secure a higher standard of observance of the obligations of Conventions." However, the delegation has finally decided against any revision of the implementation procedures. The reasons for this decision, stated in the report of the delegation, are worth quoting:

> The conclusion which [the delegation] has reached is that the problem is primarily one of national standards of law enforcement and that international action must therefore be directed towards promoting the progressive development of more effective national administrative machinery, a more vigorous insistence on the part of trade unions on the strict enforcement of the law, and a whole-hearted willingness on the part of employers to cooperate fully in maintaining the standards agreed upon in the common interest rather than towards measures which would inevitably be regarded as unwarranted international interference with national affairs. The influence of international action of this type will necessarily be slow, since national standards of law enforcement are an expression of a complex of political, social and economic conditions which are rarely susceptible of rapid improvement.[9]

The counsel, to expect no quick results from such action, has in the meantime been fully justified. The Labor Inspection Convention of 1947, intended to promote the "development of more effective national administrative machinery," has so far been ratified by only ten member states, most of them countries of high social and administrative standards.

Similar considerations account for the fact that the constitutional revision of 1946 has toned down the original provisions on enforcement proper. Indeed, collective enforcement of labor conventions by economic or other measures is practically out of question whatever the provisions of the constitution might be. For the international and national risks involved in taking effective actions would be out of all proportion to such advantages as can reasonably be expected to result from them. It would be absurd for an organization designed for attaining social justice as a guarantee of universal and lasting peace to pursue policies likely to disturb international relations.

Thus the organization and its members have apparently resigned themselves to dispensing with the international machinery of implementation and enforcement provided for in the constitution. To the extent to which they actually try to secure the performance of labor conventions, they resort instead to the more informal and more flexible methods of open and secret diplomacy.

The limits, indeed, have proved to be very narrow, within which uniform international regulation of domestic social policies has a fair chance of being accepted and made effective with a view to securing economic and social rights of the workers. The relevancy of this experience for the idea of an international bill of economic and social rights is obvious. If the International Labor Organization has, according to the testimony of its highest officer, so far failed to fulfill its legislative task satisfactorily by successive acts of strictly limited scope, and if it has been unable to secure the adequate performance of the treaties it has promoted, it is not very likely that the United Nations, a body more heterogeneous than the organization of Geneva, shall succeed in agreeing on and giving effect to an elaborate system of precisely formulated economic and social rights by which working people of all countries would actually benefit. But the lesson seems to be pertinent to the idea of an international bill of civil and political rights as well.

II

The system of international minorities protection, established after World War I for securing certain basic rights of members of racial, linguistic, and religious minorities against their own state, has been less of an innovation than the system of international labor conventions. Treaty stipulations designed for such purpose have figured in the public law of Europe throughout modern history. Especially in the nineteenth century they were characteristic of arrangements imposed by the Concert of Powers upon small newcomers to the society of nations.

The stigma of inequality was attached also to the minorities system of Versailles. It was a special regulation applying to special states, and not a general system for the protection of minorities everywhere. In fact, not even all of those states whose dominion has been extended by the peace treaties had to accept international control over their relations with their newly acquired minorities. That the number of countries subject to the special regime was comparatively large, and that there were among them countries of considerable size and importance, could hardly be a consolation for the states affected, particularly not if they were or felt themselves entitled to a significant role in international politics. Nor was the main feature of the new system, the guarantee of the League of Nations, apt to lessen their resentment. It is true that they, themselves, formed part of the supervising international organization. But the very purpose of the collective guarantee, to make international control more effective than it had proved to be in similar cases before, could hardly endear it to them.

If the system of international minorities protection was less novel than the extension of international law to domestic labor relations, its political significance was so much the greater. For it was to regulate "what constitutes the most sensitive sphere of the political life of a country,"[10] the constitutional relationship between states and citizens with potentially centrifugal tendencies. The subject matter of the international regulation was the most explosive political issue in eastern and southeastern Europe, the region to which it was to be applied. No wonder that the system has had such a stormy and short-lived career.

The far-reaching political implications of the scheme, which the principal Allied and Associated Powers, boasting of "the success of their arms," imposed after 1918 upon some fifteen states, are impressively suggested by the elimination of international minorities protection from the present plans for a covenant on human rights. What has been accepted under duress as a special regime is not voluntarily acceptable even as a general scheme. The universality of the covenant has to be bought at the price of omitting from it any provisions specifically aiming at the protection of minorities of any kind. To be sure, so far as the covenant is going to secure the equality of all men before the law, it will rule out any legal discrimination on racial, linguistic, or religious grounds, and thus uphold one of the main principles of the system of international minorities protection. But it will not guarantee in any form the differential treatment to which members of minorities feel entitled with a view to the preservation of the group to which they belong as a distinct cultural entity. The guarantee of positive equality and its implementation by public services to be provided by the state for the benefit of its minorities was undoubtedly the most radical feature of the system of 1918.[11]

On the other hand, the political conditions seemed then to be propitious to the bold undertaking. The system was established and to be maintained by a politically homogeneous body of great powers and was to be applied to countries desiring, to put it in the words of the preamble of the minorities treaties, to make their institutions conform with "the principles of liberty and justice." Moreover, at least some of the states, subject to the regulation, entered upon their new political career with legal traditions that qualified them well for conducting a government by law. Accordingly, each of the treaties contained a bill of rights immediately binding upon the so-called minorities states, whereas the constitution of the International Labor Organization formulated merely guiding principles for the future attainment of economic and social rights by subsequent acts of international legislation.

An objective attempt at appraising the actual results of the system of international minorities protection requires a clear realization of the basic conceptions underlying it and of the principal purposes which it was intended to achieve. In the words of one of the best experts in the field:

> . . . the primary objective is the peace of the world; the means through which this is to be attained, and thus the indirect objectives of the Treaties is the internal stability of the Treaty states; and the means through which this, again, is to be achieved is the well-being of the minorities, which shall make them contented and loyal citizens of the states of which they form part. The welfare of the minorities is thus, in a sense, relegated to the third place. It is, however, the foundation upon which the whole system is built up, and is thus, in practice, the first of the three objects to be attained.[12]

In accepting this statement of the philosophy of international minorities protection, we must, however, be careful not to overlook the subjective element involved in the question whether the third purpose of the system has been realized. For the contentment and loyalty of the members of minorities are not a mere function of the degree of their wellbeing. The attitude of citizens toward their state is never exclusively dependent upon their objective situation, political, cultural, or economic. Particularly, the fervor of modern nationalism is due to the impact of political ideas and sentiments rather than to unsatisfied needs, objectively justified. In short, the degree of well-being is only one of the factors that determine the attitude of minorities toward their state. Nevertheless, it is an important factor.

There is, of course, no way of assessing accurately the extent to which the minorities treaties have actually contributed to the welfare of the minorities in the several states. But we may draw certain conclusions relevant to this question from the way in which the treaty states have tried to conform their laws and institutions to the legal obligations undertaken by them.

The authors of the treaties have refrained from spelling out in detail the fundamental rights to be respected. Apart from the provisions stipulating positive services and special privileges for the benefit of the minorities each of the instruments merely obligates the respective minorities state to assure full and complete protection of life and liberty to all inhabitants without distinction of birth, nationality, language, race, or religion, as well as the equality of all before the law and their equal enjoyment of the civil and political rights. If those minimum obligations are stated in terms that lack precision where no traditional body of jurisprudence can be resorted to for defining their meaning, they are on the other hand not qualified either by an emergency clause, or by a blanket limitation or any specific limitations. Only the right to the free exercise of religion is qualified by the provision that its practice must not be inconsistent with public order or public morals. Furthermore, the treaties provide that their stipulations "shall be recognized as fundamental laws, and that no law, regulation, or official action shall conflict or interfere with these stipulations, nor shall any law, regulation or official action prevail over them."

It seems that the attempt at imparting by international treaty to treaty law the standing and force of municipal constitutional law has been least successful. According to Dr. Robinson's painstaking study on the operation of the minorities system, the minorities states, basing themselves on traditional views of legal theory, have maintained, on the one side, that the treaties required, for becoming applicable to their individual beneficiaries, transformation into domestic law. On the other side, most of them have deliberately failed to effect their outright transformation.[13] This attitude disposed in a convenient way of the ticklish question whether the national courts were under the constitution of the respective country authorized to test the alleged conformity of a municipal law, constitutional or other, with what according to the treaties were to be the fundamental laws overriding all other legal norms and acts.

The degree to which municipal law—constitutional and statutory law—was actually in conformity with the treaty stipulations varied a great deal from country to country. Even strict conformity, however, did not necessarily mean that the administration of the laws was consistent with the obligations of the treaties. After all, in every country of the world, laws, including constitutional laws, are often honored by breach rather than observance. Conversely, the administration of laws was in some cases more in conformity with the treaties than the laws themselves.[14]

Thus the effectiveness of the international regulation was in each state dependent primarily and fundamentally upon factors which the minorities treaties did not, and could not, reasonably undertake to regulate: the general legislative and administrative standards and the specific legal remedies, judicial and administrative, by which citizens can assert the rights and privileges due them under general rules.

However, contrary to the development under the constitution of the International Labor Organization, the implementation of the minorities treaties has not remained a matter of national agencies alone. In fact, efforts to secure the performance of the "obligations of international concern," as the treaties characterized the provisions concerning the rights of the members of minorities, formed an essential part of the activities of the League of Nations, and especially of the Council. The protective stipulations having been placed by the treaties under the guarantee of the League of Nations, the Council declared it not only its right, but its duty as well, to "ascertain that the provisions for the protection of minorities are always observed."[15]

The tacit assumption of this declaration was that the performance of the treaties was an interest of the organized international community as a whole rather than of the individual parties to the treaties. Accordingly, the Council rather than the respective parties had to secure the observance of those instruments. In fact, the separation of the function of guarantee from individual states and its transfer to the central organ of the international community have been considered to be the principal advantage of the new system as against similar devices of the past. They would, it was hoped, effect the de-politicalization of the procedures intended to secure the performance of the protection clauses. Quasi-judicial proceedings rather than political procedures should effect the observance of the minorities treaties.

The Council has made serious efforts to protect the interest of the international community in the contentment of the minorities, and to guarantee objective modes of dealing with their complaints. This is the more notable as the treaties themselves were not entirely propitious to such attempts. All of them stipulated that only member states of the Council "shall have the right to bring to the attention of the Council any infraction or any danger of infraction" of the obligations undertaken by the minorities states. This provision limited the possibility of venting grievances as much as it endangered the impartiality of international implementation. The Council tried to remedy these defects by granting to states not represented on the Council as well as to the minorities themselves the right to petition the League with a view to inducing a member of the Council to put the subject matter of the respective communication before the Council and call upon it to intervene. Moreover, by establishing the Committee of Three and charging it with the examination of the petitions, the Council succeeded in practically substituting for the individual action of a Council member the concerted action of three of its members. In fact, most of the issues raised in petitions have actually been settled definitely one way or the other by the Committee of Three without ever reaching the Council itself.[16]

Impartial decisions in accordance with the treaties on the legal claims of members of minorities seemed to be assured, especially thanks to a provision of the treaties by which the minorities states agreed to accept in advance the jurisdiction of the Permanent Court of International Justice for settling between them and a member of the Council any difference of opinion as to questions of law or fact that might arise out of the treaties. In addition, the Council was authorized to refer to the court any dispute or question related to minorities matters, in order to obtain an advisory opinion on the legal issues involved.

However, in spite of all legal provisions for impartial procedures, the approach of the League to minorities matters throughout the years of its existence was a political and not a juridical one. Nothing is more suggestive than the fact that the Permanent Court of International Justice has had the opportunity to render altogether only three advisory opinions and one judgment. The settlements actually reached either by the Committee of Three or by the Council itself were political compromises rather than applications of the pertinent treaty law.

It would be a mistake to attribute the attitude of the Council to the lack of specific enforcement powers under the treaties. Governments, regardless whether they act on their own behalf or that of the international community, are always inclined to resign themselves to the infraction of treaties rather than to take extreme measures, unless vital national interests compel them to run the risks involved in such steps. Therefore the Council, or, more correctly, the members of the Council would not have acted differently, if armed with legal enforcement powers. The fact is that the prevalence of political over legal considerations, evidenced by the practice of the Council in dealing with complaints of minorities, reveals an inherent weakness of the system of international minorities protection.

The practice has affirmed what is hardly surprising. States, as members of an international organization, entrusted with the collective guarantee of the rights of foreign citizens against their own governments, act fundamentally in the same way as they do as individual guarantors. In either case, they interpret their legal obligation as well as their legal right to protect citizens of another country in accordance with their own national political interests, rather than with the spirit and letter of the pertinent rules of international law. In short, the attempt to internationalize the protection of minorities did not result in the de-politicalization of the minorities question. Instead the system became itself an object of international strife. If the system was characterized in its first period by the tendency of the Western powers to restrict their obligations of protection, in the second period Germany tended to abuse such rights of protection as she had acquired as a member of the Council.

The inclination of the Council members to limit the responsibilities and risks involved in implementing the collective guarantee of the League had a paradoxical consequence. The energy displayed by the Council in settling minorities matters in accordance with the treaties has been in inverse proportion to the relative importance of the issues at stake. Minor cases were more likely to be decided in conformity with the treaties than cases of great legal and political significance for the minorities concerned, because they were of great relevance for their respective governments as well. The melancholy truth is that the Council was least energetic and successful when faced with flagrant treaty violations of the most serious kind, "measures of violence, repression and terror applied by the authorities against minorities."[17]

Nonetheless, the Council could plead attenuating circumstances even in cases that seemed to call for its outright condemnation. It was, first of all, often difficult to ascertain whether the hostilities between governments and minorities were caused by one side or the other. There are ruthless governments, but there are seditious, intractable minorities as well, often incited by outside influences for selfish purposes. Moreover, the protection of minorities was conceived to be only a means for assuring the internal stability of the treaty states with a view to securing through such stability international peace, the primary objective of the system. Thus whenever there was uncertainty about the respective guilt of governments and minorities, the Council was strongly tempted to give the benefit of doubt to the former rather than to the latter.

But even assuming that in a particular case all indications pointed to the full responsibility of the government, one may sympathize with the Council. For it found itself confronted with the formidable task of reconciling in practice what cannot easily be reconciled in theory: peace and justice. That the interests of peace and justice always necessarily coincide is a pious wish rather than a fact. In domestic as well as in international politics we are constantly compelled to weigh their respective merits, the one against the other, and we constantly sacrifice on one occasion justice in order to save peace, and on another peace in order to attain justice. In fact, time and again we have to establish an uneasy balance between them even in our daily private life.

No doubt, the interests of peace often were only a pretence of the Council when neglecting its duty to secure the rights of minorities, confided to its care. But we would fail to realize the complexity of political and human affairs, if we should interpret all of the Council's omissions in opportunistic terms alone. There is an impressive ring of sincerity in the words Briand once exclaimed in a discussion on the minorities problem. He said:

> No movement must be allowed to persist which, under cover of unexceptionable sentiments, would lead to widespread unrest in the world or breed fresh insecurity. However worthy of respect certain doctrines and propaganda may be, one thing stands before them all—peace. No special circumstances, no individual aspirations, however justifiable, can be allowed to transcend the interests of peace. Peace must prevail, must come before all. If any act of justice were proposed which would disturb world peace, and renew the terrible disasters of yesterday, I should be the first to call upon those prompting it to stop, to abandon it in the supreme interest of peace.[18]

The complexity of the undertaking to secure domestic justice by international treaties and by their international implementation has been illustrated also by the effect of the minorities system upon the relationship between the governments of the treaty states and their minorities.

The system exposed the treaty states to the lawful interference by the agencies of the League in their dealings with part of their own citizens. The liberal rules on the right of petitioning the League tended to make this interference a more or less regular feature of the public life of those countries. By introducing into it a neutral, outside element, the fathers of the treaties hoped to further the final political reconciliation between the several governments and their respective minorities. But one may wonder whether the actual results corresponded to those expectations.

Contrary to the intentions of its authors, the system, first of all, made it possible for single powers to clothe with the semblance of legality attempts at fostering for their own national purposes the discontent of minorities. To that extent it rendered the adjustment of the relations between governments and minorities more, rather than less, difficult. In fact, it encouraged disloyalty of the members of minorities towards their governments and made, conversely, those governments more reluctant to forego discriminatory policies against their minorities. However, the introduction of a third element has very likely, in other cases as well, lessened rather than increased the chances of an honest compromise on the fundamental issues between the contending nationalities. The readiness of opposing groups to come to an agreement by mutual concessions depends upon a realistic appraisal by them of their respective strength. The hope of the minorities to redress in their favor by international outside support the balance of the internal political forces was a futile one. All the same it blurred the realization that their fate would and could be decided ultimately by the normal procedures of domestic politics alone. Nor, on the other side, were the governments of the treaty states ready to trust the good faith of their minorities, as long as the latter were inclined to turn at any moment internal issues into foreign issues.

There was, therefore, much force in the argument set forth by the representatives of the treaty states from the very beginning that the system of international minorities protection was apt to render their internal consolidation more difficult, and thus not likely to further international peace as its primary objective.

The relevancy of the attempt to internationalize the protection of minorities to the idea of internationalizing human rights is self-evident. Already at the time when the minorities system was not yet buried under the ruins of World War II, the establishment of a universal system of human rights, intended to protect all men against all governments, was looked upon by statesmen and publicists as the logical culmination of the idea launched by the peacemakers of Versailles. However, the lessons we can learn from the minorities system are somewhat more involved. It is probably more correct to characterize its actual result as limited failure than as limited success. Be that as it may, from the point of view of international politics and international law its main significance lies undoubtedly in what has been the most novel feature of the system, the operation of a collective guarantee by an international organization. Whereas the constitutional provisions for the implementation of labor conventions have remained a dead letter, the implementation machinery improvised by the Council of the League for securing the observance of the minorities treaties has been utilized fully. But the use of this machinery has not only yielded meagre results in absolute terms; it has had adverse effects on international and national politics as well. Thus the system has raised more problems than it has solved.

III

Throughout human history periods of devastating wars have been productive of great designs, intended to redeem mankind once and for all from the curse of bloody and ruinous strife by devising a more just and stable international order. Revulsion against the horrors of World War II has brought into existence the United Nations of today. Its primary and paramount purpose is to maintain international peace and security by collective actions of the organized international community. To the United Nations has, however, been assigned the still more ambitious task of attaining domestic justice in all its member states as well. The origin of World War II in infamous tyranny seemed to confirm the democratic belief that to end tyranny was also a means for ending war. Thus the conference of San Francisco has charged the organization with assuring the conditions of peace by promoting "universal respect for, and observance of human rights and fundamental freedoms for all without distinction as to race, sex, language, or religion." Complying with this mandate, in 1946 the United Nations Commission on Human Rights went to work on a covenant on human rights.

The United Nations embarked upon its formidable undertaking in the temper of revolutionaries who refuse to accept any lessons from the past. Neither the experience of the International Labor Organization in the field of economic and social rights nor the experience of the League of Nations in trying to secure civil and political rights of minorities was held to have any bearing upon what the United Nations Commission on Human Rights was expected to accomplish. Nevertheless, the members of the commission were soon faced with problems and difficulties of the same nature as those organizations that had before more or less vainly been struggling with them.

In fact, the magnitude of the problems and difficulties the commission was to encounter proved to be the more terrifying, as its goal was set even higher than the objectives of the International Labor Organization and of the League. In addition, contrary to both of them the United Nations harbors under its wings antagonistic political ideologies. They are split over the very questions a covenant on human rights is designed to regulate uniformly. Thus, what was to be made the subject matter of a treaty for establishing a universal system of basic rights was bound to become in the very process of negotiating the treaty the means of ideological warfare.

This more than anything else accounts for the apparently sweeping character of the Draft First International Covenant on Human Rights, which the commission submitted to the General Assembly in 1950.[19] Any attempt of one side to adapt the covenant to the political realities of today was liable to be exploited by the other side as a betrayal of the ideal set up by the Charter of the United Nations. Considerations of this kind account also for the decision of the General Assembly at its fifth session directing the commission to reconsider the draft with a view to inserting into it economic and social rights, assuring its application to federal states as well as to trust territories and nonselfgoverning territories, and improving the methods of implementation.

But tactical reasons alone do not explain the policy of the member states of the United Nations. A covenant which is merely a least common denominator of existing constitutional standards would, first, not fulfill its main purpose of extending the range of freedom and justice. Moreover, and still worse, it might appear to be an endorsement by the world organization of the lowest standards and lack any inspirational value. This consideration speaks in favor of a more ambitious goal. However, there arises immediately another question, familiar to the authors of international labor conventions. Is such a covenant going to be ratified by the very states whose domestic policies it is intended to amend? And if it is ratified by them, are they going to give effect to it?

It is true, the draft covenant fails to include, not only the economic and social rights, but some of the civil and political rights as well that are proclaimed in the Universal Declaration of Human Rights of 1948. However, the declaration is only *un text simplement dogmatique* without obligatory legal force, whereas the covenant is intended to be an instrument of international law binding each state party thereto "to respect and to ensure to all individuals within its territory and subject to its jurisdiction the rights recognized in this Covenant." It corresponds as to content and scope more or less to the traditional municipal bills of rights, and is more comprehensive than the enumeration of civil and political rights of the usual type in the minorities treaties. As a matter of fact, it even stipulates "effective remedies" for securing the internal enforcement of the various substantive rights. Nonetheless, the covenant lacks, and is in view of its subject matter bound to lack, the character of a genuinely uniform regulation. Nor does it provide for an international machinery of implementation that might reasonably be expected to develop uniform rules in applying the covenant.

Whatever the philosophical foundation of a municipal bill of rights is considered to be, and regardless whether a constitution states the rights of individuals in absolute or relative terms, there is practically no right whose exercise is not subject to limitations. It is the very function of the state to adjust conflicting rights among its citizens as well as to reconcile with one another conflicting claims of society and individual. Indispensable as such limitations upon the rights recognized or granted by the constitution are, they are, on the other hand, liable to render those rights illusory. In fact, to deprive by more or less lawful limitations a bill of rights of its reality, and yet maintain its semblance, is the time-honored technique of arbitrary government under constitutional disguise. It is therefore essential for securing freedom that the ultimate determination of the compatibility of limitations upon rights with the purpose and spirit of the constitution guaranteeing rights should rest in each case with an impartial authority. The system of judicial review of legislation is undoubtedly best suited for effecting this control, unless a country may, as Great Britain, expect its parliament to exercise its legislative functions with the circumspection a High Court would use.

Limitations forming an indispensable part of any municipal system of rights, it was then practically out of the question to internationalize human rights without internationalizing exceptions as well.[20] The great struggle in the Commission on Human Rights was not over the principle of limitations, but over their form and scope. The draft covenant on human rights contains three types of limitations. To the first category belong the limitations incorporated into the formulation of the several rights. They are specific limitations insofar as each of them is related to a particular right, but they are rather general in their scope, as can, for example, be seen from Article 15 of the draft: "The right of peaceful assembly shall be recognized. No restrictions shall be placed on the exercise of this right other than those imposed in conformity with the law and which are necessary to ensure national security, public order, the protection of health or morals or the protection of the rights and freedoms of others." The second type of limitations is represented by Article 2, the so-called derogation article. It authorizes the signatories in a state of emergency or of public disaster to take measures derogating, to the extent strictly limited by the exigencies of the situation, from the obligations stipulated in about half of the articles of the covenant. The third limitation, the antifascist clause of Article 18, is also general and is a legal formulation of the principle that the guarantee of rights stated in the covenant does not imply the recognition of a right to destroy rights.

No doubt, the nature and scope of the exceptions internationalized by the covenant are no less sweeping than those of the rights themselves. It is true, the first and second type of limitations are either expressly stated or tacitly implied in practically all democratic constitutions. But it is true also that they have time and again been employed for destroying democratic constitutions, and are making sweeping bills of rights satisfactorily workable in totalitarian countries. More ominous still is the antifascist clause, a novel feature in what is intended to be a constitutional document of democracy. Be that as it may, a covenant on rights without limitations of this kind or another would not be likely to be ratified even by the most advanced democratic nations. For, however easily the powers impliedly granted by those stipulations lend themselves to political abuse, they are at the same time essential requirements of the governance of states and men.

Thus the task to be solved by the authors of the draft covenant would have been to prevent possible abuse by providing for the establishment in each state of adequate institutional safeguards against it. However, compliance with such obligations would require far-reaching changes in the constitutional machinery of states that lack institutions of this kind, and they are therefore not acceptable to them. As a matter of fact, the practical value of uniform procedural safeguards provided for by an international treaty must not be overrated. For their actual operation would in each country be an expression of a complex of traditions, habits, and conditions beyond the reach of international legislation. At any rate, according to the draft covenant, the question whether a person may test through constitutional procedures the conformity of laws limiting his rights with the stipulations of the covenant, is a question to be answered solely by municipal law. Similarly, the covenant leaves it to the organ authorized by the municipal constitution of the respective state to determine the conditions under which the article of derogation may be applied, without subjecting the agency to any control, legislative or judicial. Such "effective remedies" as the covenant stipulates, are at best apt to secure the conformity of administrative acts with statutory law, but not of statutory law with the covenant itself.

If the adaptation of the covenant to the political realities of today fails to find expression in the number of rights, it is the more conspicuous in the qualifications of rights expressly stated or tacitly admitted by the covenant. The covenant, if ever adopted, is therefore to all practical intents and purposes very likely to be another more or less pious declaration of guiding principles rather than a genuinely uniform legal regulation effecting the equalization of constitutional practices on a high level. This character of the covenant is most strikingly suggested by the provisions concerning its implementation by international procedures.

The objective of the draft covenant on human rights is infinitely more ambitious than the purposes of the systems of international labor conventions and international minorities protection. But its provisions for international implementation are far from betraying even an equal zeal in securing its performance. Like those two devices, the system of internationally guaranteed human rights presupposes and is intended to protect the interest of the international community as a whole in attaining its objective. However, in opposition to the implementation provisions of the constitution of the International Labor Organization as well as to those laid down by the Council of the League, the covenant recognizes only the states parties to the covenant as legitimate representatives of the community interest. Neither states that have not ratified the covenant nor nongovernmental organizations or, least of all, private persons are to be granted by the covenant a legal standing in the proceedings of implementation. As a matter of fact, the covenant assigns not even to the United Nations as a whole the collective guarantee of its stipulations. The tendency to restrict the implementation of what is by its contents a revolutionary document in the history of international law to traditional procedures of old-time diplomacy is revealed by one more symptom. The covenant does not speak of complaints, but merely of matters one state may bring to the attention of another state which is not giving effect to a provision of the covenant both of them have ratified.

No less conservative are the other features of the third part of the draft covenant. The Human Rights Committee, composed of seven members, nationals of the treaty states, is authorized to deal with a matter, referred to it by the one or by the other of the parties to the dispute, only after adjustment by bilateral negotiations between them has failed. The committee is primarily a fact-finding body with the right to call upon the states concerned to supply any relevant information, but without the right to make investigations on the spot. Article 41 of the draft covenant purposely directs the committee only to make available its good offices to the states concerned, and confines the report the committee shall draw up to a statement on "its conclusions on the facts." The Commission of Enquiry, provided for by the constitution of the International Labor Organization, shall make "such recommendations as it may think proper as to the steps which should be taken to meet the complaint." Similarly, the Council of the League was entitled to propose concrete terms of settlement of minorities matters. But no right of recommending a specific solution is granted by the draft covenant to the Human Rights Committee. It is, in addition to its fact-finding function, an agency of mediation rather than of conciliation. It is the clear implication of the draft covenant that human rights are, to the extent to which they are regulated by it, a matter of international concern. Nonetheless, they are, as regards their implementation, treated as matters which are essentially within the domestic jurisdiction of the parties. Accordingly, the draft covenant fails to make provisions for settling issues arising out of its application, or nonapplication rather, by the International Court of Justice or any other international judicial tribunal. The Human Rights Committee being merely empowered to establish facts and mediate between the contending parties, the proceedings of implementation do not result in a legal decision of a superior authority which would lend itself to collective enforcement.

It is true, the provisions of the draft covenant concerning the composition and the procedures of the Human Rights Committee are intended to guarantee the impartiality of the body to which it proposes to entrust its international implementation. All the same one fails to see how the committee should be able to accomplish what is one of the most essential purposes of the internationalization of human rights, namely to remedy the ineffectiveness of their national protection by an effective system of international protection. For the only weapon with which the committee is armed by the draft covenant is the publication of its factual report. This brings up historical recollections. In 1914 Secretary of State Bryan was busy propagating his cooling-off treaties which provided for commissions of inquiry and conciliation as means of preventing war. "The sum and substance" of these treaties, said President Wilson at that time, was "that whenever any trouble arises the light shall shine on it for a year before anything is done; and my prediction is that after the light has shone on it for a year, it will not be necessary to do anything; that after we know what happened, then we will know who was right and who was wrong."[21] The Human Rights Committee of the draft covenant not only resembles the commissions of inquiry and conciliation of the Bryan treaties, but is founded upon their philosophy as well.

The international implementation, envisaged by the draft covenant on human rights, is thus a combination of old-fashioned mediation with the main instrument of twentieth-century diplomacy, the appeal to what is called the world court of public opinion. If this is hardly an adequate way of enforcing human rights, it is the more suitable for turning their protection into a weapon in the struggle of ideas which today threatens the peace of the world. Negligible as are the accomplishments of such a system in terms of its very objective bound to be, its effect upon international relations is considerable.

IV

Noninterference in the domestic affairs of foreign nations is a concomitant of the doctrine of sovereignty. The disrepute into which this notion has in recent times fallen—not unjustifiably to the extent to which sovereignty has been interpreted and used excessively—has therefore affected also the appreciation of the principle of nonintervention. However, it is the only principle which can secure the peaceful coexistence of different groups in international society no less than in national society. Only the recognition and clear delimitation of their autonomous spheres makes possible their coöperation with one another in the pursuit of common interests. For these reasons modern international law, essentially a law between collective entities, has abhorred dictatorial interference of one state in the internal affairs of another state and has tended to restrict the milder forms of interference, too. The more eager a state has been to maintain friendly relations with other states, the more anxious it has been not to burden its international relations with matters extraneous to foreign policy proper. The validity and the wisdom of the principle of noninterference have been challenged only by religious and political movements that were inspired with the missionary zeal to extend their ideas and systems beyond the confines of their own states.

The current tendency to transform domestic matters into international matters by making them the subject of international treaties is therefore the very negation of the conceptions that have been prevailing in international law and diplomacy throughout the last centuries. Whatever the subject of international regulation might be in a concrete case, all these schemes have one thing in common. To the extent to which they narrow the scope of legally internal matters, they enlarge the sphere of lawful mutual interference in what in legal terms are not any longer domestic matters. Thus they widen at the same time the range of possible international frictions by blurring the comparatively sharp lines of demarcation which separated the internal spheres of states from one another in former times.

To be sure, this trend is largely the mere expression of the growing interdependence of the nations of the world. We are rejoicing at the beneficial results of this process, and we have therefore to accept its untoward effects as well. However, the tendency also has purely ideological roots. In particular, the idea of internationalizing human rights is a manifestation of the universalism characteristic of the dominant political religions of the day—democracy and communism. It would be naive to expect that we could eliminate from current world politics its explosive ideological ingredient by forsaking the ideal of international protection of human rights. But it would be most dangerous on the other hand not to beware of the effect this pathetic effort might easily have of heightening rather than lessening international tensions. Briand's exhortation is as pertinent to the question of human rights today, as it was to the minorities question some twenty years ago. The primary and paramount purpose of the United Nations is the maintenance of international peace, and not the realization of domestic justice, mostly impervious to international action short of war.

The danger that the effort to secure the protection of human rights by international law is likely to impair rather than to further international peace is due to the same reason that is bound to deprive the system of its effectiveness. International law has in the last decades made deep inroads upon the province of municipal law. If the covenant on human rights is going to materialize in one form or another, international law will have conquered constitutional law, the citadel, as it were, of municipal law. But the technical structure of international law and international society has remained basically unchanged. The beneficiaries of human rights are to be individual persons. However, technically they are going to be the objects only of a covenant on human rights. States alone will be authorized to bring an infraction of the covenant to the attention of states which are not giving effect to its provisions. Human rights are made the subject matter of international law because the international community as a whole is assumed to have a vital interest in their observance by all states. But the international community, though organized today as a confederation, lacks genuine governmental powers, and must therefore, in trying to secure the performance of the covenant, rely on the coöperation of the very state which is alleged to have violated it. As Bourquin remarks in a penetrating analysis of the problem, one finds in the contents of international treaties regulating relations within nations no truly interstate matters. "Mais si, au lieu de considérer l'objet de l' opération, nous portons nos regards sur son aspect technique, le tableau change radicalement. Les bénéficiaires du régime disparaissent. Il n'y a plus en scène que les Etats."[22]

There is, of course, nothing immutable about the traditional structure of international law. The classical view that only states can be subjects of rights and duties under international law has gone by the board together with many other nineteenth-century notions, not any longer tenable in the face of recent developments in positive law. If the parties to the covenant on human rights want to grant to individuals not only the right of petition, but the status of a party before an international tribunal of human rights as well, they can do so. Nor does international law as such block the conferment of enforcement powers on agencies of the international community. The fact is that the individual as subject of international law would in terms of physical power still have less chance than a protector state to effect the performance of the covenant by his own government; and the establishment of a supranational government strong enough to enforce the covenant against a recalcitrant state is politically out of the question.

As it has repeatedly been observed,[23] the covenant on human rights is designed to impose upon the states parties thereto limitations upon their power over their own citizens which under the American constitutional system have by and large been imposed upon the states of the union only after the Civil War had overthrown the political power structure expressed in the Constitution of 1787 and the first ten amendments. As a matter of fact, the nationalization of liberty through the vehicle of the fourteenth amendment has been accomplished not earlier than in our time. The first ten amendments to which the covenant on human rights corresponds in contents were intended to protect American citizens against arbitrary actions of the newly established federal government and not of the historically older state governments. As regards the Constitution itself, the federal limitations upon state powers were to serve the uniform regulation of inter-state relations rather than of relations within the single states. The only provisions of the federal Constitution intended to protect American citizens against encroachments upon their rights and freedoms by their own state governments are those of Article I, Section 10 forbidding the states to "pass any bill of attainder, *ex post facto* law, or law impairing the obligation of contracts . . ."

The parties to the prospective covenant on human rights are thus aiming at an objective American history has proved to be attainable only under a federal government of a highly centralized type. Nor does any other historical experience support the hope that an international system of human rights and freedoms can secure men in their actual enjoyment. Be that as it may, the great significance of the idea cannot be doubted. It is one of the many symptoms of the profound crisis that international society and international law, as they have evolved in modern times, are going through today.

The idea of human rights and freedoms under international law is a challenge to and a denial of practically all basic concepts upon which international law has during the last centuries been resting. It refutes the traditional doctrine on the contents of international law as well as the division of powers between the international community and its members to which that doctrine corresponded. It implies the rejection of the traditional notions on the structure and the subjects of international law. Last, but not least, it is in fundamental opposition to the concept of sovereignty, the very core of modern international law. In short, the idea is the most radical manifestation of the tendency to develop the law of nations into world law.

Nor are the symptoms of this crisis confined to the theory and practice of modern international law. In fact, the latter are rather the expression of moral, political, and economic forces incessantly working and undermining the foundation of the nation state, the basic unit of modern international society. Indeed, many trends in the realm of ideas and of facts recall the period of transition from the ancient city state to wider forms of political organization, based on new principles of human association. The picture Fustel de Coulanges has drawn of this transformation seems to describe our century as well.[24]

The end of the road leading through the present period of crisis and transformation is shrouded in the mists of the future. All history suggests is, unfortunately, that such periods of transition are not ages of peace. Thus it gives little comfort to see the United Nations indulging in grandiose visions of human rights, as long as it does not attempt to restore the humane laws of war that have been the great achievement of modern times, but are abandoned now. International law of today, we are told, recognizes and asserts, contrary to the traditional international law of the past, the worth and dignity of the human being. The claim obliges us to apply humanitarian principles also to the regulation of warfare, once one of the proudest accomplishments of traditional international law.

Part Three: Special Studies

ARTHUR NUSSBAUM

Forms and Observance of Treaties in the Middle Ages and the Early Sixteenth Century

FORMS AND OBSERVANCE of agreements are closely correlated matters—not only in the sense that forms are designed to strengthen observance, but also because the historical forms may furnish indications of what contemporary parties to a convention mutually expected from each other. Multiplication of solemnities in treaty making is not a propitious symptom. This observation applies especially to the Middle Ages with which the present study is primarily concerned. No more is intended, however, than to indicate, on the basis of a number of conspicuous examples, some distinctive lines of medieval state practice in treaty matters.[1]

From the outset, one cannot expect that in the Middle Ages oral or written promises alone should have been recognized as binding—such recognition was absent in classical Roman law and, under the "consideration" doctrine, is still absent in common law. Nevertheless, one should assume that within the orbit of Christianity any oath would have offered ample assurance for the keeping of a promise. But this was not the view of medieval covenanters. A corporeal action had to accompany and to strengthen the oath[2] *(juramentum corporaliter praestitum)*.[3] What was required at least was to place a hand on the Gospels, a form practiced not infrequently also in our day. There was some medieval casuistry on this point; for instance, that the sacred book must not only be present but must be touched directly by the hand and not only by any part of the body.[4] While this is easily understandable, one is baffled by an elaboration such as is found for instance in the celebrated Peace of Tordesillas (1494) by which the sovereigns of Spain and Portugal divided between themselves the newly discovered, or to be discovered, areas of the Western World.[5] The substantive provisions of the treaty were followed by this statement: "For the greater security and stability of the aforesaid, they (the authorized representatives of the sovereigns) swore before God and the Blessed Mary and upon the Sign of the Cross on which they placed their right hands, and upon the words of the Holy Gospels wheresoever they are written at greatest length . . ." The high contracting parties were afraid, it seems, that the swearing person would place with great dexterity his hand on the margin of the text and thereby nullify the oath.[6]

The Peace of Madrid between the Emperor Charles V and King Francis I of France (1526) expressly states that the *serment solonnel* was made *corporellement aux Saints Evangiles de Dieu en présence de la vraie Croix.*[7] The latter reference points to a sacred relic.[8] Generally, however, the employment of relics in oaths belongs to an earlier period. An extraordinary instance is connected with the name of William the Conqueror. Having made, in 1064, Harold of England a prisoner, he would release him only upon Harold's sworn promise to surrender, after the death of Edward the Confessor, the throne of England to William. Harold had to place one hand on the Gospels and the other on an altar covered with a golden cloth. After the oath was duly taken, Harold was told that relics of saints were hidden in the altar so as to make the saints guardians of the oath.[9] Harold was dismayed but not to such an extent as to keep the promise. The invocation of saints as guardians of an oath seems to have been a widespread custom of contemporaneous France; St. Lô d'Angers enjoyed a particularly high reputation in this respect because people who had violated an oath taken on his cross were said to have died in the same year.[10]

Despite all solemnities, oaths, as indicated before, did not prove in any way an effective obstacle to violation. Flimsy pretexts were sometimes used to cloak violations. The Middle Ages were a bit more naïve in this respect than later times. Guy de Lusignan, Latin King of Jerusalem, having been captured by Sultan Saladin, was freed by the latter on the sworn promise "not to bear arms" against the sultan, but he felt that he did not violate his promise by hanging his sword at the saddle of his horse.[11]

More important, there were broad legal limitations on the efficacy of sworn promises. Those limitations were derived from canon law as the oath was (and is) considered a *sacramentum* subject to the jurisdiction of the church. Under this theory, canon law developed numerous rules under which an oath would lose its binding force and could or should be broken without sin and punishment. Canon law engendered, on moral grounds, the conception of the *clausala rebus sic stantibus,* which means that a promise, sworn or not, loses its binding force when the circumstances under which it was given have vitally changed.[12] This conception, however, was originally one of private contracts and was introduced into international law only by Alberico Gentili in his *De Jure Belli* (1598).[13] It does not affect the period contemplated in the present study. Other canon law dilutions of oaths followed from theories which would stress the inner will of the promising in contrast to the expression used, invalidating therefore an oath taken with a *reservatio mentalis;*[14] or which would read into a promise a tacit condition the deficiency of which would dissolve the promise.[15] Again, these types of nullification were more important outside the sphere of international law although we shall encounter an instance of *reservatio mentalis* in an international agreement. Far more momentous was a rule laid down by Innocent III (1198–1216) and incorporated in the *Corpus Juris Canonici,* that an oath taken contrary to the interests of the Church did not hold good.[16] *A fortiori,* this would be true of plain promises. To this Urban VI added, in 1382, a decree according to which all agreements with princes heretic, schismatic, or otherwise in some way separated from the Roman Church, were illicit and, *ipso facto,* void even though the separation had occurred subsequent to the making of the agreement. The Catholic princes were even forbidden to keep those agreements and they were told to see to it that others did not keep them either.[17] It was in the spirit of these decrees that the church council of Constance (1415) invalidated the solemn safe conduct granted by Emperor Sigismund to John Hus so that Hus could be burned at the stake.[18] No international law proper was involved here but, on the same ground, treaties concluded with princes considered as heretics were considered invalid by the popes.[19] It was consistent with this doctrine and was clearly implied by the decree of Urban VI that the ecclesiastical authorities should exert pressure upon Catholic princes to disregard obligations undertaken by oaths toward non-Catholics.[20]

Between Catholic princes the Church would intervene on another basis—through dispensation from oaths or other promises. Supreme dispensing power was vested in the pope; numerous high dignitaries of the Church possessed limited dispensing power, or they would obtain it by papal delegation.[21]

The frequency of such dispensations[22] and the ensuing feeling of uncertainty about the value of treaty obligations, led to a remarkable reaction of international law proper. Catholic princes invented clauses to protect themselves from possible dispensation. An early instance is the Treaty of Brétigny (1360) between Edward III of England and John of France. There the parties pledged themselves not to apply for dispensation from the oaths taken in confirmation of the peace but, on the contrary, to do everything in their power to prevent the giving of such dispensation.[23] Furthermore, in an alliance concluded in 1370 between Charles V of France and Robert II of Scotland directed against England, it was said that "the Pope should release the Scots of all the oaths they had taken in swearing to the truce with the English, and that he should promise never to release the French or the Scots from the oaths to be taken in swearing to the new treaty. . . ."[24] The Treaty of Tordesillas exhibits a clause of a more refined character. Having narrated the abovementioned solemnities of the oath, the text goes on: "And under the same oath they swore not to seek absolution or release from it from our most Holy Father or from any other legate or prelate who could give it to them. And even though it should be given to them *proprio motu*, they will not make use of it. . . ."[25]

Various ways of "legally" eliminating a sworn treaty can be studied from the example of the above mentioned Peace of Madrid. Before signing the treaty, Francis I made before the Archbishop of Ambrun and other French notables a protestation against the oath allegedly forced upon him.[26] The protestation was carefully kept secret from the emperor; only after the latter, relying on the oath, had released the king from captivity, was protestation made public. This is an early instance of the use of a *reservatio mentalis* in international relations. Yet the king's indulgence in a deceptive procedure was hardly reconcilable with his knightly honor which he had likewise pledged by the treaty, and had so proudly claimed for himself after his military defeat.[27] Hence, it seemed advisable to look for another escape. Dispensation would have been too crude an offense to the emperor, especially as Pope Leo X, in 1521, had excommunicated Francis I for unjust aggression committed against the emperor.[28] Therefore, Clement VII, successor to Leo X, chose another way. His nuncio, Count Castiglione, told Francis I in a letter that treaties made under duress need not be kept *(non stant foedera facta metu)* implying, of course, also the nullity of the oath.[29] Immediately afterwards, Clement VII concluded with Francis I, Venice, Florence, and Milan, the Ligue Sainte de Cognac as a threat to the emperor, thereby conspicuously corroborating the view set forth by his nuncio. It is not necessary to expatiate on the invalidity of the argument used by the nuncio,[30] as most peace treaties are agreed upon by the defeated party under duress, and, often enough, under extreme duress. The argument runs counter even to an old canonical theory.[31]

On the other hand, sovereigns sometimes sought papal confirmation of their treaties in order to obtain for their stipulated rights the protection of canon law. Thus in the Treaty of Tordesillas the parties "entreat our most Holy Father that His Holiness be pleased to confirm and approve this agreement . . . and that he order his bulls in regard to it to be issued by the parties or to whichever of the parties that may solicit them . . . and that he lay his censures upon those who shall violate or oppose it at any time whatsoever."[32] In the Treaty of Zaragoza between Charles I of Spain and John of Portugal (1549) a similar clause was inserted; but it was tightened by the proviso that under a bull to be requested from the pope a prospective offender should suffer excommunication *ipso facto*.[33] Nevertheless, this threat did not prevent Philip II from seizing the islands, called after him Philippines, which under the demarcation line drawn by the treaty, were situated within the zone reserved to the Portuguese.[34]

On the whole, the Western World presented in the Middle Ages and the early sixteenth century, a gloomy picture of practices undermining faith in treaties; the infusion of religious elements into legal relations of a secular character, proved confusing as well as harmful.

Within the orbit of the Eastern Orthodox Church the way of confirming an oath was uniformly after the Byzantine model, the kissing of the cross.[35] Though kissing of the Gospels occurred occasionally in Western Christianity,[36] the kissing of the cross was felt in the West as something strange. Characteristically, when in 1392 the Lübeck alderman, Niebuhr, concluded a treaty for the Hanseatic League with the prince of Novgorod, the treaty came to be called in Germany, Niebuhr's Kissing of the Cross *(Niebuhrs Kreuzküssung)* because Niebuhr in confirming the agreement, had to act the same way as the prince of Novgorod.[37] Dispensation by ecclesiastics of the Orthodox Church was granted only in rare cases and without the basis of a systematic theory.[38] But it would certainly be rash to conclude that observance of treaties was better in the East.[39]

In the Islamic world the oath seems not to have played as large a role as in Christianity for the purpose of treaty confirmation, but it was so used sometimes, especially in agreements with Christian princes.[40] The Koran contains an express provision against the breaking of an oath.[41] More important is the attitude of Islam toward promises in general. A famous precept of the Koran obligates the believers to keep their covenants even toward pagans (polytheists) to the end of the term, provided the pagans have not defaulted toward the Moslem in anything and did not help anyone against them.[42] All the more the same rule applies to

Christians and Jews who, as "peoples of the Book," enjoy under the Koran a preferential position.[43] In addition to the precept of the Koran, a celebrated proclamation by Abu-Bekr, Mohammed's immediate successor, (d. 634), has often been cited.[44] In that proclamation, Abu-Bekr told his followers: "Let there be no perfidy, no falsehood in your treaties with the enemy; be faithful in all things proving yourselves ever upright and noble, and maintaining your word and promises truly." No dispensation from treaty obligations on religious or other grounds is provided by Islamic doctrine, nor did Islam develop during the Middle Ages any casuistry comparable to the contemporaneous Christian one regarding the *ipso facto* invalidity of oaths or promises. The main impact of Islamic doctrine on treaty making resulted from the theory that, fundamentally, Islam was considered to be in a permanent state of war with the nonbelievers. Consequently, there could be only truces and no real peace with the nonbelievers; though an agreement might be called peace, it had to be limited in time. The prevailing opinion among the learned in the law was that ten years were the maximum. Actually one encounters, especially in the postmedieval era, longer periods, for instance, in the Turco-Austrian Treaties of Zsitva Torok (1606), twenty years, and of Carlowitz (1699), twenty-five years. More objectionable, from the viewpoint of modern international law, is the Moslem doctrine that even before the end of the term agreed upon, the treaty may be canceled in the interest of Islam; formal denunciation, however, was required unless the other party was the first offender.[45] Still there are few reports of such treaty *repudiation*, and they belong to the postmedieval epoch.[46] Undoubtedly there have been many violations of promises especially in connection with the so-called "capitulations,"[47] but, generally speaking, the record of Islam is very good as far as the keeping of promises is concerned. This applies particularly to the era of the Crusades. The Crusaders, though aggressors, acted on the principle that no faith need be kept with the infidels.[48] Says the noted English historian, Lane-Poole: "The virtues of civilization were all on the side of the Saracens."[49] As a matter of fact, the Crusades coincided with the flourishing of Arabic civilization, whereas Western civilization had then not fully recovered from the ravages of the Dark Ages.

COVEY T. OLIVER

Thoughts on Two Recent Events Affecting the Function of Law in the International Community

TWO THINGS seem essential to the viability of any particular human institution: fairly common agreement as to the concept of the institution and the probability that it will be used for the purposes for which it was designed. Other papers in this series have recognized the great credit due Professor Kelsen with regard to the development of useful theory about the concept of international law[1] and for his detailed studies[2] of international law in action. My tribute takes the form of an attempt to analyze the nature and implications of two mid-century developments which seem to impugn the concept of an international rule of law and at the same time to raise formidable institutional obstacles to any reliance on legal techniques in the solution of international tensions. These developments are (1) the publication of Mr. George F. Kennan's *American Diplomacy 1900–1950*[3] and (2) the conduct of the Security Council concerning the interim order of the International Court of Justice in the Iranian-oil case. The first development imprecisely strikes at the concept of the international rule of law as many, including Kelsen, have seen it,[4] associates law through the intimacy of a hyphen with morality,[5] and attributes to this alliance the chief errors of our foreign policy for the past fifty years. The second development is a study of the frustration of a judicial technique at the enforcement level. The two developments appear to me to be interacting ones and the net effects of interaction to be predictably quite serious in spheres outside those of strict law, unless close analysis can detect errors of observation as to the concepts involved, and of technique in using the concepts institutionally.

I. The Concept of International Law: Selected Current Views from Kelsen to Kennan

This is not the place to review problems of beginning students about the nature of law, the Austinian preoccupation with sanctions, naturalism and positivism, monism and dualism. To many of these questions Professor Kelsen, with some straining of his Pure Theory of Law, has addressed himself.[6] Professor Kelsen's legal philosophy about international law requires for its most basic assumptions belief in the existence of an international community which is more than the arithmetical sum of the national states of the world, whereas classical positivism could exist as a theory without more than this minimal concept of the international community. Kelsen's hierarchy of norms requires a monistic view of national and of international law, and the attribution—to the extent permitted by the principle of effectiveness[7]—of superiority to the international legal order. All of this assumes an existent, though presently relatively decentralized, international community.[8] Additionally and in keeping with his general philosophy of law, Professor Kelsen keeps his international law "pure," i.e., sharply separated from the ethical value judgments implicit in "morality" and "justice."[9] In summary it need only be said that Professor Kelsen's norm system has the effect of providing a countertheory to meet the sanctions problem and of elevating international law (such as it is) to the highest position in the norm structure, thus leading the casual reader to a concept of international law somewhat more grandiose than that provided by classical positivism, with its emphasis on the absolute sovereignty of states and its concept of international law as something existing only in those small areas of almost universal state consent. To this extent Professor Kelsen, in Hollywood terminology, might be called a "glorifier" of international law: ". . . the most important means of international policy is international law."[11]

Another great scholar, Professor Edwin D. Dickinson, has focused attention on an aspect of international law which Kelsenian theory tends not to emphasize in connection with the study of either national or international norms. This is the problem of the "hole in the law." In his memorial lecture, "What is Wrong with International Law?"[12] Professor Dickinson used the well-known story of how "Judge" Roy Bean,

"The Law West of the Pecos," acquitted the killer of a friendless Chinese, in a situation where the "power relationships" did not augur well for the effectiveness of a decision to the contrary, to illustrate his point about international law:

> While it is unlikely that Roy Bean ever read a treatise on the law of nations, his realistic sensitivity to surrounding circumstances, his improvised procedures, his caution in the presence of armed force, his discreet recourse to the cooling-off interval and his profound discovery that there was "want of law" relating to the corpus delecti were deserving of a more stately setting.
>
> May I develop a little the suggestion that international law, like law "West of the Pecos" *has been a system of juridical pretensions which ill conceal an underlying political disorder.*[13] This is not to suggest that the society of nations bears even superficial resemblance to what once passed for society in western Texas. It is to suggest, however, that it has retained down to our time the attributes of loose organization, social instability and prevalent apprehension which characterized the frontier community.[14]

Proceeding, then, to review well-known international adjudications like the cases of the *Lotus*[15] and the *David,*[16] Professor Dickinson uses them to demonstrate that, "very largely it [international law] has responded to the frictions and discords of international life by affirming that there was 'want of law' relating to them."[17]

Having made a realistic appraisal, Professor Dickinson then proposes a general line of solution: to remedy

> . . . the tragic lack of essential agencies and procedures of amelioration and adjustment, in which the constant threat of force has worn many disguises and has led ultimately to the madness of war.[18]

Remedy them through the then only recently negotiated Charter of the United Nations:

> The Charter, in brief, is the latest and in all respects the firmest expression of a common determination to have justice under law in international relations. If we have only the will and the persistence to implement it effectively and to make it serve, we may have the firm beginnings of a true law in our time.[19]

Professor Dickinson's latest book, *War and Peace,* develops the same theme in greater detail.[20] This presentation is, in a popular sense, more "realistic" than Kelsen's, because the existing international law described by Dickinson is hardly susceptible of being called, to any degree, a "super" norm. Also, it makes more of the substantive deficiencies of international law to cope with particular tensions and hence involves, indirectly, the selection of values as to what law ought to deal with, an exercise which Kelsen places outside the science of law. Common ground exists as to the assumption of an international community and with respect to the role law is capable of performing in it, the central idea of the latter being legal decision as a workable alternative to the individualized national use of force (war).

Another recognized authority, also writing post-Charter,[21] finds in the United Nations version of the international community the opportunity and the need for the development of a modern law of nations. Like Dickinson, Professor Jessup's approach is through the improvement of legal doctrine, which in its present state of "isness" is found fairly deficient, especially in its want of rights for individuals.[22] The chapter "Rights and Duties in Case of Illegal Use of Force"[23] assumes, following the Charter plan, that the international organization shall have a force monopoly, except in self-defense, "and then only as a preliminary matter until the organized power of the international community could be brought to bear."[24] Thus, formerly legitimate uses of force—by way of intervention, retaliation, reprisals, naval demonstrations, and so forth—in furtherance of national interests (such as the protection of nationals) are no longer legal. But unlike Dickinson, and with greater kinship to Kelsen, Professor Jessup seems to be deëmphasizing the judicial processes in the international community. Jessup, however, carries his concept of international law beyond the point of Kelsenian concurrence when he asserts,[25] in disagreement with Professor Morgenthau,[26] that there is no division between law and diplomacy. Jessup's concept of law is obviously far removed, also, from the Austinian; it includes the dialectical use of "principles of international law" at the diplomatic conference table;[27] it emphasizes that in many matters international law is followed as a matter of course; it minimizes the threat to the concept which arises from the notorious headline instances of breach: aggressions, oppression of the weak by the strong, and the like.[28] One cannot escape the feeling that in the author's mind the deficiencies are too frequently highlighted, to the disservice of the potentialities of an expanded, effective rule of law, especially in matters of human rights, carrying with it regulation of the use of force, and compelling the decline of the concept of absolute sovereignty.

In sharp contrast to the concepts of the scholars discussed heretofore, we find the views of Professor Morgenthau, to which Jessup in one fundamental particular took exception. For the purposes of this comparison, we may take the thesis of Professor Morgenthau's article "Diplomacy":[29] a legalistic school has sought to supplant the older power-politics–national-interest diplomacy with a "new diplomacy," which is essentially an effort to apply legal rules to international conflicts. Morgenthau insists that the adherents of the "new diplomacy" deny separate functions to diplomacy and to law. He then asserts that the very terms of the Charter reject this "legalistic monism." Having satisfied himself that "legalistic monism" will not do, Professor Morgenthau proceeds to administer a left-handed *coup de grace* to the role of law in international affairs, and thus to establish himself as a monist (though a diplomatic monist) after all. Thus he writes:[30]

> The *legal decision*,[31] by its very nature, is concerned with an isolated case. The facts of life to be dealt with by the legal decision are artificially separated from the facts which precede, accompany, and follow them and are thus transformed into a 'case' of which the law disposes 'on its merits'. . . .
>
> The parties to the conflict were well aware of the law in the Ethiopian case of 1935, in the case of the Sudetenland in 1938, of Danzig in 1939, and of Iran in 1946. What they wanted to know was whether and how the law ought to be changed. Hence, what is at stake in conflicts of this kind is not who is right and who is wrong but what ought to be done to reconcile the particular interests of individual nations with the general interest in peace and order. The question to be answered is not what the law is but what it ought to be, and this question cannot be answered by the lawyer but only by the statesman.

It does not require a trained student of jurisprudence to detect that this statement fairly bristles with points of view about (a) the law (note, "legal decision"); (b) the relationship of moral values to law (note, "right and wrong"); (c) reconciliation of interests (diplomacy) versus legal decision as to which interests are to prevail (note especially here the examples chosen!); (d) a categorical imperative for aggressors (one infers that Mussolini was interested in "changing the law"!). This viewpoint seems to assume an almost monolithic completeness to law; it does not recognize the primitiveness of international law which Kelsen has emphasized, the "holes in the law" or the shabbiness of pretensions about international law which Dickinson has called attention to, or the need for growth of law under the new United Nations organization, which is Jessup's basic thesis. It assumes that the procedural technique for the use of law is confined to that of courts handing down decisions in particular cases. This thesis goes further, and this is emphasized, because it foretells a favorite point of Mr. Kennan's:[32]

> On the international scene we have not stopped paying for our forgetfulness since 1914, and we seem to be resolved to pay with all we have for the privilege of continuing to disregard the lessons of history. For here our first appeal is always to the law and to the lawyer, and since the questions which the law and the lawyer can answer are largely irrelevant to the fundamental issues upon which the peace and welfare of nations depend, our last appeal is always to the soldier.

The implication here seems to be, in part, not only that lawmen cannot function effectively, to any degree, in solving the basic issues of our times, but also that, in some unspecified way, legal conceptions have been responsible for our "forgetfulness since 1914 . . . of the lessons of history." Of this suggestion we shall hear more later. But there is a final word pointing the way: "search for the rules of the political art which, in foreign affairs, is but another name for the traditional methods of diplomacy well understood." For these "rules of art," for the "traditional methods well understood" we must look elsewhere.

The last range of imagery about international law which I wish to discuss under this heading before turning to Kennan is best stated by Professor Myers S. McDougal in his "The Role of Law in World Politics."[33] Professor McDougal's thesis may be outlined as follows:

1. Law is a variable in the world power process, but there are many confused notions about the relationship between this variable and many others. Lawmen, just as other specialists, tend to emphasize the critical importance of their particular interests and skills in solving international problems.

2. The traditional conception of international law as doctrine is unrealistic and inadequate. Kelsen, Brierly, Jessup, Moore, and Borchard are among those criticized for continuing and developing the doctrinaire approach.

3. Law must be related to the world power process. Doctrine has its place, for "we must recognize that the symbols by which men organize and express all their perspectives do have a powerful effect on their behavior."[34] But the role of doctrine must not be overestimated; the skilled advocate, "whether he is trying to persuade himself or others, seldom need be without a base in legality."[35] A realistic concept of law requires its definition in terms of both values and institutions. Thus "any realistic description of International Law must locate both doctrine and practice (how doctrine is applied) in the total world power process in which they play a part in the shaping and distribution of values."[36] Such a view of law, the author adds, has the effect of making the role of doctrine considerably smaller than it appears in a more traditional concept of law; in fact, "doctrine comes to be regarded as composed not of autonomous absolutes but rather of symbols whose functions are to serve the total policies of their users."[37]

4. The national state is no longer the sole, although admittedly still by far the most important, participant in the world power process of which international law is a part. Other groups participating in the world power process are international governmental organizations, transnational political parties, transnational pressure groups, transnational private associations and individual human beings. Each participant will take his attitude toward technical, legal doctrine largely in terms of where he is located in the power structure and of what he is trying to do. One result is that "the often alleged distinction between 'legal' questions and 'political' questions becomes one not so much of rationality as of arbitrary compromise in specific contexts. The whole function of legal doctrines is to shape and apply power; they are an integral and indispensable part of that process, ordinarily called 'political' by which all values are shaped and distributed."[38]

5. Existing doctrines of international law are inadequate as devices for the shaping and distribution of major values, such as power, security, wealth, respect for human dignity, enlightenment, and so on.

6. The doctrines which are inadequate developed in a completely different environment from our contemporary one, whose most striking and urgent characteristic is the interdependence of all values for all peoples everywhere. The people of no country can be secure unless all people everywhere are, nor unless there is a rising standard of living elsewhere.

7. An appropriate redistribution of power is the foremost, but not the only essential, precondition of the democratic world order under law, which the new fact of interdependence makes (rationally) necessary. Law is one of the alternatives which rational policy says we should explore and attempt to use in the process of developing the effective world community.

The contrast between McDougal's thesis, just abstracted, and that of Kelsen is quite marked. The former takes into account, but in a different way, some of the things Dickinson and Jessup are pointing out. It is poles away from Professor Morgenthau's idea of the legal decision as the sole symbol of law. It may not be far away, however, from what Morgenthau considers as the role of diplomacy in building toward a new distribution of world power.[39] McDougal simply substitutes his type of "operator," a lawman who is not a pettifogger by any stretch of the imagination, for Morgenthau's "operator," an old-line diplomat. Over-all, McDougal stakes out a modest role for law, an interacting, coöperative role, as power is building up, a more comprehensive role later. Implicit in his philosophy is the idea that international law would be a poor thing indeed if the national state should not lose its overwhelmingly preponderant position as a participant in the world power process. The thesis is somewhat lost in the sociological jargon; but, nevertheless, a concept of valid law is accepted. The proposals for its continued development and use in the solution of international problems are vaguer.

This essay, so far, has probed the writings of a selected group of recognized American scholars, all writing after World War II, for the purpose of noting their concepts of international law and their estimates of its actual, probable or hoped-for contribution to the resolution of the pressing problems of our times. A range of currently influential views, rather than complete coverage, has been the objective.[40]

The stage is thus set for consideration of the views of Mr. Kennan, who has been referred to as "the most learned of our officials, the most experienced of our scholars."[41] At the outset it must be noted that Mr. Kennan, unlike the other scholars discussed, commands more effective media than they for the rapid, wide dissemination of his ideas. Teachers communicating to students and with each other through learned journals and monographs must expect to wait some time before the ideas they toss cause ripples to spread across any large areas of water. Mr. Kennan's views, however, have received widespread, almost popular, recognition. Weekly newsmagazines,[42] newspapers,[43] foreign-affairs study groups,[44] the house organ of the American foreign service,[45] and a magazine of literary criticism[46] have figured among the media through which his thesis has been presented, and sometimes criticized in one or more of its aspects. The aspect which I want to focus upon, however, does not seem to have been caught very clearly in the commentaries I have read. I wish to call attention to Mr. Kennan's concept of international law and its role—past, present, and future—in the adjustment of the tensions which arise between peoples.

One does not have to read beyond the dust jacket of Mr. Kennan's book to find out what his thesis is, for there it is said:

> During this period [1900–1950] America has participated in two destructive and seemingly futile world wars; if a third awaits us, its destructive power will be unparalleled. How has this country, so secure in the world of 1900, become so insecure in 1951? A key to this riddle, Mr. Kennan feels, may lie *in the basic concepts and characteristic methods that have dominated our diplomacy.*
>
> With a view to evaluating these concepts and methods, Mr. Kennan examines certain major phases of United States foreign policy over the past half-century. He considers the premises and results of our policy in the Far East, beginning with the 'Open Door' notes of John Hay. He describes the orientation of the diplomacy which carried us through the Spanish American war and two world wars during the course of 50 years.
>
> *Mr. Kennan concludes that certain malformations of method and concept have chronically distorted the conduct of American foreign relations. We Americans, he feels, have exaggerated the role that moral and legal principles can usefully play in international life*[47] and have accordingly neglected the realistic analysis and pursuit of our own national interest.

It is obvious, even from this much, that Mr. Kennan has a concept that concepts are of the greatest importance. With this I certainly agree, and this is why I think it important to look very carefully at Mr. Kennan's concepts of law, the international community, diplomacy, and national interest. It is important to keep in mind, also, that Mr. Kennan blames what he calls an American "legalistic-moralistic approach to international problems"[48] for our past mistakes in foreign policy. This certainly is 180 degrees out of phase with people who have had the idea that the past errors may have resulted in part from lack of law and its organized application, rather than from overdoses of "legalistic moralism."

Mr. Kennan does not oblige us with so succinct and revealing a glimpse of his concept of law as Professor Morgenthau does.[49] (The influence of the latter, however, on Kennan's thinking is unmistakable to me, though not provable by the texts). Therefore, we must look, first, to Kennan's analyses of the major blunders of our foreign policy during the period 1900-1950. Perhaps there we shall see, as he tells us what was wrong, what he thinks law (and for that matter, morality) is.

Mr. Kennan's account of the Spanish-American War certainly does not show that a "legalistic-moralistic" approach was at work, as I read his words. It seems to me that the legalists were those who argued that expansion into empire was unconstitutional.[50] The Spaniards who offered to arbitrate the case of the *Maine*,[51] not the Americans who ignored the Spanish proposal, appear to have been the more mindful of certain avenues offered by international law for the settlement of disputes. The seizure of the Philippines as a result of "a very able and quiet intrigue by a few strategically placed persons in Washington"[52] hardly seems the sort of thing one could blame law for. And, finally, what is the congruity between Mr. Kennan's general conclusion under examination and this specific one about the Spanish-American War:

> This decision [war] seems rather attributable to the state of American opinion, to the fact that it was a year of congressional elections, to the unabashed and really fantastic warmongering of a section of the American press, and to the political pressures which were freely and bluntly exerted on the President from various political quarters.

Mr. Kennan then turns his attention to the Far East and accepts the interesting thesis that the Open Door policy was a rather happenstantial sort of thing which a zealous Britisher in the Chinese Customs Service, for reasons of his own and against the emerging national interests of the United Kingdom, induced Washington to get enthusiastic about and announce as a great diplomatic and moral victory. As a matter of fact, Mr. Kennan goes on, it was nothing of the sort, because (1) it was not a new policy but an outworn British one which its originators were casting off, (2) it was given only mumbling lip service by the other interested countries, and (3) within five months after the great operation, the United States was trying for a Chinese coaling station itself and was telling the Japanese that we would not join them to prevent Russian violations of the Open Door in Manchuria. But, where, in this, are we to find substantiation for the basic Kennan charge? I do not see that Mr. Kennan tells us in his chapter on the Open Door. To remark, quite properly I think, that it was undesirable for the American people to be swept away by the notion that all of this was a "major diplomatic achievement"[53] cannot make this instance prove the main point, unless Mr. Kennan's idea of what passes for law or morality in America is that it is something akin to the sound and fury of a Fourth of July oration at the turn of the century!

In his third chapter, Mr. Kennan moves on from an episode of Far Eastern policy to a more general consideration of America and the Orient. Here specific charges begin to emerge. The first is a tilt at the legalistic concept of statehood implicit in the phrase "the territorial and administrative integrity of China." China was not really a state in the sense of the Western concept of international law, says Mr. Kennan, and in particular China was not particularly sovereign in Manchuria. Therefore, he stresses, Russian interest in Manchuria could not be expected to "disappear behind a polite deference to Western concepts of state sovereignty and international amenities."[54] Russian interests could not be opposed effectively by the legalistic sovereign, China; Japan was the only power factor which could oppose Russia in Manchuria. Result: China nominally sovereign in Manchuria, but Russia dominant in the north and Japan in the south. Hence: the Open Door doctrine and "the territorial and administrative integrity of China" could not usefully be made the bases of a foreign policy, because they were not clear and precise *"as political principles."*[55] Therefore, these phrases, the Open Door Notes, and so on, are manifestations of

> . . . the tendency to achieve our foreign policy objectives by inducing other governments to sign up to professions of high moral and legal principle. . . . [This is also linked with] the pronounced American tendency to transplant legal concepts from the domestic to the international field: to believe that international society could—*and should*—operate on the basis of general contractual obligation, and *hence to lay stress on verbal undertakings* rather than on the *concrete* manifestations of political interest.[56]

Kennan goes on to say that this stress frequently misled the American public into thinking that there is a community outlook among nations, which did not really exist. (Even the pre-World War I Americans? The anti-League Americans? The pre-Pearl Harbor isolationists? Were they all misled?). More grave, says Mr. Kennan, was the bewilderment of foreign statesmen: they just knew those general propositions were too imprecise to mean anything, and they assumed our diplomats knew this too; so, naturally they suspected us of ulterior motives. (One wonders whether these bewildered souls were professionals, peers of Mr. Kennan, or individuals indulging in that, to Mr. Kennan, regrettable American habit of "diplomacy by dilettantism.")[57]

The main vice of a legalistic-moralistic Far Eastern policy, however, is that in the period between the two world wars it prevented us from appreciating realities with respect to Japan's interests in China. The evidence Mr. Kennan has seen leads him to assume that "whatever was uttered or urged in the name of moral or legal principle bore with it no specific responsibility on the part of him who urged it."[58] The thesis seems to be that for legalistic and moralistic reasons "we hacked away, year after year, decade after decade, at the positions of the other powers on the mainland of Asia, and above all the Japanese."[59] We never stopped to consider Japan's problems, the weakness of China, or practical ways of countering the ambitions of "other" (than Japan?) powers. This development seems to reveal several of Kennan's concepts: (1) the China of the 1930's was the same nonsovereign state of the Boxer Rebellion (a questionable assumption); (2) we acted against our national interests in opposing Japan on the Asian continent, and it was the legalistic-moralistic orientation of our foreign policy which caused this blindness to what was best for us. (Again, this is questionable: is there not the alternative possibility that legalistic-moralistic techniques based upon contract were simply the manner in which we sought, futilely as history has shown, to implement a policy arrived at on other grounds?)[60] Later in the chapter Mr. Kennan suggests that our Far Eastern policy may have been colored by a certain sentimentality toward the Chinese. This may be a clue. Perhaps "morality" and "sentimentality" are not too far apart in Mr. Kennan's thinking. The chapter is then concluded with this inversion of the main theme:

> If, . . . we were able to refrain from constant attempts at moral appraisal—if, in other words, instead of making ourselves *slaves of the concepts of international law and morality,* we would confine these *concepts to the unobtrusive, almost feminine, function of the gentle civilizer of national self-interest in which they find their true value*—if we were able to do these things in our dealings with the peoples of the East, then, I think, posterity might look back upon our efforts with fewer and less troubled questions.[61]

Mr. Kennan's rather poetic concept of the role of international law and morality may be not far removed from the function the former, at least, may be expected to serve at a given level of governmental effectiveness. It is submitted, however, that the Scotch verdict, "Not proven," properly describes his assertion that these concepts have been our masters, commanding us and thus limiting what we might have or should have done in Asia. The truth of the matter seems to be that the concepts have been our rather poor and inadequate servants; that they have been boys sent to do men's work; that we finally had to send men to die to do the job; that having had to resort to force, we prefer not to do it again, provided we can get something more effective out of the alternative instrumentalities than we have had heretofore.

Whether our concept of the national interest in the Orient was wrong or not is another matter, one upon which the minds of experts definitely differ.[62] In view of the ponderosity, heat, and detail of the experts' debates, Mr. Kennan's analysis seems a little too facile in its implied assumptions of over-all error.

In his chapter on World War I, Mr. Kennan makes it clear that this blood bath was a monstrously futile thing, that World War II grew inexorably out of it, and it may yet be the point at which the end will finally be said to have begun. Here he begins to answer the question with which the book began: Why are we so insecure now when we were so secure in 1900? One gains the impression that America's security, in Kennan's appraisal, began to erode away when we took territory outside our continental limits and adopted a particular policy line for the Far East; the landslides started when we entered World War I, and they continue at an awful, accelerating, dreadfully interacting rate. Why did we subject ourselves to the risk of this landslide? Not because of the origins or issues, says Mr. Kennan, citing Wilson in statements in 1916 to show "the same denial we saw in the case of the Far East—of the legitimacy of the real interests and aspirations of other peoples, the same dismissal of these things as unsubstantial and unworthy of our attention. . . ."[63] We entered World War I over the issue of neutrality, involving legalisms which were oblivious to "the new modalities of warfare and of weapons." It is extremely doubtful whether it was in our national interest to risk so much for these legalisms. If Mr. Kennan's analysis of our real reason for entering the war is correct, he has made a point against hyperlegalism, although if he is correct here, his other charge based on Wilson's 1916 utterances seems a little unfair. Mr. Kennan leaves the "error" of our getting into the war at that point and concentrates on our attitude after we got in. The concept of total victory was the great error. After we got in, channels for the settlement of the war were closed, our earlier intentions for a moderate peace were not carried out,[64] we moved ahead with the destruction of the European balance of power and the substitution therefor of the idea of an "organized common peace," "a community of power." The shift to this high goal gave us justification, "both for continuing the war to its bitter and terrible end" and "for refusing to preoccupy ourselves with the practical problems and maladjustments to which the course of hostilities was leading."

What should we have done? With respect to our prebelligerency period, Mr. Kennan says we should have known what was brewing and when it happened we should have "ignored the nonsensical timidities of technical neutrality and used our influence to achieve the earliest possible termination of a war that nobody could really win."[65] (Granted, except the implication that technical neutrality was what restrained us). Once in, for reasons of national interest, including prevention of British collapse, we should "have refrained from moralistic slogans . . . from picturing [our] efforts as a crusade," and so forth. We should have moved at a proper time for a negotiated peace, and we should have restored the balance of power. The end result might not have been any better, says Mr. Kennan, but it could not have been any worse than what happened, either.

Mr. Kennan's chapter on World War II is both logically and historically a continuation of his study of World War I. Mr. Kennan sees the errors of World War I and its aftermath as drastically limiting the choices of the anti-Axis powers in World War II, and the Western Allies' mistake of allowing the Axis to get stronger than they (thus making collaboration with Russia to win a war essential) as a further restriction. Even so, it is suggested, if we had guided the Weimar republic, instead of leaving it to its own devices, had won the respect of the Soviets, and more carefully worked toward avoiding war with Japan, the story might have been different. However, Mr. Kennan is careful not to be categorical here. Once war came, it was to be expected that we would let it be brought to us, although our pre-Pearl Harbor conduct was certainly a contrast with that of 1916. The wartime conferences were not the source of the evils popularly attributed to them. Nor were the decisions made in the heat of battle. The continuance of Lend-Lease to the Soviet Union, he suggests, was possibly a mistake. The major mistake, reflecting a general American lack of understanding of the basic nature of this war, was the "failure to appreciate the limitations of war in general—any war—as a vehicle for the achievement of the objectives of the democratic state."[66] Is this lack of understanding an aspect of the fatal "legalistic-moralistic" concept? Even with allowance for an understandable and very human revulsion against modern war, the very definite impression at this point is that Mr. Kennan believes our "legalistic-moralistic" conceptualism prevents us from reasoned, wise responses where force is an element. Thus:

> Force, like peace, is not an abstraction; it cannot be understood or dealt with as a concept outside of the given framework of purpose and method. If this were better understood, there could be neither the sweeping moral rejection of international violence which bedevils so many Americans in times of peace

nor the helpless abandonment to its compulsions and its inner momentum which characterizes so many of us in times of war.[67]

This is a theme to be developed in the final chapter. From this initial version of the motif it is to be noted that Mr. Kennan is loyal to his own preachments: "force" is "force." Americans do not serve their interests well by reacting against bad or illegal "international violence" in peacetime or by going all out against "it" (the antecedent is revealing) in wartime.

It is in chapter vi that Mr. Kennan draws the indictment which has been the subject of the foregoing analysis of the earlier chapters. In my view Mr. Kennan has not made his case as to the past, and his uncritical indictment has marred an otherwise brilliant, if somewhat general, presentation. What of the future? What dangers does Mr. Kennan see of our making even graver errors if we do not avoid legalistic-moralistic conceptualism? The future evils of legalistic moralism seem to fall into the following pattern:

1. This conceptualism, setting up legal criteria for the conduct of states and based on the unrealistic assumption that conflicts of national interest can be repressed legally, blinds us to the realities of the national interest and encourages the avoidance of negotiated settlements of conflicts "on their merits."[68]

2. The subordination of states to an international juridical regime actually tends to entrench the present national states and to increase the power-in-law of many beyond their power-in-fact. Mr. Kennen sees the international legal order as a "legal strait jacket," impervious to change. Yet change must be reckoned with. Diplomacy "in the most old-fashioned sense of the term" is the way to reckon with it. Law is not the way, because " . . . law is too abstract, too inflexible, too hard to adjust to the demands of the unpredictable and the unexpected."[69]

3. Legal rules do not exist about such things as ideological attack, puppet statecraft, penetration (presumably economic as well as political), and, most importantly, internal matters. Mr. Kennan points out that the law assumes that civil wars will remain civil, that people can solve their own internal problems without affecting the international environment, that each nation is competent to construct a government qualified to speak for it, "in short, that domestic issues will not become international issues and that the world community will not be put in the position of having to make choices between rival claimants for power within the confines of the individual state."[70]

4. The concept of an international legal order creates the illusion that general, collective action to enforce norms against misbehaving

states is something more than the great power alliances which were and are the reality of control. The dissipation of this illusion brings us "right back in the realm of the forgotten art of diplomacy from which we have spent fifty years trying to escape."[71]

5. "The *inevitable* association of legalistic ideas with moralistic ones"[72] results in adoption of the concepts of total war and total victory. A lawbreaker is bad. One does not negotiate with a lawbreaker. He is punished. "A war fought in the name of high moral principle finds no early end short of some form of total domination."[73]

To this prognosis of continued failure in foreign affairs if we do not mend our ways of thinking about international relations there are many possible rejoinders. As to alleged evil number one, it might be asked, just what is the national interest of the United States with respect to the rule of law? Is there some reason to believe that international law is not in the national interest? Even the most casuistic might see that a "have" nation—seeking to dissimulate, to the degree the niceties of diplomacy make desirable, its overwhelming material power—would find the doctrine of the equality of sovereign states useful, without being thereby led astray. Longer-range thinkers might even hope that democratic international organization under law might prevent the rise of that "universalist state," which, Toynbee warns, is a dominant sign of a disintegrating civilization.[74] Certainly the present bipolar world, ever threatening to become unipolar, one way or the other, is something of a portent. The actuality of the bipolarity of world power is, incidentally, something Mr. Kennan does not seem to admit in his book, although it appears to be implicit in his celebrated articles in *Foreign Affairs*.[75]

With respect to evil number two, Mr. Kennan will convince me when I see "old-line diplomats" digging into the internal affairs of some sensitive small state, without some sort of legal backing, such as that given by the dependent-peoples provisions of the Charter,[76] or by the precedent of the Security Council's consideration of the Indonesian case as a threat to peace or security, despite the Netherland's assertion of "internal question"[77] as a bar.

As to evil number three, Professor Dickinson has taken up the same gaps, but his conclusions are that we should improve and grow, not throw up our hands and retreat. Further, I wonder if it has been the inhibitions of legality that have prevented us from taking courses other than the ones we did in such civil conflicts as, say, the one in Spain or the recent one in China. Some observers might wish to say that diplomats not particularly expert in international law, and therefore, presumably, not inhibited by it, did not solve either conflict to the entire satisfaction of the American national interest.

Evil number four will not necessarily remain an evil if we recognize—and perhaps this is why Mr. Kennan brought it up in the way he did—that we are faced with the power realities he mentions. But in recognizing them, I cannot see that anything in logic, law, fact, or morality requires us to assume that the "international juridical order" cannot be an *instrumentality* having utility in dealing with aggression and threats to peace. Surely there must be some practical significance in our sudden return to the United Nations instrumentality at the time of the Korean crisis, after a period in which our foreign policy seemed to be by-passing the United Nations. Surely the American initiative with respect to the General Assembly resolution, Uniting for Peace,[78] must have been based on an appraisal of the usefulness to us of diplomatic leadership through the instrumentality of a rather large international conference (the General Assembly) in which a heavy majority seemed to agree with our point of view. No such suggestions, however, are to be found in Mr. Kennan's book.

We are still too close to the working out of the application of what I would admit to be the moralistic (puppet statecraft masking aggression is bad) and legalistic (force except in self-defense or through the Security Council is illegal) bases of our action in Korea to say that Mr. Kennan's fears are groundless. It does not seem at this writing, however, that, despite exhortations and skillfully applied pressures, popular adoption of legalistically begotten drives to total war and total victory are going to force us beyond limited objectives consistent with a minimal national interest. If Mr. Kennan fears that we would insist upon the unconditional surrender of the Soviet Union in the event of a major war, let him take comfort from fairly widespread knowledge of history and of geography and, in an oblique way, from the fantastic issues of a mass-consumed national magazine on the subject, "The War No One Wants,"[79] a major objective of which seemed to be to drill into us that we could not fight the U.S.S.R. in the same way and to the same finish as we did Germany.

But, in a graver sense, Mr. Kennan is dangerously wrong. The struggle against man's greatest fear and his greatest threat requires more than the intellects and the professional skills of our diplomatists. The power realities of democracy make that apparent. It requires dedication, faith, and determination from peoples everywhere. You cannot muster that dedication, that faith, and that determination without connecting with that greatest of earthly power sources, man's belief that Good (as in the aggregate he sees it) should be supported and Evil (as in the aggregate he sees it) should be opposed. Absolute Good and Absolute Evil may or may not be beyond us, depending on how we look at ethics. But the relative values of an existing (but not necessarily static) order are tremendous forces, and that engine called "law" may do useful work when connected to that energy source, rather than exploding into the blinding short-circuit Mr. Kennan has written about. It would seem that diplomats who have had to attempt their professional tasks without a connection to this energy source—as in Europe after the disappearance of the American Army in being before the Potsdam conference—would realize this. At the other extreme, it will not do for the majority of us to be unconcerned, as Kelsen, the scientist, says he is, with the energy sources themselves, and concentrate attention to seeing to it, as he does so thoroughly, that the parts of the law motor mesh well. This is only to say that in addition to a great master mechanic for the law motor, we need other skillsmen; and with this I am sure Professor Kelsen will heartily agree.

II. The Anglo-Iranian Oil Case: Want of Law, Misuse of Law, or Disregard of Law

At most this will be an epilogue, if not merely an extended footnote. The basic subject is still speculation about the role of law in international life, but here the aspect taken up is the operational. The questions to be asked about the developments in this case are: How do the concepts we have discussed relate to an actual legal event? What reorientations of older concepts may result from the manner in which the case was treated (a) by the International Court of Justice, (b) by the Security Council? Where, as a result of the foregoing, do we stand regarding international law and its function in the international community?

The Case Before the Court

After the Iranian Oil Nationalization Law of April 30, 1951, was enacted and before the assumption of physical control by the Iranian authorities over the installations in Iran of the Anglo-Iranian Oil Company, the British government, on May 26, 1951, referred the dispute to the International Court of Justice. Jurisdiction was posited on British and Iranian acceptance of compulsory jurisdiction under Article 36 (2) of the statute of the International Court of Justice.[80] On June 22, 1951, the United Kingdom filed a request for an indication of interim measures in the case, basing itself upon Article 41[81] of the statute of the Court and the allegation of irreparable injury to the interests of its national, the Anglo-Iranian Oil Company, if the Iranian government were not restrained, pending determination of the case on its merits, from ousting the company from control, requiring its employees to become employees of the newly created National Iranian Oil Company, damaging the productivity of the fields and the refinery at Abadan, and claiming the proceeds of all sales since June 11, 1951. The basic British theory of action was that its national was threatened with a denial of justice, as a result of the unilateral denunciation by Iran of the concession convention of 1933, between the company and the Iranian government. This convention contained provisions against unilateral termination and for the arbitration of differences. Although it is not clear whether Iran, after the institution of the proceeding, sought to withdraw its acceptance of compulsory jurisdiction with respect to this case,[82] Iran did not appear by agent but telegraphed the court that it considered the controversy beyond the competence of the court, because (a) the United Kingdom had no international claim against Iran arising out of the dispute between the company and Iran, and (b) the dispute was exclusively within the national jurisdiction of Iran because it involved the exercise of the sovereign rights of Iran.

In its opinion of July 5, 1951, the court granted the British request for an interim order. The view of the majority was that the court could grant an interim order before the determination of the issue of its general competence or decision on the merits, where "it cannot be accepted *a priori* that a claim based on such a complaint falls completely outside the scope of international jurisdiction."[83] The order of the court commanded the following:

1. Both governments should ensure that no action should be taken to prejudice the rights of the other in respect of the carrying out of any decision on the merits.

2. Both governments should ensure against aggravation or extension of the dispute.

3. Both governments should ensure that the Anglo-Iranian Oil Company's commercial and industrial operations, as they were carried on before May 1, 1951, should not be hindered, pending decision on the merits.

4. The company to continue under its management but subject to modification directed by the board of supervision.

5. A board of supervision, with two Iranians and two British representatives and a national of a third state, chosen by agreement of the governments or in default of agreement, by the president of the court, should have the following duties, pending final decision on the merits:

a. Auditing revenues and taking custody of revenues in excess of normal operating expenses.

b. Ensuring that the company's operations are carried on in conformity with the interim order.

The dissenting opinion of Judges Winiarski and Badawi Pasha was confined to the point that, in their opinion, the court was not authorized by Article 41 to make interim orders unless the court should consider its competence "reasonably probable."[84] In view of Iran's refusal to appear or to admit jurisdiction, the dissenters did not believe that the required reasonable probability existed.

The Case Before the Security Council

After the order of the court diplomatic negotiations were resumed, and the United States extended good offices through Mr. Harriman. Following the breakdown of efforts for a negotiated settlement, the seizure of the refinery at Abadan on September 27, 1951, and the related expulsion order, the United Kingdom on September 29, 1951, requested that Iranian noncompliance with the interim order be considered by the Security Council. A United Kingdom draft resolution of the same date proposed that the Security Council call upon the government of Iran to obey the interim order.[85] Reference to the Security Council was, of course, based upon Article 94 (2) of the Charter.[86] The result of the Security Council debate in October, 1951, is well known. Iran, represented by its premier, insisted that neither the court nor the Security Council was competent to deal with an internal matter of national sovereignty. The British resolution was progressively watered down,[87] in an effort to get agreement to support resumption of negotiations and to take into account that the company's representatives had in the meantime left Iran, until it finally eliminated all reference to the ground upon which the controversy had been submitted to the Security Council. Even this did not result in Security Council adoption of any proposal on the issue other than that discussion be adjourned at the Security Council until after the court had decided upon the question of its jurisdiction.[88]

The Security Council discussion was notable for the almost complete absence of any serious discussion of the legal problems involved, which, chiefly, were:

(1) Does the court have the power to issue an interim order without having decided the question of jurisdiction?

(2) Is such an order within the purview of Article 94 of the Charter?

The United Kingdom presentation, following the revision of the British resolution, focused upon the competence of the Security Council to recommend the continuance of negotiations.[89]

The United States representative, in replying to an initial U.S.S.R.–Yugoslav objection ("internal question") to the inclusion of the item on the agenda of the Security Council, stressed that the Security Council should consider the dispute because it was a subject of litigation before the court.[90] The American emphasis during the debate in the Security Council shifted, however, as no doubt was required in view of the revision of the British resolution, away from action under Article 94 to the provisions regarding the pacific settlement of disputes. Thus we find Ambassador Austin on October 17, 1951, stressing the existence of a dispute between the United Kingdom and Iran likely to endanger international peace and security.[91]

The representative of the Netherlands appears to be the only member of the Security Council who seemed to feel that the references in the proposed recommendation to the competence of the court should not be watered down.[92] The press reported one South American representative as having rather loftily referred to the "political character" of the Security Council, implying that legal issues involved in the enforcement of the court's order[93] were rather a bother, if not *infra dig.*

What Are the Implications?

Technical evaluation of the legal aspects of the development outlined has begun,[94] and it is likely that several more words are still to be said. Here, however, general reactions seem more relevant to the basic approach being taken. The following are illustrative:

> In this state of the case before the Court the Security Council's action on October 19 can be accounted for only as an effort to evade its responsibility for dealing with the question on its agenda. . . .[95]
>
> This [speaking of the Security Council's disposition] may well create a most serious precedent for the future. The tendency will surely be to diminish the prestige of the Security Council, of the International Court of Justice and of the United Nations itself.[96]
>
> The only relevance of all this is that it illustrates the triumph of tactics over principles, of the immediate over the long range, and of the expedient over the moral in the current conduct of international relations.[97]

To these the following observations may be added:

Far from finding a want of law, the International Court may actually have pioneered.[98] Its order reads like that of a national court, instead of one of the cautious, "a little something for both parties" awards so familiar to those who study the adjudications of international tribunals. Perhaps the court may actually have expected that its order would be enforced by the Security Council. Writing in 1949, the president of the court stressed that the tribunal was not hampered by the veto principle and that its decisions might be enforced by the Security Council.[99] The judges, even if Mr. Dooley's dictum does not apply to them, have certainly found no encouragement here for any assumption that their institution may have a significant and effective role to play in the settlement of international tensions. The result may be what Mr. Justice Brandeis feared would happen to administrative agencies, back in the days when the United States Supreme Court required a *de novo* court review of their orders: a corrosive irresponsibility caused by frustration of institutional effectiveness might set in. The "Roy Bean approach" Professor Dickinson has so well caught[100] may return to international legal life.

Administratively, the order of the court seemed to cover adequately the legal rights of the parties. One observer has said that the court's proposal was the only sensible one made in the whole controversy.[101] That may or may not prove to be the case, but its good sense was not good enough to make the order effective.

In a broader sense the whole United Nations power process, which is "law" to Professor McDougal, failed to settle the dispute. So far, so has Mr. Kennan's "diplomacy," even "in the most old-fashioned sense of the term." However, the ball is back to the diplomats.

Mr. Kennan seems to be "one up" also, with respect to the role played here by the legal conceptualisms involved in "the equality of states" and "internal questions." Yet we must realize that in another sense a legalism may have had a major part in keeping international violence out of this controversy so far. The British resort to the court was welcomed with relief by those who had found reason for concern in certain British hints, during the summer of 1951, that measures of self-help might have to be taken to protect British lives and property in Iran. Who can deny that Charter inhibitions on the use of force to protect interests or enforce treaties, a use so clearly legal under traditional international law, was a factor in keeping the conflict peaceful? This is not to say that the law alone accomplished this. It is to say that the concept of a law against the use of force in these situations becomes itself a significant factor in the power relationships—and a good thing this was, too, many would add.

But Kelsen's Principle of Effectiveness may be a rule of institutional life, as well as a convenient jurisprudential theory for maintaining the purity of law. Who can say that another great power, sometime, somewhere, may not find the Charter restraints intolerable, when the institutions of international life give it no alternative means of asserting or defending its interests against a smaller and (in its eyes) irresponsible state hiding behind the United Nations force monopoly? There is the possibility that *rebus sic stantibus* might win over *pacta sunt servanda,* even with respect to that multilateral treaty known as the Charter of the United Nations. An intermediate result might be the return to professional diplomacy in the most old-fashioned sense of the term, but the institutional restraint would be gone, and with it an important fire-wall against the conflagration of war.

A somewhat wistful final point is that so much of the damage which has been done might have been unnecessary. Some[102] have condemned the British for overstraining a weak institution. That is not quite what I mean. The law about interim orders; the law about whether any international reclamation against a nationalizing country other than for compensation will lie; the law about whether an order of the court can be enforced under Article 94 unless there were a further Security Council finding under Articles 41 or 33,[103] to list some of the doubtful points —all are sufficiently disputable to have permitted a resolution of the impasse along the lines of preserving the prestige and the integrity of institutions not yet quite adequate to do the job, but worthy of being kept viable against the day of development or of overwhelming change of conditions. This is a process which lawyers and domestic courts know well, it is a part of the concept of institutional infallibility, which, while it may often be a fiction, is a fiction which has frequently been found useful in institutional life. This may be a legalism, and perhaps it is not a very moral one; but certainly it is almost as flexible in its way as the diplomacy Mr. Kennan wants us to return to. Yet, it is an institution, not an art or a science, and that means there is something there, other than craftsmanship, to fall back on when needed or useful.

III. The Summing Up

A popular presentation by a persuasive and authoritative personality has blamed law and morality for our past mistakes and predicted that these concepts would cause us even greater trouble in the future, if we did not abandon them. A legal institution and its legal technique for helping toward the solution of an international tension were ineffective, because the enforcement mechanism did not operate, except to show the disrespect or disregard for the International Court and its order. The legalism of collective police action to put down aggression and a threat to peace and security has become to far too many minds for comfort, indistinct[104] from, or merely a euphemism for, old-style war (including, in popular thinking, "just" and "unjust" sides).

This paper has attempted to point out errors of observation regarding the concepts of international law held by Mr. Kennan and his partial precursor, Professor Morgenthau. It has sought to raise questions as to the expertness and wisdom with which United Nations instrumentalities were used by national representatives in a particular case.

It is a pity that the most popular of the writers discussed here has, apparently, taken the least pains to study the institution he blames for our ills,[105] that his denunciations appear little short of biased, although the reasons for this reaction are not given and can only be surmised. It is more regrettable and in the long run probably more significant, that those with professional competence in international law and in philosophy of law generally, continue (a) seemingly at loggerheads about basic concepts, (b) quixotically optimistic or just plain arrogant about law's place in the whole picture, and (c) wedded to media ill-adapted to any effective communication with the main bodies of citizenry or, for that matter, as Mr. Kennan's self-revelations may have shown, with other professional groups working in the same fields.

As to concepts, it seems fairly plain that "law" is coming more and more, in the international field especially, to refer to the whole power process within the political order. "Law is concerned with social management, and social management is government."[106] Only Morgenthau thought of law as judicial decision alone. Jessup stressed law as a part of the very fabric of the conventions of international intercourse. Kelsen's norms are a little harder to fit into the broader view of law, but it can be done. Rigidity and lack of compromise in law, which Morgenthau and Kennan fear, are phantasms to the empirical observer or denied as a matter of faith by American pragmatists and neorealists. A good current statement, serving for both schools in this regard is found in Professor Grant Gilmore's review of a new edition of Professor Karl Llewellyn's *Bramble Bush:*[107]

> The Bramble Bush, as manifesto, tells us that the law is not a self-contained set of logical propositions; that rules of law do not explain results at law; that the stated reasons for decision regularly mask the inarticulate major premise; that facts are slippery things with a nasty habit of changing shape and color, depending on who is looking at them; that judges are not automatons who announce the law, but human beings, possibly neurotic; that juries are barely human; that the truth is not in the law books, which should nevertheless still be studied; that we don't quite know yet where the truth is, but it is somewhere—in economics, sociology, or anthropology or psychology, or in the murky reaches of Freudian theory.
>
> These ideas no longer excite us, which is more our good fortune than their fault. *They are the ideas which destroyed classical jurisprudence.*[108] They are the ideas which set us free. They are the ideas which have served their time and passed out of controversy.

For lawmen, perhaps, but they do not appear to have reached very far outside the profession.

If the concept of law is expanded, it is also necessary to define the relationship of the older, more traditional types of law (judicial decisions, and the like) and its specialized practitioners to the whole process. Kelsen, Dickinson, Jessup, and McDougal, all see a large place for "law" in international life, but they do not tell us very clearly just what the lawman's part in the whole power structure is. The implication from many of these presentations is that his is the dominant role. Certainly here, as to so many other points of contact with related disciplines and techniques, it would not hurt the cause of the rule of law if lawmen were a bit more modest about their contribution to the over-all, a little more willing to pull in harness, rather than to gallop in splendid isolation with somewhat faded banners, not all won in real battles. It would be interesting to have a study, for example, on the extent to which particular techniques of law-trained men might help in the conduct of diplomatic negotiations, in sifting the relevant from the irrelevant in appraising the national interest with respect to particular choices of foreign policy, or, in improvising institutions or adapting concepts for particular ends—in short, the instrumental use of law. It would be most useful, also, to have studies showing us how, when, and to what extent, lawmen and their "legal minds" have hampered, or, as a result of their professional limitations, distorted, foreign policy made under their leadership—in other words, the factual study Mr. Kennan promised but did not deliver.

The third need is for more popular presentations by legal scholars. The reader of a weekly newsmagazine can keep up with new ideas in science and in medicine. Not so with law. In the field of international law, matters of substantive development appear sufficiently static or sufficiently well under research that the further intensive cultivation of this extraordinarily well-plowed field might, temporarily at least, be deferred, in order to release more time for contact, not with the small corps of brother professionals, but with those most important elements of any legal order, the individuals living out their lives under its rule.

HEINRICH BRANDWEINER

The International Status of Austria

THE PRESENT POSITION of Austria within the international community is determined by a state treaty, in the making of which she herself took no part. This treaty is the so-called Second Control Agreement, which the four occupying powers—the Union of Socialist Soviet Republics, the United States of America, the United Kingdom of Great Britain and Northern Ireland and the French Republic—signed on June 28, 1946.[1] It assumes the existence of supreme Austrian legislative and executive organs ("the Austrian government"), of subordinate authorities, and of a federal constitution, and subordinates all Austrian national organs, in principle, to the directions of an organization of the four powers, which bears the title "Allied Commission for Austria" (Article 1*a*). This commission consists of:

(1) An Allied Council consisting of four high commissioners, one appointed by each of the four powers;

(2) An Executive Committee consisting of one high-ranking representative of each of the high commissioners;

(3) The staffs appointed respectively by the four powers (Article 2*a*). Their decisions must be taken unanimously and the chair is occupied by each power in turn (Article 2*a*).

The powers of the Allied Commission, in matters concerning Austria as a whole, are exercised by the Allied Council, by the Executive Committee, or by the staffs, working in coördination. The high commissioners must guarantee, within their zones, the execution of the decisions of the Allied Commission, and supervise the carrying out of the directions of the central Austrian authorities. The high commissioners must further ensure within their zones that actions of the Austrian provincial authorities, deriving from their autonomous functions, do not conflict with the policy of the Allied Commission (Article 2*b*).

The Allied Commission acts through the Austrian government or other appropriate Austrian authorities, with the following exceptions:

I. To maintain law and order, if the Austrian authorities are unable to do so;

II. To carry out its own directives if the Austrian government or other appropriate Austrian authorities do not;

III. To accomplish the following purposes through direct measures:

(1) Demilitarization and disarmament (military, economic, industrial, technical, and scientific);

(2) The protection and security of the Allied forces in Austria, and the fulfillment of their military needs;

(3) The protection, care, and restitution of property belonging to the governments of any of the United Nations or their nationals;

(4) The disposal of German property;

(5) The care and evacuation of, and exercise of judicial authority over, prisoners of war and displaced persons;

(6) The control of travel into and out of Austria until Austrian travel controls can be established;

(7) The tracing, arrest, and handing over of certain war criminals sought by the United Nations (Articles 2*c* and 5).

Should the Allied Council take no measures, the four high commissioners may, in any such case (see I-III, above), do so independently in their respective zones (Article 2*d*). Concerning the zones of occupation, an earlier treaty (July 9, 1945) between the four powers remains in force[2] (Article 2*e*). The principal tasks of the Allied Commission for Austria are:

I. To ensure the enforcement in Austria of the provisions of the Declaration on the Defeat of Germany signed at Berlin on June 5, 1945;

II. To complete the separation of Austria from Germany, and to maintain the independent existence and integrity of the Austrian state and pending the final definition of its frontiers to ensure respect for them as they were on December 31, 1937;

III. To assist the Austrian government to recreate a sound and democratic national life based on an efficient administration, stable economic and financial conditions, and respect for law and order;

IV. To assist the freely elected government of Austria to assume as quickly as possible full control of the affairs of state in Austria;

V. The establishment of a progressive long-term democratic educational program (Article 3).

The right of direction, expressed in general terms in Article 1*a*, is more clearly defined in Article 6 for the sphere of legislation and for the international agreements which Austria will sign in the future. All acts must be submitted to the Allied Council before they are made public and come into force. For constitutional laws, the written approval of the Allied Council is required. For other laws, the approval of the Allied Council may be assumed if, within 31 days of the submission of the bill to the Allied Commission, it does not inform the Austrian government of its objection.

International agreements concluded between Austria and one of the four powers must, after signature, be brought to the notice of the Allied Council. All other treaties negotiated by Austria are, in the same way as bills other than those pertaining to the constitution, subject to the veto of the Allied Council, which must be unanimous and must be communicated to the Austrian government within 31 days. In the absence of such veto, they come into force for Austria.

Austria may, according to her own judgment, establish diplomatic and consular relations with the members of the United Nations. The establishment of such relations with other governments requires the prior approval of the Allied Council. Diplomatic missions in Vienna have the right to establish direct liaison with the Allied Council (Article 7).

Consideration of the peculiar situation created by the Second Control Agreement might, at first sight, prompt the question whether, in the circumstances, it is appropriate to speak of Austria as a state at all. The answer to this question, however, is very definitely in the affirmative. Indeed, the present Austrian legal order is derived from the unanimous will of the four powers, as expressed through the Second Control Agreement. It is, however, in no way subordinated to another, higher legal order (except to that of international law) but is an order in its own right; an order which, no doubt because of the presence of the forces of the four powers, is also effective and which possesses a certain territorial, temporal, and material sphere of validity. Austria is certainly not a part of the United States because of its American Zone, nor does its French Zone make it a constituent part of the French Republic. Is it then a state within the meaning of international law? If we accept Lauterpacht's conception of a state as possessing "independent government, effective authority and defined territory,"[3] or if we follow Kelsen and take the fact for granted in a situation where an independent government proclaims, over a definite inhabited territory, a coercive order whose rule is effective, that is, that the coercive order receives general and lasting obedience,[4] then we must, at any rate in the beginning, answer our question in the negative. For Austria has no independent government which includes supreme legislative and executive organs not subordinated to a will other than her own—the Austrian federal president, the federal government, and the other supreme organs of the state are subject to the above-mentioned restrictive clauses in the Second Control Agreement. But the Allied Council, as far as its members are concerned, is also subject to directives and therefore not independent. Finally, no one of the four powers is in any respect this "independent government" of Austria because the will of each of the four powers, with regard to Austria, is likewise limited and restricted by the wills of the three others. Only through the unanimity of the four powers within the framework of the Second Control Agreement is a new will created, which is in fact supreme in Austria. But even this, as we have seen, is not completely free—for instance, even with the unanimity of the four powers, the validity of a treaty concluded by Austria could not be made to depend upon the written approval of the Allied Council, unless they agreed to amend or to revoke the Second Control Agreement. For Austria has, on her part, acquired certain rights through this treaty, as will yet be shown.

The definition of the "state in the sense of international law" embraces only the so-called sovereign state. This sovereignty, however, is limited in Austria;[5] limited—and this is the deciding factor—not by reason of a foreign national legal order but by an international treaty, in which, however, Austria herself did not take part. Nevertheless, Austria is a state. She was recognized by more than half of the nations of the world, including the most important ones. However this recognition may be formulated, it is certain that the recognizing nations intended the recognition of Austria as a state and not the recognition of her government. This is all the more true since recognition of governments is applicable only to so-called *de facto* governments. It should be clear, without further proof, that the Austrian government is not a *de facto* government, that is, one which has come to power through the interruption of the continuity of the national legal order.

Westlake writes at one point: "It is not necessary for a state to be independent in order to be a state of international law."[6] Austria may conclude international treaties with each of the four powers without the consent of any other power (Article 6). Thus far she is doubtless subordinated only to International Law, that is *völkerrechtsunmittelbar*. But she may conclude such treaties with other states only when the four powers raise no unanimous objection, that is, merely with the tacit approval of at least one of the four powers. But even then this limitation of her capacity for action under international law *(völkerrechtliche Handlungsfähigkeit)* is not dependent upon a foreign national legal order; for it can be altered only by action in accordance with international legal procedure.[7] That Austria is *völkerrechtsunmittelbar* or, in other words, a subject of international law, that is, possessor of rights and duties under international law, is shown by considering who must bear the consequences in the event of Austria's committing a breach of international law. Assuming the general principle of international responsibility, Austria could, in my opinion, free herself from such responsibility only if she proved that a particular one of the four powers has provoked, through the mechanism provided by the Second Control Agreement, the measure causing this responsibility. This is so because the restrictions of Austria's capacity for action under international law, caused by the clauses of the Second Control Agreement, are known to all states. The limitation of her capacity for action corresponds to the limitation of her responsibility.

As Austria is limited in her capacity for action under international law—though this does not mean that she is only partly *völkerrechtsunmittelbar*—she can best be described as a protected state. She stands under the protection of the four powers.[8] This is clearly shown by a consideration of the tasks which the four powers have assumed in Article 3 of the Second Control Agreement—to effect the complete separation of Austria from Germany, to maintain her independent existence and integrity, to guarantee her frontiers, and to support the Austrian government in the fulfillment of its duties.

There are precedents in international practice for Austria's present position. It is approximately similar to the status of the city of Cracow which was established as a state under the common protection of Austria, Russia, and Prussia, in accordance with Article 6 of the *Schlussakte* of the Congress of Vienna on June 9, 1815. The facts are even clearer in the Free City of Danzig, set up in 1919. The constitutional laws of Danzig required the approval of the high commissioner appointed by the League of Nations. Danzig stood expressly under the protection of the League of Nations. In her foreign affairs she was severely restricted by her ties with Poland, forced upon her by treaty. Nevertheless, in her relations with Poland itself, she had complete capacity for action under international law, and Poland could not sign treaties for Danzig without previous consultation with the Free City. In her internal affairs also—with respect to customs, waterways, harbors, certain railways—she was restricted in favor of Poland. Despite this, she was undeniably recognized as a state in the sense of international law,[9] and thereby as a subject of international law; a state restricted in its capacity for action under international law and standing under the protection of the League.[10]

The Second Control Agreement does not simply impose restrictions upon Austria; it also contains clauses in her favor. Through it Austria has obtained the legal right that the four powers shall guarantee her existence and her frontiers, and support her within the framework of the clauses of Article 3. In the same way, Austria may claim all those rights which are hers in accordance with the status created by the Second Control Agreement; for instance, the right to establish diplomatic relations with certain states, to conclude treaties within the framework of the clauses of Article 6, with one of the four powers without further formality. These rights have been granted to Austria without her being empowered to take part in the treaty. The clauses of the treaty, however, are, by their nature and in accordance with the will of the concluding parties, of such a kind that Austria has thereby obtained inalienable rights which are valid so long as the treaty remains in force.

Essentially, however, the Second Control Agreement is a treaty *zu Lasten Dritter*—obligating a third party. It restricts Austria's constitutional autonomy as well as her capacity for action under international law. Treaties *zu Lasten Dritter* are contrary to the principle of treaty autonomy, which is a general rule of international law.[11] *Pacta tertiis nec nocent nec prosunt.* Despite this, international practice does admit treaties *zu Lasten Dritter*. This result is brought about by an international territorial statute, based on a treaty, and in general by any settlement which determines territorial rights.[12] On the other hand, we must agree with Verdross when he states that only the exercise of these treaty-based rights affecting third states can become effective.[13] Further, the law of state succession contains norms which, under certain conditions, oblige third states to allow treaties, concluded by their territorial predecessors, to remain in force against themselves. Certain treaties, however, limiting the states' capacity for duties and for action under international law (*Rechts- und Handlungsfähigkeit*) produce results also concerning third states which must accept a changed legal situation, for example, that brought about by a protectorate established by agreement. Finally, federal treaties and agreements aiming at collective security are occasionally of importance for third states.[14]

All these cases, however, do not apply to Austria in relation to the Second Control Agreement. Is it then contrary to international law? The answer is in the negative.[15] To begin with, the Second Control Agreement aroused no protest from the Austrian side, but earned the thanks of the federal government[16]—which in case of an open breach of international law would scarcely have happened and so may be regarded as proof. But then, there do exist, in fact, treaties *zu Lasten Dritter,* which are outside the narrow limits of the exceptions mentioned above. These are the treaties *from which new states emerge.* These treaties may, according to the wish of the signatory states, prescribe limits to the freedom of the unit to be created. Now, strictly speaking, the emergence of a new state on the basis of an international treaty must be looked upon as an event in which the treaty itself has only the quality of a norm necessary to the creation of a state. The organ named in the treaty then creates the actual new legal order.[17] Should this become effective—in particular through the creation of the supreme directing organs of power, the "government"—then the new state is born. It is then subject to the restrictions which the founding states have imposed upon it at its birth. But once the new national legal order is created, then all—the founding states, the new state, and third states—are obligated by its existence and, in particular, the founding states cannot revoke the existence of the new state, for example, by *contrarius actus.*[18] They may destroy it by depriving its legal order permanently of its effectiveness, but, by doing so, they commit a breach of international law. The creation of the new order brings permanent rights and duties to the founding states, the new state, and third states.

The Second Control Agreement is certainly a treaty *zu Lasten Dritter,* but Austria does not owe her existence to this treaty. As was emphasized at the beginning, it already presupposes her existence as a state. In its preamble, however, the treaty refers back to another treaty which the Second Control Agreement has replaced.[19] This earlier treaty is the so-called First Control Agreement, which the four powers concluded on June 4, 1945. It is this treaty alone which laid down the conditions for the emergence of Austria as a state. It created those organs which enabled the new Austrian legal order to become effective; only after that date, at the moment when the legal order became effective for its whole territorial sphere of validity, did the Austrian state come into existence.

The First Control Agreement[20] established an Allied control system which was to function in Austria until the setting up of a freely elected government recognized by the four powers. As the present Allied Commission for Austria, it consisted of the Allied Council, the Executive Committee, and the staffs appointed by the four powers (Article 1). The Allied Council consisted of four military commissioners, appointed by each of the four governments, who were at the same time the supreme commanders of their countries' occupation forces. The supreme power in Austria was exercised by them for questions concerning Austria as a whole, in their capacity as members of the Allied Council and in accordance with the instructions of their governments. With this reservation, each military commissioner, as supreme commander of the occupation forces placed at his disposal by his government, exercised supreme power in his own zone of occupation. The Allied Council met at least once every ten days or, in addition, at the request of any one commissioner. Its decisions were taken unanimously and the chair was occupied in turn (Article 2). On the basis of the directives which each commissioner received from his government, the Allied Council worked out plans concerning the most important military, political, economic, and other questions affecting Austria as a whole, and took decisions on them. In addition, it guaranteed a measure of uniformity of action in the occupation zones (Article 5). The Executive Committee, acting in its name, guaranteed the carrying out of the decisions of the Allied Council, coordinated the activities of the departments of the Allied Commission, and examined all questions passed on to it by the Allied Council (Article 6). The departments of the Allied Commission—that is, the subordinate staffs—acted in an advisory capacity and carried out the decisions passed on to them by the Allied Council (Article 7).

The chief tasks of the Allied Commission for Austria were as follows:

(a) to ensure the endorsement in Austria of the provisions of the Declaration on the Defeat of Germany signed at Berlin on June 5, 1945;

(b) *to effect the separation of Austria from Germany;*

(c) *to establish an Austrian central administration as soon as possible;*

(d) *to make preparations for the setting up of a freely elected Austrian government;*

(e) in the meantime, to take all proper measures adequately to ensure the working of the Austrian administration (Article 8).

During the period before the establishment of the offices of an Austrian central administration—a period which was to be as short as possible—the decisions of the Allied Commission, so far as they required action to be taken in the various zones, were carried out by the occupation authorities (Article 9). As soon as the offices of an Austrian central administration were in a position to take adequate action, the exercise of their respective functions, with regards to Austria as a whole, was handed over to them (Article 10). The necessary liaison with the governments of other especially interested members of the United Nations was ensured by military missions, which these governments established with the Allied Council (Article 12). Finally, Article 14 alluded to a future treaty, which was envisaged after the setting up of the national legal order: "A separate agreement between the four powers lays down the nature and scope of the instructions and advice which the Allies must give Austria after the establishment of a freely elected government recognized by the Four Powers." This new treaty is the Second Control Agreement which thereby, as well as by its own preamble, is derived from the First Control Agreement.

A short time later, the Potsdam Conference examined a Soviet proposal, which had as subject the extension of the authority of the Austrian provisional government. This had been set up on April 27, 1945—that is, before the end of the war—under the leadership of the later head of state, in Russian-occupied Vienna, and was under Soviet control. On August 2, 1945,[21] the conference resolved to reëxamine the question after the entry into Vienna of British and American forces. After this entry and after the so-called Provisional Conference *(Länderkonferenz)*, which was held in Vienna from September 24–26, the Allied Council sent a memorandum to Chancellor Dr. Karl Renner.[22] This contained the information that the four powers had approved the extension of the authority of the Austrian provisional government to all Austria, under the following conditions:

(1) The Austrian government should exercise its function under the guidance and control of the supreme authority in Austria—the Allied Council. The control over the ministries and departments would be exercised through the machinery of the Allied Commission. Certain functions of government would be reserved to the Allied Council—the chancellor would be informed of these.

(2) The Austrian provisional government should hold free elections as early as possible and not later than December 31, 1945.

(3) The provisional Austrian government was empowered to enact laws applying to the whole of Austria, provided that they were first submitted for approval to the Allied Council and did not limit any law in force in the Soviet Zone, unless by a law to be applied to the whole of Austria.

The Allied agreement, communicated to Austria by this memorandum, weakened the First Control Agreement at some points without, however, destroying its validity.

From all this there emerges the compelling conclusion that, at the time of the signing of the First Control Agreement (July 4, 1945), an Austrian state, that is, an effective legal order extending to the entire territorial sphere of validity, was not yet in existence; that it required first the completion of the separation of Austria from Germany (Article 8*b*), that there were as yet no supreme directing organs with authority extending over the whole national territory, and that this extension took place only after October 20, 1945.

It should not be thought, because of this, that the importance of the proclamation of the three political parties on April 27, 1945,[23] is in any way diminished. It brought into existence the Austrian provisional government, which later became the supreme organ of the international legal order. Legally it did not have as a consequence the establishment of a revolutionary national legal order, for there was absent the essential attribute of any real, that is, victorious . . . revolution—effectiveness. In the Vienna of those days there was only one effective order, that of the Soviet Union.

When, however, did the First Republic cease to exist? On March 12, 1938, German military forces occupied the whole federal territory of Austria, without meeting resistance.[24] This occupation was preceded on March 11, 1938, by the happenings made familiar by a long list of events and publications, and culminating in a short-term ultimatum presented to Austria by Germany. On the evening of March 11, Germany forced the resignation of the Schuschnigg cabinet and the setting up of a National Socialist Austrian federal government. On the same night the entry of German troops began. Thereby Germany violated a number of international treaties,[25] guaranteeing the independence of Austria and restricting the use of force. By doing so she committed a breach of international law.

On March 13, 1938, Austria was formally incorporated into the German Reich, that is, declared an integral part of Germany. A "Reichsgesetz" of that day expressly states: *Österreich ist ein Land des Deutschen Reiches.*[26] By this, Germany quite clearly and unmistakably expressed *animus domini* with regard to Austria, over whose entire territory she had by military means already established an effective rule. This was nothing else than an *annexation,* that is, an extension of the territorial sphere of validity of the German legal order over the whole former national territory of Austria. However, it was covered up by the purposely chosen method of issuing parallel laws—a law of the German Reich and a federal Austrian constitutional law, passed by a federal government which, because of the complete occupation of the country, no longer really possessed the quality of an organ. This method was used in order to give the true state of affairs the appearance of an international agreement, subject of which was the so-called *Anschluss* to Germany. Subsequently, an attempt was made to legalize the completed annexation by a plebiscite. But this was no less an offense against international law than was the occupation of the country itself. Here Germany committed a further international crime.

It is proved that Hitler for a long time had contemplated the annexation of Austria. At a meeting in Berlin on November 5, 1937, Hitler, in the presence of Göring, Neurath, Raeder, Blomberg, Fritsch, and others, made pronouncements[27] with respect to a plan to conquer Austria; in his opinion the annexation of Austria would ease Germany's political and military position. This emerged in the Nürnberg trials. The order to the German forces to march into Austria has also been preserved. It includes the instruction to crush any resistance that might be offered "with the greatest ruthlessness and by force of arms." There was then also present on the part of Germany an *animus bellandi,* should the use of force prove necessary—although Hitler, to mask the true state of affairs, disavowed any intention of "waging war against a brother people."

Subsequently, Germany put into force in Austria the most important German laws; where Austrian laws were still valid, they were so by delegation from the German legal order. The German legal order had therefore become fully effective *(wirksam)* for the entire territory of the former federal state of Austria. *Thereby Austria had ceased to exist as a state.*

By virtue of the primacy of international law over national laws, the former[28] determines when a state "dies" or "is born." International law determines when a state in the meaning of international law actually comes into existence. This happens when an independent government issues a coercive order for a definite inhabited area, and *when this order is effective,* that is, receives general obedience. In this context, Kelsen says:

> Under what circumstances does a national legal order begin or cease to be valid? The answer, given by International Law, is that a national legal order begins to be valid as soon as it becomes—on the whole—efficacious; *and it ceases to be valid as soon as it loses this efficacy.* The legal order remains the same as long as its territorial sphere of validity remains essentially the same. . . .[29]

And earlier he says:

> A state remains the same as long as the continuity of the national legal order is maintained, that is to say, as long as the changes of this order, even fundamental changes in the contents of the legal norms or of the territorial sphere of validity, are the result of acts performed in conformity with the constitution; *provided that the change does not imply the termination of the validity of the national legal order as a whole.*[30]

Should the legal order of State A cease to be effective, on the whole, then State A ceases to exist; should it be replaced by another legal order, that of State B, we say (personifying and inadequately defining) "the territory belongs to State B," or "State A has been incorporated or merged or annexed." This "acquisition of territory," itself, as a happening wholly dependent on its effectiveness, must be distinguished from the legality or illegality of the acts which brought it about. It can happen either in accordance with or contrary to international law. Guggenheim rightly says:[31]

> Von der Völkerrechtsgemäszheit und Völkerrechtswidrigkeit des Gebietserwerbes ist die Erstreckung des räumlichen Zuständigkeitsbereiches durch den gebietserwerbenden Staat deutlich zu scheiden. Der Erwerb des Gebietes erfolgt nämlich unabhängig von dem Umstand, ob es mit oder ohne Zustimmung des Altstaates an den Folgestaat übergeht. Die Effektivität der Gebietserstreckung begründet den Gebietserwerb.[32]

And later:

> Das primitive Völkerrecht erscheint technisch nicht fortgebildet genug, um einer wirksamen, auf rechtswidrigem Wege zu Stande gekommenen permanenten politischen Macht die Rechtsverbindlichkeit abzusprechen.[33]

Now international law seems to allow exceptions which contradict the principle of effectiveness. If in war a state completely occupies the territory of its enemy, or of a neutral state,[34] and the occupation is effective, that is, militarily effective, then undeniably the legal order of the occupying power has replaced that of the occupied state. In this case, however, doctrine asserts that the occupied state remains in existence and it declares annexation during war to be "invalid." But this so-called *occupatio bellica* has provisional character not only because of the relevant norms of Articles 42–56 of the Hague regulations. Its explanation is once again to be found in the principles of effectiveness, which is paramount in international law. So long as the war is not victoriously concluded, we cannot regard the rule of the occupying power as "firmly established,"[35] for a change in the fortunes of war makes possible at any time the loss of the occupied territory. In this case, the international legal order regards the occupied state as still existing, although the term "state in the sense of international law" is no longer applicable. As the legal order of the occupying power can never be "firmly established" until the end of the war, that is, until the cessation of hostilities, positive international law has invented a fiction to cover this case—an *als ob* the occupied state still existed. For, "in reality," that is, in legal reality, it no longer exists, since its legal order as a whole is no longer effective; it is destroyed by that of the occupying power—where it "remains in force," it is based upon the legal order of the occupying power, from which the foundation of its validity is to be derived.

But it is this fiction which allows us to speak of the identity of a state before, during, and after an *occupatio bellica*. It exists so long as the state does not "perish" in the sense of international law, for example, by annexation by the occupying power or another state after the end of the war. It is customary to mask the facts by the use of legal formulas, by claiming that the state retains its *Rechtsfähigkeit* and has lost only its *Handlungsfähigkeit*. But this is incorrect, or at least inaccurate. The state has also "perished" by the *occupatio bellica*, but is treated as being in existence for as long as this occupation lasts, and this thanks to the same principle of effectiveness to which it owes its end. For a situation is "effective" only so long as it lasts. But whether the power of the occupying state will last is always questionable during the war; at all events, it is not "firmly established." The legal order of the conquered state has lost its effectiveness through the occupation; the legal order of the occupying power has not yet gained effectiveness so long as the war continues. For this period, therefore, the occupied state remains in existence. But when the war has been terminated or, more exactly, at the cessation of hostilities, then the principle of effectiveness regains its power; the static nature of peace stabilizes the dynamic changes of war in the position in which it finds them. If the wholly occupied state remains in the hands of the victor, and if this victor intends to incorporate it, to extend its own territorial sphere of validity over the territory of the conquered state, and if it carries out this intention, then the new situation has become effective and the occupied state "no longer exists." For the rule of the victor is now "firmly established," and makes impossible, because unobtainable, every *als ob*, every fiction of continued existence. In Anglo-American literature this is expressed in the formula, "Annexation turns the conquest into subjugation,"[36] in which by subjugation is understood the legal annihilation of the enemy state. In essence, this is identical with the doctrine of Continental authors that the *debellatio* accomplishes the annihilation of the state only through the subsequent annexation.

Now, according to accepted doctrine there is war only when at least two opponents resort to the use of force, but not when an armed attack meets with no resistance, as in Austria.[37] Consideration of the grounds for this ruling, reached through international law, shows us, however, that it is of no importance whatever whether the occupation takes place in the course of a war or in connection with an armed invasion in time of peace. For a war too may be started contrary to existing obligations under international law, and it is then a breach of international law in just the same way as an unresisted invasion. Thus Kelsen writes:[38]

Provided that a unilateral act of force performed by one state against another is not considered to be war in itself (war being, according to traditional opinion, "a contention between two or more states through their armed forces"[39] and hence a bilateral action) *annexation is not only possible in time of war, but also in time of peace.*[40] The decisive point is that annexation, that is, taking possession of another state's territory with the intention to acquire it, constitutes acquisition of this territory even without the consent of the state to which the territory previously belonged, if the possession is firmly established. It makes no difference whether the annexation takes place after an *occupatio bellica* or not. . . . If the extension of the efficacy of a national legal order to the territorial sphere of validity of another national legal order, the efficacious annexation of the territory of one state by another state implies a violation of international law, [*sic*] the guilty state as pointed out exposes itself to the sanctions provided by general or particular international law. *The fact that the act of annexation is illegal does not prevent, however, the annexed territory from becoming part of the occupying State's territory,*[41] provided that the annexation is firmly established. *Ex injuria jus oritur.* This follows from the legal principle of effectiveness prevailing in International Law.

And likewise, Kelsen says: *"Nach dem Rechtsprinzip der Effektivität richten sich Beginn und Ende der Rechtsgeltung staatlicher Ordung."*[42] The very case mentioned by Kelsen above, namely, illegal annexation which nevertheless—because it is effective—causes the annexed territory to become part of the annexing state, clearly answers the question for Austria.

In its essence this was always a definite part of the doctrine of international law, for example, see Franz von Holtzendorff,[43] Karl Strupp,[44] and Christian Meurer;[45] similarly also Liszt-Fleischmann[46] who—rightly—simply declared the announcement of annexation before the establishment of effective rule over the annexed territory to be contrary to international law. Verdross,[47] however, considers the principle of effectiveness alone insufficient in the acquisition of territory as such, even when *animus domini* is present. "Der allein angerufene Grundsatz der Effektivität kann nämlich als Beweis nicht hinreichen, da die Effektivität nur in dem Rahmen neues Recht begründen kann, den ihr die Völkerrechtsordung anweist." But Verdross acknowledges *debellatio* as a title for acquisition and understands by it "die vollkommene Zerstörung der Staatsgewalt des besetzten Staates."[48] This, however, is nothing else than the loss of force *(Unwirksamwerden)* of the legal order of the occupied state, caused by the gaining of force *(Wirksamwerden),* that is, the effectiveness, of the legal order of the occupying state. Recognition of *debellatio* always implies recognition of the principle of effectiveness, only under another name. The position taken up by Verdross regarding this problem is obviously affected by considerations *de lege ferenda.* It is not in accordance with accepted international law.

The consequence of a breach of international law is always a sanction directed against the state[49] to which are imputed the actions which are contrary to international law. An annexation, as an actual occurrence, is divisible into a host of actions of individuals, the legality or illegality of which, taken together, varies according to that of the annexation itself. Such legality or illegality is then imputed to the state, and entitles other states to apply sanctions against the offender, and, indeed, in certain circumstances, oblige them to do so. Thereby, however, the annexation does not become "invalid." Only a norm can be "valid" or "invalid" —human behavior can not. It is quite permissible to speak of valid legislation, of a valid treaty, of a valid legal transaction, because the legal order sets up norms which lay down the conditions under which the creation of new norms may proceed. Should these conditions not be fulfilled, then we speak in this sense of invalid treaties, invalid laws, invalid legal transactions. Annexation is, however, not a procedure of law creation and still less is it a norm. It is human conduct, legal or illegal, and to be imputed to the state; in our case illegal and therefore an offense. Offenses, however, by their nature, can only be answered by a sanction. According to international law, this sanction is reprisal or war. Now Oppenheim-Lauterpacht[50] claim that unilateral actions, for example, annexation, taken contrary to international law, are "invalid" and can have no legal consequences. "In such cases the act in question *is tainted with invalidity and incapable of producing legal results*[51] beneficial to the wrongdoer in the form of a new title or otherwise." But Lauterpacht[52] has himself to admit: "An illegality cannot, as a rule, become a source of legal right to the wrongdoer. *This does not mean that it cannot produce any legal results at all* for it gives rise to a legal liability of the law-breaker . . ."[53] But that is precisely Kelsen's opinion. *Ex factis jus oritur,* even when the *facta* are illegal. Then the law breaker must simply bear the consequences of his offense, consequences which, because of the primitive nature of international law, can only be reprisal or war.

International law recognizes other cases, where the facts are similar. If a state goes to war when warfare is expressly prohibited, then it commits an offense, but the war is "war" in the legal sense—"a legal result"— and brings into force the *jus in bello.*

The vague formula of Oppenheim-Lauterpacht contained in the following: "Insofar as these instruments[54] prohibit war, they *probably*[55] [*sic*!] render invalid conquest on the part of the state which has resorted to war contrary to its obligations"[56] at best gives expression to a desideratum *de lege ferenda.* Legally it is untenable. For it fails to recognize that "conquest," that is, the extension of the victor's legal order, if effective, by its very nature *can* only be valid, for every national legal order is valid only by delegation from the superior legal order of international law; the latter, however, only permits the validity of the former as far as it is effective.[57] We shall not go far wrong if we take it that in Oppenheim-Lauterpacht's fundamentally dualistic position is to be found the reason for their irreconcilable contradiction.[58]

The list of authors who follow the same doctrine of the prevailing importance of the principle of effectiveness can be lengthened still more. Along with Fischer Williams there is now most recently Alf Ross. He writes:

> It follows from the effectivity principle that *the only fact* which can prove the acquisition of territory is the *lasting effective taking possession of it*. . . . In the case of a conquest by war the transition does not take place until the hostile resistance—from the enemy himself or his allies—has practically been finally put down.[59]

Let us now return to the object of our inquiry. Whether or not there was war on March 12, 1938, at all events there was peace from March 13 onward, and the rule of Germany was "firmly established" over all Austrian territory. The fact that a state of political tension continued which, as was latter shown, could at any time have turned into open conflict, makes no difference. *Inter pacem et bellum nihil est medium,* says Cicero. In positive law there is no reason to doubt this even today.[60] The best proof of this is the present world situation, which is frequently characterized by the expression "cold war." But who would think of doubting the effectiveness of the established orders, especially that of the two which stand opposite each other in this so-called cold war? Both are really "firmly established." War, in the sense relevant here, therefore, means war in the legal sense or actual hostilities. From March 13, 1938, until the outbreak of the Second World War there was neither war with Germany, nor did the latter become involved in actual hostilities during that period. The annexation of Austria was "firmly established"; the First Republic had ceased to exist. There is therefore no national identity with the present Austria.[61]

It is now of importance to inquire what position the rest of the world had taken up toward the events of March 12 and 13, 1938. That the occupation and annexation of Austria was a breach of international law on the part of Germany has been repeatedly stressed. Many states have given expression to this view, some even in the form of protests. However, and this deserves to be remembered, *no state* other than Austria herself has yet taken the view that Austria was not annexed nor formally incorporated. International practice and foreign literature on international law are unanimous in this.

Mexico's[62] protest speaks of the "political death of Austria" and of the fact that Austria "has ceased to exist as an independent nation," and, later, once again of the "death of its fatherland" when referring to the Austrian people. Chile's declaration speaks of the "disappearance of a member state of the League of Nations."[63] The Spanish delegate to the 19th session of the General Assembly of the League of Nations several times refers to the "disappearance of a member state."[64] At the same session, Litvinov spoke of the fact that Austria had "lost her independent existence," and that she had "disappeared."[65] Even the Austrian envoy in Washington announced that "Austria had ceased to exist as an independent nation and had been incorporated in the German Reich."[66] On March 16, 1938, Lord Halifax, then foreign minister of Great Britain, declared in the House of Lords: "The Government . . . are bound to recognise that the Austrian State has been abolished as a national entity and is in process of being completely absorbed into the German Reich."[67] Cordell Hull declared on July 27, 1942, that the United States had never recognized the "annexation" of Austria and once again expressly described it as "annexation."[68] Finally, the Moscow declaration of October 30, 1943, also contains the expression "annexation." Austria was to be "reëstablished" (*sic!*).[69] In Proclamation No. 1 of the Supreme Allied Commander of the Mediterranean theater of operations it is stated expressly that Austria had waged war "as an integral part of Germany."[70] Supplement C of the Nürnberg indictment frequently mentions "annexing" *(einverleiben),* referring to Germany and Austria, and once also mentions the compulsory "surrender of Austrian sovereignty."[71] The Nürnberg sentences speak of the "seizure" of Austria and of "annexation."[72] It is interesting to note there the abovementioned statement that Hitler himself, as early as 1937, spoke of "conquest and annexation" of Austria, which is of importance for the proof of Germany's intention of annexation. We may mention in passing that even the Austrian proclamation of April 27, 1945, twice contains the expression "annexation." In its declaration on Austria of October 28, 1946, the U.S. State Department similarly speaks of "formal incorporation," "Anschluss," and "annexation."[73] In a resolution of its 21st ordinary session on April 21, 1946,[74] the League of Nations, before its dissolution, in reply to Austria's intention of having herself represented as a member in the General Assembly on April 8, 1946, merely invited her to send observers. The preamble of the projected so-called international treaty likewise contains the declaration that "Austria was forcibly *annexed* by Hitler Germany on the 13th of March, 1938, and *incorporated* in the German State."[75]

To this overwhelming mass of proof taken from international practice can be added similar proof from literature. Thus Oppenheim-Lauterpacht state: "In 1938 Austria was *annexed* by Germany."[76] Guggenheim likewise says: "Österreich wurde 1938 von Deutschland *annektiert.*"[77] Lauterpacht speaks of the *"annexation* of Austria" and discusses the nature of the American and British recognition of this annexation.[78] In the same sense Fenwick in the *American Journal of International Law* wrote an article entitled "Fuit Austria." He calls the *Anschluss* "the *complete assimilation* of Austria into Germany." "Austria is henceforth to be a mere province of Germany . . . *treaties made with Austria come to an end.*"[79] In the same periodical and in the same year there appeared an essay by Garner on "Questions of state succession raised by the German *annexation* of Austria."[80] In the same volume of this periodical Garner wrote another, smaller, essay on "Germany's responsibility for Austria's debts."[81] Likewise in the *American Journal of International Law* Wright published an inquiry into "The Legality of *Annexation* of Austria by Germany."[82] Garner's first-named essay and that of Wright are the only foreign scientific inquiries[83] dealing with the subject—with the exception of Kelsen, of whom I shall speak later. Wright was only interested in the question of the legality of the annexation; in addition, he gives an analysis of the events of the decisive days. Garner describes the diplomatic activity between the United States and the German Reich; he also mentions the declaration of the last Austrian envoy in Washington, stating that Austria had ceased to exist as an independent nation and had been incorporated into the German Reich. Garner also states that the United States recognized the annexation of Austria—*de facto* on March 19, 1938 and *de jure* on April 6, of the same year. ("On March 19th, however, the Secretary of State issued a statement accepting as a fact the disappearance of Austria as an independent state, which was tantamount to a *de facto* recognition of the German annexation and, as stated above, this was followed by a formal *de jure* recognition on April 6th.")[84] He even speaks of a general recognition by states of the annexation in connection with the cessation of Austria's membership of the League of Nations (". . . the general recognition by states of the *annexation* of Austria to Germany and *its consequent extinction as a state* would seem to remove any possible basis for the contention that Austria any longer sustains even a *de jure* relation to the League.").[85] Of the international treaties concluded by Austria, Garner says:

Turning now to the effect of the *annexation* upon treaties of Austria and even upon those of Germany herself, we may note that among the treaties to which

Austria was a party at the time *her juridical existence as a state came to an end* were at least six with the United States. . . . The vast majority of writers on International Law who have discussed the subject maintain that treaties in such cases, subject to some possible exceptions to be discussed later,[86] are *automatically terminated by the act of annexation,* or at least are terminable at the option of the annexing states.[87]

After careful consideration of international practice and doctrine, he comes to the conclusion that all bilateral treaties concluded by Austria were canceled:

In the light of this practice and doctrine we venture the conclusion that *all bilateral treaties* between Austria and other states in force at the time of its annexation to the German Reich, unless there be some which establish obligations inseparable from the territory *will have to be recognized as terminated* in case Germany elects to so regard them.[88]

Garner's view that the United States had, *de facto* and *de jure,* recognized the annexation[89] is, however, not shared by Lauterpacht.[90] In any event, however, there are American decisions which describe the question as controversial;[91] one even states: "The Anschluss has in no wise been disavowed by the Department of State."[92]

However, according to all the doctrine that has been pronounced so far—which, as can be seen, is by no means represented only by authors under Kelsen's influence but which has received its scientific basis from him—it is not the recognition which is important. Kelsen says:[93]

A State may declare "not to recognize" [*sic*] the annexation of another State by a third State because the annexation involves a violation of International Law. If, however, the annexation is effective, that is to say, firmly established, the government of the non-recognizing State cannot maintain that the incorporated community still exhibits all the elements essential to a State in the sense of International Law. *Then, the 'non-recognition' cannot imply the opinion of the non-recognizing government that the illegally incorporated community continues to exist as an independent State.*[94] The 'non-recognition' may have a political significance. It may express a certain disapproval on the part of the non-recognizing government and its wish to see the illegally annexed community restored as an independent State. *To impute to such a non-recognition the meaning that the community concerned has not ceased to exist as a State implies a fiction, in contradiction to legal reality determined by the principle of effectiveness.*[95]

Likewise Guggenheim, when discussing nonrecognition in international practice, says: "Die tatsächlichen Verhältnisse erwiesen sich stärker als der Grundsatz der Nichtanerkennung gewaltsamer Veränderungen des Staatsgebietes."[96] We are dealing with nothing else than a postulate *de lege ferenda,* the basis of which is to be sought in the absence of the obligations of states to recognize changes in the territorial sphere of validity of other states. The Kellogg pact gave the further impetus to the development of nonrecognition, the most successful manifestation of which was the so-called Stimson Doctrine. But even it, and the well-known resolution of the League of Nations General Assembly of March 11, 1932 were unable to effect the carrying out in practice of the nonrecognition of Manchukuo. As was stated earlier: The primitive nature of positive international law permits no such solution.

Even the declaration of nonrecognition contained in the Moscow Declaration has no other significance. To this Kelsen says:[97]

> The refusal by the Powers in the Moscow Declaration to recognize the annexation of Austria by Germany has hardly more than a political character. Nonrecognition of the annexation means that the Powers are willing to restore a legal status which, in their opinion, has been changed illegally; *but this nonrecognition cannot alter the fact that at the moment of Germany's surrender the former Austrian territory will still be an integral part of the German Reich. That Austria never ceased to exist as an independent state is a political fiction which will be very difficult to maintain at the moment of Germany's surrender,* since at this time no Austrian government will probably exist.[98]

The attempt to replace the principle of effectiveness, a principle inherent in the international legal order, by that of legality—for that is fundamentally our question—must always fail so long as no world state exists. But then there would be no longer international law. Yet only then could the principle of effectiveness be eliminated from the legal relations of the national legal orders subordinated to the world government. The world government itself, that is, the world legal order whose supreme organ it would be, would in turn only be based upon the fact that it is—as a whole—efficacious, that is, once again simply upon the principle of effectiveness!

This is the crux of all international legal problems and there can be no avoiding it. It is also decisive in the case in question. One of the many consequences of this is that Austria is not bound by treaties concluded by the First Republic and has to assume no obligations which were imposed on it.

So far little has been published in Austria itself about the problems emerging from a consideration of her present international status. The control agreements,[99] and the four-power declarations in connection with them, have not yet been the subject of theoretical legal inquiry; the preliminary question, that of the legal judgment of the events of March, 1938, has to date been scientifically tackled twice.[100] In 1947 Verosta contributed a short introduction to his *Quellensammlung*,[101] in which he endeavors to base the theory of occupation, in its essentials, upon the claim that there has arisen a new norm of customary international law which states that the international personality (*Völkerrechtsobjektivität*) or a state does not perish, even if the occupation lasts for a long time—indeed several years—irrespective of whether the occupation took place in peace or in war.[102] He tries to give proof of this claim by analogous quotation of the principle of international law according to which constitutional changes, whether brought about by peaceful or by revolutionary means, have no influence upon the international personality of the state in question. In other words, this principle means that a legal order is to be recognized as a state in the sense of international law for that territory within which its norms find general obedience. This principle is, however, nothing else than the expression of the principle of effectiveness, which Verosta claims to apply "analogously" to the state occupied *animo domini* in time of peace. Logically, however, this application must lead to the conclusion that the state ceases to exist, and not the contrary!

Finally, when Verosta tries to prove that the three so-called elements of the state—territory, people, and power—were preserved, it may well be objected that the modern theory of international law has learned to regard "territory" as being the territorial sphere of validity of the legal order. To describe the people as "Austrian" simply means, from a legal standpoint, that they were subject to the Austrian legal order; and this was certainly not the case for the period 1938–1945. That it also remained "physically identical"—in reality this is quite impossible—has nothing to do with the problem of the identity of the state. Finally, that large parts of the Austrian legal order remained untouched cannot, legally, be seriously maintained. The legal order is a system of norms, which is either valid or invalid, and the validity of the system depends upon the fact that it is effective as a whole. The fact that former Austrian laws were left in force by the German legal order means no more than an adoption, a technical measure which caused certain norms of the earlier state, by virtue of their grounds for validity, to become part of the new legal order. Verosta's attempt to prove the "existence" of Austria from 1938 till 1945 must therefore be classed as a failure.

The April, 1950, issue of the Austrian *Monatshefte* contained an extensive inquiry *von besonderer Seite* into the same subject.[103] In that part of his argument which deals with international law, the anonymous author relies essentially upon a passage in Verdross[104] (which I discussed in detail above) and upon the arguments of Oppenheim-Lauterpacht[105] concerning the "invalidity" of the acquisition of territory contrary to international law. However, they contradict the generally accepted principle of effectiveness—the governing principle of international law; it is only necessary here to refer to the above detailed refutation of these authorities. Quite incomprehensible is the anonymous author's statement that Germany had issued no declaration of annexation. A clearer one than the words "Austria is a Province of the German Reich" can scarcely be imagined. It is equally untrue that the recognition of Austria after 1945 applied only to her government. Only a *de facto* government can be recognized. The present Austrian government, however, did not come to power through the interruption of the national legal continuity, but owes its position to the unanimous will of the four powers.

Lastly, Werner's attempt[106] to prove the legal continuity from the standpoint of the internal legal order does not agree with the logic of law. For it is not for the internal legal order, but for international law alone, to establish the norms for the beginning and end of its (the internal legal order's) validity. That a law contains a formula revealing that its authors have proceeded from the theory of legal continuity is of no importance. Such statements—like their opposites—deny the primacy of international law, from which our own positive legal order is also derived.[107] Recognition of this primacy, however, is the logical and legal consequence of the principle of effectiveness. To have pointed this out is one of the many outstanding services rendered by Kelsen,[108] whose voice should not have been allowed to go unheard in that same Vienna in which "the greatest jurist of the XXth century"[109] began his career, and where he founded his Vienna School.

EDVARD HAMBRO

A Case of Development of International Law Through the International Court of Justice

THE INTERNATIONAL COURT of Justice is more closely linked with the United Nations than was the Permanent Court of International Justice with the League of Nations. The present court is the principal judicial organ of the organization. Great interest surrounded the establishment of the court and the election of its members. Yet, although the members were elected in February, 1946, the first case was brought before the court only on May 22 the following year. In retrospect, it seems strange that a delay of less than a year and a half should have seemed so long. No great concern seems justified, as some hesitation was to be expected before states used this new organ, and two years is not a very long period in the history of an international organization. However, even at that time it was feared that the judicial organ of the organization would be completely silenced by the use of the political organs of the United Nations, and during the second session of the General Assembly in New York in 1947 a resolution was adopted, on the proposal of the Australian delegation, in which the General Assembly, recommended *inter alia:*

> . . . that organs of the United Nations and the Specialized Agencies should, from time to time, review the difficult and important points of law within the jurisdiction of the International Court of Justice which have arisen in the course of their activities and involve questions of principle which it is desirable to have settled, including points of law relating to the interpretation of the Charter of the United Nations or the constitutions of the Specialized Agencies,

and, if duly authorized according to Article 96, paragraph 2, of the Charter, should refer them to the International Court of Justice for an advisory opinion.

It is interesting to note the first recital in the resolution: "Considering that it is a responsibility of the United Nations to encourage the progressive development of International Law."

Nobody would object to this consideration, but it might be asked whether it was necessary or even natural to include it in a recommendation concerning greater use of the court.

It might be argued that this particular field is covered by Article 13 of the Charter, which entrusts the responsibility of developing international law to the General Assembly. That body has instituted an international law commission for this very purpose. Is it really the duty of the International Court of Justice to develop international law? Is not such a concept incompatible with the structure of the organization? Is it not even contrary to the Charter? Is it not contrary to the usual function of a court of law? Would it not be wiser to state that the main function of a court is not to develop law but simply to apply the law as it is? Article 38 of the statute states in particular that the function of the court "is to decide in accordance with international law." Therefore one would perhaps to a certain degree be justified in saying that the only duty of the court is to find out what international law is. This attitude would, however, be very restrictive indeed, and it would not be in conformity with the realities of international life or with the essence of any law since law is always a function of the community. International public law is the law of the international community, a turbulent, alive, constantly changing community. Law changes and develops with the community in which it functions. In that way law is dependent on the political, social, and economic trends in society. On the other hand, law in its turn influences the changes in that community. This was stated with admirable clarity by the court in its advisory opinion on reparation for injuries suffered in the service of the United Nations: "Throughout its history, the development of international law has been influenced by the requirements of international life and the progressive increase in the collective activities of States has already given rise to instances of action upon the international plane by certain entities which are not States."[1] New situations arise and new rules must be molded to suit them. A law that could not be adapted to changing circumstances would be a dangerous law indeed. There is a constant tension in every law between the static element—the need for security which creates stability—and the progressive element which responds to the changes in society. These two tendencies are intensified in the law of nations. The static element is strengthened by the fact that most of the subjects are states, whose sovereignty must be spared, and because great prudence must be shown in the creation of judge-made law when the parties to a lawsuit are states, since the states might show a certain reluctance to accept a judgment based on "new" law, and since enforcement action should be resorted to very rarely. On the other hand, the need for judge-made law is greater where there is no real legislative body. The creation of law by judges takes more often than not the form of interpretation of treaties.

Professor Kelsen, who probably has done more to encourage clear thinking in the international-law profession than any other writer in this generation and who has aroused stronger loyalties and greater hostility than any other founder of a school in the field of law has written searchingly on interpretations:

> The view, however, that the verbal expression of a legal norm has only one "true" meaning which can be discovered by correct interpretation is a fiction, adopted to maintain the illusion of legal security, to make the law-seeking public believe that there is only one possible answer to the question of law in a concrete case. Unfortunately, the contrary is true. That there is almost always a possible interpretation different from that adopted by the law-applying organ in a concrete case, is made clear by the practice of courts, such as the Permanent Court of International Justice and the International Court of Justice, which publish both majority and dissenting opinions. In examining the decisions of these Courts one must inevitably conclude that in most cases the arguments of the dissenting judges are logically at least, equal in value to those which motivate the majority decision of the Court.[2]

The abundant literature on the interpretation of the Charter of the United Nations has shown beyond the shadow of a doubt that different meanings may be attributed to the same paragraph and that a legal term may have one meaning in one provision of the Charter and quite a different meaning in another. Furthermore, it is not excluded that exactly the same meaning may be covered by different expressions in different parts of the Charter. This has also very clearly been brought out by Professor Kelsen:

> The fact that the legal norms as formulated in words having frequently more than one meaning is the reason why every legal instrument has its own life, more or less independent of the wishes and expectations of its begetters. That the law is open to more than one interpretation is certainly detrimental to legal security; but it has the advantage of making the law adaptable to changing circumstances, without the requirement of formal alteration.[3]

It is reasonable—we submit—to use the same basic principles in the interpretation of the Charter as in the interpretation of any other legal document, whether the Charter be called a treaty or a constitution.

Prolonged and detailed discussions took place at the San Francisco conference concerning the interpretation of the Charter, and a resolution was adopted envisaging as one possibility the request for advisory opinions by the International Court of Justice. The relevant San Francisco document states:

> If two Member States are at variance concerning the correct interpretation of the Charter, they are of course free to submit the dispute to the International Court of Justice as in the case of any other treaty. Similarly, it would always be open to the General Assembly or to the Security Council, in appropriate circumstances, to ask the International Court of Justice for an advisory opinion concerning the meaning of a provision of the Charter.[4]

It is true that an advisory opinion of the International Court of Justice is not legally binding on the other organs of the United Nations or on the members of the organization. It is, therefore, not correct to call such an opinion an "authentic interpretation." It is, indeed, doubtful whether one can ever talk about an authentic interpretation, since, if the interpretation is really binding, it is in fact a new law-creating act. Kelsen says:

> Authentic interpretation, whether general or individual, is a law-creating act. This is obvious in case of a general interpretation made by the legislator, but an act of individual interpretation has also a law-creating character. The decision of a judicial or administrative authority applying a general norm—which has several meanings—to a concrete case can correspond only to one of these meanings and must thus exclude the others. It is by the decision that one of several meanings of the applied norm becomes binding in the concrete case; and it is mainly, although not only with respect to its interpretative function that a judicial or administrative decision has a law-creating character.
>
> The meaning of a legal norm which becomes binding by authentic—general or individual—interpretation is neither more nor less 'true' than the other meanings, excluded by this interpretation. By authentic interpretation any meaning of the norm thus interpreted may become binding. Hence, the function of authentic interpretation is not to determine the true meaning of the legal norm thus interpreted, but to render binding one of the several meanings of a legal norm, all equally possible from a logical point of view.[5]

When the International Court is called upon to give an interpretation of a stipulation of the Charter, the opinion it renders is important in two different ways. First, it settles—or it is hoped that it settles—a dispute concerning the application of the stipulation in question. Second it creates law. It lays down rules of interpretation, it improves the technique of international law and thereby develops the law. It may, indeed, be that the law-creating function of the court in the long run is more important than the actual decisions. The pronouncements of the court whether in contentious or advisory cases have importance far above the actual disputes, important though the latter may be.

It may be difficult to select one case submitted to the court as being preëminently a contribution to the development of international law. On the other hand, it will probably not be out of place for a student of international law to show a certain preference for one case even though recognizing that all the cases decided by the court have been of fundamental importance.

The most characteristic example of progressive development of international law so far, is, in the opinion of this writer, the advisory opinion on reparation for injuries suffered in the service of the United Nations. It is fitting, therefore, to make a few comments on that decision in order to illustrate the approach which the court has taken to some of the more important aspects of the constitutional law of the community of nations, as it is today.

The questions put to the court by the General Assembly in the resolution of December 3, 1948, were:

I. In the event of an agent of the United Nations in the performance of his duties suffering injury in circumstances involving the responsibility of a State, has the United Nations, as an Organization, the capacity to bring an international claim against the responsible *de jure* or *de facto* government with a view to obtaining the reparation due in respect of the damage caused (a) to the United Nations, (b) to the victim or to persons through him?
II. In the event of an affirmative reply on point I (b), how is action by the United Nations to be reconciled with such rights as may be possessed by the State of which the victim is a national?[6]

The court gave its decision on April 11, 1949. The attitude of the court was revealed in the very beginning of the opinion where it is stated that "the Court understands the word *agent* in the most liberal sense."[7] The leitmotif thus introduced in the overture is ever recurring in different forms.

The first question that the court was called upon to answer was whether the organization could be regarded as possessing international legal personality. There can be no doubt that the organization possesses legal personality in regard to the national law of the members of the organization. That is quite clearly stated in Article 104 of the Charter. But no definite rule was laid down in the Charter concerning the international legal personality of the organization. The reason for this may be that it was self-evident that the organization had international personality. A formal article to this effect might have been "another glimpse of the obvious." Or the reason might have been the opposite. In all probability, the explanation is that nobody thought a formal statement either way worth a real fight. It is quite obvious that it is possible for an organization to possess national but not international legal personality.

The court approached its examination of this problem in the most practical and progressive spirit. It stated that this question was not answered by the actual terms of the Charter and that it was necessary to consider what characteristics were intended to be given to the organization. The court, furthermore, stated that it was possible for the subjects of law in any legal system to be different in their nature or in the extent of their rights. It stated that these rights and the nature of the legal personality would depend upon the needs of the community. After having examined the aims and functions of the organization, the court came unanimously to the conclusion that the organization has international personality. It stated:

> In the opinion of the Court, the Organization was intended to exercise and enjoy, and is in fact exercising and enjoying, functions and rights which can only be explained on the basis of the possession of a large measure of international personality and the capacity to operate upon an international plane. It is at present the supreme type of international organization, and it could not carry out the intentions of its founders if it was devoid of international personality. It must be acknowledged that its Members, by entrusting certain functions to it, with the attendant duties and responsibilities, have clothed it with the competence required to enable those functions to be effectively discharged.[8]

It seems difficult to dispute the fact that the court has, in this instance, accepted a functional or sociological conception of international law. Instead of examining who are subjects of international law on the basis of old precepts or established doctrine, the court approached the question from the other end. Instead of asking in the abstract what constitutes legal personality, it asked which powers must be given to the international organization in order to make it fulfill its task or its functions. Thereby, the court also expressed in very clear terms the rule of effectiveness as a guiding principle of interpretation. After having examined the character of the organization, the court ends this part of its opinion with the following words:

> The functions of the Organization are of such a character that they could not be effectively discharged if they involved the concurrent action, on the international plane, of fifty-eight or more Foreign Offices, and the Court concludes that the Members have endowed the Organization with capacity to bring international claims when necessitated by the discharge of its functions.[9]

Having thus cleared the ground for the positive and constructive solution of the problems before it, the court examined the possibility of protecting agents and of claiming reparation for the damage suffered by the organization in the person of its agents. After having stated that the organization may clearly sue for damages if the loss has been sustained by itself, the court proceeds to examine whether the organization can claim damages suffered not by itself, but by its agents. In this particular field also the court breaks new ground. In traditional international law, individuals are protected not as individuals, but as subjects of a state. The protection extended to them is therefore generally known as "diplomatic protection of citizens." Now, in this particular case, it is quite obvious that the protection could not be called "protection of citizens" because the organization would not protect its own citizens, there being no citizenship of the United Nations. Furthermore, it might be stated that the protection would not be diplomatic, since the organization does not possess a diplomatic corps, in the old meaning of the phrase. The court quite openly recognized this, and stated that a new situation had in fact arisen and that it must be examined in a new way, but on the basis of recognized principles of international law.

The court started by inquiring whether the provisions of the Charter concerning the functions of the organization and the part to be played by its agents implied the power to protect the agents by bringing claims on their behalf for the damage they might have suffered in the performance of their duties.

The cardinal principle laid down by the court was that:

> Under international law, the Organization must be deemed to have those powers which, though not expressly provided in the Charter, are conferred upon it by necessary implication as being essential to the performance of its duties. This principle of law was applied by the Permanent Court of International Justice to the International Labour Organization in its Advisory Opinion No. 13 of July 23rd, 1926 (Series B., No. 13, p. 18), and must be applied to the United Nations.[10]

In the passages immediately following, the court stated that the organization in actual fact had found it necessary to entrust agents with important and dangerous missions which involved great personal dangers. The court also found that the damage thus suffered often would be of such a character and have happened under such circumstances that the national governments of the agents would feel reluctant to take any steps for the protection of the agent or for collecting any reparation due to him. The most striking pronouncement in the whole opinion is probably the following:

> Upon the examination of the character of the functions entrusted to the Organization and of the nature of the missions of its agents, it becomes clear that the capacity of the Organization to exercise a measure of functional protection of its agents arises by necessary intendment out of the Charter.[11]

It would be superfluous to stress that here again the court followed the functional approach to international law. The court has cut through old traditions and helped actively in the creation of international law.

It has been seen now that the court has increased the strength of the organization as a subject of international law, that it has applied the functional interpretation of law and reinforced the principle of effectiveness as a guiding rule of interpretation; but this opinion has broken new ground also in two other fields of international law.

The agents of the United Nations are protected by the organization, and they are protected as agents and not as citizens. The court has stated that the nationality of the agent is irrelevant for this purpose. Whether his state be weak or strong, great or small, the protection extended to him will be the same. The principle that the agent is protected as agent and not as a citizen of a nation state leads to the protection of stateless persons in the same way as citizens of a member state. Furthermore, not only will stateless persons be protected, but an individual will also be protected even if the damage he has suffered has been caused by the state of which he is a citizen. It seems clear that thereby the importance of the individual in international law has been recognized to an extent which has never happened before.

The court was also called upon to examine the relationship of the organization to third-party states. It stated:

> Accordingly, the question is whether the Organization has capacity to bring a claim against the defendant State to recover reparation in respect of that damage or whether, on the contrary, the defendant State, not being a member, is justified in raising the objection that the Organization lacks the capacity to bring an international claim. On this point, the Court's opinion is that fifty States, representing the vast majority of the members of the international community, had the power, in conformity with international law, to bring into being an entity possessing objective international personality, and not merely personality recognized by them alone, together with the capacity to bring international claims.[12]

This statement is of great theoretical interest as it clearly indicates that a multilateral treaty like the Charter of the United Nations may be binding also on third-party states. Another of the traditional concepts of international law has thus been given a death blow. It will, in the future, be more difficult than ever before to contend seriously that treaties can never confer rights or impose obligations on third-party states.

I believe that, in the future, this decision of the court will be referred to more and more, as it contains an astonishing amount of progressive, restatements of international law—if such a term will not be considered self-contradictory. This advisory opinion shows very clearly that the

International Court of Justice is fully aware of the need for, and the possibility of, developing international law so that it shall not become a strait jacket to stop, prevent, or slow down the beneficial development of international law concepts. Thereby the court has taken its place at the front of the organs which will make of international law in the future a living, growing body of rules, developing in accordance with the dynamic necessities of the present-day international community.

The court—as all courts—had to choose between a conservative and static view and a progressive and dynamic one. Kelsen has said: "The choice of interpretation as a law-making act is determined by political motives. It is not the logically 'true,' it is the politically preferable meaning of the interpreted norm which becomes binding."[13]

If the word "political" is taken in its widest sense, this statement under the pen of the founder of the Pure Theory of Law seems unobjectionable. As a lawmaker, the judge must needs be influenced by "meta-juridical" arguments. Very often he has the choice between a static and conservative conception on the one hand and a dynamic and progressive interpretation on the other. It augurs well for the future of international law that the most august law applying body in the world in this important case has chosen the progressive way.

ALWYN V. FREEMAN

The Political Powers of the OAS Council

WHILE THE SECURITY COUNCIL of the United Nations has enjoyed the prominent headlines which its paramount position in a world of tension assures it, another council, less heralded and sometimes even unnoticed, is quietly but effectively building the foundations of a more harmonious society in the Western Hemisphere. Sitting continuously in Washington and prepared to cope with new problems as they emerge, the Council of the Organization of American States has already found a way to dampen the fires of potential conflict in at least two instances. Events of the past few years have gone far toward confirming the aspirations of Bogotá. However loosely knit the structural organization of this regional unit may be, however restricted may appear the influence of the Council in comparison with that of the Security Council, nevertheless in one significant respect the OAS is rooted in a foundation of greater strength and stability than the United Nations—the elements of solidarity which unite the American republics in a common brotherhood and purpose far beyond that yet achieved by the San Francisco Charter.

In executing those functions assigned to the Council of the OAS by instruments which define its activities, the inevitable question of the extent of its jurisdiction ultimately arose—as it did with the Security Council. The thorny problem of the OAS Council's powers was painstakingly examined at the first meeting of the Inter-American Council of Jurists held at Rio de Janeiro, May 22–June 15, 1950. This topic had been placed on the agenda of the meeting by a resolution of the Council of the OAS requesting its legal organ (the Council of Jurists) to prepare a technical study which would assist the parent body in disposing of issues of a political character such as that raised in two notes from the

Chilean and Guatemalan governments concerning former President Betancourt's political asylum in the Colombian embassy at Carácas. After the Venezuelan representative had challenged the Council's jurisdiction to examine the question, it was submitted to a subcommittee which proposed that the Council of Jurists be asked for its views.[1] At Rio, however, the latter body was unable to complete its deliberations on the general topic by the close of the conference, nor reach agreement on the formulation of basic principles to guide the Council. It was, accordingly, resolved (Resolution XII) that study of the subject should be continued at the Council of Jurists' second meeting to be held in Buenos Aires.[2]

Thus the question of the Council's powers radiates more than a mere academic interest. It is in fact its practical aspects which are of such great importance to the nations of the Western Hemisphere, whose governments have vested in a permanent body attributes that profoundly affect their mutual relations.

Historical Background of the Council: The Governing Board of the Pan American Union.—While the general prerogatives of the Council are set forth in provisions of the charter of the Organization of American States signed at Bogotá on May 2, 1948,[3] an accurate evaluation of those prerogatives can only be made in the light of other international instruments incorporated into the charter by reference (Article 50), together with an examination of the preëxisting powers of the governing board of the Pan American Union, which was supplanted by the Council at Bogotá. It is useful, therefore, to discuss at the outset the evolution of functions formerly vested in the governing board so that the Council's new, enlarged role may be viewed in just perspective.

I

The outstanding characteristic of the resolutions and agreements under which the Pan American Union operated during its first fifty years' existence was the nonattribution to that institution of so-called "political" functions. Its modest aims hardly went beyond those of a clearing house of information. Early in its history serious apprehensions were manifested against entrusting political powers to an international agency which could handle possible future questions of indeterminate gravity. This reluctance to create an effective body with jurisdiction over disputes and problems of a political complexion persisted until World War II, and, indeed, was not confined to nations in the Western Hemisphere. Constantly nourishing it was a zealous desire within the

American republics to safeguard their sovereignty and freedom of action, a consideration which was as vital for the United States of America as for the other governments.[4] But whatever the basic reasons inspiring such diffidence, originally the Pan American Union was installed as a simple medium for the collection and distribution of commercial information.

By a resolution of the first International Conference of American States (1889–1890) a Commercial Bureau of the American Republics was established in Washington for the "collection, tabulation, and publication . . . of information as to the productions and commerce, and as to the customs, laws, and regulations of their respective countries."[5] Such continued to be the normal role of the bureau, despite subsequent revisions in its nomenclature, procedure, and management. At the second conference of American states in Mexico City (1901–1902) its administration and control were placed in the hands of a governing board, consisting of the secretary of state of the United States as chairman, and the diplomatic representatives of member states accredited to Washington.[6] A resolution of the third conference at Rio de Janeiro (1906) broadened and delineated more precisely the activities of the bureau with respect to reporting and distributing commercial information, and directed it to "prepare reports on questions assigned to it by the resolutions of International American Conferences; to assist in obtaining the ratification of the resolutions and conventions adopted by the Conference; [and] to carry into effect all resolutions the execution of which may be assigned to it by the . . . Conferences." A further power to act as the permanent committe of the conference[7] was confirmed at the fifth conference of Santiago, in 1923 with modifications.[8] The resolution was reënacted with minor changes at the fourth conference in Buenos Aires (1910), vesting control of the now "Pan American Union" in a governing board consisting of the diplomatic representatives of all governments accredited to Washington and the secretary of state of the United States. A government not so represented was entitled to designate a member of the board to act for it. Article XV of the same resolution provided that the Pan American Union should be governed by the regulations prepared by the governing board in accordance with the resolution, rather than as previously formulated by the 1906 conference.[9]

The composition of the governing board was fundamentally modified at the fifth conference in Santiago. It was agreed that the governing board could thereafter elect its own president and vice-president. More important, a provision was adopted (Article V of the resolution on organization of the Pan American Union) giving to any American republic not having a diplomatic representative accredited to Washington, the right to appoint a special representative on the governing board.[10] This provision grew out of a proposal by the Costa Rican delegation which would have vested the government of the Pan American Union in a board composed of representatives of the American governments accredited to the Pan American Union. Considerable dissatisfaction had existed with the formula of membership in the union theretofore prevailing, as it not only operated to disenfranchise a nation not enjoying relations with the United States but also unduly restricted the rights of member states to name those whom they desired to serve on the board.

It seems important to observe that the Costa Rican proposal (which was made the subject of a recommendation for further study and presentation by the governing board of a draft resolution or convention to the sixth conference)[11] aimed at the establishment of the governing board as a separate organization. Discussion of the proposal revealed that one of its purposes was to transform the board into the nucleus of a possible future council of an American League of Nations. Support for the Costa Rican proposal was given, wholly or in part, by the delegations of Colombia, Cuba, Guatemala, Haiti, Honduras, Panama, El Salvador, Santo Domingo, and Venezuela;[12] but the United States delegation thought it would be both unwise and impracticable to set up a separate political body to deal with Pan American Affairs.

Another resolution of the same conference entrusted to the governing board the special task of studying the bases which may be proposed by one or more of the governments of the republics "to make their mutual association closer and in order to promote common interests."[13] Two eminent Latin American publicists consider that the change effected at Santiago marked a turning point in the union's history, toward formation of an American League of Nations;[14] but this rather premature appraisal seems to be somewhat clouded by developments at the sixth conference of Havana in 1928. Here, finally, the regime of the Pan American Union came under the aegis of a formal convention. At the same time the conference went out of its way to refute the notion that the union was either a superstate, or that it enjoyed functions of a "political character." In the preamble to this convention the "moral union" of the American republics is declared to rest upon their juridical equality and on the "mutual respect of the rights inherent in their complete independence." Then follows a statement of their desire to promote efficaciously "the increasing conciliation of their economic interests and coordination of their social and intellectual activities" for which purpose the parties agree "to continue their joint action of cooperation and solidarity by means of . . . organs established by virtue of international agreements and through the Pan American Union." The impact of the Costa Rican proposal at Santiago was manifested in Article 3 which vested the government of the union in a board "composed of the representatives that the American Governments may appoint." But the most significant part of the convention is Article 6 which begins as follows: "Both the Governing Board and the Pan American Union shall discharge the duties assigned by this Convention *subject to the condition that they shall not exercise functions of a political character.*"[15]

Under paragraphs 1–4 the union is directed:

1) to compile and distribute information and reports concerning the commercial, industrial, agricultural, social and educational development as well, as the general progress of the American Republics; 2) to compile and classify information referring to the conventions and treaties concluded among the American Republics and between these and other States; 3) to assist in the development of commercial, industrial, agricultural, social and cultural relations, the study of the problems of labor and the furtherance of a more intimate mutual acquaintance between the American Republics; and 4) to act as a Permanent Commission of the International Conferences of American States . . . to assist in obtaining ratification of the treaties and conventions; to carry out and facilitate the execution of the resolutions adopted by the International Conferences of American States, within the limits of its powers; and to prepare in agreement with the Governments the program of the International Conferences of American States."[16]

Now, however, after having posited the flat prohibition against political functions and restated the specific duties to be performed by the union, paragraph 5 of this article declares that the organization shall:

perform such other functions entrusted to it by the Conference or by the Governing Board, by virtue of the powers conferred upon it by this convention. *Whenever a State believes that its vital interests are involved in a question, or that an obligation may thereby be imposed upon it, such State may require that the resolution of the Board be adopted by unanimous vote.*

The draftsmanship of several parts of this article is, to be charitable, somewhat bewildering. Paragraph 5 when read in conjunction with the positive prohibition against "political functions" must surely kindle disputes over interpretation. Aside from the fact that nowhere in the convention is that unhappy phrase defined,[17] it is difficult to see how the union could "assist in the development of commercial, industrial, agricultural, social and cultural relations . . . and the furtherance of a more initmate mutual acquaintance between the . . . Republics" without coming suspiciously close to precincts which, today at least, are considered to be tinged with a political color.

Still more curious is the "vital interests" provision of paragraph 5, which by implication virtually emasculates the prohibition with which Article 6 opens. Just what interests of a state would be "vital" without being "political" is not immediately apparent. If, in the performance of its functions the governing board may enter into matters involving a state's vital interests, then, to that extent, it is exercising a political function; and this technical attribution is none the less real because of the requirement of unanimity, even though the obvious consequence would be that action taken by the board would not be obligatory upon a state without the latter's consent.

But whatever the effect of these contradictory provisions, they failed to attain the stature of a treaty norm because the convention itself never received the requisite ratification. On the other hand, the prohibition against political functions (which originally had been sponsored by the Mexican delegation) was incorporated in a resolution of the same conference containing provisions concerning the organization of the Pan American Union which were to remain in force pending approval of the convention. This resolution made immediately operative the more important modifications contained in the convention, including changes in the method of appointing members to the governing board.[18]

Although not always discernible, the increasing tasks assigned to the Pan American Union and reports of prior conferences give evidence in reality that two competing forces had begun to influence the evolution of Pan-Americanism. One was the realization that the interests of all republics would be better served by a more closely knit organization patterned to some degree after its Geneva counterpart, which would be better adapted to the needs of the American community. The other was the traditional reluctance to surrender sovereign powers to an international agency, as already noted earlier in this study. In this connection, it is perhaps neither fair nor accurate to say that the Latin American republics were hostile to the vesting of political powers as such in an international organization; for in fact many had assented to the solution of political disputes in the covenant of the League of Nations, whereas it was the United States of America which, during that period, steadfastly refused to do so. It must be remembered that much of the fuel generating the second force we have referred to came from the fear that an American political agency would be converted into an instrument for intervention by stronger powers into the domestic or foreign affairs of the weaker. Since that fear has gradually been dispelled by repeated denials of the right of intervention in conventions and resolutions dating from the seventh conference at Montevideo,[19] the force itself slowly has diminished. This plus the changing facts of international life compel the conclusion that the wave of sentiment against vesting political functions in the union reached its high-water mark at Havana and has steadily receded thereafter despite an occasional resurgence.

The seventh conference at Montevideo (1933) limited itself to a statement (Resolution LXIV) that the program of the eighth international conference should include the topic of possible modifications of the organization of the Pan American Union with a view to rendering its operation more effective.[20] Three years later occurred the Inter-American Conference for the Maintenance of Peace at Buenos Aires which adopted two treaties and eight conventions, an additional protocol relative to nonintervention and sixty-two resolutions, recommendations, and declarations, embracing a variety of matters from the maintenance and preservation of peace to artistic and cultural coöperation.[21] The result was to increase substantially the work load of the union, impelling the conference to adopt Resolution LIV recognizing that proper fulfillment of the instruments adopted at Buenos Aires required greater scope to be given to its functions and requesting the governing board to make a study thereon for presentation to the eighth conference.[22]

Two projects for the creation of an American League of Nations had been presented to the 1936 conference, one by Colombia, the other by the Dominican Republic. Neither was approved on the ground that the topic was not yet ripe for consideration in view of the complexities it presented. Nevertheless, it was resolved to include the subject in the program of the eighth conference at Lima, the Colombian and Dominican governments which had drafted projects being urged to come to an agreement and to consult with the other states with a view to presenting a report on it.[23] This was done, the two governments submitting a joint draft in March, 1938, to the Pan American Union for presentation to the Lima conference. However, at Lima it was decided to refer the project to the International Conference of American Jurists for more thorough study and another report to the Pan American Union, as the basis of action at the ninth international conference[24]—action which the Panamanian delegation at Bogotá described as purely evasive measures.[25]

Although the Lima conference gave further impetus to the steadily expanding range of activities of the union,[26] no major departure from its basically apolitical role took place until the Inter-American Conference on Problems of Peace and War at Mexico City in 1945. After Mexico City it became increasingly difficult to demonstrate the absolute incapacity of the central organ of the inter-American system in political matters, always, of course, in accordance with such directives as might be given it by the conferences. This does not signify that the opposing trend had lost all its vitality. It was in evidence both at Mexico City and at Rio and had not unconditionally surrendered at Bogotá. Certainly the vagueness of the formula adopted in 1945 did not settle the problem. It was worded as follows (Resolution IX):

In addition to its present functions the Governing Board of the Pan American Union

a) Shall take action, within the limitations imposed upon it by the International Conference of American States or pursuant to the specific direction of the Meetings of Ministers of Foreign Affairs, *on every matter that affects the effective functioning of the Inter-American system and the solidarity and general welfare of the American Republics.*[27]

Accompanying this extension of competence was a significant change in the composition of the governing board which, under the resolution, was to be composed of one *ad hoc* delegate designated by each of the American republics. Members of the board were given the rank of ambassadors, but they were not to be part of the diplomatic mission accredited to the government of the country in which the Pan American Union has its seat.[28] The board, moreover, was given authority by majority vote to convoke the annual meetings of the ministers of foreign affairs, an absolute majority being required for exclusively emergency questions (paragraph 4); and a supervision over other inter-American agencies was entrusted to it. Finally, the resolution directed the Pan American Union to prepare a draft charter for the improvement and strengthening of the Pan-American system.[29]

At this important conference, the Mexican delegation introduced a draft resolution on the reorganization of the union of American republics which is a significant illustration of the extent to which thinking in the Americas had progressed. That draft envisaged a system composed of four essential organs consisting of the Council, the conferences, the meetings of consultation, and a permanent secretariat (an arrangement reproduced with a few additions in the Bogotá charter). Although the Council's functions were to be "especially of an executive character," it would have jurisdiction, in the words of the draft, "*the same as will the Conferences, for considering any question that may affect continental peace, solidarity, or welfare.*" Meetings of consultation were to have a permanent status, but only for the purpose of dealing with those emergency questions for which they were instituted. They were to be governed in their functioning by Resolution XVII (Procedure on Consultation), adopted at the meeting of Havana in 1940.[30] This latter resolution requires some comment because of the light it throws on the procedure for consultation of foreign ministers which had developed during the war years, and which figures so heavily in later instruments. The consultation machinery was originally instituted by the Buenos Aires and Lima conferences of 1936 and 1938 for the purpose of providing a speedy and effective means of dealing with threats to the peace in the Western Hemisphere. As no definite method had been adopted for convoking the meetings, which were called under pressure and under emergency conditions, some systematic device was required. Accordingly, it was provided at Havana that any government desiring to initiate consultation in cases contemplated by relevant inter-American instruments would address its request to the governing board of the Pan American Union, together with the questions proposed for consideration. The governing board would then transmit the request to the other member governments, inviting their suggestions and observations. On the basis of this information, the board was to determine the date and place of meeting, draft regulations, prepare the agenda, and take other necessary measures. But it was not empowered to investigate the facts motivating a particular request to determine whether the situation was sufficiently serious for a meeting of consultation. To fill this gap required merely a logical extension of powers already vested, without which the mechanism lacked equipment for prompt and effective action in both clear and doubtful cases.

II

Such was the evolutionary framework on which the Rio de Janeiro Inter-American Treaty of Reciprocal Assistance, and the Bogotá charter of the Organization of American States came to be superimposed. Both of these instruments will now be examined with a view to ascertaining the general competence which they confer upon what is now the Council of the organization.

THE RIO TREATY

The Inter-American Treaty of Reciprocal Assistance was a direct outgrowth of the conference of Mexico City which had produced the declaration known as the Act of Chapultepec. In that document it was stipulated that every attack of a state against the integrity or the inviolability of the territory, or against the sovereignty or political independence of an American state shall be considered as an act of aggression against the other states. The act further provided for consultation among the American states to determine the measures which would be taken in case of acts of aggression or the preparation of such acts.[31] These principles were given permanent form by the Rio treaty in which an effective implementation procedure was inserted. The parts of this treaty relevant for our purposes are as follows:

Article 3

2. On the request of the State or States directly attacked and until the decision of the Organ of Consultation of the Inter-American System, each one of the Contracting Parties may determine the immediate measures which it may individually take in fulfillment of the obligation [of mutual assistance] . . . and in accordance with the principle of continental solidarity. *The Organ of Consultation shall meet without delay* for the purpose of examining those measures and agreeing upon the measures of a collective character that should be taken.

Article 6

If the inviolability or the integrity of the territory *or the sovereignty or political independence* of any American State should be affected by an aggression which is not an armed attack or by an extra-continental or intra-continental conflict, *or by any other fact or situation which might endanger the peace of America, the Organ of Consultation shall meet immediately in order to agree on the measures which must be taken . . . for the maintenance of the peace and security of the Continent.*

Article 11

The Consultations to which this Treaty refers shall be carried out by means of the Meetings of Ministers of Foreign Affairs of the American Republics which have ratified the Treaty, or in the manner or by the organ which in the future may be agreed upon.

Article 12

The Governing Board of the Pan American Union *may act provisionally as an organ of consultation until the meeting of the Organ of Consultation referred to in the preceding Article takes place (en tanto no se reúna el Organo de Consulta).*

Under Article 13, consultations shall be initiated at the request addressed to the governing board of the Pan American Union by any state which has ratified the treaty. The governing board is likewise designated as the liaison agency between the treaty parties *inter se,* and between those states and the United Nations (Article 15). Decisions of the board under these last two articles are to be taken by absolute majority. However, a two-thirds vote of states ratifying the treaty is specified for decisions of the organ of consultation (Article 17). Finally, the instrument contemplates eventual incorporation of its fundamental provisions, in the future organic pact of the inter-American system (Article 26).

I believe that a better perspective of the council's political competence is obtained by examining the appropriate provisions of the charter of Bogotá in conjunction with those of the Rio treaty; but a few preliminary comments are indicated with respect to the latter. In the first place, it will be observed that nowhere in the treaty is the area of action open to the board demarcated with precision. Its powers are set forth in the barest of general terms, leaving a number of important questions to interpretation. When the board acts provisionally as an organ of consultation does it enjoy the plenitude of powers conferred upon the organ of consultation (i.e., the meetings of ministers of foreign affairs)? Article 12 authorizes the governing board to act *provisionally* as "an organ of consultation" (the Spanish version says *como organo de consulta*). Is this identical with acting as *provisional* organ of consultation? Does the meeting of foreign ministers have to ratify measures taken by the governing board acting *provisionally,* or are these measures valid and definitive until or unless impeached by the organ of consultation? Articles 3 and 6 declare that when certain circumstances exist the organ of consultation shall meet "without delay" or "immediately" to determine what measures shall be taken. Under Article 13 consultations shall be initiated at the request of a member state addressed to the board. Does this refer to consultation of the organ (foreign ministers), or of the board acting provisionally? Or does it mean that the governing board, upon convoking the meeting of foreign ministers, then proceeds to act provisionally? What if the board, after examining the facts, concludes that a case has not been presented warranting convocation of the organ of consultation? Must the board always convoke that organ? Is it sufficient for the board to issue a *pro forma notice* of convocation without setting a date? What if, after notice has been given, the meeting of foreign ministers does not convene, for whatever reason? Or suppose, between the time of convocation and the time of actual assembly of the principal organ, the board settles the case? What, in that connection, are the powers which the board enjoys between initiation of the request under Article 13, and the issuing of convocation? Just how far may the board go in that twilight period? May it appoint an investigating committee to ascertain facts upon which it may determine whether to proceed?

Finally, does the board have any implied powers—powers that are not expressly conferred upon it by the terms of the treaty? And who has the ultimate authority to decide matters of jurisdiction, to determine whether in a given situation the board possesses competence? When one state advances the plea of no jurisdiction, does this block further action and must the question then be put to immediate vote, or may the board conduct its own investigation to determine, from the facts, whether competence exists?

Unfortunately, clear-cut answers to every one of these inquiries are not found in the recorded debates of the Rio conference. But the major problems of the role to be performed by the board and the capacity it was to enjoy were examined in sufficient degree to leave little doubt as to the intent of the delegates on broad questions of principle. Before analyzing the proceedings for this purpose, however, a word may be said about some of the views embodied by various governments in their early drafts, and later in proposals to the conference itself, on the selection of an organ of consultation. These various proposals as well as the debates themselves clearly refute the thesis that the board was designed to be an agency of limited powers, without capacity to take effective political action.

Of a number of drafts originally submitted for the treaty in 1945, the Bolivian and Ecuadorean projects would have instituted the governing board of the Pan American Union as the medium of consultation (Articles 5 and 3–5 respectively). These drafts likewise empowered the board to determine or direct the adoption of provisional measures by parties to a dispute. They both would have charged the board with certain responsibilities in determining the aggressor state (Articles 8 and 2), a proposal also contained in the Mexican draft (Article 10). Bolivia's draft would have referred to the board "any controversy or situation, whatever its origin, which adversely affects the general welfare or the friendly relations among the American Nations." Acting as an "agency of security" the board would then propose appropriate measures of investigation, conciliation, or mediation (Article 4). Panama urged creation of a special organ to undertake political activities, arguing that the board should not exercise security functions. Five other drafts (those of Chile, Brazil, Mexico, Uruguay, and the United States) left the choice of mechanism to the parties in each instance.[32] In the United States proposal, the provision was worded as follows:

> The consultations and measures referred to in the preceding articles shall be carried out through such procedures and agencies as are now in existence, or as may hereafter be established by agreement of the High Contracting Parties.[33]

A revised Mexican proposal submitted to the Conference provided that the regular forum of consultation would be the meetings of foreign ministers, except that in urgent cases, "the Governing Board of the Pan American Union, at the request of any of the signatory States, shall ask the Ministers of Foreign Affairs to authorize the delegates of their respective countries on the Governing Board of the Pan American Union to have the said Board act as a security organ."[34] Nothing could better illustrate the conflicting elements pressing down upon the American governments than the draftsmanship of this article: desire to have these cases decided at the top levels of responsibility; realization that the meetings of foreign ministers might not be appropriate in all situations, particularly for effective action in urgent circumstances; and the long-held reluctance to vest political functions in the governing board, to grant to it effective power in advance of specific cases. A number of other proposals submitted directly to the conference, however, exhibited no such reluctance. Thus Article 4 of a Guatemalan proposal introduced on August 21, 1947, contemplated that the governing board would be *the* agency of consultation, to which requests from the interested governments would be directed.[35] A revised draft of the Urguayan government was in the same vein. This courageous document gave to the board authority to decide by a majority vote upon the "adequate collective measures" which would be taken to ensure compliance with the treaty whenever peace was threatened, and specified several different types of sanctions which it could initiate (Articles 7, 8). Not content with this sweeping grant, however, it included an article which would have empowered the board to apply the system of consultation, upon request of any of its members, to such serious violations of the fundamental rights and freedoms of the human person as were susceptible of threatening the maintenance of peace.[36] On the other hand, a Peruvian proposal to include extensive provisions on pacific settlement entrusted the governing board with the task of "promoting the meeting of consultation" for that purpose.[37]

These varying positions were reflected during the proceedings of the conference itself. The Peruvian delegate objected to granting capacity to the governing board to act even *provisionally* as the organ of consultation, because he was opposed to the exercise of political functions by the Pan American Union.[38] The Dominican Republic wanted the governing board to be the executive organ of the treaty;[39] whereas the Paraguayan and Ecuadorean delegations would have preferred that the meeting of foreign ministers be described as the "principal" organ of consultation.[40] By a vote of 15 to 4 it was finally decided that in view of the serious character of the action contemplated in the pact, the meeting of foreign ministers should be the normal organ of consultation unless some other mode was agreed upon in a future treaty.[41] Lest the significance of this heavy majority be misconstrued, it should be emphasized that the issue was not whether the governing board or some new body should be given capacity to operate as *an* agency for observance of the treaty, either in a provisional or any other manner, regardless of the nature of the case presented. If that had been true, Article 12 would have been meaningless altogether. What was involved was a selection as between the meeting of foreign ministers and the board, of the agency through which consultations should, in principle, be carried out. In fact, however, a certain degree of inconsistency is found between Articles 11 and 12 when the proceedings of the conference are scrutinized. It was recognized in the debates on Article 12 that the meeting of foreign ministers in many cases would not be held at all. In the words of Sr. Fusco, the Uruguayan delegate,

> . . . in practice it will happen that in ninety percent of the cases the provisional character attributed to the intervention of the Governing Board of the Pan American Union will extend to the complete solution of the disputes, whenever the latter are not of the type to justify the Meeting of Foreign Ministers.[42]

A similar understanding is contained in the report of Sr. Augusto Ramirez Moreno as *relator* for the Third Committee which recommended the articles to the conference:

> . . . as supreme organ of consultation we have established the Meeting of Foreign Ministers. The Committee is not unmindful of the excellence . . . of the Governing Board . . . but considers that the *unleashing of active measures* ought to be the direct responsibility of the Governments. . . . The Governing Board . . . will have to assume the role of Organ of Consultation in cases of inevitable urgency, or in others in which the subject matter, without being insignificant, does not justify the meeting of Ministers. [43]

If this is so then the language used in Article 12 does not accurately portray the true sense of the conference. How can an agency which, it is anticipated, will function perhaps 10 per cent of the time, be described as the normal organ of consultation? The adverb "provisionally" hardly fits the activity which the draftsmen seem to have had in mind for the board. The inconsistency adverted to—more real than apparent—springs from the curious fact that while the *relator* acknowledges that application of sanctions in situations of gravity should be the responsibility of the governments, yet the grant of effective authority to the board is justified partly upon the ground that the organ of consultation will not be available in at least one group of situations ("inevitable urgency") which motivated selection of the meeting of foreign ministers as that organ in the first place. It probably would have been better to describe the meeting of foreign ministers as the "supreme" organ. To have done so would be consonant with the explanation made by the drafting subcommittee of Committee III, when it insisted that the system established must be sufficiently effective and practical so that the inter-American mechanism would not be paralyzed by delays or inaction in urgent cases.[44] This was unquestionably the reason why a proposal of the Peruvian delegation which would have prevented the governing board from acting provisionally, except "upon express delegation," was rejected.[45]

From the foregoing summary of preparatory materials it would seem reasonably certain that the solution finally adopted constituted a compromise. For situations of extreme gravity, recourse will be had to the meeting of foreign ministers; whereas the board is endowed with effective power to settle all disputes which, for one reason or another, do not merit consideration by the foreign ministers. Moreover, since it results from the debates that there is a class of cases which would never go to that body, there is ground for maintaining that it was not the intention of the conference to have the meeting of foreign ministers convoked in every case. It would seem, also, that the decision to convoke is itself one which properly comes within the purview of board action. Whether it would follow that the board may proceed even without convoking when the facts so warrant—a logically defensible position—is not clearly apparent from the language of Article 13. In this the interests of each government are adequately protected, for every representative will be in sufficiently close contact with his foreign office to be able to determine the seriousness with which the home state views a given situation.

Once the governing board has taken cognizance of a request, its powers of investigation and settlement are no less complete than those enjoyed by the meeting of foreign ministers itself. The point was raised during a session of the Third Committee of the conference. It had been argued by the Chilean delegate that no advantage was gained from converting the governing board into an organ of consultation, since each country could send instructions just as speedily to its permanent diplomatic representative in Washington, who could then act (this could hardly be regarded as a "meeting of foreign ministers"!), or it could send direct instructions to its representative on the board.[46] Whereupon it was pointed out that the nomination of special delegates with full powers for every case would prejudice the flexibility of the consultative mechanism. The subcommittee, said Sr. Zuleta of Colombia, had chosen the governing board because it was composed of the ambassadors of 21 states familiar with Pan-American problems. These representatives would naturally act in agreement and in close and frequent contact with their own chancellories.[47] Until the meeting of foreign ministers, the governing board would act as the "representative of the respective Governments."[48]

Although the phraseology of Articles 11 and 12 might leave doubt as to the precise effects which are to be given to the resolutions and recommendations of the governing board acting "provisionally," much of this uncertainty is dispelled by the proceedings of the conference. The *relator* of the Third Committee had described the relationship of the board to the meeting of foreign ministers as a subsidiary one, stating that the latter could always revoke decisions of the former.[49] This, however, did not signify that action taken by the board had to be approved by the foreign ministers:

> . . . the fact that the Governing Board . . . can act provisionally as organ of consultation does not signify that the resolutions which it adopts are also provisional and require later ratification, even though the Meeting of Ministers, should it take place later, might revoke or modify resolutions of the Board.[50]

Another major point is likewise clarified by the debates. The treaty does not in terms enact fixed limitations upon the privilege of a state to raise a given matter before the board, under pretext that it falls within the treaty. According to the *relator,* even if this gave rise to requests which were ill-founded, the prestige of the organization would be preserved by the requirement of a majority vote, before consultation would be initiated.[51] No standard is provided for measuring whether a situation or fact is "of such a nature as might endanger the peace of America." This, it seems, is a matter which the board becomes competent to determine, by virtue of the very fact that the question is raised by a member state. There is nothing particularly outrageous in this procedure. The problem, which frequently confronts international agencies, was early faced by the Council of the League of Nations under Article XV, paragraph 1, of the Covenant, establishing jurisdiction over disputes "likely to lead to a rupture." It was deemed sufficient if one of the parties believed that the dispute was likely to lead to a rupture for the Council to be properly seized of the matter. Nor was the Council even compelled, before inquiring into any point, to determine in advance whether such belief was well-founded.[52]

It should be noted in passing that when the subcommittee reported on Article 15 (under which the governing board is authorized to act as a liaison organ between the member states) it was careful to underscore an aspect of that article which might easily escape detection. This function, said the subcommittee, "does not exclude the sovereign autodetermination of peoples to arrive at understandings among themselves, in the absence of intermediaries."[53] From this it would seem to follow that the board would lack jurisdiction to entertain a request for consultation when other means of negotiation had already been initiated by the parties. A plea to the jurisdiction by an interested state would consequently have to be sustained.

Considerable space has been taken up thus far discussing the powers of the governing board, or more accurately, the Council of the Organization of American States since Bogotá, in application of the Rio treaty. But many of the problems involved in the question of competence are common to the functions of the Council under both the charter of the organization, and the treaty. Before pursuing any further, therefore, the investigation of these general principles which guide the Council, consideration must now be given to the applicable provisions of the charter.

THE CHARTER OF BOGOTÁ

With the complete reorganization of the inter-American system at Bogotá, the governing board was separated from the Pan American Union and was made the Council of the Organization of American States. This change was partly due to a recognition that the board had come to assume greater substantive responsibilities and was no longer a merely administrative office. It also reflected the executive character assigned to the board by the ninth conference, which consolidated its political, advisory, and coördinating functions.[54]

Few issues of the conference received greater attention than the determination of the limits of these political functions which the Council was to possess. In the Draft Organic Pact prepared by the Pan American Union in compliance with Resolution IX of the Mexico City conference of 1945, Article 11 substantially incorporated by reference the Rio de Janeiro Inter-American Treaty of Reciprocal Assistance. Article 12 designated the meetings of foreign ministers as the organ of consultation, and the Governing Board as provisional organ "until the former meets." Article 7 provided that, in a dispute between American states declared to be suceptible of endangering continental peace and security, the organ of consultation shall recommend that the parties settle it by peaceful means of their own choice. Failure to settle the dispute in this manner empowered the organ of consultation to "indicate an adequate procedure for the settlement of the dispute" (Article 8). Requests for meetings of consultation were to be directed to the governing board, which would decide by majority vote whether the meeting should be called. The remaining articles pertinent to our study were thus conceived:

Article 35

The Governing Board takes cognizance, within the limits of this Pact and the Inter-American Treaties and agreements of any matter which may affect the functioning and purposes of the Inter-American System.

Article 36

The Governing Board shall act as a provisional organ of consultation when the circumstances foreseen in Article 12 of this Pact arise [e.g., the Consultations contemplated under Chapters II and III dealing with pacific settlement and collective security].

These articles resulted in a thorough-going reëxamination of the entire political competence issue. The broad grant contained in Article 35 was unacceptable to the conference, which exibited a serious division of partisan views. A number of delegations flatly took the position that the board should have no political powers at all. Argentina, Chile, and Panama would have repealed the authority given the board in the Rio de Janeiro treaty to act provisionally as organ of consultation. The Argentine delegate insisted that to attribute to it other than administrative duties would invade the province of the conferences, tend to the creation of an undesirable "superstate," and pave the way for intervention in the internal affairs of each country.[55] While the Chilean delegate was not apprehensive of the development of a "superstate," he was likewise opposed both to the grant of new political functions, and to the continuance of those previously accepted under the Rio treaty, which, he argued, would bring about the downfall of the system. In place of the governing board a new organ should be established, the treaty being modified so as to constitute as organ of consultation the diplomatic corps accredited to any one of the American republics, on a rotating basis.[56] Objection to extending political functions to the board was voiced also by the Paraguayan and Venezuelan delegations.[57]

At the opposite extreme were the delegations of Brazil, Cuba, Colombia, and Costa Rica. The Brazilian representative favored the retention of all powers conferred on the governing board in the Pan American Union's draft:

> It is not possible . . . for the organization to be without a permanent central organ or it will otherwise revert to the status of an information office as it was in the beginning, if the powers that have been conferred upon it in the course of time, and particularly at Chapultepec and Rio de Janeiro are taken away. If it is deprived of these functions the Governing Board will have to seek some other organ to perform them.[58]

Colombia's delegation saw no reason why political powers should be denied the Pan American Union[59] after such powers had already been granted to the Security Council of the United Nations. An intermediate formula was proposed by the Mexican delegation, which would have confirmed powers exercised by the governing board up to the Rio treaty; withheld new powers except those expressly delegated to it by the "essential" organ of consultation for concrete cases, or by the inter-American conferences; and rewritten Article 12 of the Rio treaty concerning the provisional aspects of the board's assignment. The principal change suggested in the Draft Organic Pact on this point was the following:

> In case of an armed attack . . . the meeting of the Ministers shall take place without delay by summons made immediately by the Chairman of the Governing Board, who, at the same time, shall convoke the Board itself for the purposes of Article . . . In any other case, the meeting may be requested by any American State. The request shall be addressed to the Governing Board, which, in consultation with the American Governments and in accordance with the opinion of the majority, shall decide whether or not to convoke the meeting.
>
> The Governing Board shall undertake such preliminary steps as may be deemed necessary as to whether the Organ of Consultation should meet.[60]

In view of the support manifested for the Mexican proposal, the matter was entrusted to a subcommittee to summarize and correlate the consensus entertained by the various delegations. This subcommittee reported as follows:

> 2. In the Organic Pact of the Organization the Governing Board should be granted only those "political" functions which were already delegated by Resolution IX of Chapultepec . . . and by the Treaty of Reciprocal Assistance signed at Rio de Janeiro (Articles 12, 13, 15 and 16).
>
> 3. The general opinion seemed to favor the argument that no new function of a political nature should be conferred on the Governing Board in the Organic Pact; because, among other stated reasons, the International Conferences of American States and the Meetings of Consultation of the Ministers of Foreign Affairs constitute the Organs within the Organization expressly authorized to carry out this type of function.[61]

The solution finally accepted by the conference was based, generally, upon the Mexican formula. By virtue of Article 43 of the charter, the meeting of consultation is to be held "without delay" in case of an armed attack, and is to be convoked by the chairman of the Council at the same time that he convokes the Council to act in an interim capacity. On the other hand, the Council still serves provisionally as organ of consultation in all cases under the Rio treaty. Its capacity under this treaty has not been diminished by the charter of Bogotá; for Article 25 of the charter (Article 11 of the Draft Organic Pact) virtually incorporates the provisions of the Rio treaty, and the express phraseology of "any other fact or situation that might endanger the peace of America," by reference. Article 35 of the draft was replaced by Article 50 of the charter:

Article 50

> The Council takes cognizance, within the limits of the present Charter and of inter-American treaties and agreements, of any matter referred to it by the

Inter-American Conference or the Meeting of Consultation of Ministers of Foreign Affairs.

It seems clear from the proceedings of Bogotá that the powers granted to the Council in the field of political action were the result of a compromise, a middle-of-the road course between the dilemma of a further grant of powers on the one hand, and a shrinking of those already conceded, on the other. A reaction had set in between Chapultepec and Bogotá against the extension of competence in relation to differences arising between the member states.

Whether such resurgence of the tenaciously held reluctance which has been described earlier in this study will in turn yield to a swing of the pendulum in the opposite direction, can not now be predicted. But it is important to emphasize that the compromise solution finally adopted at Bogotá did not slam the door on the question of the Council's political capacity. The charter not only does not prohibit the exercise of political functions (even beyond those it reaffirms under the Rio treaty), but it expressly contemplates that additional functions may be given to it by the two highest levels of the inter-American system. Moreover, in a number of other fields of action embraced by the charter, provision is made for the Council to undertake duties of a quasi-political character, above and beyond its usual responsibility with respect to the administration of the Pan American Union (Article 51), approval of the union's budget (Article 54), and general supervision over the activities of its three organs (Articles 57 and 58). Thus, the Council is charged with the duty to draft recommendations to the governments, the inter-American conference, the specialized conferences or the specialized organizations for coördination of the activities and programs of such organizations after consultation with them (Article 53*b*); to conclude agreements with the inter-American specialized organizations to determine the relations that shall exist between the respective agency and the organization; and to enter into similar agreements with other American organizations of recognized international standing (Article 53*c* and *d*). Finally, and of considerable importance, is the position enjoyed by the Council under Articles XVI and XLV of the American Treaty on Pacific Settlement known as the Pact of Bogotá. Article XVI, which directs the Council to convoke the Commission of Investigation and Conciliation upon request of a party to a dispute which has been submitted to the procedure of peaceful settlement under Article II, provides that pending convocation of the commission the Council "may make appropriate recommendations to the parties" so that they will refrain from any act which might make conciliation more difficult. Under

Article XLV, failure of a party to designate an arbiter within a specified time gives the other party the right to request the Council to establish the arbitral tribunal.

To summarize, the Council enjoys two general sources of competence, one derived from Rio, the other from Bogotá, both being blended together in the charter. The existence or nonexistence of such competence in particular cases depends, of course, upon the interpretation to be given to the provision involved. According to Article 12 of the Rio treaty the Council acts provisionally as the organ of consultation whenever the conditions required by that treaty (particularly Articles 3 and 6) prevail. This is basically the same competence which is reënacted in Article 25 of the charter, as already noted. In addition, Article 52 of that instrument provides that the Council "shall serve provisionally as the Organ of Consultation whenever the circumstances contemplated in Article 43 arise," for example, in an "armed attack within the territory of an American State or within the region of security delimited by treaties in force." It may be noted that the phraseology differs from that of Rio's Article 3 which refers to an "armed attack by any State against an American State."

Up to this point the respective areas of competence conferred upon the organ of consultation and the Council acting provisionally are identical, as are their powers to investigate and settle cases properly brought before them. But the charter in Article 39 grants to the meeting of consultation a competence which it withholds from the Council, namely, "to consider problems of an urgent nature and of common interest to the American States." The Council's power in this field is limited under Article 40 to deciding by a majority vote whether a meeting of consultation will be held. On the other hand, by retaining the provision of the Rio treaty which qualifies the Council to assume jurisdiction whenever the "sovereignty" of any American state is affected by "any other fact or situation that might endanger the peace of America," the Bogotá conference—designedly or not—ensured that many a dispute which could not otherwise be brought before the Council (under Articles 39–40) might still be disposed of under the Rio provisions. And that dragnet is very broad, indeed. For example, in the situation confronting the Council in the Venezuelan-Chileno-Guatemalan controversy over the diplomatic asylum granted to former President Betancourt in the Colombian embassy, the competence of the Council was challenged on the ground that it lacked jurisdiction to concern itself with violations of treaties.[62] Even if this were conceded as a general proposition, it is nevertheless true that a "fact or situation" may be produced precisely because of the violation of an international convention, as well as of customary international law. It is impossible to maintain that because a dispute involves the violation of a treaty, the Council is rendered impotent. And even a case of asylum may give rise to a factual situation such as that envisaged in the Rio treaty.

For these reasons it does not seem possible at the present time to lay down categorical principles in advance determining that a given matter does or does not fall within the Council's jurisdiction. Whether it does will depend upon future developments no less than upon a careful interpretation of the provisions of the charter and other documents. To assert unqualifiedly that the Council enjoys no "political" functions other than those specifically granted to it is meaningless, for one is immediately faced with the necessity of defining further, and of determining what limits attach to the powers conferred. Moreover, the phrase "political functions," which is susceptible of varying meanings, is too vague to be of practical utility as a juridical concept. Finally, as already observed, not only does the Council enjoy a number of extra-Rio-treaty attributes which partake of a political flavor, but the charter has expressly left the road open to further grants of competence by the higher organs of the American system. No formula that might now be drafted would be adequate or accurate enough to embrace the varying and unpredictable types of situations which may eventually fall within the Council's cognizance. To the solution of this problem the Council itself must contribute, always, of course, within the boundaries of the charter, through a "gradual process of . . . inclusion and exclusion, as the cases presented for decision shall require."[63]

In this connection, it is well to inquire whether the Council possesses any so-called "implied" powers. It may be argued that the essence of those functions derived, principally, from the Rio treaty, is such that the instrument should receive a strict construction, particularly as the powers themselves are in derogation of sovereignty and in a domain long withheld from inter-American action. But whether reliable guidance is furnished by the application of such *a priori* principles of interpretation to the situation now considered, is doubtful. The problem is rather to give effect to the intention of the conference, so far as that intent can be ascertained from available sources. What the framers clearly wanted was an effective instrument to reduce threats to the peace. Accordingly, the powers of the Council can be most accurately ascertained, I believe, by interpreting ambiguous or doubtful language in the light of this fundamental purpose.

There has been some apprehension voiced during meetings of the

Council that it might be prone to assume the attributes of an international arbitral tribunal which would pronounce judgment upon the actions of the member states. Wherefore Ambassador Acciolly, the great Brazilian jurist, found it necessary to remind Council members in a brilliant address of the proper limitations to be placed upon the mandate they were charged with executing.[64] The difficulty, of course, is that by the very nature of its functions action by the Council in a specific case may be equivalent to a finding that there has been a violation of customary or conventional international law. Beyond this, there exists no resemblance to judicial process. The Council does not pass judgment upon the parties; it does not render an award in favor of one and against another; and its action does not preclude later submission of the same issue to an international court or arbitral tribunal. The action which it takes is designed to remove a threat to the peace. If in the course of its labors it ascertains facts which justify and demand Council action, any implication of a violation of international law would seem to be incidental to the effective discharge of its principal business.

III

Some Special Problems.—Must the Council, before applying the Rio treaty and convoking the organ of consultation, first determine that a given group of circumstances comes within the purview of the treaty? The point was raised in a Costa Rica–Nicaragua dispute involving the alleged invasion of the former's territory by armed forces proceeding from Nicaragua.[65] Costa Rica contended that the Council was not required to pass upon the validity of charges made before convoking the organ of consultation. This position was concurred in by various members of the Council.[66] It would seem to be sufficient to justify Council action in these cases that the complainant state has made out a *prima facie* case. If it has, the next inquiry is: just what is the authority of the Council prior to convocation of the meeting of foreign ministers, or in the possible alternative, after it decides that convocation is unnecessary? Assume that a request has been received, but that no decision has been reached on convoking the organ of consultation. May the Council immediately undertake an examination of the substantive aspects of the dispute with a view to settlement? *No.* And yet at the same time it appears indisputable that the Council may have to ascertain the existence of certain facts in order to conclude whether convocation is necessary, whether it is warranted in acting provisionally at organ of consultation. May it appoint a committee of investigation to do so? When it acts provisionally as organ of consultation, of course, it may investigate the facts in any manner it deems appropriate, through committee action, or otherwise. But does this same power exist in the initial phase of the procedure? To deny it this right could easily hamstring the processes contemplated by the treaty; it might compel the Council to make preliminary decisions on the basis of inadequate information; and it is flatly repugnant to the intent evidenced during proceedings of the Rio conference. To avoid futile consultations, which could easily jeopardize the value of the mechanism for truly grave issues, the Council must be permitted to determine as a preliminary question whether a sufficiently colorable case exists to warrant consultation. Moreover, independently of the attributes given to it by the Rio treaty, the Council's capacity to investigate pertinent facts seems to derive equally from the faculty recognized in Article 40 of the charter to decide if a meeting of consultation should be called "to consider problems of an urgent nature and of common interest to the American States" (Article 39). Satisfactory fulfillment of the functions conferred in Article 40 necessarily presupposes that the Council undertake such an investigation of the facts as may be required in order to arrive at a decision. This implied power in investigation, of course, in no way implies authority for it to take action with respect to the substance of the question presented. Nevertheless, a salutary consequence of the facts revealed by the Council's investigation under Article 40 may well be to bring the disputants together in a voluntary, amicable adjustment of grievances.

The Council may certainly require a complaining state to come forward with any additional information deemed necessary. But it may go much further. In the Costa Rica–Nicarague dispute, the Council adopted a resolution (December 12, 1948) directing the president to seek further information from sources he deemed useful, postponing further deliberations for forty-eight hours.[67] Pursuant thereto information was collected from the member governments, including the parties to the dispute. There would seem to be no principle inhibiting the Council's choice of means for such purpose; and if a special committee is required in its judgment, one may be appointed. In the dispute between Haiti and the Dominican Republic, the Council as Council, and not acting provisionally as organ of consultation, appointed a special committee to draft the resolution in which convocation was refused, the Council limiting itself to an exhortation that the friendship and good relationship between the parties would be strengthened and reaffirmed.[68]

Once the Council begins to operate provisionally as organ of consultation, it can create such committees as it needs to assist in the substantive disposition of the case. In the Costa Rica–Nicaragua dispute, a Committee was appointed to investigate facts on the spot.[69] A similar committee was appointed to investigate facts in the dispute between Haiti and the Dominican Republic arising out of a charge that the latter was encouraging revolutionary activities by a former Haitian army officer, Colonel Roland—specifically, in permitting violent broadcasts from a radio station in the Dominican Republic.[70]

A somewhat confusing aspect of the interlacing relationship between the charter and the Rio treaty is offered by the question of a nonratifying state's right to vote in the deliberations of the Council. While the charter is silent on voting procedures (other than prescribing a two-thirds majority in budgetary matters), the Rio treaty (Article 14) specifically limits voting to representatives of the signatory states which have ratified the treaty. It consequently makes considerable difference whether an issue is brought before the Council under the charter or under the Rio treaty. In the Costa Rica–Nicaragua dispute, the Council unanimously confirmed the distinction, voting on basic resolutions as well as ancillary matters of procedure being restricted to "ratifying members."[71] However, other members were not thereby precluded from giving the Council the benefit of their views.[72] In the same way the Council took the position that the member of a nonratifying state was eligible to serve on a committee of the organ of consultation acting provisionally.[73]

Although, as pointed out earlier in this study, there is a definite basis for maintaining that convocation of the meeting of foreign ministers is not essential in every case to "provisional" Council action, the Council itself has acted upon the assumption that convocation is a prerequisite to such action. It did so in the Costa Rica–Nicaragua dispute, despite the fact that the requesting state had sought only immediate convocation of the Council (in its provisional capacity as organ of consultation), without a meeting of foreign ministers.[74] As a device of expediency the concept is probably unobjectionable, though it seems to have been commonly anticipated at the Rio conference that in a large majority of situations it would be sufficient for the Council to render a determination that convocation was not necessary. That the Council has been fully aware of this is illustrated by its practice of passing a resolution to convoke the meeting of foreign ministers, without, however, setting either a date or a place for the meeting.[75] *A fortiori,* if the "provisional" activity of the Council of the organization culminates in a solution of the problem presented to it, the actual meeting of foreign ministers, convoked *sine die* would become unnecessary.[76] The obvious disadvantage of the Council's practice in this type of *pro forma* convocation is that it would appear to open the way to a discontented state thereafter to insist that the dispute be submitted to the meeting of foreign ministers—the very fact of convocation carrying with it an implication of later submission; whereas, a decision by the Council that convocation is unwarranted would bar that path entirely. On the other hand, failure of the Council to settle a controversy within a reasonable time would probably deprive that body of any reason for delaying further the meeting of foreign ministers.

One paramount inquiry remains. When the competence of the Council is challenged with respect to any matter brought before it, what organ is qualified to rule finally that jurisdiction does or does not exist? Is it the Council *qua* council or *qua* organ of consultation, the meeting of foreign ministers, or the inter-American conference? It seems beyond cavil that the Council should be recognized as qualified *in the first instance* to pass upon its own competence. Every agency of governmental administration will be confronted sooner or later with the necessity of harmonizing its activities with what it conceives to be the scope of its authority. When Committee IV/2 was asked at the San Francisco Conference on International Organizations "how and by what organ or organs of the Organization should the Charter of the United Nations be interpreted?" it replied:

> In the course of the operations from day to day . . . it is inevitable that each organ will interpret such parts of the Charter as are applicable to its particular functions. This process is inherent in the functioning of any body which operates under an instrument defining its functions and powers. . . . Accordingly, it is not necessary to include in the Charter a provision either authorizing or approving the normal operation of this principle.[77]

Yet it is equally certain that the final determination of the extent of the Council's competence must reside necessarily with the inter-American conference as the supreme organ of the Organization of American States—or else with such other organ as the governments themselves may see fit to vest with that power.[78] Under Article 33 of the charter, it is the conference which "decides the general action and policy of the Organization and determines the structure and functions of its organs." Until, therefore, the conference delegates this authority to the Council, any decisions made on it by the latter will be valid only as long as they are not repudiated by the higher organ. In the absence of such repudiation, a strong presumption would seem to arise in favor of the validity of the Council's determinations in matters of competence. For, it is reasonable to presume that a body of such stature as the Council would not construe its capacity except on the basis of a most careful analysis of the legal instruments which gave it life.

To anyone who has followed its development during the brief years since Bogotá the Council appears to hold great promise for the future of Pan-Americanism, in the prevention and settlement of differences which could easily cloud the sensitive atmosphere of the Western Hemisphere. Its maturity is not yet such as to permit a prediction of the exact degree of influence which the Council may come to exercise. But a sturdy structure is there; its skeletal framework is being filled out with the flesh and blood of experience and achievement; and the prospects for its future health are enhanced by what at the current phase of inter-American organization appears to be a happy balance between the forces of closer collaboration and the traditional resistence to restraints upon sovereign action.

JOSEF L. KUNZ

The Geneva Conventions of August 12, 1949

AT THE TIME of writing* nothing has been published in the United States[1] on the new Geneva conventions. It is not proposed to give here a full discussion of all the norms of these conventions. Such task would not only require a book, but is hardly yet possible, as important materials are not yet available.[2]

This study will present the history and legal status of these conventions, will relate them to the subject of the laws of war and will give a general evaluation of the progress achieved. It will show how far the innovations, positive and negative, were influenced by the modern conditions of war and, especially, by the experience of World War II. It will, finally, study their relations to the law of war crimes, the law concerning the conduct of war, and the international law of neutrality.

I

Despite the general neglect of the laws of war since 1920,[3] the Red Cross has at all times made great efforts to revise and expand the international law for the protection of the victims of war,[4] and was instrumental, together with the Swiss government, in bringing into being the two Geneva conventions of 1929.[5] The one was the convention concerning the amelioration of the condition of the wounded and sick in the armed forces in the field,[6] the other that concerning prisoners of war.[7] The Geneva Conference of 1929 recommended unanimously that a careful study be made in preparation for a convention for the protection of civilians. The idea of "security zones" had already appeared in 1929; and in 1931 the association Lieux de Genève was founded in Geneva.[8]

*Summer, 1951.

To the XV International Red Cross Conference, Tokyo, a draft treaty for the protection of civilians (so-called Tokyo Draft) was submitted; this conference recommended also the study again of the Monaco Project,[9] which had been elaborated by the 8th Congress of Military Medicine and Pharmacy. The International Committee of the Red Cross started new studies on the revision of the Geneva conventions of 1929 on the basis of experience gained in the Italian-Ethiopian War and the Spanish Civil War. A revised draft of the 1929 conventions was considered by the XVI International Red Cross Conference, held in London in 1938. All these studies were transmitted to the Swiss government, which intended to convoke a diplomatic conference in Geneva in 1940. This conference could not be held because of World War II.

But on February 5, 1945, while the war was still going on, the International Committee of the Red Cross sent a memorandum to the national Red Cross societies and the governments of the world. The United States actively supported this initiative in 1945 and later.[10] The national Red Cross societies held a preliminary conference in Geneva from July 26 to August 3, 1946.[11] It was followed by a conference of governmental experts, held at Geneva April 14–26, 1947.[12] At the XVII International Red Cross Conference, held at Stockholm, August 20–30, 1948, the four new draft conventions were approved.[13]

Finally, the Swiss government convoked a diplomatic conference which took place at Geneva April 21–August 12, 1949. There were four principal committees: the Joint Committee,[14] dealing with the articles common to the four conventions; Committee I,[15] dealing with the first two conventions; Committee II,[16] dealing with the third; and Committee III,[17] dealing with the fourth. This conference produced the four new Geneva conventions,[18] namely: 1) Convention for the amelioration of the condition of the wounded and sick in the armed forces in the field; 2) Convention for the amelioration of the condition of wounded, sick, and shipwrecked members of the armed forces at sea; 3) Convention relative to the treatment of prisoners of war, and 4) Convention relative to the protection of civilian persons in time of war.[19]

The conventions were open for signature until February 12, 1950, by the powers represented at the 1949 conference and, with regard to the first three conventions, also by powers not represented there, but parties to the earlier conventions.[20] The four conventions have been signed by sixty-one states.[21] The conventions further provide[22] that they shall be ratified and come into force six months after two instruments of ratification have been deposited. The first ratification was deposited by Switzerland on March 31, 1950, the second by Yugoslavia on April 21,

1950. The four conventions came, therefore, into force on October 21, 1950. At the time of writing the following states, in addition to the first two, have ratified, in chronological order: Monaco, Liechtenstein, Chile, India, Czechoslovakia and the Vatican. Only the ratifications by Yugoslavia and Czechoslovakia contain reservations, identical with those made at the time of signature.[23] From the time of coming into force—October 21, 1950—accession is open to any power in whose name the conventions have not been signed.

Naturally, the importance of the new conventions depends, in the first place, on their ratification by the states of the world.

II

The Diplomatic Conference of Geneva of 1949 was the most universal international conference that it was possible to hold in recent years. Very small states, usually not seen at international conferences or as members of international organizations, were represented, including the Vatican. The ten Soviet states found it possible to participate at this conference. Bielorussia and the Ukraine took part at the conference as separate members; their partial sovereignty is, hence, not restricted to the ambit of the United Nations. States, not members of the United Nations, did take part, including Spain. Only very few states were absent: some Arab states (Iraq, Jordan, Saudi Arabia, and Yemen), Indonesia, Germany, and Japan.

In view of the atmosphere of hostility against the laws of war which has so disastrously prevailed since 1920, the International Red Cross is all the more to be congratulated for having kept to the great work of preparing the new conventions. The Swiss government, too, deserves credit. Even at the 1949 conference, despite the unanimous agreement to conclude these conventions, some doubted the wisdom of the action, because of the impression on public opinion. But the Swiss Foreign Minister Max Petitpierre stated[24] that it is a necessity and an imperative duty to establish such conventions in time of peace; that it is of the utmost urgency to do so in order to prevent the repetition of the terrible horrors perpetrated in World War II. In a speech of December 8, 1949, he added that the conventions were signed "on the unhappy assumption that a new war is not impossible." On the other hand, Resolution VIII, adopted at the conference, "affirmed its earnest hope that in the future governments may never have to apply the new Geneva Conventions."

The Geneva Diplomatic Conference of 1949 was exclusively based on work carried on, and on proposals made, by the International Red

Cross.[25] The Red Cross acts within the framework of international law and, particularly, of the laws of war. Organizationally it consists of the National Red Cross societies, the association of these societies, and the International Committee of the Red Cross. All these organs are legally private organizations, but recognized and regulated by international treaties; at the International Red Cross conferences participate also delegates of the states, members of the Geneva conventions. Article 24 of the League of Nations Covenant dealt with the Red Cross. The Geneva conventions of 1929 spoke only of "voluntary aid societies," but those of 1949 specifically mention the "National Red Cross Societies." Their staff is placed on the same footing as military neutral personnel exclusively engaged in the search for, collection, transport, or treatment of the wounded and sick, or in the prevention of disease. The norms[26] concerning the "distinctive emblem" of the Red Cross,[27] its use, and measures against its abuse have been strengthened.

The International Committee of the Red Cross, composed (interestingly) entirely of Swiss citizens, is a juridical person under Swiss municipal law, but exercises functions recognized or conferred upon it by international law; it negotiates with governments, sends direct appeals to them, concludes agreements, and fits out vessels. It acts independently, without the authority of any state, and on its own initiative sends its delegates; it matters not whether a certain entity with which it must deal is or is not a state, or whether or not the state or its government is recognized. The committee will try to function in all situations where large-scale fighting and suffering occur, however abnormal the situation may be from a legal point of view. Guggenheim treats the committee as a "juridical person, directly subordinated to particular international law." Werner asked whether the time has not come to recognize the committee as a "person" in international law. Verdross sees in it already a particular subject of international law.

The international position of the International Committee of the Red Cross, already recognized by the Prisoners of War Convention of 1929, has been greatly strengthened by the new Geneva conventions.[28] It is entitled to establish and to run a Central Prisoners of War Information Agency in a neutral country, and it is provided that "its special position in this field shall be recognized at all times." With regard to prisoners of war, it has the same prerogatives as the representatives or delegates of the protecting power; similar prerogatives are given to the committee by the fourth convention. Resolution XI, adopted at the 1949 conference, requires the committee to be ready at all times and in all circumstances to fulfill the humanitarian tasks entrusted to it by the conventions. The conference also recognized the necessity of providing regular financial support of the committee.

III

The new Geneva conventions deal with the protection of "war victims," that is, with the protection of persons outside of the fighting formations (civilians), or with persons of the armed forces who are at the time or permanently not able to fight. This is the proper sphere of action of the Red Cross conventions within the larger framework of the laws of war. It is important to emphasize that the laws of war in general and the Geneva conventions in particular are a chapter in the international protection of human rights. Present-day efforts at this international protection of human rights stand in strange contrast with the growing inhumanity of total war and the neglect of the laws of war. The dignity of and respect for the human personality[29] is the very basis of the Geneva conventions.[30] It is possibly for this reason that the conventions[31] speak of the "rights conferred upon the individuals" and state that they "may in no circumstances renounce in part or in entirety the rights secured to them."[32] This means that such renunciation is legally void. This norm expresses the intention of protecting war victims against undue pressure to renounce their rights. But, although the conventions give some limited rights of petition to the individuals concerned, these rights constitute primarily duties for the ratifying states. Violation of these rights or refusal to grant them make the states internationally responsible. Intervention by the protecting power or the International Committee of the Red Cross will then be necessary. That is why it is hardly tenable to assert that the conventions have made of the individuals subjects of international law, although the idea of the "expanding sphere of international law" can be found in some parts of the reports of the committees.

Even those most opposed to the continuance of the laws of war agreed with Nicola Politis in the League of Nations—and so do present-day opponents of the laws of war—that, at least, these humanitarian norms of the Geneva conventions must and should continue to be positive law and to be revised and expanded. Some writers today assert that the continuance of these norms can be defended, because they are "compatible with total war," whereas norms for the conduct of war are not. But this reasoning is fallacious. Total, lawless war will even make impossible the working of the norms of the Geneva Conventions, as the International Committee of the Red Cross in a memorandum to all governments has tersely warned the states.

IV

The new Geneva conventions deal with the protection of "war victims." But it is not correct to speak of these norms, as is sometimes done, as of the "humanitarian" norms of the laws of war. On the one hand, the laws concerning the conduct of the war are also inspired by humanitarian motives. On the other hand, even the norms of the Geneva conventions are based, as they should be, on practical and realistic considerations, striking, in the words of the Swiss foreign minister, an equilibrium between humanitarian ideals and the cruel necessities of war.

Although all the preliminary work had been done by the Red Cross, the task of the Geneva Diplomatic Conference of 1949 was not an easy one. The humanitarian views of the Red Cross societies had to be reconciled with the views of the governments. And, within the latter, many divergent views had to be brought into a formula, acceptable to all. This explains the long duration of the conference and the fact that, apart from the four principal committees, many subcommittees and working parties were at work, many proposals and amendments were presented, many drafts made. Neutral and belligerent states were present; among the latter were states which had heavily suffered under enemy occupation or those which feared enemy occupation in a new war and other states with quite different experiences. Naturally, every state looked at every problem from the point of view of its own experience and necessities.

The new Geneva conventions of 1949 are not wholly ideal and without weaknesses, but, in general, they represent progress. Such progress moved in three directions, namely, according to Professor Maurice Bourquin, in enlarging, strengthening, and adapting the former conventions to the present conditions of war.

Progress lies in the field of legal technique, in the attempt at a clear statement, so as to avoid ambiguities or *lacunae,* which may give rise to different interpretations or *mala fide* circumventions. True, the wish to state everything fully has led to repetitions, particularly in the third and fourth conventions — to a certain lack of legal elegance. Further, certain technical difficulties arose from the fact that the conventions are equally authentic in English and French.

Further progress realized by the Geneva conventions lies in the abolition of the *clausula si omnes.* Article 2, paragraph 3, of all the conventions lays down that, although one of the powers to the conflict may not be a party to these conventions, not only do the others remain bound among themselves, but also toward the said power, if the latter accepts and applies the provisions. Everywhere the effort can be seen to make the law of the conventions as binding as possible.

A great advance in legal technique, and sometimes also in contents, can be seen in the fact that certain groups of norms of a general scope have been put together, clarified, and amplified. These common norms are, to a great extent, identical in all four conventions. Apart from the norms already mentioned, dealing with the Red Cross emblem, the following groups of norms are analyzed here:

1) Final provisions,[33] dealing with signature, ratification, coming into force, accession, and notification of accession. In case of armed conflict or civil war, ratifications deposited and accessions notified shall immediately go into effect. A denunciation made at a time when the denouncing power is involved in a conflict shall not, as generally, take effect one year after the notification to the Swiss Federal Council, but only when peace has been concluded and after operations connected with release and repatriation of the protected persons have been terminated.

2) Execution of the conventions.[34] Each contracting party, acting through its commander in chief, is not only bound to assure the detailed execution of the conventions, but also to provide for unforeseen cases in conformity with the general principles of these conventions.

3) Repression of abuses and infractions.[35] Identical articles establish the duty for each contracting party to complete its national legislation by the incorporation of penal provisions for the repression of acts constituting a breach of the conventions; also, to apprehend persons charged with acts contrary to the conventions, regardless of their nationality, and to refer them for trial to their own courts or, if necessary, to those of another contracting state. The conventions distinguish between grave breaches and other infractions. The "grave breaches" are not defined, but a list of acts, committed against protected persons or property is given, a list which shows the bitter experience of the last war: wilful killing, torture or inhuman treatment, including biological experiments, wilfully causing great suffering or serious injury to body or health, and extensive destruction and expropriation of property, not justified by military necessity and carried out unlawfully and wantonly.

The Geneva conventions carefully avoid the term "war crimes," and contain nothing about the so-called "Nuremberg principles." This is a consequence not only of the controversial nature of these principles which have not and do not constitute general international law and, up to now, do not even constitute United Nations law, but also of the legally decisive fact that these subjects were outside of the competence of the Geneva Diplomatic Conference of 1949. In these respects, the rapporteur stated,[36] it "was considered advisable to proceed very cautiously." A special article discussed grave breaches, but "without any reference to an international jurisdiction; it is not the duty of this Conference to form rules of International Penal Law."

An innovation is the article, inserted at the suggestion of the Italian delegation, according to which no contracting party shall be allowed to absolve itself or any other contracting party of any responsibility incurred by itself or by another contracting party with respect to grave breaches of the conventions. This article, as the report of the Joint Committee[37] states, is designed to make the norms compulsory and "to render null and void, in advance, any contractual exemption by which a victor State could prevail upon the conquered State to cease to hold the victor responsible for any violation of the Conventions committed by the organs of the latter." The norm is legally interesting, as containing obligations, not for the war, but for the peace treaty.

4) Settlement of disputes. The conventions contain two norms in this respect. The one deals with violations of the conventions and establishes a procedure of inquiry. The other establishes a conciliation procedure for disagreements in the application or interpretation of the provisions of the conventions. If such a dispute cannot be settled otherwise the parties are encouraged to agree between themselves to refer it to the International Court of Justice (Resolution I).

5) General Provisions.[38] The most important ones will be discussed later. The protecting power,[39] with whose coöperation and under whose scrutiny the conventions shall be applied, has the duty to safeguard the interests of the parties to the conflict. The experiences of World War II, especially the situation of French prisoners of war after the fall of France and of German prisoners of war after unconditional surrender, inspired the article concerning substitutes for the protecting power. The same experiences led to the last paragraph of this article that "no derogation from the preceding provisions shall be made by special agreements between Powers one of which is restricted, even temporarily, in its freedom to negotiate with the other Power by reason of military events, more particularly where the whole or a substantial part of the territory of said Power is occupied."

The quoted article refers to special agreements. The technique of special agreements appears often in the conventions. As a rule the norms of the conventions are obligatory, but some are optional in the sense that they may be created by special agreements, which the parties may, but need not conclude.[40] But "no special agreement shall adversely affect the situation of the protected persons nor restrict the rights conferred upon them."[41] On the other hand, Annexes I and III to the third convention and Annex III to the fourth convention apply obligatorily in the absence of special agreements between the powers concerned.

V

The new Geneva conventions contain not only groups of common, identical norms, but are also legally closely related among themselves. Thus, the articles concerning procedural safeguards for persons accused of grave breaches of the conventions refer to Articles 105 ff. of the third convention. Article 20 of the first convention disposes that hospital ships, protected by the second convention, shall not be attacked from the land. On the other hand, Article 23 of the second convention provides that establishments ashore, entitled to protection under the first convention, shall be protected from bombardment or attack from the sea. Retained religious, medical, and hospital personnel of hospital ships shall, under Article 37 of the second convention, be subject, immediately on landing, to the provisions of the first convention. Under Article 14 of the first convention, sick and wounded, and, under Article 29 members of the auxiliary personnel who have fallen into the hands of the enemy shall be prisoners of war and enjoy the protection of the third convention. Personnel, designated in Articles 24 and 26 of the first convention shall, if they fall into the hands of the adverse party, at least benefit by the provisions of the third convention. A good part of the fourth convention is modeled after the third convention.

The fourth convention, relative to the protection of civilian persons in time of war,[42] creates new international law. The first three conventions are revisions: The first convention replaces the Geneva conventions of August 22, 1864,[43] July 6, 1906,[44] and July 27, 1929.[45] The second convention replaces the tenth Hague convention of October 18, 1907.[46] The third convention replaces the Geneva Prisoners of War Convention of July 27, 1929.[47]

The Geneva Diplomatic Conference of 1949 had no competence to deal with the international law of neutrality, to change the fifth or twelfth Hague conventions of 1907, dealing with neutrality land and maritime warfare. The conference was without competence, with respect to the general or particular treaty law concerning neutrality. Now, it has often been asserted since 1920 that neutrality is a thing of the past, an outmoded concept, which has no more standing, in law and in fact, under the new concept of collective security. Undoubtedly, there are certain duties for members of the former League of Nations and the present United Nations, which are legally incompatible with neutrality. But, apart from nonmembers, even members of the United Nations may, for the time being, be neutral, in the case of legal use of force under Articles 51 and 106; or they may not participate in a military enforcement action, either because a binding decision of the Security Council has not called upon them, or because they do not heed a nonbinding recommendation of the Security Council or Assembly. For this and other reasons the law of neutrality is today in a chaotic state.

What position do the new Geneva conventions take toward neutrality? In view of the prominent role of the International Committee of the Red Cross and of Switzerland, it is not surprising that the conventions presuppose the continuation of the law of neutrality. "The humanitarian aim of the Red Cross," Judge Huber has stated, "presupposes complete neutrality, absolute impartiality, full independence vis-à-vis all national, supra-national, political, social or confessional organizations, and the will to put oneself equally at the service of all."

Neutrality has, therefore, a broad place in the conventions. That the general law of neutrality still exists has been shown by World War II, and has been confirmed by the practice of states, recent treaties, and national and international judgments. In 1949 no participating state raised any objections to the concept of neutrality, as used in the conventions.

The protecting power—a neutral power—plays an important role in all four conventions. It is equally a neutral state or organization which may be agreed upon as a substitute for the protecting power. A Central Prisoners of War Information Agency shall be created in a neutral country; equally, a Central Information Agency for protected civilian persons, in particular, for internees, shall be created in a neutral country. To the neutral International Committee of the Red Cross far-reaching rights of supervision are given. These instances of neutrality are vital for carrying out the conventions, especially the last two.

While neutrality under international law continues, and while neutrality holds such a prominent place in the conventions, it is, of course, thinkable that in a future world war no neutral country may be left; this is a question of fact, not of law. This hypothesis was referred to at the 1949 conference by the French delegation, which, therefore, proposed to establish a "High International Committee," consisting of thirty persons whose duty it would be, in the event of a conflict, to "supervise and ensure the respect for the Conventions." But various objections were raised, during the discussion, with regard to the practical difficulties which the High International Committee would encounter. The whole problem also seemed too difficult for the conference. That is why no article was inserted to this effect into the conventions; but Resolution II was adopted, which, under the hypothesis that there may be no protecting power in a future conflict, recommends that consideration be given, as soon as possible, to the advisability of setting up an international body, the functions of which shall be to perform the duties of a protecting power, if there is no such protecting power.

Article 109 of the third convention contains the norm that throughout the duration of hostilities the parties to the conflict shall endeavor, with the coöperation of the neutral powers concerned, to make arrangements for the accommodation in neutral countries of seriously wounded and sick prisoners of war, and to conclude, in addition, agreements for direct repatriation or internment in a neutral country of able-bodied prisoners of war, who have undergone a long period of captivity. Annex I gives the text of a model agreement. Article 110 contains categories of prisoners of war who may be accommodated in a neutral country. Article 111 foresees special agreements for internment of prisoners of war in a neutral country until the close of hostilities. The mixed medical commissions of Article 112 and Annex II shall consist of three members, two of whom shall belong to a neutral country. Article 132 of the fourth convention foresees special agreements for the accommodation of civilian interned persons in a neutral country.

The protection of the first two conventions is also due to wounded, sick, and shipwrecked neutral persons.[48] Article 4 of the first, and Article 5 of the second convention prescribe that these conventions shall be applied by analogy by neutral powers to the protected persons received or interned in neutral territory, or to dead persons found. "A neutral government can, without being deemed to interfere improperly in the conflict, authorize a recognized relief society of its country to bring assistance to one of the belligerents; it may authorize such a society or even an individual to place a hospital ship at the disposal of the belligerent. This assistance carries with it certain duties."[49] In addition to the activity which neutral powers may engage in beyond the limits of their territories, they also have rights and duties on their own territory. They must care for the wounded, sick, and shipwrecked persons who may reach their neutral territory. The neutral powers will not retain medical and religious personnel, but will send them back to the belligerent of their service. Such persons may take with them their clothing, personal articles, valuables, and instruments.[50]

The conventions abound in articles involving neutrality. They deal with societies of neutral countries;[51] the marking of medical units of neutral countries;[52] the taking of wounded, sick, or shipwrecked persons on board a neutral warship or a neutral aircraft;[53] the landing of wounded, sick, or shipwrecked persons in a neutral port;[54] appeals to the charity of commanders of neutral merchant vessels, yachts, or other crafts to take on board and care for wounded, sick, or shipwrecked persons, and to collect the dead;[55] and hospital ships utilized by relief societies and private individuals of neutral countries.[56] Military hospital ships and hospital ships of relief societies of parties to the conflct or of neutral countries are not assimilated to warships, as regards their stay in a neutral port.[57] On board ships used for the conveyance of medical equipment neutral observers may be placed by agreement among the parties to the conflict.[58] The second convention has also retained the norm that neutral vessels, which have taken wounded, sick or shipwrecked persons on board, shall enjoy special protection and may, in no case, be captured; but that "they shall remain liable to capture for any violation of neutrality they may have committed."

New is the norm that allows, under certain conditions, medical aircraft of parties to the conflict to fly over the territory of neutral powers, land on it when necessary, or use it as a port of call.[59] In the 10th Hague convention of 1907 it was provided that, if wounded, sick, or shipwrecked persons are taken on board a neutral warship, or if such persons are landed in a neutral port, "every possible precaution must be taken" to see that they take no further part in operations of war. Here we see in the first two conventions the impact of changes in the law of neutrality, brought about by treaties such as the United Nations Charter. For the corresponding Articles 15 and 17 of the new second convention provide that "it shall be ensured, *where so required by international law,* that they can take no further part in operations of war." In the same way, Article 37 of the first and Article 40 of the second convention provide that, if in a flight of a belligerent medical aircraft over neutral territory, wounded, sick, or shipwrecked persons are disembarked with the consent of the local authorities on neutral territory, they shall be detained by the neutral Power, where so required by international law, so that they cannot again take part in operations of war.

The only strange thing in the conventions is that Article 4 B/2 and Article 122 of the third convention speak of "neutral *or non-belligerent* Powers." "Nonbelligerency," as introduced by Mussolini, later used by Franco Spain, is a political, not a legal concept: international law does not know nonbelligerency.[60]

VI

As already observed, the Geneva conventions cautiously avoid any reference to the term "war crimes" and the so-called "Nuremberg principles."

Article 85 of the third convention prescribes that even prisoners of war, prosecuted and sentenced for acts committed prior to capture—particularly offenses against the laws and customs of war—retain the benefits of this convention. Long discussions turned around this point. A minority of delegations felt that prisoners of war, sentenced on the basis of the Nuremberg principles should no longer be subject to this convention. But a great majority held to the contrary, just as under any mature national legislation the lawbreaker remains under the benefit of such legislation, without prejudice to his punishment.[61]

Article 99 of the third convention forbids trial and condemnation of prisoners of war, except for acts forbidden by the law of the detaining power or by international law in force at the time the act was committed. In view of the *ex post facto* legislation of the Nuremberg Charter, which constitutes strictly particular international law, it is to be emphasized that the principle *nullum crimen sine lege* is added to the fundamental principles, and that the phrase "international law" is to be understood to mean its "generally recognized provisions."[62]

The Geneva Diplomatic Conference of 1949 had no competence to legislate in the field of the laws concerning the conduct of war. With regard to the latter, the convoking government and the place of the conference by precedent have been different. International conferences concerning the law for the protection of the victims of war have been traditionally convoked by Switzerland in Geneva; those for the international law concerning the conduct of war, by The Netherlands at The Hague. It was for this reason of lack of competence that the Soviet proposal at Geneva to ban the atomic bomb was not accepted.

According to Article 135 of the third convention this convention "shall be complementary to the IVth Hague Convention of October 18, 1907, Section I, Chapter II of the Regulations annexed"; these Articles 4–20 deal with prisoners of war. According to Article 154 of the fourth convention, this convention "shall be supplementary to the IVth Hague Convention of October 18, 1907, Sections II and III of the Regulations annexed." Articles 22–41 deal with the conduct of war, Articles 42–56 contain the norms concerning belligerent occupation. The formulation of Article 154 of the fourth convention "was a question of great difficulty." The "cautious wording" ("supplementary"—not "replace") "does not attempt to indicate any limitation between the Civilians Convention and the Hague Conventions; neither does it seek to establish a hierarchy; any such attempt, in a field as complex as this, would be a singularly dangerous undertaking."[63]

This lack of competence as to the laws concerning the conduct of war was again and again emphasized at the conference. Thus "Committee I did not consider itself competent to interpret international law, concerning survivors who had been landed on neutral territory";[64] nor was this committee "prepared to give a precise definition of the notion of "enemy territory or enemy-occupied territory. It did not regard as part of its business the definition of the rules applying to territorial waters or so-called battle-zones."[65]

The third Committee noted that the treaties governing means of combat "are entirely irrelevant to our convention."[66] "As to Article 33 of the fourth convention, the majority felt that "regulations governing property in time of war were within the terms of reference of the laws and customs of war on land, and that we should refrain from any encroachment, our task being confined to protection of persons."[67] Committee III remarked that the prohibition of pillage and collective penalties in Article 33 of the fourth convention are merely restatements from the Hague regulations; that Article 51, concerning labor, incorporates the main provisions of Article 52 of the Hague regulations; that with regard to requisitions (Article 55 of the fourth convention) "we were anxious to avoid any conflict with the Hague Regulations."[68]

Being without competence to legislate in the field of the law concerning the conduct of war, the Geneva diplomatic conference of 1949 tried to avoid any conflict with the laws of war as they stand, and with the new conventions which may replace them. The Hague rules actually in force concerning the conduct of war and, particularly, the norms with regard to prisoners of war and to the law of belligerent occupation, constitute, therefore, the framework within which the Geneva conference operated. This is also true with respect to the fourth convention, although it creates new law concerning the protecting of war victims. On the other hand, the conference could not ignore modern conditions of warfare, which are so different from those prevailing at the time of the first and second Hague conferences. It is also clear that the delegates stood, to a very high degree, under the impression of the experiences and atrocities perpetrated in World War II. Perhaps these experiences dominated them too much, and it may well be that the new conventions will not suffice in the event of another world war with atomic weapons.

Generally speaking, the conventions try to strengthen the law actually in force, by clearer definitions, more detailed regulations, unambiguous wording, and try to avoid any contradiction with the Hague rules. Modern conditions of warfare are amply taken into consideration, but as matters of fact, voicing no opinion as to their legality or illegality. The bitter experiences of the last war are often made use of by writing into the conventions definitive prohibitions of certain acts; here no conflict with the Hague rules had to be feared, as these atrocities have been and are illegal. But in some respects the conventions introduced innovations which either go beyond the Hague rules or are even in contradiction with them.

Some norms clearly show the wish to stay within the Hague rules. Thus Article 28 of the second convention retains the protection of sick bays, should fighting occur on board a warship, in conformity with Article 7 of the tenth Hague convention of 1907, although writers have argued that this clause is hardly of any importance under modern conditions of naval warfare. Similarly, the norm of Articles 10–12 of the Hague regulations on land warfare, concerning the institution of release of prisoners on parole, has, at the request of several delegations, for the first time been inserted as Article 21 of the third convention, although the release on parole has little practical importance, as most states do not allow the members of their armed forces to accept release on parole.

Modern conditions of war have in some respects exercised a negative influence, either by making impossible the conclusion of certain conventions for which the International Committee of the Red Cross had made preparatory studies, or by allowing only optional norms. Thus, no convention concerning the protection of the whole civilian population against all dangers and in all circumstances was enacted, nor a convention concerning protection against aerial bombardment. Also, the long-cherished project for the creation of hospital or neutralized zones in the belligerents' own territories or in occupied areas, in time of peace and after the outbreak of hostilities, organized to protect the wounded and sick—or the civilian population—could not be realized as an obligatory norm;[69] it is left to the discretion of the contracting parties to establish such zones and, upon the outbreak and during the course of hostilities, mutually to recognize them by optional agreements.

In some respects modern conditions of warfare have forced a retreat, as compared with the more liberal norms of earlier conventions. Thus, the permanent members of the medical service of the land, sea, and air forces and of the national relief societies of the belligerents have been reduced from their former particularly privileged legal position. The reasons were, on the one hand, that the medical service has become, through many functions going beyond the care for the sick and wounded, an integral part of the armed forces and plays nowadays a prominent role in contributing to the maintenance of the numerical strength of the troops; on the other hand, retreat from liberal norms of earlier conventions was forced by the enormous number of prisoners of war and the long duration of captivity.[70] If medical personnel falls into the hands of the enemy, they are no longer to be returned obligatorily, but may be retained;[71] they constitute a new category, are not prisoners of war, and benefit, at least, by the provisions of the third convention; hence the new Article 33 in this latter convention. If auxiliary medical personnel falls into the hands of the enemy, they shall be prisoners of war.[72] But medical personnel belonging to neutral countries,[73] as well as the religious, medical, and hospital personnel of hospital ships,[74] remain fully protected.

As a consequence of these changes and under the impact of modern war as warfare of movement, far-reaching changes concerning medical buildings and material came about. The buildings, material, and stores of fixed medical establishments of the armed forces shall remain subject to the laws of war. The material of mobile medical units that fall into the hands of the enemy will no longer be returned, but shall be reserved for the care of wounded and sick.[75] Equally important alterations concern transports or vehicles of the wounded and sick and of medical equipment. If such transports fall into the hands of the enemy, they will no longer be returned, but shall be subject to the laws of war.[76] But ships used for the conveyance of medical equipment may not be captured, nor the equipment carried seized, provided that the particulars regarding their voyage have been indicated to and approved by the adverse party.[77]

To the less liberal norms belongs also Article 52 of the third convention; a prisoner of war may now be employed on labor of an unhealthy or dangerous nature, if he volunteers—a rather unhappy norm in view of the very different interpretations of "volunteers." Contrary to the report of Committee II, Article 52 now provides that the removal of mines or similar devices shall be considered as dangerous labor.

It is to be noted that the conference accepted the internment of civilian persons, in the belligerents' own territory and in occupied territory.[78]

Many norms of the new Geneva conventions show the impression of the atrocities, perpetrated during the last war. Here belongs—in full harmony with present-day efforts at international protection of human rights—the prohibition against any discrimination of protected persons, "founded on sex, race, nationality, religion, political opinion, or any similar criteria."[79] Here belongs also the norm that strictly forbids "any attempts upon the lives of the protected persons or violence to their person; in particular, they shall not be murdered or exterminated, subjected to torture or to biological experiments; they shall not wilfully be left without medical assistance and care, nor shall conditions exposing them to contagion or infection be created."[80] "Future generations," said the rapporteur,[81] "will certainly be astounded that, in the midst of the twentieth century, it was considered necessary to embody such elementary moral rules in our conventions. The vivid recollection of recent indescribable atrocities is, however, sufficient evidence that this was necessary."

Other bitter experiences of World War II are reflected in many norms of the new Geneva conventions. Such are, for example, the norms, protecting the aged and infirm, and expectant mothers among the civilian population;[82] or the norms relating to child welfare, especially children under fifteen, who are orphaned or are separated from their families.[83] The special Article 26 of the fourth convention was inspired by the tragic experience of civilian families dispersed by the war. Article 109 of the third convention which prescribes that no sick or wounded prisoner of war, eligible for repatriation, may be repatriated during hostilities against his will, as well as Article 45 of the fourth convention, laying down that "in no circumstances shall a protected civilian person be transferred to a country where he or she may have reason to fear persecution for his or her political opinions or religious beliefs," are also due to experiences of the last war. The Western powers did not send back soldiers of the Polish Army in Italy or persons in refugee camps in western Germany or Austria to the countries of their origin or nationality against their will, as such sending back would often have meant a death sentence.

Article 44 of the fourth convention is also closely connected with manifold experiences of the last war; it was inserted at the proposal of the Israel delegation. During the last war tens of thousands of persons took refuge in an enemy country, either because they were strongly opposed to the regime of their own country or because they were forced to leave by the regime of their own country. Such persons, for example thousands of German and Austrian Jews, bitterly opposed to, expelled and no longer protected by, the regimes of their own country, but still possessing its nationality, found themselves in the country of asylum in the paradoxical legal position of alien enemies. That is why Article 44 provides as follows: "The Detaining Power, in applying the measures of control, shall not treat as enemy aliens exclusively on the basis of their nationality *de jure* of an enemy State, refugees who do not, in fact, enjoy the protection of any government."

Of great importance is the principle of direct responsibility of the detaining power for the treatment given to prisoners of war or any protected civilian person.[84] The detaining power cannot, therefore, shift responsibility for infractions to its agents. An entirely new norm, inspired by the experiences of the last war, has been inserted, concerning the transfer of prisoners of war or of protected civilian persons by the detaining power to another power.[85] Transfer to a power which is not a party to these conventions is absolutely forbidden; transfer to another power, party to these conventions, is allowed only after the detaining power has satisfied itself of the willingness and ability of such transferee power to apply the convention. Responsibility then rests on the power accepting these persons. But if this power fails in any important respect, the transferring power shall, upon being notified by the protecting power, take effective measures to correct the situation or shall request the return of the protected persons. While, therefore, the principle of joint responsibility was not accepted, the principle of the transferring power's contingent responsibility was adopted.

After the experience in the last war the provision of Article 47 of the fourth convention, concerning the inviolability of rights of the protected civilian persons, is of great importance. The article prescribes that these persons in occupied territory shall in no case or manner be deprived of the benefits of this convention by any change made, as the result of the occupation of a territory, in the institutions or government of said territory, nor by any agreement concluded between the authorities of the occupied territory and the occupying power, nor by annexation by the latter of the whole or part of the occupied territory. During the last war Germany and Italy annexed certain parts of occupied territory. Such annexations of occupied territory *pendente bello* are illegal under general international law. Nor can the argument of conquest and subjugation be applied, as long as allies of the occupied state continue fighting.

Many norms of the new Geneva conventions show the influence of modern conditions of warfare, without taking any stand about their legality. Thus the fact that women are nowadays enrolled in the armed forces is reflected in norms specially mentioning women and providing that they shall be treated with all consideration due to their sex.[86] The great importance of collective and individual relief shipments to prisoners of war and protected civilian interned persons has led to detailed regulations.[87] Profound changes had to be introduced with regard to the problem of the financial resources of prisoners of war, because it was necessary to take into account the more rigid financial and monetary systems which now exist in many countries.

The influence of modern aerial warfare is of the utmost importance on the norms of the Geneva conventions. Here belong the special norms, concerning medical aircraft[88] and concerning markings of hospitals, hospital ships, prisoners-of-war or civilian-internees camps, "so as to be clearly visible from the air."[89]

Article 23 of the third convention and Article 88 of the fourth convention provide for air-raid shelters in prisoners-of-war and civilian-internees camps. The term "shipwrecked" persons means "shipwrecked" from any cause and includes forced landings at sea by or from aircraft.[90] Medical establishments and units shall, as far as possible, be situated in such a manner that attacks against military objectives cannot imperil their safety.[91] Hospital ships may not possess or use a secret code for their wireless or other means of communication.[92]

Of particular importance is Article 18 of the first convention which was inspired by the "lamentable experiences of the war of 1939–1945." The military authorities of occupied territories may appeal to the charity of the inhabitants voluntarily to collect and care for the wounded and sick under the direction of the authorities. But no pressure must be brought upon these inhabitants, nor is the occupying power relieved of its obligation to give both physical and moral care to the wounded and sick. On the other hand, the same article authorizes the inhabitants spontaneously to collect and care for the wounded and sick of whatever nationality, even in invaded and occupied territories. The civilian population shall respect these wounded and sick, and, in particular, abstain from doing them violence. No one may ever be molested or convicted for having nursed the wounded or sick. This article is, particularly in view of aerial warfare, far-reaching. It protects wounded fliers, who land in enemy territory, against violence by the civilian population. This proviso was, further, inserted "to apply more particularly to wounded fliers or parachutists of their own or allied armies of the population of the occupied territory or even to members of resistance movements, whom this population was frequently prohibited to assist and care for in the last war, subject to extremely severe penalties."[93]

The influence of total war, the vanishing dividing line between armed forces and civilian population can be seen in a number of norms of the new conventions. Draft agreements, although purely optional, provide that hospital zones and localities, shall be far removed and free from all military objectives or large industrial or administrative establishments; hospital-zone lines of communications and means of transport shall not be used for the transport of military personnel or materiel, even in transit. And "no person residing in whatever capacity in such zone shall perform any work, either within or without the zone, directly in connection with military operations or the production of war materiel."

The extension of humanitarian activities of medical units or establishments of the armed forces to the care of civilian wounded and sick shall not deprive these establishments of their guaranteed protection.[94] On the other hand, civilian hospitals, organized to give care to the wounded and sick, the infirm and maternity cases, shall at all times be respected and protected and shall not lose their protection because of the fact that sick or wounded members of the armed forces are nursed in these hospitals.[95] Thus, "the hard and fast distinction between military and civilian hospitals, drawn under the 1929 Convention, will be abolished."[96]

VII

A great number of norms of the new Geneva conventions strengthen the earlier norms, but remain fully within the law actually in force concerning the conduct of war. Among them are, for example, the much more detailed rules with respect to search for casualties, recording and forwarding information, prescriptions regarding the dead, graves, and registration service.[97] Other such norms are the new definition of hospital ships,[98] the recognition of officially recognized lifeboat institutions for coastal rescue operations,[99] the norm that any hospital ship in a port which falls into the hands of the enemy shall be authorized to leave.[100] New and interesting is the norm that merchant vessels which have been transformed into hospital ships cannot be put to any other use throughout the duration of hostilities.[101]

The third convention contains many more detailed norms concerning questioning, property, and evacuation of prisoners of war. The rules concerning internment have been greatly strengthened and amplified, as far as quarters, food, bathing, hygiene, medical attention, and religious, intellectual, and physical activities are concerned; often new ideas and standards have been introduced. Greatly improved is the section on the labor of prisoners of war. Entirely new is the section on their financial resources. Strengthened are the sections on the relation of prisoners of war with the exterior and the authorities. It deserves mention that Article 88—an innovation—gives to prisoners of war the *unrestricted* right to apply to the representatives of the protecting power, in order to draw their attention to any points on which the prisoners may have complaints to make regarding their conditions of captivity. Of far-reaching importance is the chapter on penal and disciplinary sanctions—a full brief code. Human rights and due process of law shall be secured to persons charged with violations. The rules are dominated by three principles: an appeal to the indulgence of the authorities of the detaining power concerning their decision as to whether to take judicial or disciplinary action; the principle of decision by military courts which have the guarantee of independence and impartiality; and the principle of allowing the judge to lighten sentences.

The fourth convention, while creating new law, also remains mostly within the framework of the rules actually in force concerning the conduct of war. Thus, Article 27, valid for the territories of the belligerent and occupied territories, is an enlargement of Article 46 of the Hague regulations; not only respect for the person and honor of civilians, but also for their family rights, for their religious convictions and practices, and their manners and customs is guaranteed, and special protection is given to women. Article 33 is a mere restatement of Articles 47 and 50 forbidding pillage and collective penalties. The norms concerning aliens in the territories of the belligerents are new. In principle, they may be allowed to leave the territory, but such permission may be refused. It is no longer compulsory to subject detained persons to the same conditions as those prevailing before the outbreak of hostilities. Certain measures of control may be applied, although, in principle, the situation of the enemy civilians shall be continued to be regulated by the provisions concerning aliens in time of peace. The severest measures of control which may be applied—and then only if the security of the detaining power makes it absolutely necessary—are assigned residence and internment, the latter being under the convention a more severe measure than assigned residence. Articles 79–135 contain the regulations for the treatment of the internees, whether in a belligerent's own country or in an occupied area; they are modeled, *mutatis mutandis,* after the rules of the Prisoners of War Convention.

Particularly interesting are the norms of Articles 47–78 concerning occupied territory,[102] in relation to Articles 42–56 of the Hague regulations.[103] Norms of the convention regulate spiritual assistance, collective and individual relief shipments; and there is a brief code of penal legislation and procedure. Article 51, concerning enlistment and labor, amplifies Articles 44, 45; Articles 55, 56, concerning prohibited destruction, correspond to Articles 55, 56 of the Hague regulations.

Some innovations are merely optional and, hence, in no contradiction with the laws of war actually in force. Thus, Article 18 of the second convention lays down the rule that the parties to the conflict shall conclude local arrangements, whenever circumstances permit, for the removal of the wounded and sick by sea from a besieged or encircled area and for the passage of medical and religious personnel and equipment on their way to that area. As the report[104] states, experience of the last war has demonstrated the usefulness and possibility of such evacuation. Similarly, Article 17 of the fourth convention recommends the conclusion of local arrangements for the removal from besieged or encircled areas of wounded, sick, infirm and aged civilian persons, children and maternity cases. Such agreements are wholly optional, at the discretion of the belligerents; for the civilian population has, under the laws of war, no legal claim to leave unmolested before or during the siege.[105]

Article 23 of the fourth convention prescribes the allowance of free passage, even by the enemy, of all consignments of medical and hospital stores and objects necessary for religious worship, intended only for the civilian population, as well as of all consignments of essential foodstuffs, clothing, and tonics, intended for children under fifteen, expectant mothers and maternity cases, if the enemy is satisfied as to certain enumerated objective conditions. This means, particularly, also passage through a blockade. The report[106] tells us that several delegations raised very decided objections to which they attached capital importance, because they said any exception to the strict enforcement of a blockade may result in contributing indirectly to enemy reinforcements. These objections were overcome and the present text reached through the proposal, by the Norwegian delegation, and acceptance of objective conditions. When the committee stated that "in modern warfare the blockade has become a powerful weapon," it obviously did not refer to a real blockade, the importance of which was not great in the two world wars, but to the so-called "long-distance blockade." Here again merely the fact was taken into consideration. For the legality of the so-called "long-distance blockade" is, to put it mildly, highly doubtful.

Article 54 of the fourth convention concerning judges and public officials in the occupied territory is in conformity with Article 43 of the Hague regulations. This is also true of the prescription of Article 64, according to which the penal legislation of the occupied territory shall remain in force; Article 43 of the Hague regulations obliges the occupying power as follows: "*... respecter les lois en vigueur dans le pays, sauf empêchement absolu.*" Article 64 of the fourth convention allows the occupying power to repeal the penal laws of an occupied territory, if they constitute a menace to the security of the occupying power or if they constitute an obstacle to the application of the convention, for example, laws providing for racial discrimination.

Article 55 of the fourth convention, concerning requisitions of foodstuffs and medical supplies by the occupying power, is in harmony with Article 52 of the Hague regulations. The new convention allows such requisitions not only for the use of the occupation forces, but also for the use of administration personnel. The restriction that such requisitions are allowed only if the requirements of the civilian population have been taken into account corresponds to the norm of Article 52 of the Hague regulations that these requisitions must be "en rapport avec les ressources du pays." Also, the norm of Article 55 of the fourth convention that the occupying power "shall make arrangements to ensure that fair value is paid for any requisitioned goods" introduces no new obligation, as this duty exists only "subject to the provisions of other international Conventions."

The detailed regulation of the problem of escaped prisoners of war is interesting.[107] These rules show again that such escape is, by no means, prohibited or made a crime by international law; to the contrary, such escape is, as the rapporteur stated,[108] "perfectly legitimate and honorable." It is not tenable to argue that the right of the detaining power to prevent such escape and to apply disciplinary measures to a prisoner who is recaptured, is a sanction for an illegal act. There are many such situations in the laws of war, such as spying, carrying contraband, breaching a blockade. They are not illegal, but because of the danger for the adverse party, the latter is allowed by international law to take preventive and repressive measures. Such acts are not illegal, but risky.[109]

VIII

Some norms of the new Geneva conventions deserve closer scrutiny from the point of view of their relations to the laws of war actually in force. The Prisoners of War Convention of 1929 already forbade reprisals against prisoners of war. This prohibition of reprisals against protected persons is now inserted into all four conventions.[110] Reprisals are not regulated by the Hague conventions. But here we have only a special prohibition of reprisals,[111] accepted by the states since 1929.

Although the second convention recommends a minimum of two thousand tons for hospital ships, this is only a recommendation; the conference did not intend to limit the protection of hospital ships to those of any particular tonnage.[112]

Of great importance is the norm of Article 49 of the fourth convention, according to which "individual or mass forcible transfer, as well as deportations of protected persons from occupied territory to the territory of the Occupying Power or to that of any other country, occupied or not, are prohibited, regardless of their motive." These deportations played a role in World War I[113] and a much greater one in the last war.[114] There is hardly any doubt that these deportations were always illegal under positive international law, but a new and clear norm, concerning the absolute prohibition of such deportations, was very much needed. Article 49 constitutes, therefore, important progress.

Article 55 of the fourth convention lays down the rule that "the Occupying Power has the duty, to the fullest extent of the means available to it, of ensuring the food and medical supplies of the population and should, in particular, bring in the necessary foodstuffs, medical stores and other articles, if the resources of the occupied territory are inadequate." The opinion has been voiced that "these provisions go very far beyond anything which is to be found in the Hague Regulations. It may possibly be thought that they go too far."[115] This writer is not of this opinion. This duty of the occupying power follows from Article 43 of the Hague regulations. It is, no doubt, a rule of positive international law that a state which takes over a territory in any form, even if this taking over is illegal, is bound to care for the population.[116] On the other hand, the norm of Article 55 of the fourth convention takes the difficulties of the occupying power fully into consideration; that is why this duty of the occupying power is qualified by the condition "to the fullest extent of the means available to it."

Article 68 of the fourth convention limits the imposition of the death penalty on protected civilian persons of an occupied territory to espionage, serious acts of sabotage, or intentional offenses which have caused the death of one or more persons, provided that such offenses were punishable by death under the law of the occupied territory in force before the occupation began. This latter proviso is hardly logical, because the martial law, proclaimed by the occupying power, has nothing to do with the local laws of the occupied territory. This proviso, further, is not in harmony with the laws of war actually in force; hence the reservations by Argentina, Canada, the United States, New Zealand, The Netherlands, and the United Kingdom.

A real innovation is the prohibition of taking hostages.[117] The Hague regulations contain nothing concerning the problem. The opinion in the literature was divided, but the practice of states resorted to the taking of hostages. It was controversial whether hostages can be put to death. Insofar as the taking of hostages is a measure of reprisals, it is already forbidden by the prohibition of reprisals against protected persons. But, as Guggenheim states, the taking of hostages is not only a measure of reprisal.[118] Hostages are also taken for securing the payment of taxes, requisitions, and contributions; further as prophylactic hostages to secure the observance of the laws of war, especially in an occupied territory. Before the present Geneva conventions, the taking of hostages and even the killing of hostages could not be proved to be forbidden by treaties or by a norm of general international law; the British *Manual of Military Law,* 1914, the American *Rules of Land Warfare* in paragraph 387 allow the taking of hostages. The taking of hostages was, therefore, not forbidden, although it was generally lamented and the urgent necessity for prohibition was stressed.[119] During and after World War II many writers argued that the taking and—*a fortiori*—the killing of hostages is prohibited under positive international law.[120] But even in most recent times no such positive rule of general international law can be shown. The London Charter in Article 6 and the Control Council Law No. 10, paragraph 1*b* of Article II recognized without qualification merely the "killing of hostages" as war crimes.[121] And here we have only particular and *ad hoc* international law, restricted to the prohibition of the killing, but not to the taking of hostages.

On the other hand, in the Hostages trial[122] the United States Military Tribunal "could not rule out entirely the possibility of the legitimate killing of hostages in order to guarantee the peaceful conduct of the populations of occupied territories." In the trial of Albert Kesselring by a British military court the judge advocate stated that "there is nothing which makes it absolutely clear that an innocent person properly taken for the purpose of a reprisal cannot be executed."[123] Even Claude Pilloud writes in 1950[124] that a positive rule of international law against the taking and killing of hostages cannot be proved. The norm of the Geneva conventions, absolutely forbidding even the taking of hostages, is, therefore, a *new* norm and constitutes great progress. This new norm of international law clearly corresponds to the conviction of the states, as shown by the fact that no signatory state entered a reservation.

Great progress has been achieved by the norms concerning the application *ratione temporis* of the Geneva conventions:

Article 5 of the first convention prescribes that the protection of protected persons who have fallen into the hands of the enemy shall apply until their *final* repatriation; the same is provided by Article 5 of the third convention with respect to prisoners of war. Of great importance, in view of the long detention of German and Japanese prisoners of war by the Soviet Union after the unconditional surrender of these two states, is Article 118 of the third convention, according to which prisoners of war shall be released and repatriated without delay after the cessation of active hostilities; this norm is merely a restatement of the positive international law already in force. Equally important is the norm of Article 133 of the fourth convention which prescribes that civilian internees—contrary to the practice of World War II—shall be released as soon as possible after the close of hostilities.[125]

IX

Of fundamental importance are the norms concerning the application *ratione materiae* and *ratione personae;*[126] they are basic and permeate all four Geneva conventions; at the same time they contain real innovations and some norms of which it is, to say the least, doubtful that they are in harmony with the laws actually in force concerning the conduct of war.

Articles 2 and 3 of all four conventions deal with the application *ratione materiae;* Article 2 with international conflict, Article 3 with "conflicts not of an international character."[127] The conventions shall, therefore, apply

1) to all cases of declared war;

2) to any other armed conflict that may arise between two or more of the contracting parties, even if the state of war is not recognized by one of them;

3) to all cases of partial or total occupation of the territory of a contracting party, even if the occupation meets with no armed resistance.

Formerly, the Geneva conventions applied simply to war. But the experiences under the League of Nations Covenant and the Kellogg pact have shown that, as a consequence of the uncertainty about the legal concept of war, it was possible to make "wars in disguise." Hence, in a great advance, from the point of view of legal technique, the United Nations Charter dropped the term "war" and replaced it with the clearer term "use of force." There is no doubt that such considerations influenced the making of Article 2 of the new Geneva conventions. But the wording is, in my opinion, not a happy one.

Logically, to "declared wars" correspond "undeclared wars." Under general international law, a war can be fully a war in the legal sense, even if undeclared. From an undeclared war must be distinguished other types of the international use of force which are not war, whether declared or undeclared, such as military reprisals, the international "punishing expedition" against the Boxers and so on. What Article 2 obviously and correctly tries to achieve is the application of the conventions to any large-scale international fighting, whether it is called war or not. But the wording is not apt to achieve this goal.

First, the Article speaks of any other armed international conflict, "even if the state of war is not recognized by *one* party." But the state of war may not be recognized by any party to the conflict; such a conflict would, under the letter of Article 2, not be included. That was exactly the situation in the so-called "China incident," where not only the Japanese, but also the Chinese were reluctant to recognize a state of war.

Second, the Article speaks of any other armed conflict, "which may arise between two or more of the High Contracting Parties." What, for example, of the fighting between the Jews and the Arabs? What of the start of the fighting by North Korea, not a state and not a contracting party? True, under Article 2, paragraph 3, the conventions will be binding, if the nonparty accepts and applies the provisions.

Third, nothing is provided for a large-scale fighting in the course of an international military enforcement action, as now going on in Korea. For this is not an armed international conflict "between two or more of the High Contracting Parties." It is clear, further, that the conventions also apply in the case of *illegal* war or *illegal* use of force. This is the norm of positive international law, which was fully recognized by the Geneva Diplomatic Conference.

In consequence, what is really meant, but not expressed, is the application of the conventions to all international armed conflicts, whether called war or not, or, to put it better, to all international use of force, be it legal or illegal. The cases of legal use of force on an international level include, then, the cases of Articles 51, 106, and 107 of the Charter of the United Nations as well as military enforcement actions by the United Nations, whether in consequence of a decision by the Security Council or a recommendation by the Assembly, or by regional organizations under Article 53.

The conventions, further apply, as mentioned, "to all cases" of partial or total occupation, even if the occupation meets with no armed resistance. That the conventions apply to belligerent occupation is clear; an extension to certain types of occupation which do not constitute a belligerent occupation in the strict sense of the term, such as the German occupation of Denmark in World War II, or the occupation of neutral countries, can easily be granted. But the occupation on the basis of an armistice or peace treaty is mostly regulated by particular international law. What about the occupation of Germany and Japan after World War II? If the fourth convention, applying to *all* cases of occupation, applies also to these types, many acts of the occupying powers are bound to be illegal under the fourth convention. It has also been argued that the German rule in Austria from 1938 to 1945 was never an annexation, but only an unlawful occupation. We see, therefore, that the application of the conventions to *all* cases of occupation is hardly tenable.

Article 3, expanding the application of the conventions to "armed conflicts not of an international character"[128] is entirely novel and, to a certain extent, revolutionary. Just as "war" in the first paragraph of Article 2, just as "occupation" in the second paragraph of Article 2, thus, the term "armed conflicts not of an international character" is not defined in Article 3. But there can be no doubt that this term means civil war. The article, as it was adopted and now stands, went for years—before and during the Geneva Diplomatic Conference of 1949—through a great many drafts, suggestions, amendments, and discussions. Some feared the vagueness of the term "armed conflict not of an international character," the lack of definition. They feared that the convention may apply even to a mere riot, rebellion, or even acts of banditry. Others took the position that even a civil war in the full sense of the term is illegal from the point of view of municipal law and that to bind the legitimate government to apply the conventions would make it much more difficult for it to suppress the rebellion. In consequence, some arged that any norm concerning the application *ratione materiae* to civil wars should be dropped; but the majority was of a contrary opinion.

There evolved, then, a set of ideas that the "armed conflict not of an international character" must have reached a certain magnitude, the status of a "real" civil war; hence, the application of the conventions should be made subject to the fulfillment of certain objective conditions, such as that the rebels had achieved certain features of a state or that the rebels had been recognized as a belligerent party by the legitimate governments. But it was objected that often these conditions are not fulfilled, or that in any concrete case there would be an endless discussion as to whether these conditions are fulfilled so as to make the conventions applicable, and that there would be no impartial judge to decide this problem with juridical authenticity.

From another point of view, two extreme positions were represented—that the conventions should not apply to civil war at all; and that they should be applied in their entirety.

A further difficulty arose. If the legitimate government shall be bound by the totality of the conventions, it is necessary that the rebels be bound too. But how is it juridically possible—apart from the political awkwardness of stipulating in an international convention duties for rebels in a civil war—to bind third, and not yet existing, parties? Hence, some suggested that the legitimate government should be bound only on condition of reciprocity.

But a new idea paved the way for the final acceptance of Article 3: the distinction between fundamental obligations, which should be obligatory, and all other obligations, which should be optional and brought about by special agreements. In order to determine the fundamental obligations, the proposed reference to the "principles of the conventions" was considered too indefinite, especially as the original idea to have the conventions preceded by a preamble, laying down their fundamental principles, was dropped. These fundamental obligations were, therefore, enumerated.

It is on this basis that Article 3 was adopted, which, in the words of a delegate, quoted by Siordet, constitutes a *convention en miniature.*

Article 3, therefore, contains an unconditional obligation to treat persons taking no active part in a civil war in all circumstances humanely, without any discrimination; violence to life and person, in particular murder of all kinds, mutilation, cruel treatment and torture, the taking of hostages, outrages upon personal dignity, the passing of sentences and carrying out of executions without previous judgment pronounced by a regular court under due process of law are prohibited. The wounded and sick shall be collected and cared for.

As far as all or part of the other provisions of the conventions are concerned, the parties to the conflict shall endeavor to bring them into force, by means of special agreements.

The fundamental obligations, then, are obligatory unconditionally and without reciprocity. In this respect Article 3—an interesting innovation—contains an individual and unilateral engagement, without counterpart.

The application of the conventions *ratione materiae* to civil war, in the sense discussed, has made it necessary to change the terminology of "belligerents" to "adverse party" or "party to the conflict" throughout the conventions.

Just because only each party to the conflict is bound, neutrals are not bound in a purely internal conflict. The distinction between armed international conflicts of Article 2 and armed conflicts not of an international character is not always clear-cut. It suffices to refer to the Spanish Civil War, where there was outside intervention on both sides, so that it could hardly longer be called a purely internal conflict. The same is true of the recent civil war in Greece. The Geneva Diplomatic Conference has taken great care in no way to invade the domains of the norms of general international law. Exactly because the legitimate government, in respect of the enumerated fundamental obligations, is bound individually and unconditionally, the last sentence of Article 3 states that "the application of the preceding provisions shall not affect the legal status of the parties to the conflict." Hence the fulfillment of its obligations by the legitimate government is not an implied recognition of the insurgents as a belligerent party, nor an obstacle to such recognition either by the legitimate government or by third powers. Resolution X states once more that the conditions under which a party to a conflict can be recognized as a belligerent by powers not taking part in the conflict are governed by the general rules of international law on the subject, and are in no way modified by the Geneva conventions.

Article 3 constitutes valuable progress. The fact that no signatory power, with the exception of Portugal, has entered a reservation, indicates that this new international law corresponds to the conviction of the states.

The real weakness of the conventions, concerning their application *ratione materiae,* lies, in this writer's opinion, in Article 2; positively, by extending their application to *all* cases of occupation, negatively, by not including clearly all cases of a use of force, legal or illegal, on an international level.

X

As to the application of the Geneva conventions *ratione personae,* we must distinguish between the fourth and the first three conventions.

The fourth convention, creating new international law, speaks of "protected persons."[129] The application of the fourth convention *ratione personae* is not the same in all norms; we have to distinguish three different groups of protected persons. The convention deals only with protected civilian persons; hence, negatively, all persons, protected by the first three conventions are *not* protected persons within the meaning of the fourth convention.[130]

Part II of that convention, consisting of Articles 13 to 26, has the largest sphere of application *ratione personae;* it applies to the *whole* populations of the countries in conflict, without any discrimination.[131] It applies, therefore, not only to alien enemies, not only to neutrals, but also to the belligerent state's *own* nationals. This is an interesting innovation, as, under traditional international law, the treatment by a state of its own nationals is considered a problem of domestic jurisdiction. That is why various delegations criticized this principle. But the norm was adopted, as it stands, although "not in entire agreement with the traditional view of international law; but [in conformity with the fact that] that law is gradually becoming wider."[132]

There are, further, two different circles of protected civilian persons, narrower than the whole population, but also different *inter se:* the protected persons on the territory of a party to the conflict and the protected persons on occupied territory, although Articles 27 to 34 are common to both circles; equally articles 79 to 141, containing the regulations for the treatment of internees, apply to both groups.

The norms of Articles 35 to 46 apply only to protected persons in the territory of a party to the conflict. Article 4, paragraph 1, of the fourth convention defines, preliminarily, protected persons as "those, who, at a given moment and in any manner whatsoever, find themselves in case of a conflict or occupation, in the hands of a party to the conflict or Occupying Power of which they are not nationals." But, in consequence of Article 4, paragraph 2, the application *ratione personae* with regard to the norms, applicable to the territory of a party to the conflict, is as follows:

Not protected persons:

1) The belligerent state's own nationals.

2) Nationals of a neutral state, while the state of which they are nationals has normal diplomatic representation in the state in whose hands they are.

3) Nationals of a cobelligerent state.

Protected persons:

1) Alien enemies.

2) Nationals of a neutral state whose country is not represented diplomatically in the normal way.

3) Stateless or denationalized persons, who are "ipso jure protected persons."[133]

Even if under these rules nationals of a neutral state are protected persons, the special norm of Article 40, concerning employment of protected persons in the territory of a party to the conflict, does not cover them, as Article 40 specifically applies only to protected persons of *enemy* nationality.

The application *ratione personae* of Articles 47–78, concerning occupied areas, is as follows:

Not protected persons:

1) The occupying power's own nationals.

2) The nationals of a cobelligerent state.

Protected persons:

1) The nationals of the state which is occupied, whether they are alien enemies or not, as the convention applies to *all* cases of occupation.

2) All nationals of neutral states.

3) Stateless or denationalized persons. This protection of stateless persons in the territory of a party to the conflict or in occupied territory is an innovation and great progress in international law. For as individuals are only protected, under general international law, by the states of which they are nationals, stateless persons found themselves without any international protection whatsoever. The number of stateless persons has tremendously increased in the last decades for many reasons. But it is not correct to identify stateless persons with "refugees"; for refugees may still technically be nationals of the state from which they have taken refuge or by which they were even forced to leave. It has happened often that, for example, German Jews took refuge in Czechoslovakia, Denmark, Norway, Belgium, France, and other countries which were successively in varying forms occupied by Germany. These persons were *not* stateless, but nationals of the occupying power, who were not protected by the convention. That is why Article 70, paragraph 2, of the fourth convention prescribes that "nationals of the Occupying Power who, before the outbreak of hostilities, have sought refuge in the territory of the occupied State, shall not be arrested, prosecuted, convicted or deported from the occupied country, except for offenses committed after the outbreak of hostilities, or for common law offenses committed before the outbreak of hostilities which, according to the law of the occupied State, would have justified extradition in time of peace."

But, with regard to the two circles of protected persons in the territory of a party to the conflict and in occupied territories, there are two general grounds of exclusion from the status of protected civilian persons:

1) Nationals of a state which is not bound by the convention. The principle of reciprocity applies. But, according to Article 2, paragraph 3, if a state, not party to the convention, accepts and applies the provisions thereof, its nationals will automatically enjoy the benefits of the convention.

2) Persons who forfeit certain rights. Article 5, introduced at the

proposal of the Australian delegation, tries to strike the balance between the humanitarian reasons working for the protection of civilians, and considerations of the security of the state in a belligerent's own territory or of military security in occupied territory. This article reflects the fact that war is nowadays not fought on the battlefields alone; that enemy agents, saboteurs, "fifth columns" are part of modern warfare.

If a state is satisfied that an individual protected person in the territory of a party to the conflict is definitely suspected of or engaged in activities hostile to the security of the state, such individual person shall not be entitled to claim such rights and privileges as would be prejudicial to the security of such state. If in occupied territory an individual protected person is detained as a spy or saboteur, or as a person under definite suspicion of activity hostile to the security of the occupying power, such person, where absolute military security so requires, shall be regarded as having forfeited rights of communication. It was recognized that the wording of this Article is somewhat vague and leaves a good deal of discretion to the state in question. But such discretion was considered indispensable for reasons of state or military security. But even such persons shall be treated with humanity and not be deprived of the rights of fair and regular trial.

The earlier Geneva conventions referred, as far as application *ratione personae* is concerned, simply to Articles 1–3 of the Hague regulations. But the 1949 Prisoners of War Convention lays down in Article 4 in great detail, the circle of persons entitled to the status of prisoners of war, introducing many innovations and giving rise, at least in one point, to serious doubts.

Article 4 of the third convention consists of three parts A, B, and C. Part A is the principal part and corresponds literally to Article 13 of the first convention and Article 13 of the second convention; here we have the main norms for the application *ratione personae* of the first three conventions.

Parts B and C of Article 4 of the third convention are to be found only in this convention. Part C stipulates negatively that retained medical personnel and chaplains, dealt with in Article 33 of this convention, are not prisoners of war, although they are entitled to receive as a minimum the benefits and protection of this convention.

Part B introduces two new groups not before included in the Geneva conventions:

1) The first group consists of persons who are already under the enemy's jurisdiction. It happened during World War II that Germany had released and liberated soldiers of The Netherlands and Belgium,

after the resistance of these countries had ended and they had been occupied, while the hostilities were going on outside the occupied territories. But later they were again arrested, especially if they made an unsuccessful attempt to regain the armed forces to which they belonged or where they failed to comply with a summons made to them with a view to internment. In such cases they were no longer considered to be prisoners of war. That is why it is provided that "persons belonging, or having belonged, to the armed forces of the occupied country, if the Occupying Power considers it necessary by reason of such allegiance to intern them, even though it has originally liberated them, shall likewise be treated as prisoners of war under the present convention."

2) The second group, also to be treated as prisoners of war, consists of those who are military personnel interned in neutral countries, without prejudice to any more favorable treatment which these powers may choose to give. "This category intentionally excludes prisoners escaped to neutral countries, and others who, in principle, should not be interned."[134]

But it is Part A of Article 4 of the third convention, identical with Articles 13 of the first and second conventions, which contains the principal norms concerning the application *ratione personae* of the first three conventions, defining the categories of protected persons and, especially the categories of persons, who, if they fall into the hands of the enemy, are entitled to the legal status of prisoners of war.

Of the six categories enumerated, category one (members of the armed forces of a party to the conflict as well as members of militias or volunteer corps forming part of these armed forces) and category six *(levee en masse* by the inhabitants of a nonoccupied territory) are in full conformity with the laws of war actually in force, that is, with Articles 1 to 3 of the Hague regulations.

Category four, concerning persons who follow an army without actually being members of it, such as war correspondents, supply contractors and so on, is equally in full harmony with the laws of war actually in force, corresponding to Article 13 of the Hague regulations. The addition of civil members of military aircraft crews is new.

Also new—a real innovation, introduced as a result of the experiences of the last war—is category five: members of crews, including masters, pilots, and apprentices, of the merchant marine, and the crews of civil aircraft of the parties to the conflict. "There was unanimous agreement that it was preferable to treat [such persons] fallen into enemy hands as prisoners of war rather than civilian internees."[135] Yet, there is a reservation: provided they do not benefit by more favorable treatment under any other provisions in international law—in view of Article 7 of the eleventh Hague convention of 1907.

Category three—members of regular armed forces who profess allegiance to a government or an authority not recognized by the detaining power—constitutes an innovation, inspired by the problem of the status of de Gaulle troops in the last war.

In category two[136] we must distinguish:

1) Members of the militias and members of other volunteer corps—that is, not forming part of the armed forces—if they fulfill the four conditions prescribed in Article 1 of the Hague regulations. There is no innovation here; this norm is in accord with Article 1 of the Hague regulations.

2) Members of organized resistance movements, belonging to a party to the conflict and operating in or outside their own territory, even if this territory is occupied, provided they fulfill the four conditions laid down in Article 1 of the Hague regulations. This is, undoubtedly, the most crucial norm of the new Geneva conventions.

In order to investigate it, it is, perhaps, useful to point, first, to forms of resistance in occupied territory, which are not protected by these conventions; proposals by some delegations to expand protection to them were not accepted by the conference. The following are *not* protected:

a) levee en masse in occupied territory;

b) unorganized resistance movements in occupied territory;

c) organized resistance movements in occupied territory which do not fulfill the four conditions of Article 1 of the Hague regulations;

d) single civilians who have taken up arms to defend their life, their health, their near ones, their livelihood, under an attack which violated the laws of war.

The new category of protected persons is spoken of under many different names, such as guerillas, franc-tireurs, partisans, maquisards, members of resistance movements. We restrict ourselves here to such forces, however called, in occupied territory. The problem is old. In the last war it arose in two different forms, actually and potentially. Actually in many German-occupied countries, but particularly, with respect to the partisans of Tito in Yugoslavia, and the FFI (Forces Françaises de l'Intérieur) in France. On July 15, 1944, the latter were declared by General Eisenhower to be a combatant force, commanded by the French General Koenig (then in London), forming an integral part of the Allied Expeditionary Force, bearing arms openly against the enemy, and wearing distinctive emblems. Of particular importance were the Russian guerillas in the rear of the German armies, who, in the words of Trainin, "fought not only with weapons, but were also political fighters, organizers, propagandists, agitators," an expression of the Soviet people defending itself.

The other problem, which arose only potentially, was the possibility of German units continuing to fight, refusing to abide by the unconditional surrender.

The Geneva Diplomatic Conference of 1949 rightly felt that the problem of the "partisans" was the most difficult one. All agreed that it was necessary to keep in harmony with the Hague regulations. That is why the four conditions, laid down in Article 1 of these regulations, were inserted verbatim. There was a tendency to add further conditions, such as that the headquarters of a resistance movement should be in proper control of the members and should, preferably, also exercise control over a definite territory; those in command of partisans should be in a position to receive communications and to reply to them. But all these additional conditions were finally dropped and the resistance movements on occupied territory simply assimilated to the militias and corps of volunteers, not forming part of the armed forces, of Article 1 of the Hague regulations.

Trainin[137] argued for the unconditional legality of the guerillas, from the Soviet point of view of a "people's war." But that was hardly an exposé of the law in force. Even now Gutteridge[138] says of this norm of the Geneva conventions merely that "it resolves a hitherto doubtful point"—a strong understatement. Guggenheim[139] equally understates the innovation brought about by this article. It is true that, on August 17, 1944, the International Committee of the Red Cross sent an appeal to the belligerent governments, asking that they give to the partisans the status of lawful armed forces; but this appeal shows exactly that this was not a recognized rule of law. Similarly it is not possible to quote the new norm of Article 4 of the Geneva conventions as a mere confirmation of an already previously existing norm. The report of Committee II itself underlines the fact that we have here an "important innovation which has become necessary as a result of the experience of the Second World War."

It is true that the Hague regulations are not clear,[140] as far as the population in occupied territory is concerned. There is, on the one hand, no direct norm; on the other hand, the preamble to the fourth Hague convention states not only that in cases not regulated here the populations and belligerents remain under the protection of the usages established among civilized nations, of the laws of humanity, and of the exigencies of the public conscience; but add also specifically that Articles 1 and 2 of the regulations must be understood in this sense.

But there can be little doubt that the population of a territory already occupied or invaded had no right of organized or unorganized armed resistance, either according to Article 2 of the Hague regulations, or according to general international law. There was no doubt that the armed resistance by the population of an occupied territory constitutes "war-rebellion," punishable by the occupying power.[141] Oppenheim-Lauterpacht[142] states that Article 2 of the Hague regulations does not cover the case, in which, therefore, "the old customary rule of international law is valid, that those taking part in such a levy en masse are liable to be shot if captured."[143] Schätzel[144] could ask in 1948 whether the franc-tireur has a right to a regular trial. He mentions that the French representative at the Nuremberg trial declared that the French "resistants" could have been brought before a military court for not having fulfilled the requirements of the Hague Convention." The court in Case VII against the German generals in command of the armies in the South East stated that the partisans there could not be considered as legitimate combatants, as they did, in their great majority, not fulfill the requirements of the Hague conventions. Winston Churchill declared on May 8, 1945, that, "if Germans should continue to resist in places the Russian troops after midnight they will, of course, deprive themselves of the protection of the laws of war."

The real innovation of Article 4 of the third Geneva convention consists in granting the status of prisoners of war to members of resistance movements in occupied territory, if they are organized, if they belong to a party to the conflict, and if they fulfill the four conditions laid down in Article 1 of the Hague regulations.

It seems that the acceptance of this norm was strongly demanded by the Soviet Union, that it was, perhaps, made a condition for ratifying the conventions. But it seems also that a number of delegations had an uneasy feeling. It is the most talked-of norm of the Geneva conventions in Continental Europe and has been the subject of critical study, as the detailed investigation by Strebel shows.[145] This author states that the mere fulfillment of the condition of "belonging to a party to the conflict" may give rise to many doubts. But it was always clear, even of the militias and volunteer corps of Article 2 of the Hague regulations, that a further condition is the belonging to some authority *de jure* or *de facto*. It is true, as Strebel states, that this new norm constitutes a strong encroachment upon the very foundations of the laws of war actually in force, especially on the law of belligerent occupation, and on the distinction between armed forces and civilian population. True, no signatory power has entered a reservation against this new norm. Yet, the real proof of its value can only be furnished by future experience. "Articles 1 and 2 of the Hague Regulations," states Oppenheim-Lauterpacht,[146] "make the greatest possible concessions regarding hostilities committeed by irregulars. Beyond the limits of these concessions belligerents will never be able to go without the greatest dangers to their troops."

Notes

Notes to Part One

QUINCY WRIGHT

[1] Law is said to have the advantages of protecting the administration of justice from uncertainty, bias, and the errors of individual judgment, and to have the disadvantages of rigidity, conservatism, formalism, and complexity. See John W. Salmond, *Jurisprudence* (London: 1902), pp. 23 ff.; Roscoe Pound, "Justice According to Law," *Columbia Law Review*, XIII and XIV (December, 1913; January and February, 1914).

[2] On the merits of different methods of political change, see Charles E. Merriam, *Systematic Politics* (Chicago: University of Chicago Press, 1945), pp. 241 ff.

[3] The question of whether law is a crystalization of principles of justice accepted by public opinion or an expression of the will of supreme authority, at issue between the historical and positive schools of jurisprudence, is not here answered. See Roscoe Pound, *An Introduction to the Philosophy of Law* (New Haven: 1922), p. 60; *Interpretations of Legal History* (New York: 1923); Quincy Wright, "The Distinction between Legal and Political Questions," *Proceedings, American Society of International Law* (1924), pp. 57 ff.; "Legal Positivism and the Nuremberg Judgment," *American Journal of International Law*, XLII (April, 1948), pp. 405 ff. The two points of view may be synthesized by recognizing that the process of crystalization involves a continuous interaction of the public opinion and the leadership of the group in which both legislatures and courts have a part. "Law is not right alone or might alone, but the perfect union of the two." Salmond, *op. cit.*, p. 55. "Whatever is considered 'just' in the sense of international morality has at least a tendency of becoming international 'law'." Hans Kelsen, *Law and Peace in International Relations* (Cambridge: Harvard University Press, 1942), p. 38.

[4] By distinguishing the validity (formal sanction) of legal rules from their effectiveness (actual enforcement) and their justice (conformity to ethical norms), the Pure Theory of Law developed by Hans Kelsen is able to describe rules as law even if they ignore the prevailing conceptions of justice and are not actually observed: Hans Kelsen, *General Theory of Law and State* (Cambridge: Harvard University Press, 1945); "The Pure Theory of Law and Analytical Jurisprudence," *Harvard Law Review*, LV (1941), 44 ff.; "Law and Peace in International Relations," *op. cit.*, pp. 3 ff.; Josef L. Kunz, "The 'Vienna School' of International Law," *New York University Law Quarterly Review*, XI (March, 1934), 1 ff.

While British analytical jurists approach this point of view—e.g., T. E. Holland, *The Elements of Jurisprudence* (11th ed., Oxford: 1910), pp. 22, 41, 42—most common-law jurists consider law inextricably linked with both justice and effective enforcement even though they recognize that particular rules of law may depart from one or both of these *desiderata*. See Salmond, *op. cit.*, pp. 11 ff., and the controversy between Bergman and Kelsen in *Yale Law Journal*, LVII (1947–1948), 55 ff., 377 ff.

[5] Quincy Wright, "Political Science and World Stabilization," *American Political Science Review*, XLIV (March, 1950), 2 ff.; "The Significance of the International Political Science Associaton," *International Social Science Bulletin*, III (Summer, 1951), 275 ff.

[6] Quincy Wright, *A Study of War* (Chicago: University of Chicago Press, 1942), pp. 382, 763; "International Law and the Balance of Power," *American Journal of International Law,* XXXVII (January, 1943), 97 ff.; "The Historic Circumstances of Enduring Peace," *Annual Report to the American Historical Association,* III (1942), 367 ff.; "Accomplishments and Expectations of World Organization," *Yale Law Journal,* LV (August, 1946), 880 ff.

[7] Wright, *A Study of War,* pp. 158 ff., 354, 885 ff.; "Modern Technology and the World Order," *Technology and International Relations* (W. F. Ogburn, ed., Chicago: University of Chicago Press, 1949), pp. 178 ff.; John U. Nef, *War and Human Progress* (Cambridge: Harvard University Press, 1950), pp. 257 ff., 382 ff.

[8] The researches of Sir Henry Sumner Maine of the conditions of law in classical antiquity, in ancient Ireland, and in India, indicated that law has frequently functioned without formal enforcement. See n. 4, above.

[9] Dictators like Napoleon, Hitler, and Stalin have sought to eliminate competing organizations and to establish a simple hierarchy of authority. According to Hitler, the parliamentary "system is opposed by the true German democracy of the free choice of a leader with the latter's obligation to take over fully all the responsibility for what he does and does not do. There will be not voting by a majority on single questions, but only the decision of the individual who backs it with his life and all he has." *Mein Kampf* (New York: Reynal and Hitchcock, 1939), p. 116. The same absolutism, but with sovereignty vested in all the people, was supported by Rousseau. "It is, therefore, essential if the general will is to be able to express itself, that there should be no partial society within the state, and that each citizen should think only his own thoughts." *The Social Contract* (Everyman's edition) Book II, chap. 3, p. 26.

[10] History discloses many instances of the difficulty of law enforcement in a state, within which are powerful feudal barons, ecclesiastical organizations, chartered municipalities, cultural minorities, historic states which were once sovereign, monopolistic corporations, or wealthy trade unions.

[11] According to Edmund Burke, effective law and essential justice are most likely when numerous subgroups exist in a complex, historically established equilibrium, maintaining general stability and permitting the law to prevent sporadic deviations from the basic stability, and gradually to introduce correctives. Addressing himself to the French revolutionists, he said, "Your constitution was suspended before it was perfected; but you had the elements of a constitution very nearly as good as could be wished. In your old state you possessed that variety of parts corresponding with the various descriptions of which your community was happily composed; you had all that combination, and all that opposition of interests, you had that action and counteraction, which, in the natural and in the political world, from the reciprocal struggle of discordant powers, draws out the harmony of the universe. These opposed and conflicting interests, which you considered as so great a blemish in your old and in our present constitution, interpose a salutary check to all precipitate resolutions. They render deliberations a matter not of choice, but of necessity; they make all change a subject of *compromise,* which naturally begets moderation; they produce *temperaments* preventing the sore evil of harsh, crude, unqualified reformations; and rendering all the headlong exertions of arbitrary power, in the few or in the many, for ever impracticable. Through that diversity of members and interests, general liberty had as many securities as there were separate views in the several orders; whilst by pressing down the whole by the weight of a real monarchy, the separate parts would have been prevented from warping, and starting from their allotted places." *Reflections on the Revolution in France, 1790* (Everyman's edition), p. 33.

[12] Emerich Vattel in the eighteenth century denied the existence of a universal society (*civitas maxima*) posited by Christian Wolff, and sought to found positive international law solely upon consent—express, tacit, or presumed—but he had to rely upon "natural law" for the rule that agreements should be observed, thus in effect reducing international law to a system of ethics. *The Law of Nations,* Prelim. (Washington: Carnegie ed., 1916), p. 9a; Wright, *A Study of War,* p. 970.

[13] James Brown Scott, *The Spanish Origins of International Law* (Oxford: The Clarendon Press, 1934), chap. 1; Wright, *A Study of War*, pp. 166 ff., 970 ff.

[14] "Tunis Nationality Decrees," Permanent Court of International Justice, 1923, *Series B, No. 4* (Manley O. Hudson, ed., *World Court Reports*, I, 143, 156); the case of the *Lotus, ibid.*, 1927, *Series A, No. 9* (*World Court Reports*, II, 20, 35); "Interpretation of Peace Treaties with Bulgaria, Hungary, and Rumania," International Court of Justice, *Reports 1950*, p. 65; *American Journal of International Law*, XLIV (October, 1950), 742, 745.

[15] The International Law Commission recommended a declaration on the rights and duties of states at its first session in 1949. *International Organization*, III (August, 1949), 492. The General Assembly submitted this to members for their observations on December 6, 1949. *Ibid.*, IV (February, 1950), 104.

[16] Kelsen, *Law and Peace* (as cited in n. 3, above), pp. 35 ff. The medieval distinction was primarily subjective, holding a war just if the motive of the initiator was to promote justice, providing that the circumstances and power situation made that result probable. The modern distinction, on the other hand, is primarily objective, starting with the presumption that the initiation of hostilities is illegal, whatever the motive, and can only be justified by jurisdiction of the area where the hostilities are conducted, by permission of the government of that area, by permission of international authority, or by necessity of self defense, individual or collective. Quincy Wright, "The Test of Aggression in the Italo-Ethiopian War," *American Journal of International Law*, XXX (1936), 52 ff.

[17] Research in International Law, Harvard Law School, *Draft Conventions . . . with Comment*, Part III: "Rights and Duties of States in Case of Aggression," printed in *American Journal of International Law*, XXXIII (1939), *Supplement*, 858 ff.

[18] See International Military Tribunal, *Trial of the Major War Criminals . . .* (Nuremberg: 1947), I, 221 ff.; Quincy Wright, "The Outlawry of War," *American Journal of International Law*, XIX (January, 1929), 76 ff.; *A Study of War*, pp. 341 ff., 891 ff.; Philip C. Jessup, *A Modern Law of Nations* (New York: Macmillan, 1948), pp. 157 ff.

[19] John E. Stoner, *S. O. Levinson and the Pact of Paris* (Chicago: University of Chicago Press, 1943).

[20] Quincy Wright, "Neutrality and Neutral Rights Following the Pact of Paris," *Proceedings, American Society of International Law*, 24th Annual Meeting (1930), pp. 79 ff.; "The Stimson Note of January 7th, 1932," *American Journal of International Law*, XXVI (April, 1932), 342 ff.; "The Meaning of the Pact of Paris," *ibid.*, XXVII (January, 1933), 39 ff.; "The Concept of Aggression in International Law," *ibid.*, XXIX (July, 1935), 373 ff.; "The Test of Aggression in the Italo-Ethiopian War," *ibid.*, XXX (January, 1936), 45 ff.; "The Rhineland Occupation and the Enforcement of Treaties," *ibid.*, III (July, 1936), 486 ff.; "The Munich Settlement and International Law," *ibid.*, XXXIII (January, 1939), 12 ff.; "The Denunciation of Treaty Violators," *ibid.*, XXXVII (July, 1938), 526 ff.; *Legal Problems in the Far Eastern Conflict* (New York: Institute of Pacific Relations, 1941), pp. 3 ff., 88 ff.

[21] "The American Republics in accord with the principles of international law and in application of the resolutions adopted in their Inter-American conferences (including one supporting the Kellogg-Briand Pact), considered unjustifiable the ruthless violation by Germany of the neutrality and sovereignty of Belgium, Holland, and Luxembourg." Declaration of American Republics, May 19, 1940, U.S. Department of State, *Bulletin*, II, No. 48 (May 25, 1940), 568.

[22] Quincy Wright, "The Transfer of Destroyers to Great Britain," *American Journal of International Law*, XXXIV (October, 1940), 680 ff.; "The Lend Lease Bill and International Law," *ibid.*, XXXV (April, 1941), 305 ff.; "Permissive Sanctions against Aggression," *ibid.*, XXXVI (January, 1942), 103.

[23] Mr. Justice Jackson, chief of the prosecution for the United States, said: "Any resort to war . . . is a resort to means that are inherently criminal. War inevitably is a course of killings, assaults, deprivations of liberty, destruction of property. An hon-

estly defensive war is, of course, legal and saves those lawfully conducting it from criminality. But inherently criminal acts cannot be defended by showing that those who committed them were engaged in a war, when war itself is illegal. The very minimum legal consequence of the treaties making aggressive wars illegal is to strip those who incite or wage them of every defense the law ever gave, and to leave war makers subject to judgment by the usually accepted principles of the law of crimes .... The principle of individual responsibility for piracy and brigandage, which have long been recognized as crimes punishable under international law, is old and well established. That is what illegal warfare is .... The idea that a state, any more than a corporation, commits a crime, is a fiction. Crimes always are committed only by persons. While it is quite proper to employ the fiction of responsibility of a state or corporation for the purpose of imposing a collective liability, it is quite intolerable to let such a legalism become the basis of personal immunity." *Trial of the Major War Criminals* . . . , II, 146-150.

[24] Quincy Wright, "The Law of the Nuremberg Trial," *American Journal of International Law,* XLI (January, 1947), 38 ff.

[25] Joseph B. Keenan and Brenden F. Brown, *Crimes against International Law* (Washington: 1950); Solis Horwitz, "The Tokyo Trial," *International Conciliation,* no. 465 (November, 1950), pp. 475 ff.; Telford Taylor, "Nuremberg Trials," *ibid.,* no. 450 (April, 1949), 243 ff., especially the Weizsaecker case, pp. 331 ff., 339. Parts of the proceedings of the latter trials have been published in *Trials of War Criminals before the Nuremberg Military Tribunals under Control Council Laws Number 10,* 15 vols., (Washington: 1949).

[26] *Trial of the Major War Criminals* . . . , I, 218-223; Wright, "The Law of the Nuremberg Trial" (as cited in n. 24, above), and n. 23, above.

[27] United Nations Charter, Art. 2. The General Assembly approved the Nuremberg principles in a resolution of December 19, 1946, and in a resolution of November 21, 1947, asked the International Law Commission to formulate these principles. The International Law Commission responded to this resolution in its second session (1950) with a report on "Principles of International Law Recognized in the Charter of the Nuremberg Tribunal and in the Judgment of the Tribunal." It assumed, as it had in the report of its first session approved by the General Assembly in 1949, that its task "was not to express any appreciation of these principles as principles of international law, but merely to formulate them." Messrs. Alfaro and Scelle made a reservation to this on the ground that in formulating the principles of the Nuremberg tribunal, the commission could not ignore the tribunal's statement that the Charter "is the expression of International Law existing at the time of its creation and to that extent is itself a contribution to international law." Judge Manley O. Hudson, on the other hand, abstained on the ground that the report had not made it sufficiently clear that it was confining itself to mere formulation. See United Nations General Assembly, *Official Records, Fifth Session, Supplement* no. 12 (1950), reprinted in *International Organization,* IV (November, 1950), 714. The General Assembly on December 12, 1950, after a debate in which different opinions were expressed on this issue and on certain formulations, passed a resolution inviting governments of member states to submit observations on the principles. *International Organization,* V (February, 1951), 169.

[28] H. Lauterpacht, *International Law and Human Rights* (New York: Frederick A. Praeger, 1951); Philip C. Jessup, *A Modern Law of Nations* (New York: Macmillan, 1948), pp. 58 ff.; Quincy Wright, "Human Rights and the World Order," *International Conciliation,* no. 389 (April, 1943), pp. 238 ff., "War Criminals," *American Journal of International Law,* XXXIX (April, 1945), 251 ff., "The Crime of War-Mongering," *ibid.,* XLII (November, 1947), 128 ff.; United Nations, International Law Commission, *Historical Survey of the Question of International Criminal Jurisdiction* (Lake Success, N.Y.: 1949), pp. 1 ff.; Harvard Research in International Law, "Jurisdiction of Crime," *American Journal of International Law,* Supplement, XXIX (1935), 569 ff., 576.

[29] *Re Drummond Wren,* Ontario Reports, 1945, p. 778; *Fujii v. the State,* (1950) 217 Pac.2d, 481; 218 Pac.2d, 595. See also *Shelley v. Kramer* and *Hurd v. Hodge* (1948), 68 Sup. Ct. 836, 849, 853 and Quincy Wright, "National Courts and Human Rights—The Fujii Case," *American Journal of International Law,* XLV (January, 1951), 62 ff.

[30] "Interpretation of Peace Treaties with Bulgaria, Hungary, and Rumania," International Court of Justice *Reports 1950,* p. 65; *American Journal of International Law,* XVIV (October, 1950), 745.

[31] See *International Organization,* IV (November, 1950), 624; V (February, 1951), 168; n. 27, above.

[32] Independence is implied by the principle of "sovereign equality" (Art. 2, par. 1 and Art. 1, par. 2); interdependence is implied by the duty of members to fulfill obligations in good faith and to insure that nonmembers observe the principles of the Charter concerning international peace and security (Art. 2, pars. 2, 6 and Art. 1, par. 3*c*); the outlawry of war is implied by the duty to settle disputes by peaceful means, to refrain from the threat or use of force and, in case of aggression, to assist the United Nations and refrain from giving assistance to the aggressor (Art. 2, pars. 3, 4, 5, and Art. 1, par. 1); and international maintenance of the rights and duties of individuals is implied by the purpose of achieving international coöperation in promoting and encouraging respect for human rights and for fundamental freedoms for all without distinction as to race, sex, language, or religion (Art. 1, par. 3). See also Arts. 13, par. 1; 64*c*); 56; 62, par. 2; 68; 73*b*; 76*c*.

[33] Eugene P. Chase, *The United Nations in Action* (New York: McGraw-Hill, 1950), pp. 37 ff., 188 ff.

[34] United Nations Department of Public Information, *Korea and the United Nations* (October, 1950); U.S. Department of State, *United States Policy in the Korean Crisis* (July, 1950).

[35] Chase, *op. cit.,* pp. 205 ff., 377 ff.; Leland M. Goodrich and Edvard Hambro, *Charter of the United Nations,* Commentary and Documents (Boston: World Peace Foundation, 1949), pp. 56 ff.

[36] For general appraisal of the United Nations from the political point of view, see Edward H. Buehrig, "United States, United Nations, and Bi-Polar Politics," *International Organization,* IV (November, 1950), 573 ff.; Charles Chaumont, "A French View of Security through International Organization," *ibid.,* IV (May, 1950), 236 ff.; Daniel Cheever, "The Role of the United Nations in the Conduct of United States Foreign Policy," *World Politics,* II (April, 1950), 390 ff. Appraisals from the sociological point of view have been made by Charles Easton Rothwell, "International Organization and World Politics," *International Organization,* III (November, 1949), 605 ff.; Werner Levi, *Fundamentals of World Organization* (Minneapolis: University of Minnesota Press, 1950) and n. 39, 40, and 41, below. These may be compared with my evaluation of the League of Nations in 1942, *A Study of War* (as cited in n. 6, above), pp. 1043 ff. and of international organization when the United Nations began operation, "Accomplishments and Expectations of World Organization," *Yale Law Journal,* LV (August, 1946), 870 ff.

[37] Each of these proposals were advocated in hearings before a subcommittee of the Committee on Foreign Relations, U. S. Senate, 81st Cong., 2d sess., *Resolutions Relating to the Revision of the United Nations Charter, Atlantic Union, World Federation, etc.* (Washington, D.C.: February, 1950).

[38] N. 11, above. A difference of opinion as to whether this advance can best be achieved by restrictive interpretation of the Charter (based on the principle that states intend to preserve their sovereignty except so far as they have explicitly accepted precise rules of international law or have conferred explicit powers upon United Nations agencies), or by an effective interpretation based on the presumption that states intend to realize the purposes and principles of the Charter, and that consequently the powers and procedures of the agencies it established should be liberally interpreted to effect that result. Restrictive interpretation gives great weight to the

intentions of the negotiators of the Charter and thus prevents its adaptation to new conditions except by the difficult process of amendment; this principle emphasizes the distinctiveness of legal and political processes. Effective interpretation permits development of the Charter by practice in the light of changing conditions and political exigencies, thus reducing the gap between legal and political processes. See Hans Kelsen, *The Law of the United Nations* (London: Stevens & Sons, 1950), pp. xiii ff.; H. Lauterpacht, "Restrictive Interpretation and the Principle of Effectiveness in the Interpretation of Treaties," *British Yearbook of International Law* (London: Oxford University Press, 1949), pp. 48 ff.; Leland M. Goodrich, "International Organizations," *World Politics,* III (April, 1951), 408 ff.; Goodrich and Hambro, *op. cit.,* pp. 21, 547 ff.; Manley O. Hudson, "Integrity of International Instruments," *American Journal of International Law,* XLII (January, 1948), 108; Quincy Wright, "National Courts and Human Rights—The Fujii Case," *American Journal of International Law,* XLV (January, 1951), 78; Myres S. McDougal and Richard N. Gardner, "The Veto and the Charter: An Interpretation for Survival," *Yale Law Journal,* LX (February 1951), 262 ff.

[39] "Policy Toward Russia," *World Politics,* II (July, 1950), 463 ff.; "Law and International Relations," *Proceedings, American Philosophical Society,* XCV, (1951).

[40] I have expanded this idea in "International Law and Power Politics," *Measure,* II (Spring, 1951), 123 ff.; "Collective Security in the Light of the Korean Experience," *Proceedings, American Society of International Law* (1951).

[41] Quincy Wright, "The Problem of Establishing and Maintaining a Stable World Society," *Perspectives on a Troubled Decade,* ed. by Lyman Bryson, Lewis Finkelstein, and R. M. McIver, 10th Symposium on Science, Philosophy, and Religion (New York: Harper and Brothers, 1950), pp. 279 ff.

[42] Quincy Wright, "Freedom and Responsibility in Respect to Transnational Communication," *Proceedings, American Society of International Law* (1950), pp. 95 ff.

PAUL GUGGENHEIM

[1] Cf. the famous statement by Judge Benjamin Cardozo: "Law never is, but is always about to be. It is realized only when embodied in a judgment, and in being realized, expires. There are no such things as rules or principles: there are only isolated dooms." (*The Nature of Judicial Process* (New Haven: Yale University Press, 1921). p. 126.)

[2] Cf. Hans Kelsen, "Naturrecht und positives Recht," *Internationale Zeitschrift für Theorie des Rechts* (1927–1928), p. 71 ff.

[3] Cf. mainly Alfred von Verdross, *Völkerrecht* (2d ed., Berlin und Wien: J. Springer, 1950), p. 24 ff.

[4] Cf. H. Lauterpacht, "Kelsen's Pure Science of Law," *Modern Theories of Law* (London: Oxford University Press, 1933), pp. 131 ff.

[5] Cf. Paul Guggenheim, *Lehrbuch des Völkerrechts* (Basel: Verlag für Recht und Gesellschaft, 1951), II, 571 ff.

[6] Henri La Fontaine, *Pasicrisie internationale* (1902), p. 364 ff.

[7] Cf. *Recueil des sentences arbitrales des Nations Unies* (Lake Success, N.Y.: United Nations, 1948–1949), II, 1013 ff.

[8] Karl Oftinger, *Schweizerisches Haftpflichtrecht* (Zürich: Polygraphischer Verlag, 1940), I, 32 f., 74 f.

[9] International Court of Justice, *Reports 1949,* p. 184.

[10] Cf. H. Lauterpacht, "De l'Interprétation des traités," *Report on the Meeting of the Institut de droit international of 1950* (Basel: Editions Juridiques et Sociologiques, 1950). Neither this report nor the excellent critical remarks in it by Sir Eric Beckett held it necessary to refer to natural law in the interpretation of rules of law.

[11] Cf. the survey of the older clauses in K. Strupp, "Le Droit du juge international de statuer selon l'équité," Académie de La Haye, *Recueil des Cours,* 33/III (1930), 355 ff.; of the newer clauses in H. Lauterpacht, *The Function of Law in the Interna-*

tional Community (Oxford: The Clarendon Press, 1933), pp. 113 ff. Cf. also M. Chailley, *La Nature juridique du traité international* (Paris: Librairie du Recueil Sirey, 1932), pp. 64 ff. Art. 15, par. 2, of the Swiss-Italian arbitration and conciliation treaty of September 20, 1924, deserves to be mentioned here.

[12] Cf. Permanent Court of International Justice, Order of December 6, 1930, *Series A, No. 24*, p. 10; Judgment of June 7, 1932, *Series A/B, No. 46*, p. 162; and the specific, although hardly convincing, "observations" of Judge Kellogg, hostile to judgments of equity (Order of December 6, 1930, *Series A, No. 24*, pp. 30 ff.).

[13] Cf. Guggenheim, *Lehrbuch des Völkerrechts* (as cited in n. 5, above), II, 639.

[14] Cf., particularly, J. Spyropoulos, *Die allgemeinen Rechtsgrundsätze im Völkerrecht* (Kiel: Institut für internationales Recht an der Universität Kiel, 1928).

[15] Cf., on this point, Verdross, *Völkerrecht* (as cited in n. 3, above), p. 115, who agrees with this interpretation, although he assigns other and conflicting tasks to these general legal principles.

[16] Cf. *Schumann v. Secretariat of the League of Nations* in *Annual Digest* (1933–1934), Case No. 203.

[17] Cf. H. Wehberg, *Das Problem eines Internationalen Staatengerichtshofes* (München und Leipzig: 1912), pp. 18 f.; an evaluation which estimates the activity of the old arbitral tribunals more highly in Lauterpacht, *The Function of Law in the International Community* (as cited in n. 11, above), pp. 139 ff. But even Lauterpacht does not succeed in finding absolutely legal values in the judgment of the tribunals.

[18] It was rejected in the judgment concerning the Alp Cravairola. See Guggenheim, *Lehrbuch des Völkerrechts*, I, 402, n. 210.

[19] "Bien que le principe que les peuples doivent pouvoir disposer d'eux-mêmes occupe une place importante dans la pensée politique moderne, surtout depuis la guerre mondiale, il convient de remarquer qu'il ne se trouve pas inscrit dans le Pacte de la Société des Nations. Et la consécration de ce principe, dans un certain nombre de traités internationaux, ne saurait suffire pour le faire considérer comme une des règles positives du droit des gens." *Official Journal, Special Supplement*, no. 3 (Geneva: League of Nations, 1920).

[20] This conception is, for instance, expressed in a statement by Judge Schücking in his dissenting opinion to the decision in the case of Oscar Chinn, Permanent Court of International Justice, Judgment of December 12, 1934, *Series A/B, No. 63*, pp. 149 f.: "Jamais la Cour n'appliquerait une convention dont le contenu serait contraire aux bonnes moeurs."

[21] On the impossibility of the concurrent existence of natural and positive law, see H. Kelsen, *Naturrecht und positives Recht*, p. 71. See also G. Radbruch, *Rechtsphilosophie* (4th ed., Stuttgart: K. F. Koehler, 1950), pp. 106 ff.

[22] Cf. Verdross, *Völkerrecht* (2d ed.), pp. 24 ff.

[23] Hans Kelsen, *Hauptprobleme der Staatsrechtslehre* (Tübingen, 1911), pp. 245 ff. This problem is discussed in Switzerland mainly in connection with the right of judicial review of the constitutionality of statutes. Giacometti in F. Fleiner and Z. Giacometti, *Schweizerisches Bundesstaatsrecht* (Zürich: Polygraphischer Verlag, 1949), p. 934, states, to the point, that the right of "judicial review" corresponds to a need, because the *political* Federal authorities fail essentially as "protectors" of the constitution. In other words a judicial organ individualizes the general norms rather in accordance with the traditional principles of interpretation than, as the political authorities do, with political principles. This is correct and is due to the greater independence of the judges from the political and administrative organs which depend on the interests of those employing them. But it does not mean that the acts of the political Federal authorities, having the force of law, can be illegal.

[24] The main objection against its legal character lies in this weakness of customary international law. Cf., particularly, W. Burckhardt, *Die Organisation der Rechtsgemeinschaft* (Basel: Helbing und Lichtenbahn, 1927), p. 383; Max Weber, *Wirtschaft und Gesellschaft* (Tübingen: J. C. B. Mohr, 1922), p. 373; cf., against this, the justified

objections of Hans Kelsen, *Reine Rechtslehre* (Leipzig und Wien: F. Deuticke, 1934), p. 118; Guggenheim, *Lehrbuch des Völkerrechts,* I, 445 f.

[25] However third states, if they are not concerned, are usually very careful in coming to a decision as to whether acts are in conformity or not with international law. Cf., for instance, the report of the Swiss Federal Council on the mass evacuation from Belgian and French territories on March 4, 1916. L. R. Salis-W. Burckhardt, *Schweizerisches Bundesrecht* (Frauenfeld: Huber & Co., 1930–1931) Vol. I, No. 38. But what is the situation if a multilateral treaty is violated to which the third state is a party?

[26] Cf. Verdross, *Völkerrecht* (2d ed.), p. 24.

[27] The introduction of a procedure for the revision of arbitral awards and judicial decisions is also possible in international law. It has already been employed in practice. Cf. Guggenheim, *op. cit.,* II, 662 ff.; also, "La Validité et la nullité des actes juridiques internationaux," Académie de La Haye, *Recueil des Cours,* 74/I (1949), 218.

[28] Cf. the references to the judicature in Guggenheim, *op. cit.,* I, 125, n. 231. See also the decision in "Admission of a State to the United Nations," International Court of Justice, *Reports 1948,* p. 63; H. Lauterpacht, "De l'Interprétation des traités," (as cited in n. 10, above), p. 12 ff.; Beckett, *op. cit.,* p. 75.

[29] Max Weber, *op. cit.* (n. 24, above), pp. 400 ff.

[30] The sociological, antinormative doctrine of law has found support in Scandinavia, particularly following the doctrines of the legal theory of Axel Hägerström. Cf. the summary view of Alf Ross, "Le Problème des sources du droit a la lumière d'une théorie realiste du droit," *Annuaire de l'Institut International de Philosophie de Droit et de Sociologie Juridique* (1934–1935), pp. 167 ff. The earlier legal-sociological studies, particularly Eugen Ehrlich, *Grundlegung der Soziologie des Rechts* (2d ed., Münden und Leipzig: Duncker & Humbolt, 1929), and Max Huber, "Beiträge zu den soziologischen Gründlagen des Völkerrechts und der Staatengesellschaft," *Jahrbuch des öffentlichen Rechts* (1910), have not progressed to a conceptual clarification of legal sociology, in spite of their ingenious content. Cf., also, Fritz Sander's attempt at an antinormative theory of legal knowledge, *Zeitschrift für öffentliches Recht* (1921), pp. 511 ff. On the other hand see Hans Kelsen, *Zeitschrift für öffentliches Recht* (1922–1923), pp. 103 ff.

[31] The reduction of legal obligation to a sociological problem is also presented by Leon Duguit, *Traité de Droit Constitutionel* (2d ed., Paris: E. D. Boccard, 1921), I, 71 f.: "Elle (referring to the "règle juridique") trouve naturellement son fondement dans l'adhésion des consciences individulles, dont l'observation détermine le contenu, infiniment changeant, continuellement variable avec le temps et le pays, mais se rattachant toujours au fait de la solidarité sociale toujours sentie et au sentiment de la justice, variable dans ses manifestations, mais permanent dans son principe."

[32] Therefore the tendency of the sociological doctrine of law to recognize adjudication as an independent source of law. See Georges Scelle, *Manuel de Droit International Public* (Paris: Domat-Montchrestien, 1943), p. 15.

[33] See Hans Kelsen, *General Theory of Law and State* (Cambridge: Harvard University Press, 1946), p. 168.

[34] Cf. the fragmentary remarks by Oskar Adolph Germann, "Präjudizielle Tragweite höchstinstanzlicher Urteile, insb. der Urteile des schweizerischen Bundesgerichts," *Zeitschrift für schweizerisches Recht* (1949), pp. 432 ff.

[35] More in Paul Guggenheim, "Relations Internationales et Droit International Public," *Mélanges Georges Streit* (1939), I, 445 ff.

[36] The content of positive international law is, of course, not limited to international treaties as a sole source of law. Critical positivism recognizes the possibility of other ways of creating law, independent of the will of the state to create law, as for instance customary international law. It obligates subjects of the law who did not participate in the creation of the norms obligating them. It is therefore not possible to reduce customary international law to a treaty tacitly consented to. But even today, positivism is often reduced to the agreement doctrine of Triepel-Anzilotti. Judge Badawi-Pascha,

for instance, in his dissenting opinion in "Columbian-Peruvian asylum case, Judgment of November 20, 1950," International Court of Justice, *Reports 1950*, pp. 305 ff.: "Sans avoir à examiner si une coutume internationale peut abroger une *régle de droit positif*, on doit admettre . . . ."

[37] Cf. Sir Cecil Hurst, "A Plea for the Codification of International Law on New Lines," *Transactions of the Grotius Society* XXXII (London; Grotius Society, 1947), 135-153. Also the excellent opening speech by Sir Arnold D. McNair at the meeting of the Institut de Droit International in Bath (1949). Cf. also M. Sörensen, *Les Sources du droit international* (Copenhague: E. Munsgaard, 1946), pp. 175 f. In a judgment in international law, just as in municipal law, a distinction has to be made between the concrete decision and the deliberations. Only the former, of course, have significance as precedents. Cf. K. Spiro, *Ueber den Gerichtsgebrauch zum allgemeinen Teil des revidierten Obligationrechts* (1948), pp. 1 ff.

[38] It is correct to hold that the creation of a large part of legal norms is predetermined in its content by religious concepts and the actuality of society. But it does not appear correct to consider them not as *fatti normativi* but to qualify them as *formazione spontanea* as is done by Roberto Ago in *Scienza Giuridica e Diretto Internazionale* (1950), p. 78. The so-called "spontaneous" formation of norms, too, takes place in a process of norm creation. This is true also for the universal and regional customary international law. It needs a constitutive statement. Cf. also Max Weber, *Wirtschaft und Gesellschaft* (Tübingen: J. C. B. Mohr, 1922), p. 397.

[39] The negotiations in 1949 of the Diplomatic Conference of Geneva on the symbol of the Red Cross are of special interest in this connection. The delegation of Israel at this conference proposed the supplementing of this provision (Article 38, paragraph 2) to include as a fourth symbol—after the exceptions of the "Red Lion" for Persia and of the "Red Crescent" for Turkey were reaffirmed—the Red Star of David. This was rejected. If it had been accepted, other states would also have demanded the recognition of their national symbols. But as the *Schweizerisches Bundesblatt* (1949), II, 1193 states, it is becoming increasingly more difficult to maintain the unity of the Red Cross symbol. This is due to the process of secularization of international law leading away from the original foundation of a Christian community of states. A red circle, a red triangle (a stylized red heart) or a red flame were proposed as "neutral" signs at the 1949 diplomatic conference. Cf. Claude Du Paquier, "Promenade philosophique autour des Conventions de Genève de 1949," *Mélanges françois Guisan* (Special Edition, 1950).

ROBERT W. TUCKER

The opinions or assertions contained herein are the private ones of the writer and not to be construed as official or reflecting the views of the Navy Department or the Naval Establishment at large.

[1] The terminology presents a certain difficulty here. The term "particular" is used to indicate the actual rules of a legal system as distinguished from the legal system as such. But the term "particular," in turn, refers to positive rules of a "general" and of an "individual" character. Thus the further distinction concerning the rules themselves is between general rules of law and individual norms. General rules of law include, of course, those rules of customary international law binding all states and may be said to include those rules created by certain treaties binding a large number of states (e.g., Charter of the United Nations). The individual norm establishes in a specific instance rights and duties for definite subjects. An example of the latter would be a treaty of cession. It need hardly be pointed out that the individual norm is always the concrete application of a general rule of law.

[2] The effectiveness of legal rules will of course vary considerably. There is no doubt that inquiry into the causes underlying the varying effectiveness of legal rules forms

a most important sociological task. This is especially true with reference to international law where little work has been done to date in this respect. On this problem see Hans J. Morgenthau, "Positivism, Functionalism, and International Law," *American Journal of International Law,* XXXIV (1940), 260–284; Georg Schwarzenberger, "Jus Pacis Ac Belli? Prolegomena to a Sociology of International Law," *American Journal of International Law,* XXXVII (1943), 460–479; W. Friedmann, "The Distintegration of European Civilization and the Future of International Law," *Modern Law Review,* II (1938–1939), 194–214; Georg Schwarzenberger, "International Law and Society," *The Year Book of World Affairs* (London: Stevens & Sons, 1947), I, 159–177; Georg Schwarzenberger and George W. Keeton, *Making International Law Work* (2d ed., London: Stevens & Sons, 1946).

[3] The content of the positive rule of effectiveness in international law refers primarily to the conditions of validity of both those rules of a general character (general rules of conventional international law) and of an individual nature (individual norms creating concrete rights and duties for definite subjects). The positive rule of effectiveness does *not* have as part of its content the rights and duties specified by these rules themselves. Thus the effective control of territory gives rise to specific rights and duties as a result of certain general rules of international law regarding territorial sovereignty. The rights and duties stipulated have nothing to do with the positive rule of effectiveness; but whether they apply in a given instance—let us say when the territory has been seized illegally—depends upon the interpretation states give to the content of this rule of effectiveness.

[4] Effectiveness, as a rule of positive law, is itself a principle of customary international law. What may be referred to as the "negative" application of the juristic presupposition referred to above is to be seen in the process whereby the rules of customary law are invalidated. If, after a certain period of time, a rule of customary law is by and large ineffective, it is no longer to be considered valid. In this connection there are certain customary rules of international law regulating the conduct of warfare and dealing with the status of neutrality which are no longer—by any conceivable test—very effective. Do these "rules" still form a part of general international law or has their ineffectiveness served to invalidate them? It would appear that a legal system in which customary law plays a considerable part, such as international law, must allow for the negative effect of custom. This is especially true the more undeveloped a legal order is from a procedural point of view.

[5] P. 31, above.

[6] But Professor Lauterpacht has written that "to admit that, apart from well-defined exceptions, an unlawful act, or its immediate consequences may become *suo vigore* a source of legal right for the wrongdoer is to introduce into the legal system a contradiction which cannot be solved except by a denial of its legal character." *Recognition in International Law* (Cambridge: Cambridge University Press, 1947), p. 421.

[7] J. L. Brierly, *The Outlook for International Law* (Oxford: Oxford University Press, 1944), p. 9.

[8] Emphasis in this paper is placed on the principle of effectiveness in relation to territorial changes which have taken place in violation of the general rules of customary or conventional international law. This for the reason that territorial changes, by conquest or otherwise, have provided the most important and most disputed application of the rule of effectiveness in recent years.

[9] Thus Lauterpacht: "International law acknowledges as a source of rights and obligations such acts and situations as are not the result of acts which it prohibits and stigmatizes as unlawful." *Op. cit.,* p. 409.

[10] It is universally recognized that occupation, in order to constitute a valid claim to territory, must be effective. Cf. "The Legal Status of Eastern Greenland," Permanent Court of International Justice, 1933, *Series A/B No. 53*; Island of Palmas award, Tribunal of the Permanent Court of Arbitration, *Hague Court Reports,* second series (1928), pp. 83 ff.

[11] Lauterpacht, *op. cit.*, p. 413.

[12] See for example E. M. Borchard and P. Morrison, "The Doctrine of Non-Recognition," *Legal Problems in the Far Eastern Conflict* (New York: Institute of Pacific Relations, 1941), pp. 157 ff. H. W. Halleck writes "By the term 'conquest' we understand the forcible acquisition of territory admitted to belong to the enemy. It expresses, not a right, but a fact, from which rights are derived." *International Law* (4th ed., London: 1908), II, 491.

[13] Lauterpacht, *op. cit.*, p. 413. See also Oppenheim, ed. by H. Lauterpacht, *International Law* (6th ed., London: Longmans, Green, 1947), I, 136.

[14] Which rules of customary international law, when violated, do form the legitimate interest of other states, to the extent that other states are entitled to take repressive measures against the violator? This is an extremely difficult question to answer. Most writers would appear to be of the opinion that states are only justified in intervening when a violation of customary international law directly affects their rights. This clearly applies in the illustration given above. But there are few illustrations of this kind. Most violations of the rules of customary law are injurious to the rights only of one state. Thus the action of a state in denying to the nationals of another state on the former's territory the treatment required by customary law. In this instance prevailing opinion of writers and the practice of states appears to warrant the conclusion that the intervention by other states on behalf of the injured states would not, according to law, be justified.

[15] Borchard and Morrison state that among the misconceptions in law underlying the doctrine of "non-recognition" are: ". . . that it is possible to tell when a particular change, territorial or otherwise, is 'legally' or 'illegally' effected, a moral and legal judgment from which the world heretofore had refrained because of its impracticability, its danger, its essential lack of criteria and the divisions and conflicts it would necessarily create; . . . that by some instrument or principle not identified the nations of the world have been authorized to pass upon the morality or legality of each others acts, even when not directly affecting them, whereas no such instrument or principle exists . . ." *Op. cit.*, p. 158. See also Sir John Fischer Williams, "The New Doctrine of Recognition," *Transactions of the Grotius Society*, XVIII (1933), 120, 128.

[16] This rule has, of course, exceptions. A state may give its consent through treaty to submit certain of its acts to the jurisdiction of another state's courts. There are other exceptions—such as espionage—but these must be established by a rule of international law restricting the normal operation of the rule that no state has jurisdiction over the acts of another state.

[17] P. 328, n. 4, above.

[18] Lauterpacht writes: "A treaty which to the knowledge of both contracting parties is contrary to pre-existing treaty obligations binding upon one or both of them is, in general, illegal, invalid, and unenforceable." *Recognition in International Law* (as cited in n. 6, above), p. 426.

[19] It may even be doubted whether a state violates international law by concluding with a third state a later treaty establishing obligations which contradict obligations of an earlier treaty. If the earlier treaty does not contain a specific obligation excluding later inconsistent treaties, it is probably more correct to say that it is not the actual act of concluding a later treaty that is illegal but rather the acts performed in carrying out the provisions of the later treaty which conflict with the earlier treaty. This point need not be pressed, however.

[20] See Joseph L. Kunz, "The Meaning and the Range of the Norm *Pacta Sunt Servanda*," *American Journal of International Law*, XXXIX (1945), 192–195.

[21] Lauterpacht's opinion.

[22] See Quincy Wright, "Conflict between International Law and Treaties," *American Journal of International Law*, XI (1917), 576 ff.

[23] Resarch in International Law, Harvard Law School, *Draft Conventions . . . with Comment*, Part III: "Law of Treaties," printed in *American Journal of International*

Law, XXIX (October, 1935), *Supplement,* 1026–1029. Also Myers, "Violations of Treaties," *American Journal of International Law,* XI (1917), 797–813.

[24] For bilateral treaties see *Costa Rica v. Nicaragua,* Central American Court of Justice, September 30, 1916, reported in *American Journal of International Law,* XI (1917), *Supplement,* 3–13; a decision that a later treaty inconsistent with an earlier treaty, while illegal, was not void. For examples of the modification or abrogation of multipartite treaties without the consent of all original parties, see Kunz, *op. cit.,* pp. 193–194, n. 67. Also the judgment in the Oscar Chinn case by the Permanent Court of International Justice, December 12, 1934, *Series A/B, No. 63;* but note the dissenting opinions of Justices Van Eysinga and Schücking.

[25] Oppenheim, *op. cit.,* I, 805.

[26] Harvard Research *Draft* (as cited in n. 23, above), p. 1024, presupposes just this situation. Art. 22(C): "If a State assumes by a treaty with another State an obligation which is in conflict with an obligation which it has assumed by the earlier treaty with a third State, the obligations assumed by the earlier treaty takes priority over the obligation assumed by the later treaty." See Hans Kelsen, *Law of the United Nations,* (New York: Frederick A. Praeger, 1950), pp. 111–121, with regard to treaties inconsistent with the Charter of the United Nations.

[27] Wright, "The Legal Background in the Far East," *Legal Problems in the Far Eastern Conflict* (as cited in n. 12, above), p. 91.

[28] See "Virginia Beach Conference of the Institute of Pacific Relations, 1939," *Legal Problems in the Far Eastern Conflict* (New York: Institute of Pacific Relations, 1941), p. 182. In "The Legal Status of Eastern Greenland," Permanent Court of International Justice, 1933, *Series A/B, No. 53,* p. 75 the court held that the Norwegian declaration of occupation, and any measures taken in this respect, was "unlawful and invalid." But the court made this decision on two assumptions: that Denmark, at the time of the Norwegian declaration, was actually exercising sovereignty over eastern Greenland (pp. 63–64); and that as a result of the Norwegian undertaking of July 22, 1919 (Ihlen declaration) Norway was under an obligation to Denmark to refrain from contesting Danish sovereignty over Greenland as a whole (p. 73). In his dissenting opinion Anzilotti asserted that the court could not declare the Norwegian occupation "invalid" if the term "invalid" signifies "null and void." But Anzilotti reached this opinion on the ground that although Norway was under an obligation not to occupy eastern Greenland, Denmark at the time of the Norwegian declaration of occupation was not actually exercising sovereignty over the area in question. His remarks are instructive: "A legal act is only non-existent if it lacks certain elements which are essential to its existence. Such would be the occupation of territory belonging to another State, because the status of a *terra nullius* is an essential factor to enable the occupation to serve as a means of acquiring territorial sovereignty. But this does not hold good in the case of the occupation of a *terra nullius* by a sovereign State in conformity with international law, merely because the occupying State had undertaken not to occupy it. Accordingly, it would have been for the Norwegian Government to revoke the occupation unlawfully carried out, without prejudice to the Danish Government's right to apply to the Court, as reparation for the unlawful act, to place this obligation on record." p. 95.

[29] Thus in the first four editions of Oppenheim's *International Law,* I, § 240: "But it must be emphasized that the validity of the title of the subjugating State does not depend upon recognition on the part of other Powers. Nor is a mere protest of a third Power of any legal weight." And even in the 6th edition of the same treatise (I, § 525) we find the statement: "Under general International Law conquest is not the result of an illegal act; on the contrary, it is the consequence of use of force permitted by International Law." If this attitude is accepted then the resort to war and consequent act of subjugation constitute normal legal powers of states, except as restricted by treaty obligations to the contrary. And if so, the results produced by the illegal acts of violence during the 1930's were valid, since they constituted the exercise of clear

legal powers, although taken in breach of treaty obligations. Professor Wright, of course, does not accept any such conclusions and for the reason that "with respect to acts of international violence . . . such acts do not constitute legal powers, the exercise of which might transfer rights under international law." *Legal Problems in the Far Eastern Conflict* (as cited in n. 12, above), p. 91. Evidently Professor Wright's interpretation concerning acts of international violence presupposes a rule of customary international law forbidding the use of force—including war—except as a measure in support of the law. But this certainly has not been the traditional opinion of the majority of writers.

[30] "Sovereignty," Justice Holmes once remarked, "is pure fact." *American Banana Co. v. United Fruit Co.* (1908), 213 U.S. 347.

[31] Thus Matthew M. McMahon, " . . . non-recognition is not a denial of the existence of the fact of conquest, since the actual invocation of non-recognition is by its very nature an admission of the fact, otherwise the formulation of such a policy would be meaningless and futile." *Conquest and Modern International Law* (Washington: The Catholic University of America Press, 1940), p. 157.

[32] This particular point is not made by some writers because of the failure to distinguish between recognition and the legal consequences, in a given instance, of recognition. See Lauterpacht, *Recognition in International Law,* p. 413; Quincy Wright, "Some Thoughts About Recognition," *American Journal of International Law,* XL (1950), p. 555 and references cited p. 555, n. 14.

[33] Some writers refer to acts of a law-creating nature as international juridical acts. Verzijl refers to international juridical acts as "actes d'Etat aux quels l'ordre juridique international reconnait le pouvoir de produire des effets juridiques conformes a l'intention de leurs auteurs," "La validité et la nullité des actes juridiques internationaux," *Revue de droit international,* XV (Paris: 1935), 302.

[34] Opposed to the above position is the interpretation of many writers that the mere declaration of "nonrecognition" is sufficient to prevent acts illegal in origin from having law-creating effects. In the terminology of these writers an illegal act, let us say the illegal seizure of territory, does not result in the creation of new rights and obligations so long as it has not been "validated" by the other states. It is sufficient that the state which refuses "to validate" does so by means of a declaration to this effect. This latter interpretation implies that to contest means that according to the opinion of the contesting state there is no legal rule attaching to the illegal act the intended legal effects. International law leaves not only the ascertainment of facts, but also the ascertainment of the rule of law attaching legal consequences to the facts, to the individual states interested in the concrete case in which the rule of law in question may apply.

The obvious result of this may be, and in fact has been on many occasions, that there is no general agreement among other interested states on whether or not the act in question has the intended legal effects. What is the law then if no agreement in this respect is reached among the states concerned? It is of no use to evade the entire problem by assigning it to the realm of politics. It is of course painfully evident that states reach a decision in such cases largely on the basis of political considerations. But if we are to affirm the existence of a legal order among states, such decisions must be subject to legal interpretation. And the only possible answer which may explain this disagreement among states is that the law is different for each state. This in turn seems to lead to the conclusion that each state has its own international law which may be different from that of other states. The law is valid only for the state which recognizes it, and as this state recognizes it. The final consequences would appear to be that international law is part of the law of each state, and not only its validity but its content as well depends on the "will" of each state.

It must be admitted that this particular interpretation is by no means excluded. Interestingly enough, however, many writers who insist upon the premises of this interpretation fail to see, or refuse to admit, the almost unavoidable consequences.

[35] Lauterpacht, *op. cit.*, p. 412.

[36] It is therefore not true to say, as does Professor Lauterpacht, that the validation of the effects of an illegal act "is no longer an act of administration of international law; it is a political function," *loc cit.* One may agree with the obervation that the extent to which a state contests an illegal act, or its effects, will depend primarily on political consideration. Still the action of the state has legal significance and must be subject to legal consideration. And this is true even with respect to the recognition of states, an act so subject to political considerations that it is dismissed by most writers as having little more than political significance. Yet Professor Lauterpacht has argued, with great vigor, that the act of recognizing new states must be considered a legal act.

[37] The relationship between the interpretation given to war by many writers as corresponding to revolution in municipal law, and the principle of effectiveness, proves interesting. Thus Professor Kunz has remarked: "While international law never could entirely ignore the problem of change, the principle vehicle of bringing about far reaching changes was war. For war in primitive international law has a double function: to enforce one's right, as a primitive way of self help, in the absence of a judgment and execution by the international community; and to bring about change of the positive law, as a primitive way of self help, in the absence of an international legislature." "The Problem of Revision in International Law," *American Journal of International Law,* XXXIII (1939), 33.

The analogy between war in international law and revolution in municipal law is theoretically untenable. This for the reason, among others, that revolution in municipal law does not represent simply a change in the law but a completely new juridical system. Not only does the constitution of the new system differ in most instances profoundly in content from the old legal order but, most important, the reason for validity of the new order is entirely different from that of the former. War in international law has certainly not the effect of producing a completely new juridical system. Nor has it the effect of changing the "constitution" of the international legal order, that is the rules of customary international law.

What appears to be implied in this interpretation of war is the belief that in a primitive legal system the principle of effectiveness must prevail. That is to say that although there are violations of the law, and war may be considered as having an illegal character, nevertheless a war once successfully waged brings about certain changes which must be accepted as creating new law. Hence a war may be characterized as illegal when waged by a state, yet may give rise to new law because of the principle of effectiveness.

[38] Lauterpacht, *op. cit.*, pp. 427–430.

[39] D. Anzilotti, for example, *Cours de Droit International* (Paris: Librairie du Recueil Sirey, 1929), pp. 337–338.

[40] If the above statement is criticized for putting forward such a vague requirement as a "certain period of time" it might be recalled that writers in discussing the operation of prescription in international law content themselves with equally vague requirements, e.g., "some length of time," etc. Kelsen's remarks in this connection appear to be justified: "Since no rule exists as regards this length of time, it is scarcely possible to distinguish 'prescription' from the general principle of effectiveness, according to which firmly established possession exercised by the possessing State with the intention to keep the territory as its own constitutes acquisition of this territory. According to the principle of effectiveness, too, possession must last for some length of time in order to be considered as firmly 'etablished'." *General Theory of Law and State* (Cambridge, Mass.: Harvard University Press, 1945), p. 215.

[41] But Professor Lauterpacht provides the following interpretation: "There is no question here of legalizing the illegal act; the question is one of disregarding the effects of the illegality. The results of an illegal act are a legal nullity; they are legally non-existent. The wrongdoer acquires no right under it. But there is no logical objection to the community acquiescing, through collective or individual acts of its members

acting in the general interest, in the assertion of a right which did not previously exist." *Op. cit.*, p. 429. It is quite correct to say that the illegal act is not legalized. But Professor Lauterpacht's position that the results of the illegal act are a legal nullity is untenable. The community acquiesces in the assertion of a legal right which came into existence by means of an illegal act; and it does so by virtue of the rule of effectiveness, which attaches to the illegal act a law-creating effect.

[42] Thus the British refusal to approve of Austria-Hungary's violation in 1908 of the Treaty of Berlin in annexing Bosnia and Herzegovina cannot be considered as having prevented a valid title. A practice grew up in the nineteenth century according to which a state, when annexing new territory, would notify other states and usually would ask for the "recognition" of this annexation. An actual requirement of notification of territorial annexation was prescribed by the General Act of the Berlin Conference of 1884–1885. But although this practice of notification and "recognition" was of considerable political importance, its legal significance is doubtful. And M. F. Lindley in his study, *The Acquisition and Government of Backward Territory in International Law*, (London: Longmans, Green, 1926), p. 300, writes: "Although the mere assent or dissent of other states does not in law affect the goodness of an otherwise valid title, it may be of considerable moment politically and diplomatically."

[43] Such an obligation of nonrecognition is stipulated in the (Argentine) Anti-war Treaty of Non-Aggression and Conciliation, signed at Rio de Janeiro, October 10, 1933. For text see Hanley O. Hudson, ed., *International Legislation* (Washington: Carnegie Endowment for International Peace, 1937), VI, 450. Art. 2 states: "They declare that as between the high contracting parties territorial questions must not be settled by violence, and that they will not recognize any territorial arrangement which is not obtained by pacific means, nor the validity of the occupation or acquisition of territories that may be brought about by force of arms."

[44] But the opinion expressed above is not shared by many writers. See, for example, Verzijl, *op. cit.*, 325–326; Lauterpacht, *op. cit.* (n. 6, above), pp. 417–420; MacMahon, *op. cit.*, pp. 150–180; Quincy Wright, "The Legal Foundations of the Stimson Doctrine," *Pacific Affairs*, VIII (1935), 439–446; J. W. Garner, "Non-Recognition of Illegal Territorial Annexation and Claims to Sovereignty," *American Journal of International Law*, XXX (1936), 679–688; C. C. Hyde, "Conquest Today," *American Journal of International Law*, 30 (1936), pp. 471–476.

Although many writers, including those cited, did not agree with regard to the effects of both the Covenant and the Pact of Paris, it generally was insisted that the obligation of nonrecognition could be implied from at least one of the two instruments. The case for the Kellogg-Briand pact was very weak. The conclusion of the International Law Association in its Budapest Articles of Interpretation that contracting parties "are not entitled to recognize as acquired *de jure* any territorial or other advantages acquired *de facto* by means of a violation of the Pact" is more than doubtful. But Professor Wright has stated that the "obligation not to recognize fruits of aggression flows—from the explicit obligation of the parties to the pact 'to *condemn* resort to war for the solution of international controversies.' This is incompatible with the *approval* of results of war involved in such recognition." *Legal Problems in the Far Eastern Conflict* (as cited in n. 12, above), p. 117. The condemnation of resort to war for the solution of international controversies is not incompatible, however, with the validation of results brought about by such a war; "recognition" as used by Professor Wright does not imply approval of the situation validated and still less of those acts which have produced the situation.

The opinion that members of the Covenant were under an obligation of "nonrecognition" was based largely on Art. 10, according to which members undertook to "respect and preserve as against external aggression the territorial integrity and existing political independence of all members of the League." The obligation here is not that of refusing "to recognize" the illegal annexation of territory but rather to guarantee against such illegal seizure of territory in the first place. The validation of an illegal seizure of territory was simply the inevitable consequence of the failure of member states to carry out their obligation under Art. 10 to prevent such a seizure.

[45] *Official Journal, Special Supplement,* no. 100 (Geneva: League of Nations, 1931), p. 8.

[46] See the brief, clear statement by Brierly, "The Meaning and Legal Effect of the Resolution of the League Assembly of March 11, 1932," *British Year Book of International Law* (London: Oxford University Press, 1935), pp. 159–160. But see, for a contrary interpretation, Wright, "The Legal Foundations of the Stimson Doctrine," (as cited in n. 44, above), p. 441. The statement of the Assembly resolution quoted above is preceded by the words "Pending the steps which it may ultimately take for the settlement of the dispute, which has been referrd to it."

[47] See Charles Rousseau, *Le Conflit Italo-Ethiopien devant le droit international* (Paris: A. Pedone, 1938), pp. 100 ff.

[48] The problem here closely parallels nonrecognition of new governments where it has in the main only a political character.

[49] On this point, see Sir Arnold D. McNair, "The Stimson Doctrine of Non-Recognition," *British Year Book of International Law,* (London: Oxford University Press, 1933), pp. 65–74; Sir John Fischer Williams, "The New Doctrine of Recognition," *Transactions of the Grotius Society,* XVIII (1933), 123–124; Chesney Hill, "Recent Policies of Non-Recognition," *International Conciliation,* no. 293 (October, 1933), 389–397. Many writers in discussing the problem of nonrecognition avoid the decisive question of the specific legal consequences to be attached to such a policy.

[50] What are, for example, the legal consequences of the refusal to validate the illegal annexation of territory? Will the nonrecognizing state treat the territory as a kind of *terra nullius* and claim to exercise jurisdiction over its nationals in such territory? Will it refuse to have treaties already concluded with the annexing state apply to the territory in question?

[51] This conclusion is not difficult to reach from a survey of nonrecognition as carried out in practice. It has been suggested that in the event of a war titles to territory not previously "recognized" by the victorious states as lawfully belonging to the defeated states may be restored to that state from whom the territory was originally taken. But a policy of nonrecognition is not necessary in order for victorious states legally to effect this result on the successful conclusion of war.

[52] This point is seldom made by those who have examined the policies of nonrecognition because nonrecognition, in the sense discussed above, was never seriously contemplated. Even in the case of Manchukou, the most successful instance of the application of the policy of nonrecognition, the recommendations of the advisory committee of the Assembly only contemplated measures which were, in the main, of an extremely mild character. Besides, the case of Manchukuo involved the problem of recognition of a new state. No special policy of nonrecognition is necessary for states to refuse to recognize the existence of a new state. More revealing, however, are those situations where nonrecognition was supposedly applied to the illegal annexation of territory. And here the policy is clearly shown to have consisted in little more than verbal declarations.

[53] "For judgments are efficacious against those who feel that they are too weak to resist; against those who are equally strong, or think that they are, wars are undertaken." Grotius, *De jure belli ac pacis,* Proleg., sec. 25. This statement is as true today as when originally made.

[54] Thus Lauterpacht: "Non-recognition is not a sanction in the nature of punishment aiming at bending the will of the wrongdoer by the overwhelming pressure of its immediate effects. Its principal function must, more accurately, be conceived as a somewhat symbolic instrument for upholding the challenged authority of international law. That function it can perform without insisting on a rigid disregard of the realities of the situation." *Op. cit.,* (n. 6, above), p. 433. For commentary on nonrecognition as a "moral sanction" see Henry L. Stimson and McGeorge Bundy, *On Active*

Service in Peace and War (New York: Harper, 1948), pp. 234–235; also Benjamin B. Wallace, "How the United States Led the League in 1931," *American Political Science Review,* XXXIX (1945), 101–116.

[55] Borchard and Morrison write, not without reason: "If some nations recognize the change as necessary if not indeed 'legal,' and others who regard the change as unpleasant refuse, who are the 'lawless' nation?" *Legal Problems in the Far Eastern Conflict,* p. 174. What is the difference between *de facto* and *de jure* recognition of the illegal annexation of territory? On the British *de facto* but not *de jure* recognition of the Soviet seizure of Estonia see the material cited by Lauterpacht, *op. cit.,* p. 435. It is hardly unfair to say, as does Starke, that in the distinction between *de facto* and *de jure* recognition, "All that is left is a difference of political character, almost verging on sophistry." *An Introduction to International Law* (London: Butterworth, 1947), p. 84. There is almost no material available on the United States "nonrecognition" of the Soviet annexation of the Baltic states in 1940. But see the article by Professor Briggs, "Non-Recognition in the Courts: The Ships of the Baltic Republics," *American Journal of International Law* XXXVII (1943), 585–596, for certain effects given to this policy in American courts.

[56] And even if the Council should be able to act in a given instance, the possibility is not excluded that the Council may decide not only to refrain from interfering in the case of, let us say, the violent seizure of territory, but to refrain from obligating members not to validate the situation brought about by the violent seizure of territory. This possibility is the direct result of the almost unlimited discretion given to the Security Council under the Charter.

[57] This is true even if the resolution of the General Assembly adopted at the fifth session, November 3, 1950, "Uniting for Peace," is taken into consideration. The recommendations of the Assembly taken under the terms of this resolution constitute, at least for the present, no legal obligations for members. The latter are free to accept or to reject such recommendations.

[58] Morgenthau states that it is. "An alleged rule of international law, against the violation of which no state reacts, and is likely to react, is proved, by this very absence of probable reaction, not to be a valid rule of international law." "Positivism, Functionalism, and International Law" (n. 2, above), p. 276.

[59] Thus it was generally conceded that by 1939 the economic sanctions had lost their obligatory character and should be considered as only optional. A declaration to this effect was made by a group of smaller states, members of the League, meeting at Copenhagen in July, 1938.

[60] See Kunz, "Observations on the *De Facto* Revision of the Covenant," *The New Commonwealth Quarterly,* IV (1938–1939), 131–143. Art. XVIII of the Covenant stipulated that treaties shall not be binding until registered with the Secretariat. Yet the constant practice was to treat ratified treaties as binding from the moment of ratification. Kunz asks: "Is this, therefore, merely an 'illegal practice' or a legal revision of Article XVIII through the subsequent conduct of the parties?"

[61] Kunz suggests (*ibid.,* p. 142) that if the question—has Article XVI of the Covenant lost its legally binding force in consequence of continuous nonapplication?—were brought before a court, the latter would probably decide that the article had not. But this manner of approaching the problem of the validity of ineffective rules reveals the difficulties involved. The absence of a court possessing such competence is the decisive mark of the absence of procedural development in international law. If this situation were different, then the very reason for raising the question discussed above would largely be lacking.

[62] This, some writers will point out, is merely the technical, or formal, reason for the weakness of international law. The real, substantive, reason for this weakness stems, it will be argued, from other reasons principally of a political or sociological nature. The point need not be labored. Both arguments look at the same problem from a different point of view; and both arguments are correct.

GEORGES SCELLE

[1] The expressions "physical personality" and "moral personality" are used in the sense of the French terminology. The physical person is the individual. The moral person, called by the Germans "legal" person, corresponds to collective activity or to a social aim. In French, physical and moral persons are both "legal" persons endowed with rights and duties and provided with competences.

[2] By "technique of law" I mean the procedures through which a legal order is materially realized.

[3] A juridical order may be composed of a single or several norms applicable to one or several subjects of law.

[4] I call "normative federalism" the superimposition of rules of law upon the successive collectivities with the most extensive priority. By "institutional federalism" I mean the process according to which the hierarchy of norms is guaranteed by that of institutions or of organs superimposed upon those of the collectivities at the base. Federalism may be general or geographic, or decentralized by order of social relations. The technique is analogous for both.

LEO GROSS

[1] Hans Kelsen, *General Theory of Law and State* (Cambridge: Harvard University Press, 1946), p. 328; *Law and Peace in International Relations* (Cambridge: Harvard University Press, 1942), pp. 61 ff., particularly pp. 78 ff.

[2] Hans Kelsen, *Peace through Law* (Chapel Hill: The University of North Carolina Press, 1944), *passim.*

[3] Hans Kelsen, *Das Problem der Souveränität und die Theorie des Völkerrechts* (Tübingen: J. C. B. Mohr, 1920), p. 320: "Denn die Vorstellung von der Souveränität des eigenen Staates ist bisher—ob mit Recht oder Unrecht—allem im Wege gestanden, was auf eine Ausgestaltung der Völkerrechtsordnung zu einer arbeitsteiligen Organisation, was auf die Einsetzung von besonderen Organen zur Fortbildung, Anwendung und Durchsetzung des Völkerrechts, was auf eine Weiterentwicklung der Völkerrechtsgemeinschaft aus ihrem Zustande der Primitivität zu einer civitas maxima—auch im politisch-materiellen Sinne dieses Wortes—abzielt. Als unendliche Aufgabe aber muss solcher Weltstaat als Weltorganisation allem politischen Streben gesetzt sein."

[4] Leo Gross, *Pazifismus und Imperialismus* (Leipzig und Wien: F. Deuticke, 1931), pp. 430–453.

[5] Kelsen, *Law and Peace,* pp. 54 ff.

[6] Kelsen, *General Theory,* p. 388: "A person whose political attitude is one of nationalism and imperialism will naturally be inclined to accept the hypothesis of the primacy of national law. A person whose sympathies are for internationalism and pacifism will be inclined to accept the hypothesis of the primacy of international law. From the point of view of the science of law, it is irrelevant which hypothesis one chooses. But from the point of view of political ideology, the choice is important since tied up with the idea of sovereignty."

[7] Percy E. Corbett, *Law and Society in the Relations of States* (New York: Harcourt, Brace and Company, 1951), p. 10.

[8] *Loc. cit.*

[9] Kelsen, *General Theory,* p. 46.

[10] Kelsen, *Law and Peace,* p. 24.

[11] *Ibid.,* p. 9.

[12] Kelsen, *General Theory,* p. 61.

[13] *Loc. cit.*

[14] *Ibid.,* p. 62.

[15] *Loc. cit.*
[16] *Ibid.*, p. 59 f.
[17] Alfred Verdross, *Völkerrecht* (2d ed., Berlin und Wien: J. Springer, 1950), p. 26.
[18] *Ibid.*, p. 26.
[19] Kelsen, *General Theory*, p. 328.
[20] *Ibid.*, p. 329.
[21] *Ibid.*, p. 330.
[22] *Ibid.*, p. 330; italics mine.
[23] *Ibid.*, p. 340; italics mine.
[24] *Ibid.*, p. 341.
[25] Verdross, *op. cit.*, p. 26.
[26] Kelsen, *General Theory*, p. 60.
[27] There may be exceptional cases of what might be called devolution of the right or duty to take action. This seems to be the notion underlying Professor C. H. M. Waldock's interpretation of the British action in the *Altmark* incident; see his article "The Release of the Altmark's Prisoners," *British Year Book of International Law* (London: Oxford University Press, 1947), pp. 216–238, at p. 236.
[28] Verdross, *op. cit.*, p. 28. Along somewhat similar lines see the observation of the French representative, Joseph Barthélemy, in the Assembly of the League of Nations with reference to the perennial question quis custodem custodiet: "Le droit existe et s'impose, mais, lorsqu'on arrive à certaines hauteurs, le droit n'a plus la sanction matérielle." Records of the Fourth Assembly, Plenary, p. 82.
[29] Kelsen, *General Theory*, p. 62.
[30] Georg Schwarzenberger, *Power Politics* (2d ed., New York: Frederick A. Praeger, 1951), p. 255 says on this subject: "International society has been described as a primitive community. It may be implied in this classification that, in due course, there will be an automatic progress towards a fully developed international community . . . . Such a diagnosis is meaningless unless its basic proposition, the conception of the primitive community, is used in a technical sense. In this case, it is fallacious to assume that primitive communities live in a state of anarchy . . . . In reality, the inter-State system is not a primitive community, but an extreme type of society relations." Corbett, *op. cit.*, p. 12 observes: "An excuse frequently offered for the weaknesses of international law in times of crisis is that it is a primitive system . . . . But the excuse is misleading. Primitive communities are commonly marked by a social solidarity and a dependence upon tradition which, with the scantiest organization, secure a high degree of law-observance."
[31] Kelsen, *General Theory*, p. 39.
[32] Kelsen, *Law and Peace*, p. 15.
[33] E.g., Walther Burckhardt, *Die Organisation der Rechtsgemeinschaft* (Basel: Helbing und Lichtenhahn, 1927), pp. 164 ff., 374 ff.
[34] Kelsen, *General Theory*, p. 22.
[35] *Ibid.*, p. 328.
[36] *Ibid.*, pp. 338 f.
[37] *Ibid.*, p. 339.
[38] *Ibid.*, p. 325.
[39] *Ibid.*, p. 331.
[40] *Ibid.*, p. 330.
[41] *Ibid.*, p. 337.
[42] *Ibid.*, p. 341.
[43] *Ibid.*, p. 325.
[44] *Ibid.*, p. 327.
[45] Kelsen, *Law and Peace*, p. 57.
[46] *Ibid.*, p. 61.
[47] *Ibid.*, p. 56.
[48] Kelsen, *General Theory*, p. 341

[49] Kelsen, *Law and Peace,* p. 56.

[50] Glanville L. Williams, "International Law and the Controversy concerning the Word 'Law,'" *British Year Book of International Law* (London: Oxford University Press, 1945), pp. 146–163, at p. 157.

[51] Corbett, *op. cit.*, pp. 40 ff.

[52] Kelsen, *General Theory,* p. xv: ". . . the pure theory of law seeks to attain its results exclusively by an analysis of positive law. Every assertion advanced by a science of law must be based on a positive legal order or on a comparison of the contents of several legal orders."

[53] Carnegie Endowment for International Peace, James Brown Scott ed., *The Hague Conventions of 1899 and 1907* (New York: Oxford University Press, 1915).

Article 2: "In case of serious disagreement or dispute, before an appeal to arms, the contracting Powers agree to have recourse, as far as circumstances allow, to the good offices or mediation of one or more friendly Powers."

Article 3: "Independently of this recourse the contracting Powers deem it expedient and desirable that one or more Powers, strangers to the dispute, should, on their own initiative and as far as circumstances may allow, offer their good offices or mediation to the States at variance. Powers strangers to the dispute have the right to offer their good offices or mediation even during the course of hostilities. The exercise of this right can never be regarded by either of the parties in dispute as an unfriendly act."

Article 27 of the 1899 convention (Article 48 in the 1907 convention): "The contracting Powers consider it their duty, if a serious dispute breaks out between two or more of them, to remind these latter that the Permanent Court is open to them. Consequently, they declare that the fact of reminding the parties at variance of the provisions of the present Convention, and the advice given to them, in the highest interest of peace, to have recourse to the Permanent Court, can only be regarded as friendly actions."

[54] Mr. Root's letter to Colonel House, August 16, 1918, printed in Charles Seymour, ed., *The Intimate Papers of Colonel House* (Boston: Houghton Mifflin, 1928), IV, 43. Also in Sir Alfred Zimmern, *The League of Nations and the Rule of Law 1918–1935* (London: Macmillan, 1939), p. 231.

[55] *Parliamentary Debates (Lords), Fifth Series,* XXIX, 506.

[56] Philip C. Jessup, *A Modern Law of Nations* (New York: Macmillan, 1948), p. 10.

[57] Georges Scelle, *Manuel de Droit International Public* (Paris: Domat-Montchrestien, 1948), pp. 21 f: "Cependant, c'est la tare originelle et persistance de l'ordre juridique international que sa carence institutionnelle. Apparemment, il n'y a pas dans la Société internationale d'organes législatif, judiciaire, exécutif . . . . Et pourtant, il faut bien que les trois fonctions essentielles de réglementation, de contrôle, de l'utilisation des compétences et de réalisation matérielle du Droit soient accomplies. Elles le sont, mais de façon imparfaite et précaire. Elles le sont à la façon dont elles l'étaient dans les milieux féodaux et quasi-anarchiques où le pouvoir, au lieu d'être centralisé et hierarchisé, restait sporadique et partagé. Ce sont les gouvernments nationaux ou étatiques qui, chacun pour son compte en même temps que pour le compte de la collectivité internationale, accomplissent, dans la limite de leurs possibilités d'action locale et matérielle, les trois fonctions indispensables: création du droit; vérification juridictionnelle; exécution. Tantôt il s'associent à cette fin et avisent d'un commun accord (congrès, conférences, Concert européen); tantôt, au contraire, ils agissent unilatéralement, et, de ce chef, entrent en compétition ou en conflit. Cet unilatéralisme peut aller jusqu'à la guerre, emploi de la force pour imposer la conception juridico-politique d'un gouvernment étatique à un autre, à plusieurs autres, ou à la totalité des autres gouvernements de la communauté internationale (impérialisme mondial) . . . . La loi du dédoublement fonctionnel est le succédané *dangereux* de l' organisation institutionnelle défaillante des ordres juridiques internationaux. C'est un pis-aller, dans le stade actuel de l' inter-étatisme. Si on ne l'admet pas, il devient impossible d'expliquer la technique des fonctions sociales

dans le milieu international. Mais cette technique traditionnelle doit progressivement faire place à une hiérarchie des institutions *correspondant à la loi de la hiérarchie des ordres juridiques*. See also Lazare Kopelmanas "La Théorie du dédoublement fonctionnel et son utilisation pour la solution du problème dit des conflits de lois," *La Technique et les principes du droit public,* Etudes en l'honneur de Georges Scelle (Paris: Librairie Générale du Droit et de Jurisprudence, 1950), II, 753 f.

[58] Verdross, *op. cit.*, p. 69.

[59] Kelsen, *General Theory*, p. 351.

[60] *Ibid.*, p. 354.

[61] *Ibid.*, p. 354.

[62] *Ibid.*, p. 344.

[63] *Ibid.*, p. 327. See also Josef L. Kunz, "The 'Vienna School' and International Law." Reprinted from the *New York University Law Quarterly Review,* XI (March, 1934), 48: "Of course, war is a primitive means; the State entitled to a right is itself the judge and the sheriff in its own cause, which must easily lead to abuses; its ultimate success does not depend so much on its right, but on its force; but exactly the same is true of blood-feud or vendetta. But a State going to war—authorized by international law to do so—is nevertheless acting as an organ of international law, as well as men taking their recourse to blood-feud under the law are acting as organs of this law."

[64] William Ballis, *The Legal Basis of War* (The Hague: M. Nijhoff, 1937), p. 107.

[65] *Ibid.*, p. 103.

[66] Professor Charles Cheney Hyde in *International Law* (Boston: Little, Brown and Co., 1945), II, 1655 says that "a State which resorts to force in order to obtain a desired form of redress from another, and by such process to settle a controversy through ways of its own devising, asserts the right not only to be the sole judge of its own cause, but also to be the enforcer by its own strong arm of demands which in its judgment are not unwarranted," and in III (1945), 1686 he says: "It always lies within the power of a State to endeavor to obtain redress for wrongs or to gain political or other advantages over another, not merely by the employment of force, but also by direct recourse to war."

[67] Verdross, *op. cit.*, p. 36.

[68] Kelsen, *General Theory*, p. 327; italics mine.

[69] *Ibid.*, p. 337.

[70] *Loc. cit.* See also Kelsen, *Peace through Law,* p. 13.

[71] Kelsen, *General Theory*, p. 338.

[72] Georges Vlachos, "Quelques considerations sur le droit et la sanction," *La Technique et les principes du droit publique,* Etudes en honneur de Georges Scelle (Paris: Librairie Générale du Droit et de Jurisprudence, 1950), II, 608, says:

" . . . dès qu'il y a 'délit,' la guerre est 'juste,' elle est 'juste' même si l'on y recourt pour se faire justice à soi-même. Et, puisque le contrôle et la vérification des situations juridiques subjectives, des prétendus 'droit subjectifs' des Etats, sont quasi inexistants, dans un droit 'primitif' comme le droit international normatif, la guerre serait toujours 'juste' si, de l'avis des intéressés eux-mêmes, il y avait une intervention délictueuse de leurs intérêts. Prétendre que ce sont les normes qui déterminent ce qui est un 'droit' et ce qui est un 'délit,' c'est changer seulement les mots, puisque en tout état de cause le sujet qui juge et applique la norme est celui-là même qui en réclame l'avantage."

[73] Panayis A. Papaligouras, *Théorie de la Société Internationale* (Zürich: Les Editions Polygraphiques, 1941), p. 174: "Selon la conception traditionnelle—et selon celle de Kelsen—chaque Etat est l'instance compétente qui décide librement dans chaque cas particulier, sans qu'il existe aucune possibilité juridique de contrôle. *Il y a donc un grand nombre d'instances parallèles, d'instances ayant la capacité de poser des normes et forcées, chaque fois qu'il y a un conflit, de poser des normes contradictoires les unes aux autres.* Selon le droit international général l'Etat A est seul compétent pour décider si une norme concrète est juridiquement valable, si un fait est existant,

s'il doit être qualifié comme guerre, comme intervention, comme nul . . . Si l'Etat A prend une quelconque de ces décisions, s'il affirme une norme, s'il qualifie un fait, etc., il pose une règle juridique, une norme appartenant au droit international. Mais l'Etat B est également compétent pour trancher ces mêmes questions et sa décision, elle aussi, pose une norme. Toutes les fois qu'il y aura un conflit international, la norme posée par l'Etat A sera contradictoire a celle posée par B, si non il n'y aurait pas conflit. Par conséquent, toutes les fois qu'il y aura la moindre divergence, il y a deux normes contradictoires qui s'opposent et qui s'annulent mutuellement. Le fonctionnement d'un droit superétatique est impossible, logiquement exclu. Dans ce sens, un droit international superétatique est inexistant."

[74] *Ibid.*, p. 186.

[75] *Ibid.*, p. 176.

[76] *Ibid.*, pp. 179, 181.

[77] *Ibid.*, p. 183.

[78] *Ibid.*, p. 184.

[79] *Ibid.*, p. 185.

[80] Georg Jellinek, *Allgemeine Staatslehre* (3d ed., Wien und Berlin: J. Springer, 1921, p. 379: "Die Staatengemeinschaft ist daher rein anarchischer Natur, und das Völkerrecht, weil einer nichtorganisierten und daher keine Herrschermacht besitzenden Autorität entspringend, kann füglich als ein anarchiches Recht bezeichnet werden, was zugleich seine Unvollkommenheiten und Mängel erklärt."

[81] Scelle, *op. cit.*, p. 22: "Quoiqu'il en soit, en droit international classique et même dans l'état actuel des choses, tout gouvernement étatique possédait et possède compétence pour dire et réaliser le droit et agir ainsi comme organe de l'ordre juridique international. On ne saurait se dissimuler ce que cela comporte d'anarchie. Mais il n'y a d'autre remède a cet état de chose que l'institutionnalisme superétatique, tel qu'il se réalise par le fédéralisme. C'est pourquoi l'ordre juridique international ne peut faire de progrès qu'en se rapprochant d'un ordre juridique supranational."

See also Alf Ross, *Textbook of International Law* (London: Longmans, Green, 1947), p. 54, who speaks of the anarchical character of international law, and Lazare Kopelmanas, *L'Organsation des Nations Unies* (Paris: Labrairie du Recueil Sirey, 1947), I, 241 who refers to the "système anarchique du droit international dans lequel chaque Etat détermine, en ce qui le concerne, la valeur des obligations internationales qu'il a contractées."

[82] J. L. Brierly, *The Law of Nations* (4th ed., Oxford: The Clarendon Press, 1949), p. 92.

[83] See Lazare Kopelmanas, *L'Organisation des Nations Unies*, (Paris: Librairie du Recueil Sirey, 1947), I, 259: " . . . le droit international classique ne connait pas la séparation des fonctions. Les Etats y conservent aussi bien le monopole de création que celui d'application des règles de droit. Il en résulte la concentration entre leurs mains des pouvoirs d'interprétation authentique, correspondant à la fonction législative, en même temps que des pouvoirs d'interprétation individuelle, correspondant à la fonction exécutive. La distinction entre les deux ne semble vraiment pas possible, car, en déterminant à propos d'une difficulté précise le contenu de son obligation internationale, au delà du cas particulier l'Etat fixe par son attitude également sa conception officielle du texte impliqué."

[84] Walther Burckhardt, *Die Organisation der Rechtsgemeinschaft* (Basel: Helbing und Lichtenhahn, 1927), p. 377: "Eine weitverbreitete Meinung lehrt nun aber, dass es ein internationales Gewohnheitsrecht gibt, nämlich im Sinne eines positiven Rechtes. Unsere Ausführungen über das Gewohnheitsrecht zeigen jedoch, dass das nicht richtig sein kann. Durch die Uebung der Rechtsgenossen allein kann verbindliches Gewohnheitsrecht nicht entstehen; es entsteht nur durch die massgebende Mitwirkung der rechtsanwendenden Behörden, als der amtlichen Organe der positiven Rechtsordnung. Nicht was die Rechtsunterworfenen unter sich befolgen, ist von Rechts wegen gültig, sondern was von der eingesetzten Vertretung der Rechtsord-

nung (ausdrücklich durch die Rechtssetzung oder stillschweigend durch die Anwendung) als objektives Recht anerkannt wird. Eine solche Vertretung gibt es aber im Völkerrecht nicht, weil die Staatengemeinschaft nicht objektiv rechtlich organisiert ist. Es gibt wohl *vertraglich* eingesetzte Gerichte (und andere Instanzen); aber sie handeln alle nur kraft rechtsgeschäftlichen Auftrages der Staaten, die sie eingesetzt haben, und ihre Entscheidungen haben demgemäss auch nur vertragliche Verbindlichkeit; sie begründen subjektive Rechtsverhältnisse, nicht objektives Recht. Die Verbindlichkeit ihrer Sprüche ist beschränkt auf die Parteien des Schiedsvertrages; sie ist bedingt, nämlich quoad titulum durch die Verbindlichkeit dieses Vertrages, quoad materiam, dem Inhalte nach, durch den Willen der Parteien; wenn die Parteien über das anzuwendende Recht übereinkommen, wie im Alabamafalle, ist das internationale Gericht daran gebunden; es ist nicht die selbständige Stimme des Rechts, wie es das Gericht im primitiven Staat (ohne gesetzgebende Behörde) ist, wo der Richter das Recht zu finden, d.h. zugleich mit der Entscheidung des konkreten Falles festzustellen hat. Wenn die positive Geltung des Rechts davon abhängt, dass eine organisierte Macht es handhabt, können vertraglich eingesetzte Behörden nicht dieses Recht schaffen: denn die Zuständigkeit der Behörden hängt selbst von einem Rechtsgeschäft ab das schon im geltenden Recht begründet sein muss, um gültig zu sein."

[85] Kelsen, *Das Problem der Souveränität und die Theorie des Völkerrechts,* p. 259. See also his *General Theory,* p. 327, where substantially the same view is expressed. P. 339, n. 68, above.

[86] Burckhardt, *op cit.,* p. 128: "Begrifflich ist es gewiss denkbar, dass die Rechtsordnung jeweilen eine vor dem Streit nicht dazu berufene Person berufe, den Streit zu entscheiden; aber nicht in der Weise, dass sie 'den Verletzten' zum Richter einsetzte. Denn um was handelt es sich? Was ist die Aufgabe der Organisation? Die Entscheidung darüber, was rechtens ist und die Durchsetzung dieses als Recht Erkannten; hier die Entscheidung eines Streites nach dem geltenden Recht und die Vollstreckung der Entscheidung. Wenn die Rechtsordnung dazu *eine* Person (oder eine einheitlich beschliessende Mehrheit) beruft, deren Entscheidung verbindlich sein soll, mag es auch eine Privatperson sein, oder besser: eine Person, die *bisher* kein Amt hatte und kein *ständiges* Amt erhält; aber es muss bestimmt sein, welche; und wenn die Rechtsordnung sagen würde: der Verletzte ist der Richter, so würde sie den Streit als entschieden voraussetzen, bevor ein Richter da war; denn um zu wissen, wer verletzt ist, muss man den Streit entschieden haben, was eben die Aufgabe des Organes sein soll . . . . Darüber muss sich eine vollständige Rechtsordnung aussprechen: nicht nur, welches die Normen des Verhaltens der Rechtsgenossen sind, sondern auch wer diese Normen anwende und die rechtsanwendende Entscheidung erzwinge, ja auch wer über die Verbindlichkeit der Grundsätze selbst entscheide. Man kann sich Verhaltungsregeln *denken* ohne diese Zuständigkeitsordnung, die Organisation; aber man kann sie sich nicht als *geltendes* Recht denken ohne solche Ordnung, und zwar nicht ohne die durch Menschen betätigte, verkörperte Organisation."

[87] Burckhardt, *op. cit.,* pp. 125 f.: "Jede Rechtsordnung muss bestimmen, wer den Zwang anzuordnen hat und in welcher Weise er anzuordnen ist. Da aber die Norm nicht in ihrer Abstraktheit erzwungen werden kann, sondern nur in ihrer konkreten Anwendung auf den einzelnen Fall, muss der Erzwingung notwendigerweise die Entscheidung vorausgehen, dass die betreffende Norm auf den vorliegenden Fall anzuwenden ist. Die Erzwingung des Rechts setzt also die verbindliche Anwendung des abstrakten Rechtssatzes auf den konkreten Tatbestand voraus; die Rechtsordnung muss daher, um erzwingbar zu sein, auch diese Zuständigkeit vorsehen; die Instanz, die in verbindlicher Weise entscheidet, dass der Rechtssatz in concreto anwendbar ist, und das Verfahren, nach dem es zu geschehen hat. Und endlich muss auch eine Instanz da sein, um die Regeln selbst zu bestimmen. Wir sind vorhin von der Voraussetzung ausgegangen, die Regeln seien gegeben und für einmal ausser Frage; das mag zu gewissen Zeiten zutreffen, wenn nämlich eine Autorität sie früher schon bestimmt hat; aber grundsätzlich kann von der Aufgabe nicht abgesehen werden, auch die

Rechtsnormen selbst, die gelten sollen, zu bestimmen. Ist das früher schon entschieden worden, so sind die damals angenommenen Normen doch nur deshalb *heute* verbindlich, weil die Autorität, die sie aufgestellt hat, noch heute anerkannt wird (was auch eine Entscheidung ist), bzw. weil die heute zuständige Behörde nichts anderes entscheidet. Es muss stets jemand entscheiden, welche Normen gelten; die Entscheidung darüber ist logisch ebenso unentbehrlich wie die Entscheidung darüber, wo die geltende Norm anzuwenden und wie die Entscheidung zu vollstrecken ist. Denn gleich wie die Rechtserzwingung die Entscheidung voraussetzt, dass das zu erzwingende konrete Verhalten rechtmässig ist, so setzt die Entscheidung, dass ein Verhalten rechtmässig (ein anderes rechtswidrig) ist, einen Rechtssatz voraus, an dem dieses konkrete Verhalten gemessen wird. Diese Aufgabe, die jede Rechtsordnung stellt, lediglich weil sie ein *rechtliche* Ordnung ist, ist die Aufgabe der Organisation."

[88] *Ibid.*, p. 124: "Denn das wäre keine Rechtsordnung mehr, die Ordnung, die grundsätzlich auf die freiwillige Befolgung ihrer Vorschriften abstellte, auf die persönliche Ueberzeugung und Gewissenhaftigkeit jedes einzelnen; die also nicht gelten wollte, so wie sie einmal lautet, ohne Rücksicht auf die individuelle Ueberzeugung der Rechtsgenossen, wie es eben zum Wesen des Rechtes gehört."

[89] Kelsen, *Das Problem der Souveränität*, p. 258.

[90] *Ibid.*, p. 266.

[91] Eastern Carelia case, Permanent Court of International Justice, Advisory Opinion of July 23, 1923, *Series B, No. 5*, p. 27.

[92] H. Lauterpacht, *The Function of Law in the International Community* (Oxford: The Clarendon Press, 1933), p. 3.

[93] Case of the *Antelope* (1825), 23 U.S. 30, in Herbert W. Briggs, *The Law of Nations* (New York: F. S. Crofts and Co., 1944), p. 15.

[94] "Frontier between Turkey and Iraq," Permanent Court of International Justice, Advisory Opinion of November 21, 1925, *Series B, No. 12*, p. 32.

[95] Judgment of November 20, 1950, International Court of Justice, *Reports 1950*, p. 274.

[96] *Ibid.*, pp. 287–288.

[97] See also arbitral award by G. Kaeckenbeeck in the dispute between Poland and Germany regarding the nationality rights of minorities of German extraction in Poland. Poland claimed the right unilaterally to determine (*constater*) whether in virtue of the Treaty of Versailles Polish nationality was acquired and that "cette constatation sera considerée comme reconnue par l'Allemagne." The arbitrator held: "Du fait que l'acquisition de la nationalité polonaise est reglée dans l'article 91 du Traité de Versailles, qui fait partie d'un groupe de dispositions relatives à la cession de territoire faite par l'Allemagne à la Pologne, résulte que cette question présente un caractère qui n'est purement unilatéral, mais qui intéresse au contraire les deux Etats contractants. . . . Mais ce caractère international, qui du fait des obligations contractées implique une certaine limitation de l'autonomie de deux Etats, n'implique nullement pour cela une co-souveraineté des deux Etats en ce qui concerne l'application. Chaque Etat agit et décide souverainement; mais, dans la mésure où il a contracté des obligations, il est tenu d'agir et de décider conformément à ces obligations. Les enfreint-il, le caractère international de la question se révèle par le fait que le co-contractant a le droit d'exiger le respect du Traité. Tant que l'infraction n'a pas eu lieu, le caractère international de la question reste pour ainsi dire latent." *Actes et Documents de la Conférence Germano-Polonaise* tenue à Vienne du 30 avril au 30 août 1924, p. 386.

[98] *Recueil des décisions des tribunaux arbitraux mixtes*, VIII (Paris: Librairie du Recueil Sirey, 1928), 425.

[99] Corfu Channel case, Judgment of April 9, 1949, International Court of Justice, *Reports 1949*, p. 35.

[100] G. G. Fitzmaurice, "The Law and Procedure of the International Court of Justice: General Principles and Substantive Law," *British Year Book of International Law* (London: Oxford University Press, 1950), p. 5.

[101] Reprinted in Denys P. Myers, *Origin and Conclusion of the Paris Pact* (Boston: World Peace Foundation, 1929), p. 355.

[102] International Military Tribunal, *Trial of the Major War Criminals* . . . (Nuremberg: 1947), I, 208.

[103] *Ibid.*, XIX, 461.

[104] Lauterpacht, *op. cit.*, p. 179 f.

[105] Advisory Opinion of December 6, 1923, *Series B, No. 8*, p. 37.

[106] Kelsen, *The Law of the United Nations* (New York: Frederick A. Praeger, 1951), p. xv.

[107] The tribunal continued: "The fact that this interpretation is given by the legislative or judicial or any other authority of one of the Parties does not make that interpretation binding upon the other Party. Far from contesting that principle, the British Government did not fail to recognize it. . . . For that reason the mere fact that a British Court, whatever be the respect and high authority it carries, interpreted the treaty in such a way as to declare the *David J. Adams* had contravened it, cannot be accepted by this Tribunal as a conclusive interpretation binding upon the United States Government. Such a decision is conclusive from the national British point of view; it is not from the national United States point of view. . . . Then the duty of this international Tribunal is to determine, from the international point of view, how the provisions of the treaty are to be determined and applied to the facts, and consequently whether the loss resulting from the forfeiture of the vessel gives rise to an indemnity." Decision given December 9, 1921. American and British Claims Arbitration, *Report* of Fred K. Nielsen (1926), p. 524, at p. 530. Quoted in G. H. Hackworth, *Digest of International Law*, V (Washington, D.C.: U.S. Government Printing Office, 1943), 268.

[108] U.S. Department of State, *Bulletin*, XXI, No. 534 (October 3, 1949), 514. The existence of a dispute was confirmed in the Advisory Opinion of March 30, 1950, International Court of Justice, *Reports 1950*, p. 65.

[109] Edward Herstlet, *The Map of Europe by Treaty*, III, 1904. The principle of 1871 was restated in the Text of Proposals drawn up by the representatives of Belgium, the United Kingdom, and Italy on March 19, 1936, in connection with the remilitarization of the Rhineland by Germany. League of Nations, *Official Journal*, 17th year (April 1936), 348.

[110] See also Arts. XVII and XX of the constitution of the Food and Agricultural Organization, and Arts. XIII and XIV of the United Nations Educational, Scientific and Cultural Organization.

[111] Report on the Interpretation of the Charter approved by Committee IV/2 on June 2, 1945. UNCIO, Doc. 887, Annex II.

[112] Kelsen, *Peace through Law*, p. 13: "As long as it is not possible to remove from the interested States the prerogative to answer the question of law and transfer it once and for all to an impartial authority, namely, an international court, any further progress on the way to the pacification of the world is absolutely excluded."

[113] Kelsen, *General Theory*, p. 369.

[114] Jessup, *op. cit.*, p .144.

[115] See Josef L. Kunz, "Revolutionary Creation of Norms of International Law," *American Journal of International Law*, XLI (1947), 119–126, to the effect that it is possible to conceive an illegal but not a revolutionary creation of norms of international law.

[116] The International Military Tribunal was an instructed tribunal as its charter contained the law to be applied in the trial. The tribunal was not free to "find" the applicable law.

H. LAUTERPACHT

[1] For an application of this principle to treaties inconsistent with previous treaties concluded by one of the contracting parties see *British Year Book of International Law* (London: Oxford University Press, 1936), pp. 54–65.

[2] I formulated these objections with what is probably an excess of emphasis in the paper printed in the *Transactions of the Grotius Society*, XX (1934), 178–202. There I maintained the view that, in the absence of express provisions to that effect in the Pact of Paris, it is not permissible to infer from that instrument any changes in the traditional law of neutrality. For a modification of this view see my edition of Oppenheim's *International Law* (6th revised ed., London and New York: Longmans, Green, 1944), II, § 292*h*.

[3] This is so, in particular in cases in which the alleged principle—such as the criminal responsibility of states or the absence of direct individual criminal responsibility in the realm of international law—affected by the major change is in itself controversial. For this reason the relevant passage in the judgment of the International Military Tribunal at Nuremberg for the trial of major war criminals, although its phraseology may be open to question on some points, constitutes an abiding contribution not only to the particular issue of criminality of aggressive war, but also to the question of the sources of international law. It is useful to cite here that passage of the judgment:

"But it is argued that the pact does not expressly enact that such wars are crimes, or set up courts to try those who make such wars. To that extent the same is true with regard to the laws of war contained in the Hague Convention. The Hague Convention of 1907 prohibited resort to certain methods of waging war. These included the inhumane treatment of prisoners, the employment of poisoned weapons, the improper use of flags of truce, and similar matters. Many of these prohibitions had been enforced long before the date of the Convention; but since 1907 they have certainly been crimes, punishable as offences against the laws of war; yet the Hague Convention nowhere designates such practices as criminal, nor is any sentence prescribed, nor any mention made of a court to try and punish offenders . . . . In interpreting the words of the pact, it must be remembered that international law is not the product of an international legislature, and that such international agreements as the Pact of Paris have to deal with general principles of law, and not with administrative matters of procedure. The law of war is to be found not only in treaties, but in the customs and practices of states which gradually obtained universal recognition, and from the general principles of justice applied by jurists and practiced by military courts. This law is not static, but by continual adaptation follows the need of a changing world. Indeed, in many cases treaties do no more than express and define for more accurate reference the principles of law already existing." *American Journal of International Law*, XLI (1947), 218, 219.

[4] This view, and the main reason underlying it, were clearly expressed in 1874 by J. K. Bluntschli in the second edition of his *Das moderne Kriegsrecht der zivilisierten Staaten*. He said: "The law of war civilises on a fully equal footing both the legal and illegal war. It is only because it ignores that distinction that it is in the position to secure its general application" (p. 519).

[5] See, e.g., Oppenheim, *op. cit.*, II, § 61. See, however, §§ 63 and 64 where it is stated that "for many legal purposes it seems now possible to distinguish between just and unjust (or lawful and unlawful) wars." And see, more emphatically, for a modification of the previous view, § 61 of the 7th edition (1952).

[6] See, in particular, Paul de La Pradelle in *Revue de droit international*, XII (1933), 511–522 and Josef L. Kunz in *Revue générale de droit international public*, XLI (1934), 43–52 and in *American Journal of International Law*, XLV (1950), 37–61. See also Hermann Mosler in *Jahrbuch für internationales und ausländisches öffentliches Recht*, II-III (1948), 333–357.

[7] Art. 3 of all four conventions.

[8] The conventions state expressly that these provisions do not affect the legal status of the parties to the conflict. In particular they do not amount to—or impose upon the lawful government the obligation of—recognition of insurgents as belligerents. The governing principle is that the respect of some fundamental human rights is no longer dependent upon the recognition of specific status. It will be noted that Art. 3

of each of the four conventions which refers to conflicts which are not of an international character, purports to impose obligations not only upon the contracting parties, but also upon "each party to the conflict." To that extent the convention, in keeping with other developments in modern international law, treats persons and entities other than states as objects of international rights and duties. For that reason it follows from a proper interpretation of the convention that while the detaining state is entitled to put to trial prisoners of war accused of war crimes and other crimes committed prior to captivity, utmost restraint must be exercised in respect of that right concerning what is in essence a political crime of treason and rebellion.

[9] Conventions II and III. These and similar provisions give expression to the principle that "toute société de guerre, dès l'instant qu'elle existe en fait, doit être aussitôt saisie par le droit": Paul de La Pradelle, *La Convention diplomatique et les nouvelles conventions de Genève du 12 Août, 1949* (1951), p. 56.

In fact there seems to be in modern conditions no justification for the tendency, which was predominant in the nineteenth century and which found to some extent expression in the compromise reached at the Hague Conference in 1899 on the subject, to brand as illegal the activities of guerilla troops on the additional ground that the continuation of the struggle after the national territory has been totally occupied by the enemy without there remaining any hope of restoring the position is a senseless act of defiance which merits reprobation. For in modern—global—warfare the complete occupation of a country may be but an episode in the campaign in which the legitimate government though compelled to withdraw from national territory continues to fulfill its responsibilities in conjunction with its allies. See for this aspect of the problem G. G. Fitzmaurice in Académie de La Haye, *Recueil des Cours,* 73/II (1948), 272–277. This was the position in World War II, when many European countries were overrun and occupied by Germany for years. Moreover, the right of the inhabitants to organize themselves spontaneously and to attack the enemy cannot be reasonably denied when the forces of the lawful government reënter the country in order to expel the invader and when, as the result, the authority of the occupant becomes precarious and is no longer uncontested. When in June, 1944, the Allied forces began the invasion of France the "French Forces of the Interior" were constituted as a military force under the command of a high French military officer. They were recognized by the supreme commander of the Allied Expeditionary Force as forming an integral part of the troops commanded by him and a formal announcement to that effect was made. In the preamble to the peace treaty with Italy of 1947 reference is made to the "Italian armed forces both of the Government and of the Resistance Movement which took an active part in the war against Germany." Moreover, the distinction which the Hague regulations established between the territory "not under occupation" (as to which the inhabitants were permitted to take up arms spontaneously on the approach of the enemy subject to the conditions laid down by the regulations) and territory under occupation is no longer as rigid as it was in the past. Large areas may be nominally occupied by rapidly advancing motorized and armored units leaving full scope for legitimate resistance by scattered and spontaneously organized groups of the population.

The above note, the insertion of which is considered useful for the better undertanding of the proposition advanced in the text, reproduces to a large extent § 60, inserted by myself, of vol. II of the 7th edition of Oppenheim's *International Law.*

[10] "Il n'est pas une armée en monde qui accepterait de traiter selon les lois de la guerre l'armée et les populations du pays qu'elle envahit, admettant d'être traitée comme une troupe de bandits par cette même armée et ces mêmes populations." Albert de Bassompierre in *Revue de droit international et de la législation comparée,* 3d ser., IV (1923), 244.

There is in this respect a measure of conflict, in a sense unavoidable, between the considerations adduced in the text above and the modern tendency to enlarge the scope of lawful combatants so as to include organized resistance movements behind the lines in occupied territory. It may be difficult to lay down in advance rigid rules likely to assist in the solution of the problem involved. In particular such assistance cannot be found either in exclusive reliance upon considerations of humanity neglectful of the safety of the occupant or in methods of terror on the part of the occupant. Neither, as is submitted below, can it be found in the distinction between lawful and unlawful wars. Decrees of the lawful sovereign in exile and the decisions of its courts after the liberation of the territory do not necessarily supply a standard capable of general application. The Dutch Royal Emergency Decree of September, 1944, gave to the "Netherlands Forces of the Interior" the status of a part of the Dutch army on the ground of "the necessity of regarding as members of the armed forces all those who during the liberation of the territory were actively engaged in expelling the enemy." In *Van Hoeve de Feyter v. Fire Insurance Company,* the District Court of Dordrecht held in 1947, *Annual Digest* (1947), Case No. 81, that even before that decree acts committed by the members of the Dutch resistance movement were "acts of war." See also to the same effect *Smulders and Piccinati v. Société Anonyme "La Royale Belge,"* decided in 1943 by the Civil Court of Liège, *Annual Digest* (1943–1945), Case No. 102, where it was held, with regard to an Italian officer killed in Yugoslavia, that in occupied territory where the partisan resistance had never ceased, an attack upon officers of the army of occupation in uniform must be regarded as an act of war not covered by the insurance policy. And see, even more emphatically, the decision given by the Belgian court in *Peeterbrock v. Assurances généralés de Paris,* in *Pasicrisie Belge,* III (1947), 15.

11 United Nations War Crimes Commission, *Law Reports of Trials of War Criminals* (London: H. M. Stationery Office, 1949), VIII, 59, 60, 77.

12 *Law Reports of Trials . . . ,* XIV, 143–144.

13 *Ibid.,* p. 144.

14 In a note appended to this case in *Annual Digest* (1948), J. H. W. Verzijl admits that the thesis adopted by the court "though fundamentally correct, might produce serious consequences during the war."

15 After World War II municipal courts of some allied countries gave decisions which endowed the so-called resistance movements with a certain degree of legitimacy as against the occupant. However, the main argument relied upon in these decisions was not the unlawfulness of the war waged by the aggressor, but the authorization by the lawful government. See p. 345, n. 9, above.

16 *Annual Digest* (1948).

17 Except, possibly, that the occupation being unlawful *ab initio* could not subsequently mature by lapse of time into legal title. The tribunal invoked the maxim of Roman law, *quod ab initio turpe est, non potest tractu tempore convalescere.*

18 *Law Reports of Trials* . . . (as cited in n. 11, above), XIII, 110.

19 See the observations made in 1946 by the chief British prosecutor, Sir Hartley Shawcross, in his closing speech before the International Military Tribunal at Nuremberg. He said: "The killing of combatants in war is justifiable, both in international and national law, only where the war is legal. But where the war is illegal, as a war started not only in breach of the Pact of Paris but also without any sort of declaration clearly is, there is nothing to justify the killing, and these murders are not to be distinguished from those of any other lawless robber band." *Proceedings of the Tribunal,* H. M. Stationery Office, XIX (1948), 423. See also *ibid.,* IV, 351 for a similar view of the French prosecutor. For the view of the German defense see *ibid.,* XVIII, 88, 89. It is reasonable to interpret Sir Hartley's observations in their context, i.e., as referring not to the responsibility of the individual members of the armed forces of the aggressor, but to the liability of those guilty of planning and instigating the unlawful war.

20 *Law Reports of Trials . . . ,* VI, 52.

21 *Ibid.,* XII, 124.

22 *Loc. cit.*

[23] *Loc. cit.*

[24] *Ibid.*, XIV, 134.

[25] *Proceedings of the Tribunal,* p. 28105.

[26] Francis Wharton, *Criminal Law* (12th ed., Rochester, N.Y.: The Lawyers Cooperative Publishing Company, 1932), I, 180.

[27] For some suggestions in that direction see Philip C. Jessup, *A Modern Law of Nations* (New York: Macmillan, 1948), chap. 8. See pp. 92–93, above, for the regulation of civil wars by the Geneva conventions of 1949.

[28] On the other hand, it was stated by the attorney-general in the British House of Commons on November 20, 1950, that the law of treason was applicable to the contest. Probably the solution of the difficulty arising from the disinclination to treat such hostilities as war in the technical sense lies in the enactment of legislation assimilating them, for certain specified purpose, to war. These include such matters as trading with the enemy, foreign enlistment, and treason.

[29] Reference may be made in this connection to yet another possible consequence of the illegality of the war on the part of one of the belligerents. Art. 84 of the Charter of the United Nations provides that it is the duty of the administering authority to ensure that the trust territory shall play its part in the maintenance of international peace and security and that, with that object in view, the administering authority "may make use of volunteer forces, facilities and assistance from the trust territory in carrying out the obligations towards the Security Council undertaken in this regard by the administering authority, as well as for local defence and maintenance of law and order within the trust territory." That provision leaves open the possibility of the total assimilation of trust territory to a region of war in hostilities in which the administering authority is engaged not inconsistently with or in compliance with its obligations under the Charter. In such situations the administering authority is entitled to use the trust territory as its own and, to that extent, the latter becomes a region of war. However, the aggressor would be adding to his principal wrong by treating the trust territory as a region of war in excess of the irreducible minimum required by the conduct of hostilities. Similarly, if the administering authority should happen to be the aggressor it would not be entitled to use the trust territory for the purposes of its unlawful war. To the extent to which it complies with that obligation the trust territory must be treated by others as remaining outside the orbit of the region of war.

[30] I put forward this view in the fifth edition of vol. I of Oppenheim's *International Law* (1937), § 499. See also to the same effect Art. 4/3 of Research in International Law, Harvard Law School, *Draft Conventions . . . with Comment,* Part III: "Rights and Duties of States in Case of Aggression," printed in *American Journal of International Law,* XXXIII (1939), *Supplement;* and G. G. Fitzmaurice in Académie de La Haye, *Recueil des Cours,* 73/II (1948), 355, 356.

[31] See my submission to this effect in the fifth edition of vol. I of Oppenheim's *International Law* (1937), § 241*a*—a view adopted in Art. 4/2 of the Harvard Research *Draft* (as cited in the preceding footnote). See also Bentivoglio, *La "debellatio" nel diritto internazionale* (1948), pp. 27–32.

[32] For an elaboration of this point of view see G. G. Fitzmaurice in Académie de La Haye, *Recueil des Cours,* 73/II (1948), 324–326.

[33] Art. 79 of the treaty with Italy.

[34] See p. 346, n. 19, above.

[35] See the observations of Professor Georges Scelle on the judgment given in 1946 by the French Court of Cassation, in the case of *Lovera v. Rinaldi* in *Clunet,* LXXVII (1950), 72–82. See also Art. 5 of the Harvard Research *Draft* (as cited in n. 30, above), which states that "by becoming an aggressor, a State loses the right to require other States to perform the obligations of executory treaties, but is not relieved of the duty to perform the obligations of such treaties." It will be noted that the proposed article is intended to apply also to the relations of the aggressor with neutral states—with

the result that those states, although remaining neutral, may participate in such sanctions against the aggressor as involve disregard of any relevant treaties.

[36] *Statutory Rules and Orders* (1941), No. 2136.

[37] For a suggestion that they may properly be resorted to for that purpose see S. W. D. Rowson in *British Year Book of International Law* (London: Oxford University Press, 1946), 352.

[38] In *Laurent v. Le Jeune* the Belgian Court of Cassation held that a requisition, not accompanied by payment, was no more capable of transferring property than theft was: *Annual Digest* (1919–1922), Case No. 343. See also *Lucchesi v. Malfatti* decided by an Italian court, *Foro Italiano,* LXIX (1944–1946), 985; *Secret v. Loizel,* decided by a French court, *Annual Digest* (1943–1945), Case No. 164; *Thiriez v. Descamps,* a decision of a Belgian court, *Pasicrisie Belge,* III (1949), 19. See also Miss Felice Morgenstern's article on the subject of belligerent occupation in *British Year Book of International Law* (London: Oxford University Press, 1951).

[39] For an account of the cases in which criminal proceedings were instituted by the French and Belgian authorities in 1919 in the Rhineland against German manufacturers who had bought machines and plant illegally carried away by Germany from France and Belgium see Marcel Nast in *Revue générale de droit international public,* XXVI (1919), 111–128.

[40] See the Flick trial, *Law Reports of Trials . . .* (as cited in n. 11, above), IX, 48; the Krupp trial, *ibid.,* 69. In all these cases German industrialists were found guilty of assisting in spoliation of private and public property in occupied territory.

[41] Misc. No. 1 (1943) Cmd 6418.

[42] The Swiss ordinance of December 10, 1945 provided that "persons who have been despoiled of movable property or securities in territory occupied by a belligerent in a manner contrary to international law by force, confiscation, requisition, or similar acts on the part of the civil or military authorities, or the armed forces of the occupant, are entitled to reclaim the property from the present possessor in good or bad faith if it is situated in Switzerland."A long series of decisions of the Swiss Federal Court gave effect to that decree. See, e.g., *Rosenberg v. Fischer* where the court held that an object seized in violation of international law was stolen property in the meaning of Art. 934/1 of the Swiss Civil Code: *Annuaire Suisse de droit international,* VI (1949), 139; *P. v. A.G.K. and P., ibid.,* VII (1950), 160; *L. M. v. Swiss Banks, ibid.,* 161.

[43] See pp. 349–350, n. 55, below.

[44] This is probably the true—and, it is submitted, the correct—*ratio decidendi* in the case of the *Adelaide Star* decided in 1947 and 1948 by Danish courts. This was a claim by the Blue Star Line against, *inter alios,* a Danish shipbuilding company, which, in pursuance of a requisition order, handed over to the German occupation authorities a ship which under a contract concluded before World War II was being built for the plaintiff company. The ship had been largely completed before the war. In conformity with the requisition order, the Danish firm completed the ship and handed her over to the German authorities. The ship was subsequently sunk in the course of war operations while in German service. The plaintiff company contended, among others, that as the German invasion of Denmark was illegal the seizure of the ship was unlawful and could not be relied upon by the defendants. The Court of First Instance rejected that argument. It said: "The Court cannot uphold the plaintiff's view that in consequence of the German invasion of Denmark being a breach of international law, it should be impossible to consider the seizure of the *Adelaide Star* as having been justified under general international law. The unlawful invasion is actually found to be analogous with an unlawful war—e.g., one waged in patent violation of a non-aggression pact—insofar as it is bound to carry with it the legal effects of war." This part of the judgment is reproduced, with illuminating comment, by Professor Ross in *Jus Gentium,* I (1949), 6–10.

The Supreme Court of Denmark, in a judgment given in 1948, upheld that part of the judgment of the court below though on substantially different grounds. It said:

"It is not necessary to define an attitude to the question whether the requisitioning of the *Adelaide Star* was contrary to international law. In view of the absolute character of the German military decision of the requisitioning of the ship . . . and the actual conditions existing in Denmark at the time concerned, it must be held that the requisitioning could not have been prevented, and the Court cannot hold that the shipyard or the Danish Government had acted in respect to the German demands in such a manner as to render them liable in damages to the appellant for the non-fulfilment of the contract": *Annual Digest* (1948). This reasoning of the court seems unobjectionable—except, possibly, that it may not have fully taken into account the allegation of the plaintiff that the defendant firm exhibited a somewhat excessive measure of coöperation with the German authorities in completing the ship for them. An Italian court —the Court of First Instance of Florence—seems to have been more rigid in disregarding the effects of an unlawful requisition. It held that such a requisition provides no defense for a bank sued by a depository whose deposit was so seized: *Weber v. Credito Italiano, Foro Italiano,* LXIX (1944–1946), I, 639; *Annual Digest* (1946), Case No. 143. In the case *In re C. van der Giessen* the Netherlands Court of Cassation held in 1948 that the accused could not plead, as a defense in the prosecution for collaboration with the enemy by completing the building of a tanker originally ordered by the Dutch government, that the contract passed to the enemy as booty of war. Only *force majeure* could excuse the performance of such acts for the benefit of the enemy: *Annual Digest* (1948).

[45] Sirey, II (1949), 141.

[46] As in the case of *Soubrouillard v. Kilbourg* where the French Court of Cassation held that although international law recognizes the right of the army of occupation to make requisitions for its military requirements, it does not give the civil authorities of the enemy the right to transfer to private individuals ownership in goods obtained by a levy on other private persons—even if compensation had been paid to the original owner and even if the subsequent transfer was accomplished for the purpose of regulating the economic life of the occupied territory: *Gazette du Palais,* 1946, (2e sem.), 90. See also, for a similar decision, *Delville v. Servais,* decided in 1945 by the Court of Appeal on Liège, *Pasicrisie Belge,* II (1945), 43; *Annual Digest* (1943–1945), Case No. 157.

[47] Annex XVII (A) to the Italian peace treaty. The provisions were limited to nationals of the United Nations.

[48] See p. 105, above.

[49] For some examples see William G. Downey in *American Journal of International Law,* XLIV (1950), 488–504. In *Vitse v. Brasser and the State of The Netherlands,* decided in 1948, the Netherlands District Court of Middelburg held that a tractor requisitioned by German forces in France, against delivery of a receipt, subsequently abandoned by them, captured by the Dutch forces and sold by them to the defendant, was the property of the latter: *Annual Digest* (1948). The court held that as the requisition was effected in accordance with Art. 52 of the Hague regulations in the matter of requisitions, it was not covered by a French decree of 1945 which declared null and void all acts of spoliation by the enemy.

[50] *Annual Digest* (1941–1942), Case No. 171. See also *Koninklijke Lederfabriek "Oisterwijk" N. V. v. Chase National Bank of the City of New York, ibid.,* Case No. 172.

[51] [1937] 1 Ch. 513.

[52] *Legal Effects of War* (3d ed., Cambridge University Press, 1948), p. 341.

[53] I examined the question of neutrality under the Charter of the United Nations in the 7th edition of vol. II of Oppenheim's *International Law* (1952), §§ 292*c*-292*i*.

[54] *De jure belli ac pacis,* Bk. III, chap. iv, § iv.

[55] Bk. II, chap. xv, § xiii, 1; chap. xxv, § iv; Bk. III, chap. x, § iii.1; chap. i, § v. 3; Bk. II, chap. ii, § xiii, 1, xiii, 4. Moreover Grotius was prepared to apply this principle to the sphere of municipal law. He asserted, in emphatic language, that the subject when called upon to take up arms in an unjust war ought to abstain from doing so: Bk. II, chap. xxvi, § iii, I. The same, he says after a careful consideration of the

dangers of disobedience, applies to cases where the justice of the war is doubtful, *ibid.*, § iv, 5, 8. With this there may be compared some judgments given by German courts after World War II. Thus the *Oberlandesgericht* of Kiel sentenced, in 1947, to a term of imprisonment a former member of the German armed forces, an opponent of the National-Socialist regime, who had been condemned to death in 1944 for desertion and who, after having escaped, was recaptured and, in an attempt to escape once more, injured the police official who had apprehended him. The accused pleaded that as the war was illegal on the part of Germany, his desertion and his further acts of resistance were justified. The court examined in detail the question—which in the case before it was probably irrelevant—whether rules of warfare apply in illegal war. It gave an affirmative answer to that question. Insofar as the accused invoked the fact of the illegality of the war as a justification of his refusal to obey the order of the then German government, the court was content to apply the controversial doctrine that rules of international law apply to states only. The judgment, which rejects the view—propounded by Grotius—that the individual is entitled to refuse obedience to his state in a war of aggression and which challenges expressly and by implication the principles of the United Nations Charter and the judgment of the International Military Tribunal of Nuremberg, provides an interesting example of the attitude of some German courts. For the judgment of the Kiel court see *Süddeutsche Juristenzeitung*, II (1947), cols. 324–340. But see *ibid.*, cols. 331–337 for a powerful criticism of the judgment of the court by Arndt. And see *ibid.*, 520, 521 for a similar judgment of the *Oberlandesgericht* of Dresden, given in 1947, where the court, while holding that in principle the laws of war applied in relation to the war waged by National-Socialist Germany, held that the accused was responsible for executing an order involving devastation which was not in fact justified by military necessity.

[56] Of this, Professor Paul Guggenheim's treatment of the subject provides an interesting example: "La Validité et la nullité des actes juridiques internationaux," Académie de La Haye, *Recueil des Cours*, 74/I (1949) 230. He expresses the view that "aussie bien l'Etat attaqué que les Etats tiers, eventuellement neutres, sont obligés d'accorder à l'Etat aggresseur le traitement par les lois et coutumes de la guerre." He relies on Grotius as an authority for the proposition that a war of aggression is not a mere nullity (Bk. III, chap. iv, § 4). But he invokes the "doctrine grotienne" in support of the view which has found acceptance in World War II and in the American practice that a war of aggression "n'obtient qu'une reconnaissance restreinte en droit international" and that neutral states are entitled to discriminate against the aggressor. In his *Lehrbuch des Völkerrechts* (Basel: Verlag für Recht und Gesellschaft, 1950), p. 779, Professor Guggenheim adopts without qualification the view that the law of war knows of no distinction between the aggressor and the victim of aggression.

J. G. STARKE

[1] See, e.g., L. F. L. Oppenheim, ed. by Arnold McNair, *International Law* (4th ed., London: Longmans, Green, 1928), I, 1.

[2] Article 15 of this treaty contains a significant reference of a regional nature; it declares that the principle of free navigation on international rivers is part of "European public law."

[3] *International Tribunals* (Washington: Carnegie Endowment for International Peace and Brookings Institution, 1944), p. 173.

[4] Cf. also the reference in the United Nations Secretariat's *Survey of International Law in Relation to the Work of Codification of the International Law Commission* (1949), p. 38, to the declarations concerning the "Latin American doctrine" of postliminium.

[5] Cf. C. K. Allen, *Law in the Making* (4th ed., Oxford: The Clarendon Press, 1946), chaps. 1 and 2.

[6] See, e.g., the numerous treaties, resolutions, etc. in *The International Conferences of American States, First Supplement 1933–1940* (Washington: Carnegie Endowment, 1940).

[7] E.g., Sir W. Eric Beckett, *The North Atlantic Treaty, The Brussels Treaty, and the Charter of the United Nations* (London: Stevens & Sons, 1950); the author is legal adviser to the British Foreign Office.

[8] See J. F. Lalive, "International Organization and Neutrality," *British Year Book of International Law* (London: Oxford University Press, 1947), pp. 72 ff.

[9] For discussion of the special character of the Council of Europe, see M. Margaret Ball, "The Organization of American States and the Council of Europe," *British Year Book of International Law* (London: Oxford University Press, 1949), pp. 150–176.

[10] "Reparation for Injuries Suffered in the Service of the United Nations," International Court of Justice, *Reports 1949*, pp. 174 ff.

[11] See, e.g., the trusteeship agreements about Tanganyika (Art. 15), French Cameroons and Togoland (Art. 14), Ruanda Urundi (Art. 15), Western Samoa (Art. 13), and the Pacific Islands Territories (Art. 10).

[12] H. Duncan Hall, *Mandates, Dependencies, and Trusteeship* (London: Stevens & Sons, 1948), p. 217.

[13] *Ibid.*, p. 233.

[14] *Op. cit.* (n. 3, above), p. 179.

Notes to Part Two

CLYDE EAGLETON

[1] Hans Kelsen, *The Law of the United Nations* (London: Stevens & Sons, 1950), p. xiv.

[2] "Law is, essentially, an order for the promotion of peace." Hans Kelsen, *Law and Peace in International Relations* (Cambridge; Harvard University Press, 1942), p. 1.

[3] *Report to the President* (Department of State Publication 2349, Conference Series No. 71, 1945), p. 84.

[4] *Ibid.*, p. 137.

[5] When the United States accepted the "optional clause," it did so with a reservation which allowed her to exclude "domestic questions," and the United States was to determine whether or not it was a domestic question.

[6] United Nations Security Council, *Official Records*, Second Year, no. 34, 127th Meeting (1947), p. 726.

[7] Hans J. Morgenthau, *In Defense of the National Interest* (New York: Knopf, 1951), pp. 101–104, *passim*.

[8] George F. Kennan, *American Diplomacy, 1900–1950* (Chicago: University of Chicago Press, 1951), p. 146.

[9] "We cannot deny that power is a factor in world politics any more than we can deny its existence as a factor in national politics. But in a democratic world, as in a democratic nation, power must be linked with responsibility, and obliged to defend and justify itself within the framework of the general good." From the message of President Roosevelt, January 6, 1945.

[10] *Harvard Law Review*, LXIV (1951), 520. Elsewhere Mr. Feller referred to the Charter as a constitution, and thus—if not from the words above quoted—conceded that the Charter is a legal instrument.

[11] *Columbia Law Review*, LI (1951), 537.

[12] *Yale Law Journal*, LX (1951), 193.

[13] *American Political Science Review*, XLV (1951), 550.

[14] Kelsen, *op. cit.*, p. xvi.

[15] United Nations Security Council, *Official Records, First Year,* first series, 13th Meeting (1946), p. 193. At one time in the dicussion, France formally moved that the Council proceed on humanitarian grounds and that the question of competence be put aside. China's proposal to refer the question to the Court was voted down. "The prevailing view seemed to be that the question was essentially a political one." Leland M. Goodrich and Edvard Hambro, *Charter of the United Nations* (Revised edition, Boston: World Peace Foundation, 1949), p. 488.

[16] United Nations Security Council, *Verbatim Records* (March 17, 1948), S/PV. 268.

[17] This debate is briefly summarized in *International Organization,* IV (1950), 98–99, with citations.

[18] United Nations Security Council, *Verbatim Records* (October 1, 1951), S/PV. 559.

[19] United Nations Security Council, *Verbatim Records* (August 16, 1951), S/PV. 552.

[20] United Nations General Assembly, *Official Records, Fifth Session,* Plenary Meetings (1950), I, 295.

[21] If it be true that the Security Council is not capable of deciding legal issues, there is nothing to prevent it from asking the advice of the International Court of Justice.

[22] O. Schachter, "Problems of Law and Justice," *1951 Annual Review of United Nations Affairs* (New York: New York University Press, 1952), pp. 190 ff.

[23] The Charter contains no such provision, but Committee IV/2 at the San Francisco Conference said in its report: ". . . it is inevitable that each organ will interpret such parts of the Charter as are applicable to its particular functions . . . . Accordingly, it is not necessary to include in the Charter a provision either authorizing or approving the normal operation of this principle." UNCIO, Doc. 933, IV/2/42 (2), vol. xiii, p. 709.

HANS J. MORGENTHAU

[1] See the detailed discussion of this problem in the author's "Diplomacy," *Yale Law Journal,* LV (1946), pp. 1073 ff.

ALFRED VON VERDROSS

[1] Hans Kelsen, *Das Problem der Souveränität und Theorie des Völkerrechts* (1920); and *General Theory of Law and State* (Cambridge: Harvard University Press, 1946), pp. 363 ff.

[2] Cf. Hans Kelsen, "Traités internationaux à la charge des Etats tiers," *Mélanges Maheim* (Paris: Librairie du Recucil Sirey, 1935), II, 164; Paul Guggenheim, *Lehrbuch des Völkerrechts* (Basel: Verlag für Recht und Gesellschaft, 1948), I, 88; Alfred von Verdross, *Völkerrecht* (2d ed., Berlin und Wien; J. Springer, 1950), p. 145.

[3] (Tübingen; J. C. B. Mohr, 1923), p. 142; cf. also Josef L. Kunz, "Revolutionary creation of norms in International Law," *American Journal of International Law,* XLI (1947), 119 ff.

[4] It is for this reason not necessary to enter into the argument whether war was or still is admissible according to *general* customary international law only as *bellum justum,* i.e., for the execution or defense of rights, or also for the realization of mere interests.

[5] Cf. Alfred von Verdross, "Le Nazioni Unite e i terzi Stati," *La Communita internazional,* II (Roma: 1947), no. 4. Also Hans Kelsen, *The Law of the United Nations* (London: Stevens & Sons, 1950), pp. 106–110.

[6] Cf. Leland M. Goodrich and Edvard Hambro, *The Charter of the United Nations* (2d ed., Boston: World Peace Foundation, 1949), pp. 517–519.

[7] See the case of the free zones, Permanent Court of International Justice, Order of August 19, 1929, *Series A, No. 22.*

[8] On the history and significance of the concept "collective self-defense" see Josef L. Kunz, *American Journal of International Law,* XLII (1948), 111.

[9] A/1481 "... l'assemblée générale examinera immediatement la question afin de faire aux membres les recommendations appropriées sur les mesures collectives a prendre, y compris, s'il s'agit d'une rupture de paix ou d'un acte d'agression, l'emploi de la force armée. ..."

[10] Paragraph 6 of the preamble.

[11] Italics mine.

[12] Italics mine.

[13] Italics mine.

[14] Cf. Kelsen, *The Law of the United Nations,* pp. 200 ff., *passim.*

[15] It was not possible to consider Kelsen's discussion in *The Western Political Quarterly,* III/4 (1950), 512–527 as it was received only after the completion of this manuscript.

[16] Cf. F. Blaine Sloan, "The binding force of a recommendation of the General Assembly of the U.N.," *British Year Book of International Law* (London: Oxford University Press, 1948), p. 1.

[17] Alfred von Verdross, *Völkerrecht* (2d ed., 1950), pp. 138 ff.

[18] Cf. Kelsen, *General Theory of Law and State,* p. 119: "If the norm remains permanently inefficacious, the norm is deprived of its validity by 'desuetudo.' 'Desuetudo' is the negative legal effect of custom."

[19] Cf. Kelsen, *The Law of the United Nations,* pp. 239 ff.; also in detail: Yuen-Li Liang, "Abstention and Absence of a Permanent Member in relation to the Voting Procedure in the Security Council," *American Journal of International Law,* XLIV (1950), 694 ff.

ERICH HULA

[1] Hans Kelsen, *Das Problem der Souveränität und die Theorie des Völkerrechts* (Tübingen: J. C. B. Mohr, 1920), pp. 124 ff.; *General Theory of Law and State* (Cambridge: Harvard University Press, 1949), pp. 363 ff.; *The Law of the United Nations* (New York: Frederick A. Praeger, 1950), pp. 770 ff.

[2] A. Esmein, *Eléments de Droit Constitutionnel Français et Comparé* (Paris: Librairie du Recueil Sirey, 1921), I, 554.

[3] International Labor Office, *Report of the Conference Delegation on Constitutional Questions on the Work of Its First Session* (Montreal: 1946), p. 32.

[4] International Labor Conference, Thirty-second Session, *Report of the Director-General* (Geneva: 1949), pp. 126 ff.

[5] *Ibid.,* p. 128.

[6] See, e.g., International Labor Conference, Twenty-ninth Session, *Reports on the Application of Conventions (Article 22 of the Constitution)* (Montreal: 1946), *passim.* The Committee of Experts on the Application of Conventions suggests that disregard for conventions has not been due to war conditions only. See *ibid.,* Report V (Appendix), p. 5.

[7] See International Labor Office, *Report of the Conference Delegation . . .* (cited in n. 3, above), pp. 37 ff.

[8] F. L. Oppenheim, ed. by H. Lauterpacht, *International Law* (6th ed., London: Longmans, Green, 1947), I, 662.

[9] See International Labor Office, *op. cit.,* p. 50.

[10] P. de Azcárate, *League of Nations and National Minorities* (Washington: Carnegie Foundation for International Peace, 1945), p. 27.

[11] *Ibid.,* pp. 59 ff.

[12] C. A. Macartney, *National States and National Minorities* (London: Oxford University Press, H. Milford, 1934), p. 275.

[13] Jacob Robinson and Others, *Were the Minorities Treaties a Failure?* (New York: Institute of Jewish Affairs of the American Jewish Congress and the World Jewish Congress, 1943), pp. 187 ff.

[14] *Ibid.*, pp. 196, 238 f.

[15] Report presented by M. Tittoni and adopted by the Council of the League of Nations on October 22d, 1920, reprinted in: League of Nations, *Protection of Linguistic, Racial or Religious Minorities by the League of Nations,* Resolutions and Extracts from the Minutes of the Council, Resolutions and Reports adopted by the Assembly, relating to the Procedure to be followed in Questions concerning the Protection of Minorities (Geneva: March 1931), p. 7.

[16] Robinson, *op. cit.*, p. 111.

[17] Azcárate, *op. cit.*, pp. 66 ff.; Robinson, *op. cit.*, pp. 122 ff.

[18] League of Nations: Ninth Assembly, *Record of Plenary Session,* p. 82 (quoted in Macartney, *op. cit.*, p. 279). Three months later, in December, 1928, Briand as president of the Council made another speech more reassuring for the minorities. He emphasized the "sacred" character of their rights and promised that minorities matters will always be considered by the Council "with the deepest respect for the interests in question." *League of Nations Official Journal,* 10th Year (January, 1929), pp. 59 f. (quoted in Robinson, *op. cit.*, p. 242).

[19] "Report of the Sixth Session of the Commission on Human Rights," Economic and Social Council, *Official Records, Fifth Year: Eleventh Session, Supplement,* no. 5 (1950), pp. 15 ff.

[20] On the question of limitations see H. Lauterpacht, *International Law and Human Rights* (New York: Frederick A. Praeger, 1950), pp. 330 ff., 365 ff.; and Zechariah Chafee, Jr., "Legal Problems of Freedom of Information in the United Nations," *Law and Contemporary Problems,* XIV (Durham, N. C.: School of Law, Duke University, Autumn, 1949), pp. 567 ff.

[21] R. S. Baker, *The Public Papers of Woodrow Wilson: The New Democracy* (New York and London: Harper, 1925–1927), I, 206. Quoted in E. H. Carr, *The Twenty Years' Crisis 1919–1939* (London: Macmillan, 1940), p. 43.

[22] Maurice Bourquin, "L'Humanisation du droit des gens," *La Technique et les principles du droit public,* Etudes en l'honneur de Georges Scelle (Paris: Librairie générale du droit et jurisprudence, 1950), I, 27.

[23] Zechariah Chafee, *op. cit.*, pp. 550 ff.; and Arthur N. Holcombe, *Human Rights in the Modern World* (New York: New York University Press, 1948), pp. 120 ff.

[24] Fustel de Coulanges, *La cité antique* (Paris: Hachette, 1912), V.

Notes to Part Three

ARTHUR NUSSBAUM

[1] To my knowledge, no earlier inquiry into this subject exists.

[2] Cf. A. Esmein, "Le serment promissoire dans le droit canonique," *Nouvelle Revue Historique de Droit Français et Etranger,* XII (1888), pp. 248 ff., 311 ff. This learned study confines itself, however, to the field of private law. "Corporeal" corrobration seems not to have been common in agreements with Moslem rulers; see n. 40, below.

[3] This term, customary in medieval law, is already found in Justinian's *Corpus Juris Civilis* (Cod. II, 28, 1) where it probably means no more than an oath taken personally rather than through a guardian or proxy. Still, in antiquity too, the promissory oath —that is, the oath confirming a promise—was ordinarily "corporeal." The swearer would drop a stone, invoking Jupiter to hurl the swearer down the same way should he violate his promise [*jusjurandum per Jovem lapidem*]. Esmein, *op. cit.*, p. 250.

[4] *Ibid.*, p. 256.

[5] Cf. F. G. Davenport, *European Treaties Bearing on the History of the United states and its Dependencies* (1917), I, 93.

[6] Regarding other evasive manipulations in the taking of oaths, see Esmein, *op. cit.*, pp. 257 ff.

[7] Jean Dumont, *Corps Universel Diplomatique du Droit des Gens*, VI/1, 463. In the Peace of Brétigny between Edward III of England and John of France (1360), it was said: "Nous ... jurons ... sur le corps de Jésus Christ Sacré et sur les Saint Evangilcs qui ci sont," Dumont, *Supp.* II, No. 39, p. 189. The first part of the oath refers to the Sacred Host, cf. Lucien de Rosny, *Recherches Ethnographiques sur les Serments* (posthumous, 1901), p. 59.

[8] See generally regarding oaths upon sacred relics, de Rosny, *op. cit.*, pp. 143, 146 ff. (with a discussion of pre-Christian precedents).

[9] de Rosny, *op. cit.*, p. 155.

[10] M. A. de Taube, "Inviolabilité des traités," Académie de Droit International, *Recueil des Cours*, 32 (1930), 345.

[11] Harold Lamb, *The Crusades, Flame of Islam* (New York: Doubleday, Doran and Co., 1945), p. 100.

[12] Cf. Fritze, "Clausula rebus sic stantibus," *Archiv für Bürgerliches Recht*, XVII (1900), 20.

[13] See Arthur Nussbaum, *Concise History of the Law of Nations* (New York: Macmillan, 1947), p. 78.

[14] The reservation may involve a mortal sin, but this would not affect the invalidity of the oath; cf. "Serment," *Dictionnaire de Théologie Catholique*, A. Vacant and E. Amann, eds. (Paris: Letouzey et Ané, 1909–1944). The doctrine of *reservatio mentalis* unfolded fully in the postmedieval era; see "reservatio mentalis," *Realencyclopädie der protestantischen Theologie und Kirche* (Leipzig: 1885, also 1904), XV.

[15] Esmein, *op. cit.*, p. 312. Thomas Aquinas had laid down the fundamental rule in these terms: "Illud quad votum fieri impediret si praesens esset, etiam voto facto obligationem aufert." *Dictionnaire de Théologie Catholique*, p. 1954. While this literally refers to vows, it applies to oaths by analogy.

[16] Juramentum contra utilitatum ecclesiasticam praestitum non tenet. *Decretals* lib. II tit. 24, c. 27. See also *Liber Sextus*, II, tit. XL c. 1.

[17] Const. III of Urban VI, *Bullarium Diplomatum et Privilegiorum Sanctorum Romanorum Pontificum, Taurinensis Editio.* ["Magnum Bullarium Romanum,"] III (1850), 584. François Laurent, *Histoire du Droit des Gens*, X (1895), 434 cites from *Bullarium Magnum*, IV/1, 129, a decree of Pope Paul III to the same effect. Laurent envisaged, most probably, Paul III's bull of 1535 condemning and excommunicating Henry VIII of England. There, in sec. 15, obligations undertaken toward this king under oath were declared invalid in strongest terms. Cf. *Magnum Bullarium Romanum*, VI (1860), p. 201. Laurent apparently cites a different Bullarium Magnum, not available to the writer (cf. *Dictionnaire*, cited in n. 14, above, under "Bullaire").

[18] The text of the invalidating declaration is found in Karl Mirbt, *Quellen zur Geschichte des Papsttums und des Römischen Katholizismus* (4th ed., 1924), p. 228. See, furthermore, Mandell Creighton, *History of the Papacy*, II (1889), 32 and, from the Catholic point of view, J. B. Schwab, *Johannes Gerson* (1858), p. 582.

[19] Laurent, *Histoire du Droit des Gens* (1865), X, 454.

[20] Examples are given by Vattel, *Droit des Gens* (1758), III, sec. 223; M. R. Vesnitch, "Le Droit International dans les rapports des Slaves méridionaux du Moyen–Age," *Revue de Droit International et de Législation Comparée*, XXVIII (1896), 329, 383.

[21] Esmein, *op. cit.*, p. 314; *Dictionnaire*, p. 1955.

[22] Cf. Laurent, X, 428 ff.; see also R. P. Ward, *An Enquiry into the Foundation and History of the Law of Nations* (1795), II, 125.

[23] Dumont, *op. cit.* (n. 7, above).

[24] François Timoleon Abbé de Choisy, *Histoire de Charles Cinquième* (1689), p. 255.

The provision apparently formed part of a secret agreement, cf., Patrick Frazer Tytler, *History of Scotland from the Accession of Alexander III to the Union* (1866), III, 8. It was already referred to by Vattel, n. 20, above, Bk. II, sec. 224.

[25] Davenport, *op. cit.* (in n. 5, above), p. 99. See also n. 32, below.

[26] The text of the lengthy protestation is found in Dumont, *op. cit.*, IV/1, 412 ff. The oath itself forms part of the peace treaty, n. 7, above.

[27] Though the famous phrase ascribed to him "all lost save honor" is not literally correct. The accurate text is found in his letter written to his mother, Louise of Savoy, after the battle of Pavia; cf. E. Lavisse, *Histoire de France* (1904), V/2, 37. Shortly before his release he had confirmed his intention to carry out the terms of the treaty, Champollion-Figeac, *Captivité du Roi François I* (1857), p. 517.

[28] The text of the bull is in Dumont, *op. cit.*, Supp. III, 12.

[29] François A. M. A. Mignet, *Rivalité de François I et de Charles-Quint* II (1875), p. 204.

[30] The question was settled in this sense by Alberico Gentili, *De Jure Belli*, Bk. III, chap. 14 (1598) [Classics ed., p. 363].

[31] Esmein, *op. cit.*, p. 265.

[32] Davenport, *op. cit.*, p. 106. Actually, the confirmation was given in 1506, that is, twelve years after the treaty was signed and ratified. *Ibid.*, p. 107. This meant another long period of uncertainty.

[33] Davenport, *op. cit.*, p. 195. It was added that "a violation could not be absolved by His Holiness without the consent of the other party"—a restriction of the Pontiff's authority certainly invalid under canon law.

[34] *Ibid.*, p. 170.

[35] This form appears everywhere in Russia's earlier diplomatic history; see, e.g., George Vernadsky, "Kievan Russia" in *A History of Russia* (New Haven: Yale University Press, 1943–1948), p. 95. For a Byzantine example [Russo-Byzantine treaty of 907] cf. H. S. Cross, "The Russian Primary Chronicle," *Harvard Studies in Philology and Literature*, XII (1930), 151.

In medieval intra-Russian treaties a remarkable way of strengthening a treaty consisted in the reciprocal assurance that the contracting princes would consider each other as "brothers" or as "son" and "father." Alexandre Eck, *Le Moyen âge russe* (Paris: Maison du livre étranger, 1933), p. 72.

[36] de Rosny, *op. cit.*, pp. 228, 231.

[37] K. L. Goetz, *Deutsch-russische Handelsgeschichte des Mittelalters* (Lübeck: O. Waelde, 1922), p. 90.

[38] de Taube, *op. cit.*, p. 358. Unfortunately, de Taube, foremost expert on the subject, did not elaborate his statement.

[39] Regarding, e.g., Byzantine conduct toward Persia, see Güterbock, *Byzanz und Persien in ihren diplomatischen und völkerrechtlichen Beziehungen* (1906), passim. De Taube, "L'apport de Byzance au Dévelopment du Droit International Occidental," Académie de La Haye, *Recueil des Cours*, 67/I (1939), 304, refers to an alleged utterance of the Byzantine Emperor Justin II, according to which the latter felt entitled to aid a Christian nation contrary to his peace treaty with Persia. But this was apparently not the real motive of his break with Persia, Güterbock, *op. cit.*, pp. 112, 114.

[40] In a treaty between King Alfonso of Aragon and the Sultan Qualaun of Egypt (1240), the king used the following form: "I, Don Alfonso, say by God, by God, by God, by the truth of the Cross, by the truth of the Madonna Maria, mother of the Light, by the truth of the four Evangiles of Matthew, Marcus, Lucas and John, by the truth of the voice which descended on the Jordan River and ascended back, by the truth of my religion, of my God and my faith . . ." The king further declared that in case of a violation of the oath he should be deemed an outcast and a deserter from his religion. The oath of the sultan was similar, but shorter: "By God, by God, by God, by the truth of the Islamic faith, by the truth of the exalted Koran, basis of the creed of the Moslem . . . I swear for me, my children and all my people . . . May God sanc-

tion my oath." But there was apparently no "corporeal" solemnity. G. Vedovato, *L'Ordinamento Capitulare in Oriente nei Privilegi Toscani dei Secoli* (1946), XII-XIV, 136, 137. Ernst Kantorowicz, in his impressive work, *Kaiser Friedrich der Zweite* (Berlin: G. Bondi, 1928), p. 176 [English ed., *Frederick the Second* (London: Constable and Co., 1931), p. 191] mentions that Frederick II, who had adopted many Arabic habits, took at one occasion an oath with the, allegedly Arabic, self-execration that he "would eat the flesh of his left hand" should he violate his oath. In the *Ergänzungsband* (1931) to the German edition where documentation is given, there is no reference supporting that statement. An inquiry undertaken by myself with competent Arabic assistance for ascertaining and explaining the use of such a formula had a negative result.

[41] Koran, Bk. XVI, chap. 91; cf. Majid Khadduri, *The Law of War and Peace in Islam* (London: Luzac and Co., 1940), p. 82 with reference to further source material in point.

[42] Koran, Bk. X, chap. 9, verse 4. Cf. Al-Haj Hafiz Ghulam Sarwar, *The Holy Qur-An* (undated, but after 1928), p. 106.

[43] The foregoing discussion is based mainly on Khadduri, *op. cit.*; Ahmed Rechid, "L'Islam et le Droit des Gens," Académie de La Have, *Recueil des Cours*, 60/II (1937) 375 ff.; Julius Hatschek, *Der Mustamin* (1919), analyzing a work by Mohammed ibn Hasan as-Saihani (749–804), concerning the law of war; Daniel B. von Haneberg, "Das Muslimische Kriegsrecht," *Abhandlungen der philosophisch-historischen Classe der Kgl. Bayrischen Akademie der Wissenschaffen*, XII/2 (1891), 217 ff. [also published separately], and *Dictionary of Islam, passim*. To Haneberg's careful study, which extends far beyond the law of war, there is annexed a translation of the Vikayah, an authoritative tract on the Islamic law of war, written in 1280 by Mahmud el Mahbab. Armanazi, *L'Islam et le Droit International* (thesis, Paris, 1929) is not helpful.

[44] See, e.g., Thomas A. Walker, *A History of the Law of Nations* (1899), p. 75.

[45] Haneberg, *op. cit.*, p. 252; Vikayah, *op. cit.*, chap. 10.

[46] Sultan Selim II, a ruler notorious for his depravity, is said to have broken, in 1571, his peace treaty with Venice, in order to invade Cyprus, after he had procured a favorable legal opinion from the Mufti Abu Suud. Again, a peace treaty with Venice was broken by the Sultan Ibrahim I in 1648. Haneberg, *op. cit.*, p. 253.

[47] Nussbaum, *Concise History of the Law of Nations* (as cited in n. 13, above), p. 38.

[48] Stanley Lane-Poole, *Saladin and the Fall of the Kingdom of Jerusalem* (1898), p. 307; Richard A. Newhall, *The Crusades* (New York: Henry Holt, 1927), p. 54.

[49] *Op. cit.*, p. 307.

COVEY T. OLIVER

[1] Hans Kelsen, *General Theory of Law and State* (Cambridge: Harvard University Press, 1945).

[2] Hans Kelsen, *The Law of the United Nations* (London: Stevens & Sons, 1950); *Recent Trends in the Law of the United Nations* (London: Stevens & Sons, 1951).

[3] Chicago: The University of Chicago Press, 1951.

[4] *Ibid.*, p. 54.

[5] *Ibid.*, p. 95.

[6] Kelsen, *General Theory of Law and State*, pp. 325–388, *passim*.

[7] *Ibid.*, pp. 121–122.

[8] *Ibid.*, pp. 325–326.

[9] See Hans Kelsen, "Science and Politics," *American Political Science Review*, XLV (September, 1951), p. 641, *passim*.

[10] His frequent comparisons between primitive law and international law, as well as his Pure Theory, preclude the attribution to Kelsen of pretensions of completeness in the system. Cf. Kelsen, *General Theory of Law and State*, pp. 339–341.

[11] Kelsen, *Peace through Law* (Chapel Hill: University of North Carolina Press, 1944), p. 18.

[12] Seventh Bernard Moses Memorial Lecture, University of California (Berkeley: James J. Gillick & Co., 1946). See also Dickinson's "International Law: An Inventory," *Calif. L. Rev.*, XXXIII (1945), 506, and *War and Peace* (Philadelphia: University of Pennsylvania Press, 1951), pp. 32–39, 89–105.

[13] Italics mine.

[14] Dickinson, "What Is Wrong with International Law?," p. 2.

[15] Permanent Court of International Justice, 1927, *Series A, No. 10* (Manley O. Hudson, ed., *World Court Reports*, II, 23).

[16] Sub. nom. Compania de Navigación Nacional *(Panamá v. United States)*, United States-Panamanian Claims Commission, 1933.

[17] Dickinson, "What Is Wrong with International Law?," p. 13.

[18] *Ibid.*, p. 18.

[19] *Ibid.*, pp. 21–22.

[20] Dickinson, *War and Peace*. See booknote George W. Miller, Calif. L. Rev., XXXIX (1951), 473.

[21] Philip C. Jessup, *A Modern Law of Nations* (New York: Macmillan, 1946).

[22] *Ibid.*, pp. 68–93, *passim*.

[23] *Ibid.*, chap. viii.

[24] *Ibid.*, p. 188.

[25] *Ibid.*, p. 3.

[26] Hans J. Morgenthau, "Diplomacy," *Yale L. J.* LV (1946), 1067.

[27] Philip C. Jessup, "The Reality of International Law," *Foreign Affairs*, XVIII (January, 1940), 244.

[28] Jessup, *A Modern Law of Nations*, pp. 6–7.

[29] Morgenthau, *Yale L. J.* (as cited in n. 26, above).

[30] *Ibid.*, p. 1078.

[31] Italics mine.

[32] *Ibid.*, p. 1080.

[33] *Miss. L. J.*, XX (1949), 253.

[34] *Ibid.*, p. 260.

[35] *Loc. cit.*

[36] *Ibid.*, p. 263.

[37] *Loc. cit.*

[38] *Miss. L. J.*, XX (1949), 269–270.

[39] McDougal credits Morgenthau with belief in the former's general goal, "World Order under Law," *Miss. L. J.*, XXX (1949), 277.

[40] There is no intention to induce inferences that only the views here abstracted are "currently influential." The effort has been toward groupings. There are many shades within the groupings. Also, it is recognized that the current concepts discussed have been influenced by many earlier studies. Cf., for example, Lauterpacht's *The Function of Law in the International Community* (Oxford: Clarendon Press, 1933) and John Basset Moore's pioneering *International Law and Some Current Illusions* (New York: Macmillan, 1924).

[41] Walter Lippman, quoted on the dust jacket of Kennan, *op. cit.* (n. 3, above).

[42] *Time*, LVIII (December 3, 1951) 20–21; "The Diplomat and the Dinosaur," *The Reporter*, V (November 13, 1951), 9-13; *The New Yorker*, XXVII (September 29, 1951), 113.

[43] *New York Times*, Lit. Supp., September 30, 1951, p. 3; *New York Herald Tribune*, book-review section, September 30, 1951, p. 5.

[44] See Mrs. Harley Stevens, book review, *Bulletin of the World Affairs Council of Northern California* (San Francisco: October, 1951).

[45] Kennan, "The National Interest of the United States," *Foreign Service Journal*, XXVIII (November, 1951).

[46] Edgar Ansel Mowrer, book review, "Who Will Counsel the Counselor?," *Saturday*

Review of Literature (September 29, 1951).

[47] Italics mine at both points in the quotation.

[48] Kennan, *American Diplomacy, 1900–1950,* p. 95.

[49] Pp. 200–201, above.

[50] Kennan, *American Diplomacy, 1900–1950,* p. 15.

[51] *Ibid.,* p. 10.

[52] *Ibid.,* p. 14.

[53] *Ibid.,* p. 37.

[54] *Ibid.,* p. 42.

[55] *Ibid.,* p. 45, italics mine.

[56] *Ibid.,* p. 46.

[57] *Ibid.,* p. 94.

[58] *Ibid.,* p. 47.

[59] *Ibid.,* p. 48.

[60] See pp. 212, 218, below.

[61] Kennan, *op. cit.,* pp. 53–54, italics mine.

[62] Cf. the bitter debate between the Beard-Barnes "historical revisionists" and the defenders of Franklin D. Roosevelt's policy toward expanding Japan, a group sometimes labeled by the former, "the court historians." A more dignified part of this dispute than the pros and cons of "he tricked the Japanese into fighting us" relates to the issue whether, regardless of provocation, we should have lost sight of Japan as the natural power for the containment "of Russia out of Manchuria [to modify a Goldwynism]."

[63] Kennan, *op. cit.,* p. 64.

[64] Mr. Kennan speaks of a shift of internal United States attitude, forcing us to fight the war "to the bitter end" (p. 67), to impose "victor's terms . . . upon the vanquished" (p. 68). But see the brilliant character sketch of Wilson receding from his high principles in telling instances under pressure from Clemenceau, in Keynes, *The Economic Consequences of the Peace* (New York: 1920). But see Etienne Mantoux, *The Carthaginian Peace* (London: Oxford University Press, 1946), pp. 49-66.

[65] Kennan, *op. cit.,* p. 71.

[66] *Ibid.,* p. 88.

[67] *Ibid.,* p. 90.

[68] *Ibid.,* p. 96. An interestingly different usage of a lawyers' phrase!

[69] *Ibid.,* p. 98. But see, Ann Van Wynen Thomas and A. J. Thomas, Jr., "Equality of States in International Law—Fact or Fiction?" *Va. L. Rev.* XXXVII (1951), 791, 821, for evidence that the doctrine of the equality of states does not fool even students of international law. I suspect that it does not too seriously mislead "old line diplomats" or the public, either.

[70] Kennan, *op cit.,* p. 99. Cf. Professor Dickinson's differing conclusions about these same inadequacies, p. 199, above.

[71] Kennan, *op. cit.,* p. 100.

[72] *Loc. cit.* Italics mine.

[73] *Ibid.,* p. 101.

[74] Arnold J. Toynbee, *A Study of History,* Sommerville Abridgement (New York and London: Oxford University Press, 1947), chap. xxi.

[75] Reprinted as appendices to the work under reference.

[76] Kelsen helps here. Cf. *The Law of the United Nations,* pp. 550–566.

[77] United Nations Security Council, *Official Records, Second Year,* nos. 67 and 68, 171st, 172d, 173d Meetings (1947); *United Nations Weekly Bulletin,* III/7 (August 12, 1947), 215–225.

[78] Resolution of the General Assembly, November 3, 1950.

[79] *Collier's* (October 27, 1951).

[80] See Louis B. Sohn, "The Jurisdiction of the International Court of Justice," *Am. Bar Assn. J.,* XXXV (1949), 924.

[81] Providing that the court shall have the power to indicate, if it considers that cir-

cumstances so require, any provisional measures which ought to be taken to preserve the "respective rights of either [sic] party," and that notice of such measures be given to the parties and to the Security Council.

[82] Recent press notices about Iran's appearance at the hearing on the merits seem in their tone to confirm the unofficial explanation made by a high Iranian official to the writer that Iran did not regard its withdrawal from compulsory jurisdiction as applying retrospectively to the current controversy.

[83] Official printing of the Order of the Court, dated July 5, 1951, p. 3.

[84] *Ibid.*

[85] U. S. Department of State, *Bulletin,* XXV, No. 641 (October 8, 1951), 584–585.

[86] United Nations Charter, Art. 94/2; see Kelsen, *The Law of the United Nations,* pp. 539–545.

[87] United Nations Security Council, Document S/2358, Rev. 2, October 17, 1951.

[88] The proposal finally adopted was made by the French representative on October 19, 1951, *New York Times* (October 20). See also *United Nations Bulletin,* XI/9 (November 1, 1951), 376, 378.

[89] *United Nations Bulletin,* XI/9 (November 1, 1951), 376.

[90] U.S. Department of State, *Bulletin,* XXV, No. 642 (October 15, 1951), 615.

[91] U.S. Department of State, *Bulletin,* XXV, No. 645 (November 5, 1951), 746–749.

[92] *United Nations Bulletin,* XI/9 (November 1, 1951), 378.

[93] James Reston, *New York Times,* October 18, 1951.

[94] Professor Manley O. Hudson, in a letter to the *New York Times,* October 28, 1951, takes the position that the French resolution, accepted by the Security Council, n. 88, above, is "based upon a misconception of the procedure of the Court," because the question of its jurisdiction will not be before the court unless Iran, before the hearing on the merits, set for January 10, 1952, objects to the jurisdiction, or, unless after that date the United Kingdom asks for a default judgment under Article 53 of the statute of the court. See, also, Professor Charles G. Fenwick's comment on the court's interim order, *Am. J. Int. Law,* XL (1951), 723, and Professor W. W. Bishop's note, *ibid.,* p. 749.

[95] Quoted from the concluding paragraph of Professor Hudson's letter, n. 94, above.

[96] Sir Gladwyn Jebb, as reported in the *New York Times,* October 20, 1951.

[97] James Reston, *New York Times,* October 18, 1951.

[98] Suggested by Professor Fenwick's comment, n. 94, above. *Cf.* Orfield, "The Use of Injunctions in International Law," *Geo. L. R.,* XL (1952).

[99] Jules Basdevant, "The Judiciary in the International Sphere," *United Nations Bulletin,* VII/9 (November 1, 1949), 503.

[100] P. 199, above.

[101] James Reston, *New York Times,* October 18, 1951.

[102] *Ibid.*

[103] Kelsen, *op. cit.,* p. 541.

[104] In a famous speech the former commander in chief of the United Nations forces in Korea seemed unaware of the differentiation.

[105] Mr. Kennan's concept of law can be gleaned indirectly; he seems oblivious to lively debate showing considerable difference of opinion on just this point.

[106] Statement of Justice Ivan C. Rand of the Supreme Court of Canada, reported in the *Harvard Law School Record,* XIII (November 11, 1941).

[107] *Yale L. J.,* LX (1951), 1251.

[108] Italics mine.

HEINRICH BRANDWEINER

[1] Text in the Supplement to the *Official Bulletin of the Allied Commission for Austria,* 1946, No. 7, and in Stephan Verosta, *Die internationale Stellung Österreichs 1938–1947* (Vienna: Manz, 1947), pp. 104 ff.

[2] Text: Verosta, *op. cit.*, pp. 71 ff.

[3] H. Lauterpacht, *Recognition in International Law* (Cambridge: Cambridge University Press, 1948), p. 26.

[4] Hans Kelsen, *General Theory of Law and State* (Cambridge: Harvard University Press, 1945), p. 219: "A new state in the sense of International Law has come into existence if an independent government has established itself by issuing a coercive order for a certain territory and if the government is effective, i.e., if the government is able to obtain permanent obedience to its order on the part of the individuals living in this territory."

[5] Cf. Ludwig Adamovich, *Grundriss des österreichischen Verfassungsrechtes* (Berlin und Wien: J. Springer, 1947), p. 43: "Österreich ist somit heute noch kein souveräner Staat." In the Moscow declaration of October 30, 1943, supplemented by a French declaration in essentially similar terms of November 16, 1943 (text: Verosta, *op. cit.*, pp. 53 ff.), the United Kingdom, the U.S.S.R. and the U.S. have taken upon themselves the solemn duty of reëstablishing the freedom and independence of Austria, that is, not merely that of effecting the separation of Austria from Germany. Rather, the powers intended the restoration of full sovereignty, which remains restricted so long as occupation forces are in the country without or against the will of the government.

[6] John Westlake, *International Law* (2d ed., Cambridge: Cambridge University Press, 1910–1913), I, 21.

[7] Cf. Alfred von Verdross, *Völkerrecht* (Berlin und Wien: J. Springer, 1937), p. 55.

[8] L. F. L. Oppenheim, ed. by H. Lauterpacht, *International Law* (7th ed., London: Longmans, Green, 1948), I, 173 ff. does not distinguish between protection and protectorate: the condition is aptly termed "a kind of international guardianship."

[9] Cf. Verdross, *op. cit.*, p. 57.

[10] The more recently established Free State of Trieste shows similar features, but here the League of Nations is replaced by the Security Council and the high commissioner by the governor.

[11] Cf. Permanent Court of International Justice, 1926, *Series A, No. 7*, p. 29: "Un traité ne fait droit qu'entre les Etats qui y sont parties"; cf., also, Permanent Court of International Justice, 1932, *Series A/B, No. 46*, p. 141; 1929, *Series A, No. 23*, p. 20; 1923, *Series B, No. 8*, p. 55.

[12] Paul Guggenheim, *Lehrbuch des Völkerrechts* (Basel: Verlag für Recht und Gesellschaft, 1948), pp. 88 ff.

[13] *Ibid.*, p. 98.

[14] Cf. Art. 2 of the United Nations Charter.

[15] Contrary to Tončič, who gives a theoretically affirmative answer with regard to the nonintervention clause of Art. 2 of the Charter and to the clauses of Arts. 103, 107 (*Salzburger Volkszeitung*, June 29, 1949).

[16] Cf. *Amtliche Wiener Zeitung*, June 29 and 30, 1946.

[17] Cf. Verdross, *op. cit.*, p. 98; also Guggenheim, *op. cit.*, p. 208.

[18] So, rightly, also Guggenheim, *op. cit.*, p. 209.

[19] I.e., in its essentials. By the memorandum of the Allied Council of October 20, 1945, Austria was informed of the alteration of several clauses of the First Control Agreement.

[20] Text: Verosta, *op. cit.*, pp. 66 ff.

[21] Text: *Ibid.*, p. 88.

[22] Text: *Ibid.*, pp. 97 ff.

[23] *StGBl.* No. 1/1945.

[24] Cf. Arnold Toynbee, *Survey of International Affairs*, 1938/1 (London: Oxford University Press, 1941), pp. 179–259.

[25] Enumerated in Verosta, *op. cit.*, p. 119.

[26] *RGBl.* I, p. 237.

[27] Text: Verosta, *op. cit.*, pp. 17–19.

[28] A principle also fundamental to the positive Austrian legal order. Cf. Art. 145 B and also Adamovich, *op. cit.* (n. 5, above), p. 44.

[29] Kelsen, *General Theory of Law and State* (as cited in n. 4, above), pp. 220–221; italics mine.

[30] *Ibid.*, pp. 219–220; italics mine.

[31] Guggenheim, *op. cit.*, pp. 404 ff.

[32] The last sentence is especially to be emphasized.

[33] Guggenheim, *loc. cit.*

[34] So far as we do not understand war as a unilateral use of force.

[35] Oppenheim-Lauterpacht, *op. cit.*, § 239.

[36] *Ibid.*, p .519.

[37] Cf. the opposite view in Guggenheim, *op. cit.*, p. 594, and the decision quoted in n. 248 on that page.

[38] Kelsen, *op. cit.* (n. 4, above), p. 214.

[39] Kelsen here cites Oppenheim-Lauterpacht, *International Law* (6th ed., 1940), pp. 166 ff.

[40] Italics mine.

[41] Italics mine.

[42] *Reine Rechtslehre* (Leipzig und Wien: F. Deuticke, 1934), p. 149, Italics mine.

[43] *Handbuch des Völkerrechts* (1886), II, 255.

[44] *Internationales Landkriegsrecht* (1914), p. 97, n. 2.

[45] "Die völkerrechtliche Stellung der vom Feind besetzten Gebiete," *Archiv des öffentlichen Rechts* (1915), III, 360.

[46] *Das Völkerrecht* (1925), p. 150.

[47] Verdross, *op. cit.* (n. 7, above), p. 126.

[48] *Loc. cit.*

[49] Except when individuals are directly responsible.

[50] Oppenheim-Lauterpacht, *op. cit.* (n. 8, above), p. 136.

[51] Italics mine.

[52] *Recognition in International Law* (as cited in n.3, above), p. 420.

[53] Italics mine.

[54] The League of Nations Covenant, the United Nations Charter, and the Kellogg pact.

[55] Italics mine.

[56] Oppenheim-Lauterpacht, *op. cit.* (n. 8, above), p. 525.

[57] Cf. Kelsen, *Reine Rechtslehre* (as cited in n. 42, above), p. 148.

[58] *Op. cit.*, § 20.

[59] *A Textbook of International Law* (London: Longmans, Green, 1947), p. 145.

[60] Cf. Josef L. Kunz, *Kriegsrecht und Neutralitätsrecht* (Berlin und Wien; J. Springer, 1935), p. 8.

[61] After the completion of this article, there appeared in the *Festschrift* in honor of Klang (1950) an article by Verdross concerning the international identity of states, in which he claims the so-called "prescription" (*Ersitzung*) as a title for justification of an illegal annexation, "for according to International Law only the permanent and undisputed rule legalizes [*saniert*] the original illegality under which this rule was exercised." He further claims that there can be no question of such rule if it is disputed by other powers. But *Ersitzung* in international law is essentially the same as the principle of effectiveness (cf. Kelsen, *General Theory*, p. 215: " . . . it is scarcely possible to distinguish prescription from the general principle of effectiveness"). But the effectiveness of rule is *not* affected by disputes or protest (cf. Oppenheim-Lauterpacht, *op. cit.*, I, 527: " . . . but after such protests and claims, if any, cease to be repeated"), but only by the *use of force*. The distinction made by Verdross between *Gebietshoheit* and *territoriale Souveränität* (cf. *Jus Gentium*, I/3 (1949), 247 ff.) is, in any case, of no importance here.

[62] Text: Verosta, *op. cit.*, pp. 32 ff.

[63] *Ibid.*, pp. 34 ff.
[64] *Ibid.*, pp. 36 ff.
[65] *Ibid.*, pp. 39 ff.
[66] Opperheim-Lauterpacht, *op. cit.*, p. 398.
[67] *Ibid.*, p. 399. This conception corresponds to the practice of the British authorities of not affixing visas to former Austrian passports, which were declared invalid by the German Reich because their holders had fled abroad. (I am indebted for this information to Professor Dobretsberger).
[68] Text: Verosta, *op. cit.*, p. 47.
[69] *Ibid.*, pp. 52 ff.
[70] *Ibid.*, p. 63.
[71] *Ibid.*, p. 15.
[72] *Ibid.*, pp. 16 ff.
[73] *Ibid.*, p. 116.
[74] *Ibid.*, pp 98-100, 102.
[75] Adamovich, *op. cit.* (n. 5, above), p. 37, n. 1. Italics mine.
[76] Oppenheim-Lauterpacht, *op. cit.*, p. 231, n. 2.
[77] Guggenheim, *op. cit.*, p. 169, n. 21.
[78] Oppenheim-Lauterpacht, *op. cit.*, pp. 397 ff.
[79] *American Journal of International Law*, XXXII (1938), 312–314.
[80] *Ibid.*, pp. 421 ff.
[81] *Ibid.*, pp. 766 ff.
[82] *Ibid.*, XXXVIII (1944), 621 ff.
[83] As well as an inquiry by Hans Klinghoffer, *Les Aspectes juridiques de l'occupation de l'Autriche* (Rio de Janeiro: Gráfica Santo Antonio, 1943), which was not available to me.
[84] *American Journal of International Law*, XXXII (1938), p. 423.
[85] *Ibid.*, p. 424.
[86] Here Garner means the obligation of the new state to obey certain treaties, concluded by its predecessor with so-called *dinglicher Wirkung*.
[87] *American Journal of International Law*, XXXII (1938), p. 432.
[88] *Loc. cit.*
[89] Most recently shared by Woolsey, in the *American Journal of International Law*, XL (1950), 133: "The United States in effect recognized the annexation of Austria in April, 1938, and agreed (which was even worse!) with Germany *to extend extradition to Austria in November, 1939.*"
[90] Oppenheim-Lauterpacht, *op. cit.*, p. 399.
[91] *Ibid.*, n. 1.
[92] v. Gude, "Land Oberösterreich," *Annual Digest*, (1940), Case No. 34, 109 F. (2d) 635. Italics supplied at appropriate points in this paragraph in quoted material.
[93] *General Theory of Law and State*, (as cited in n. 4, above) pp. 224–225.
[94] Italics mine.
[95] Italics mine.
[96] Guggenheim, *op. cit.* (n. 12, above), p. 192.
[97] "The international legal status of Germany to be established immediately upon termination of the war," *American Journal of International Law*, XXXVIII (1944), 689 ff.
[98] Italics mine.
[99] Adamovich gives the text of the Second Control Agreement; *op. cit.*, (n. 5, above) pp. 42 ff.
[100] In smaller articles:
(a) For the occupation theory:
Tončič, "Die völkerrechtliche Stellung Österreichs und ihre politischen Folgen," *Salzburger Volkszeitung*, June, 1949 (published also in *Die Abwehr*, 1950), and "Die falsche Annexions theorie," *Österreichische Monatshefte*, 1950, pp. 232–237; Plochl,

"Okkupation, Annexion und Konkordat," *Die österreichische Furche,* 1950, no. 14; and Gschnitzer, "War der Anschluss, Annexion oder Okkupation? Gilt das Konkordat?" *Der Volksbote,* March 19, 1950.

(b) For the annexation theory:

Kleinwaechter, "Ist Österreich für den Krieg verantwortlich?", *Die Presse,* February 8, 1947; Brandweiner, "Österreichs völkerrechtliches Schicksal," *Austria,* 1948, no. 4; Schärf, "Gilt das Konkordat? War der Anschluss Annexion oder Okkupation?" *Die Zukunft,* 1950, pp. 34–37, and "Gilt das Konkordat? Ein Nachwort zur Debatte," *ibid.,* 1950, pp. 177–125.

[101] *Die internationale Stellung Österreichs, 1938–47* (Vienna: Manz, 1947).

[102] *Ibid.,* p. 9; cf., also, p. 8.

[103] "Gilt das Konkordat? War der Anschluss Annexion oder Okkupation?" pp. 195–321.

[104] Verdoss, *op. cit.* p. 126

[105] Oppenheim-Lauterpacht, *op. cit., pp.* 136–137 and pp. 524–525.

[106] "Das Österreich vom 13. März 1938 und vom 27, April 1945—eine Untersuchung über das Problem Kontinuität oder Diskontinuität der österreichischen Rechtsordnung," *Juristische Blätter* (1946), pp. 2–7, and "Das Wiedererstehen Österreichs als Rechtsproblem—ein staatsrechtlicher Rückblick," *ibid.,* pp. 85–93 and 103–108.

[107] Cf. Art. 145/B1-VG.

[108] *Reine Rechtslehre* (as cited in n. 42, above), pp. 147 ff.

[109] Josef L. Kunz, *Österreichische Zeitschrift für öffentliches Recht,* I (1948) 290.

EDVARD HAMBRO

[1] International Court of Justice, *Reports 1949,* p. 178.

[2] Hans Kelsen, *The Law of the United Nations* (London: Stevens & Sons, 1950), p. xiv.

[3] *Loc. cit.*

[4] UNCIO, Doc. 933, IV/2/42 (2), vol. xiii, p. 709.

[5] Kelsen, *op. cit.,* p. xv.

[6] International Court of Justice, *op. cit.,* p. 175.

[7] *Ibid.,* p. 177.

[8] *Ibid.,* p. 179.

[9] *Ibid.,* p. 180.

[10] *Ibid.,* p. 182.

[11] *Ibid.,* p. 184.

[12] *Ibid.,* p. 185.

[13] Kelsen, *op. cit.,* p. xv.

ALWYN V. FREEMAN

[1] *Handbook, First Meeting of the Inter-American Council of Jurists, Rio de Janeiro, May 22, 1950* (Washington, D.C.: Pan American Union, 1950), pp. 143–144.

[2] *Final Act of the First Meeting of the Inter-American Council of Jurists, Rio de Janeiro, May 22–June 15, 1950* (Washington, D.C.: Pan American Union, 1950), pp. 25–26. See also the *Report of the Executive Secretary of the Inter-American Council of Jurists* (Washington, D.C.: Pan American Union, 1950), pp. 12–17.

[3] See p. 268 ff., below.

[4] See M. M. Ball, *The Problem of Inter-American Organization* (Stanford: Stanford University Press, 1944), p. 22.

[5] *The International Conferences of American States,* ed. by J. B. Scott, Carnegie Endowment Series (New York: Oxford University Press, 1931), p. 36.

[6] *Ibid.*, p. 92.
[7] *Ibid.*, pp. 124–125.
[8] *Ibid.*, p. 268.
[9] *Ibid.*, pp. 173–174.
[10] *Ibid.*, p. 178, Art. IV.
[11] *Ibid.*, p. 270, Art. V.
[12] *Report of the Delegates of the United States of America to the Fifth International Conference of American States held at Santiago, Chile, March 25–May 3, 1923* (Washington, D.C.: Government Printing Office, 1924), pp. 3 ff.
[13] Final Act of the Santiago Conference, No. 43. See also *The International Conferences . . . , op. cit.*, pp. 267–268.
[14] J. M. Yepes et Pereira da Silva, *Commentaire théorique et pratique du pacte de la Société des Nations et des statuts de l'Union Pan Americaine* (Paris: A. Pedone, 1934–1939), I, 46.
[15] Italics mine.
[16] *The International Conference . . . , op. cit.*, pp. 400–401. See also *Report of the Delegates of the United States of America to the Sixth International Conference of American States, held at Habana, Cuba, January 16–February 20, 1928* (Washington, D.C.: Government Printing Office, 1928), pp. 234–235.
[17] "Political functions" could embrace almost every effort of collaboration among the American nations—"any action whereby a joint policy is determined." On the other hand, this might just as well refer to the settlement of disputes between them, although it seems clear that the phrase is used in a much broader sense. A typical conception is formulated by Ricardo J. Alfaro, in his *Commentary on Pan American Problems* (Cambridge: Harvard University Press, 1938), p. 5, where he defines "political problems" as those which concern "the juridical equality, the territorial integrity, the national independence, the international obligations, and the rights of the American states." Included therein are likewise "the codification of international law, the organization of an American League of Nations, the creation of an Inter-American Court of Justice, and all such kindred questions as the pacific settlement of international conflicts, the definition of the aggressor, the exercise of neutrality, and the maintenance of peace in the continent." Few really important issues would escape even this attempt to define the indefinable.
[18] See *Report of the Delegates . . . to the Sixth Conference* (as cited in n. 16, above), Appendix 17, p. 239.
[19] See "Convention on Rights and Duties of States" (1933), Art. 8 in *The International Conferences of American States, First Supplement 1933–1940* (Washington: Carnegie Endowment, 1940), p. 122; see also "Additional Protocol relative to Non-Intervention" signed at the Buenos Aires Conference for the Maintenance of Peace (1936), *ibid.*, p. 191. This protocol was ratified by the United States which refused to accept any such obligation as late as the Habana conference. Cf. the address of the Hon. Charles E. Hughes to the delegates, printed in *Report of the Delegates . . . to the Sixth Conference, op. cit.*, pp. 14–15.
[20] *Final Act*, p. 27. See also *The International Conferences . . . , First Supplement, op. cit.*, p. 81.
[21] The instruments are collected in *The International Conferences . . . , First Supplement, op. cit.*, pp. 141 ff.
[22] *Ibid.*, p. 181.
[23] Resolution X of the conference, *The International Conferences . . . , First Supplement, op. cit.*, p. 147. See also *Report of the United States Delegation to the Eighth International Conference of American States,* Lima, Peru, December 9–27, 1938 (Department of State Publication 1624, Conference Series No. 50, 1941), p. 185.
[24] Resolution XIV of the conference, *The International Conferences . . . , First Supplement, op. cit.*, p. 243; *Report of the United States Delegation to the Eighth International Conference, op. cit.*, p. 185.

[25] *Diario de la IX Conferencia Internacional Americana,* April 1, 1948 (Bogotá: Ministerio de Relationes Exteriores, 1948), p. 80.

[26] Resolutions were adopted directing the governing board to broaden its economic activities in accordance with prior conference action (Resolution VI); referring certain projects on the consolidation of peace to the Pan American Union for classification and transmittal to the American governments (XV); entrusting the Union with the study of an organic statute for the Inter-American Commission of Women (XXIII); approving certain rules adopted by the governing board relative to deposit of ratifications of multilateral treaties (XXIV); directing the Pan American Union to proceed with a comparative study of legislation existing in the American republics on the preservation of historic sites (XXXVII); to prepare a draft convention on literary and artistic copyright for presentation to and signature by the American republics (XXXIX); and charging the governing board with the promotion of scientific social welfare programs (LXXXIII) as well as with initiating consultations with members of the union toward convening a Congress of Criminology and Penology (LXXXIV).

To these ends, Resolution CV recommended to the governing board that it decide upon the administrative organization that would best enable it to discharge its functions and propose to the governments the increase in appropriations necessary to maintain the services rendered. *The International Conferences . . . , First Supplement, op. cit.,* pp. 304–305. The other resolutions referred to are found on pp. 235–291, *passim,* and in the appendix to *Report of the United States Delegation to the Eighth International Conference . . . , op. cit.* See also *Report on the Results of the Eighth Conference,* Pan American Union Pub. No. 27, pp. 37 ff.

[27] Pan American Union Congress and Conference Series No. 47 (Washington, D.C.: 1946), p. 34.

[28] It was thought that special representatives would be in a position to exercise greater freedom of action in questions arising before the board.

[29] Par. 9. On the Mexico City conference generally, see *Report of the Delegation of the United States of America to the Inter-American Conference on Problems of War and Peace, Mexico City, Mexico, February 21–March 6, 1945* (Department of State Publication 2497, Conference Series No. 85, 1946).

[30] See *Report of the Secretary of State on the Second Meeting of Ministers of Foreign Affairs* (Department of State Publication 1575, Conference Series No. 48, 1941), p. 22. See also *The International Conferences . . . , First Supplement, op. cit.,* p. 362.

[31] *Report of the Inter-American Conference on Problems of War and Peace,* Pan American Union Congress and Conference Series No. 47 (Washington, D.C.: 1946), p. 30.

[32] See Report of the Delegation of the United States of America, *Inter-American Conference for the Maintenance of Continental Peace and Security,* Quitandinha, Brazil, August 15–September 2, 1947 (Department of State Publication 3016, International Organization and Conference Series II, 1948), p. 183.

[33] *Ibid.,* Art. 4, p. 122.

[34] *Diário das Sessões, Conferencia Interamericana para a mantenuçao da paz e da segurança no continente,* 23 agosto 1947 (Rio de Janeiro: Relacões Exteriores, 1947), p. 110, henceforth referred to as *Diário das Sessões.*

[35] *Ibid.,* 26 agosto 1947, p. 93.

[36] *Ibid.,* p. 92.

[37] Report of the Delegation . . . (as cited in n. 32), p. 101.

[38] *Diário das Sessões,* 28 agosto 1947, p. 118.

[39] *Loc. cit.*

[40] *Loc. cit.*

[41] *Diário das Sessões,* 28 agosto 1947, p. 118.

[42] *Ibid.,* 29 agosto 1947, p. 168.

[43] *Ibid.,* 1 setembro 1947, p. 168.

[44] *Ibid.,* 28 agosto 1947, p. 119.

[45] *Loc. cit.*

[46] *Ibid.*, 29 agosto 1947, p. 130.

[47] *Ibid.*, 28 agosto 1947, pp. 118–119.

[48] *Ibid.*, 29 agosto 1947, p. 131.

[49] *Ibid.*, 1 setembro 1947, p. 169.

[50] Remarks of Sr. Fusco, the Uruguayan delegate, which were inserted in the record of the Third Committee as the interpretation generally accepted by members of the committee. *Diário das Sessões*, 29 agosto 1947, p. 140.

[51] *Ibid.*, 1 setembro 1947, p. 169.

[52] See T. P. Conwell-Evans, *The League Council in Action* (London: Humphrey Milford, 1929), p. 13; A. N. Mandelstam, "La Conciliation Internationale," Académie de La Haye, *Recueil des Cours*, 14/IV (1926), 361; and, generally, C. E. Rousseau, *La Compétence de la Société des Nations* (Paris: A. Pedone, 1927), chap. 1.

[53] *Diário das Sessões*, 1 setembro 1947, p. 169.

[54] Report of the Delegation of the United States of America, *Ninth International Conference of American States*, Bogotá, Colombia, March 30–May 2, 1948 (Department of State Publication 3263, International Organization and Conference Series II, 1948), p. 11.

[55] *Diário de la IX Conferencia International Americana*, Anexo I (Bogotá: Ministerio de Relaciones Exteriores, 1948), p. 285.

[56] *Ibid.*, p. 284.

[57] *Loc. cit.* The Venezuelan position is set forth in Document CB–255–C. C. II–Sub. A–6.

[58] *Diário de la IX Conferencia . . .*, p. 296.

[59] *Ibid.*, p. 304.

[60] *Ibid.*, p. 296.

[61] *Ibid.*, p. 299.

[62] The divergent attitudes which exist within the Council itself on the general scope of its political competence are portrayed in two memoranda submitted by the Mexican and United States representatives on the occasion of the diplomatic-asylum issue to which reference has been made above. The Mexican document, which is a tightly reasoned clarification of the compromise proposal made by the Mexican government at Bogotá, seeks a formalistic solution of an extremely complex problem. In the United States memorandum, the position taken is that "it is undesirable if not impossible for the Council to draw up rigid rules regarding its competence over subjects of a certain type, since each case must be considered in the light of the circumstances under which it is presented to the Council." *Handbook, First Meeting of the Inter-American Council of Jurists* (as cited in n. 1, above), pp. 145, 150.

[63] *Davidson v. New Orleans* (1878), 96 U.S. 97.

[64] Extraordinary session of the Council, April 8, 1950; Council. Doc C–a–54/50, p. 724.

[65] The Costa Rican note of December 11, 1948, which brought the matter before the Council, asked for immediate convocation of the provisional organ of consultation under Art. 6 of the Rio treaty. Council Doc. OPC–d–1, p. 2.

[66] Council Doc. C–a–12/48, p. 394.

[67] Council Doc. C–a–11/48, p. 374.

[68] Council Doc. C–d–13/49.

[69] Resolution of December 12, 1948, Council Doc. C–a–12/48, p. 474.

[70] Council Doc. C–a–44/50, p. 87. This, it was charged, was an aggression of a "moral order." For a discusion of this case see Fenwick in XLIII *American Journal of International Law* (1949), and the *Inter-American Juridical Yearbook* (Washington: Pan American Union, 1948), p. 149.

[71] See Council Doc. C–a–12/48, pp. 437, 463, 467–469; also Doc. OPC–a–8/49, pp. 122, 134, 155.

[72] Council Doc. C–1–12–48, pp. 456, 458, 462.

[73] Council Doc. OPC–a–2/48, pp. 20, 23, 28.

[74] See Council Doc. OPC–d–1/49, p. 71, and Doc. C–a–11/48, pp. 366, 376. Costa Rica contended that once the Council had been notified by its communication that the situation contemplated by Art. 6 had arisen, it was the imperative obligation of the Council to convoke the meeting of consultation; but that the Council could not indulge in debate on the propriety or impropriety of the consultation C–a–12/48, pp. 394–395.

[75] Council Doc. OPC–a–9/49, pp. 222, 225.

[76] See the report of the secretary-general, Alberto Lleras, to the Council of the OAS, of November 13, 1948. *Annals of the Organization of American States,* I, 35.

[77] *Documents of the United Nations Conference on International Organization,* XIII, 709. This elementary principle was rejected, however, by the Inter-American Juridical Committee in a confused opinion on the competence of the Council prepared in May, 1950. *Amplitud de las Facultades del Consejo* (Washington, D.C.: Pan American Union, 1950), pp. 5—10, *passim;* and cf, generally, the report of the executive secretary of the Inter-American Council of Jurists on its first meeting (Washington, D.C.: Pan American Union, 1950), pp. 12–17.

[78] See the report of the committee on the competence of the Council, approved by the Council on April 21, 1949, Doc. C–l–25; *Handbook, First Meeting of the Inter-American Council of Jurists* (as cited in n. 1, above), p. 142.

JOSEF L. KUNZ

[1] The only study in English is, up to now: Joyce A. C. Gutteridge, "The Geneva Conventions of 1949," *British Year Book of International Law* (London: Oxford University Press, 1949), pp. 294–326. For literature in other languages see in general. Fred Siordet, "La Conférence Diplomatique de Genève," *Revue Internationale de la Croix Rouge* (hereafter cited: *R. I. Cr. R.),* XXXI (1949), 475–484; Maurice Bourquin, "Les Conventions de Genève du 12 Aout 1949," *R. I. Cr. R.,* XXXII (1950), 90–103; Claude Du Pasquier, "Promenade philosophique autour des Conventions de Genève de 1949," Mélanges François Guisan (special edition, 1950). The new Geneva conventions are already fully worked into the book: C. Raja Gabaglia, *Guerra e Direito International* (Sao Paulo: Saraiva, 1949) and are treated in detail by Paul Guggenheim, *Lehrbuch des Völkerrechts* (Basel: Verlag für Recht und Gesellschaft, 1951), II, 902–922.

[2] The proceedings of the Geneva Diplomatic Conference of 1949, which are being prepared by the Swiss government, have not yet been published. The same is true of the 1950 lectures at The Hague Academy of International Law by Jean S. Pictet, *La Croix Rouge et les Conventions de Genève.*

I want to express my obligation to the International Committee of the Red Cross, Geneva, for the receipt of the French text of the conventions, a list in French of the reservations, and the mimeographed reports of the four principal committees of the 1949 conference.

[3] See Josef L. Kunz "Plus de lois de la guerre?" *Revue générale de droit international public* XLI (Paris, 1934), 22–57, "The Chaotic Status of the Laws of War and the Urgent Necessity for their Revision," *American Journal of International Law,* XLV (January, 1951), 37–61.

[4] The Xth International Red Cross Conference, 1921, recommended the prohibition of mass deportations and of the taking of hostages by the military occupant. The XIth Conference, 1923, called for a convention concerning the protection of civilians. The XIIth Conference was concerned with the protection of civilians on the territory of the enemy state. The XIVth Conference was occupied with preparatory work for the protection of the civilian population against aerial bombardment.

[5] *Actes de la Conférence Diplomatique de Genève, Juillet 1929,* 1930.

[6] Text in *Revue Générale de droit international public,* XXXV (1929), 595–601 and

in *American Journal of International Law,* XXVII (1933), Doc. pp. 43–59. See Josef L. Kunz, *Kriegsrecht und Neutralitätsrecht* (Berlin und Wien: J. Springer, 1935), pp. 73–75; Paul des Gouttes, *La Convention de Genève du 27 juillet 1929* (Geneva: Comité international de la Croix Rouge, 1930); H. Bakker, *De Conventie van Genève van 27 juli 1929* (The Hague: 1937).

[7] See Kunz, *op cit.,* pp. 69–72 with bibliography 1868–1928. See also Clemens Plassmann, *Zeitschrift für Völkerrecht,* XV (1929–1930), 410–445; Gustav Rasmussen, *Code des prisonniers de guerre* (Copenhagen: Levin & Munksgaard, 1931); André Charpentier, *La Convention de Genève du 27 juillet* (Saint-Brieuc: Imprimerie moderne, 1936).

[8] General R. Debeyre, "Localités et Zones Sanitaires en temps dc guerre," *Revue générale de droit international public,* XIII/5 (1939), 600–615.

[9] See Jules Voncken, *Le Droit des gens de la guerre* (Paris: Les Editions internationales, 1937); René Clemens, *Le Projet de Monaco* (Paris: Librairie du Recueil Sirey, 1938); Julius Beinhauer, "Monaco-Konferenz. Neugestaltung des Kriegsrechts," *Zeitschrift für Völkerrecht,* XXI/1 (1937), 115–125.

[10] See U. S. Department of State, *Bulletin,* XVI, No. 416 (June 22, 1947), 1205; XIX, No. 484 (October 10, 1948), 404; and the article by William H. McCahon, *ibid.,* XXI, No. 531 (September 5, 1949), 339–340.

[11] See the report in *R. I. Cr. R.,* XXVIII (1946), 721–757, 879–940, 976–1015, and XXIX (1947), 1–40.

[12] See the report in *R. I. Cr. R.,* XXIX (1947), 544–597.

[13] Resolutions of this conference: *R. I. Cr. R.,* XXX (1948), 747–780. Text of the draft conventions, *ibid.,* pp. 701–725, 790–842, 895–914; XXXI (1949), 141–146, 214–224.

[14] Chairman: Maurice Bourquin (Belgium); rapporteur: Claude Du Pasquier (Switzerland). *Report of the Joint Committee* CDG/Plen. XCII, (July 26, 1949), 13.

[15] Rapporteur: General R. Lefebvre (Belgium). *Report of Committee I,* CDG/Plen. XXXV (July 19, 1949), 26, 16.

[16] Chairman: Maurice Bourquin (Belgium); rapporteur: S. Sederblom (Sweden). *Report of Committee II,* CDG/plen. LXXVI (July 23, 1949), 37.

[17] Chairman: Cahen-Salvador (France); rapporteurs: Claude Du Pasquier (Switzerland), and G. V. Hart (United Kingdom). *Report of Committee III,* CDG/Plen. LXXI (July 27, 1949), 74.

[18] French text: *Les Conventions de Genève du 12 août 1949,* Geneva, 1949. English text: *The Geneva Conventions of August 12, 1949,* Geneva, 1949. See also: *Geneva Conventions of August 12, 1949, Final Act of the Diplomatic Conference of Geneva 1949,* (Department of State Publication 3938, General Foreign Policy Series 34, 1950), p. 255. The fourth convention is also reproduced in French (with an introduction by St. Tchirkevitch) in *Revue générale de droit international public,* LIV (1950), 97–158 and in German translation in *Archiv des Völkerrechts,* II/4 (1950), 446–490.

[19] These conventions will henceforth be referred to in the footnotes as *Conv. I, II, III, IV.*

[20] *Conv. I,* Art. 56; *II,* Art. 55; *III,* Art. 136; *IV,* Art. 151.

[21] Definitive list of signatory states in *R. I. Cr. R.,* XXXII (1950), 184–186.

[22] *Conv. I,* Arts. 57, 58; *II,* Arts 56, 57; *III,* Arts. 137, 138; *IV,* Arts. 152, 153.

[23] Twenty-five states made reservations at the time of signature. The ten Soviet states made practically identical reservations; on the other hand, Argentina, Canada, Holland, New Zealand, the United Kingdom, and the United States made reservations to Article 68 of the fourth convention.

[24] See his speech at the closing session, *R. I. Cr. R.,* XXXI (1949), 549–553.

[25] See Gustave Moynier, *La Croix Rouge, son passé, son présent, son avenir* (Paris: Sandoz & Thuillier, 1882); Max Huber, *Rotes Kreuz, Grundsätze und Probleme* (Zürich-Berlin: Atlantis-Verlag, 1941); Max Huber, "Principes d'action et fondements de l'oeuvre du Comité International de la Croix Rouge, 1939–1946," *R. I. Cr. R.,* XXIX (1947), 45–80; Jean S. Pictet, *Le Droit international et l'activité internationale de la Croix Rouge en temps de guerre* (Genève, 1943); Auguste R. Werner, *La Croix Rouge*

et les Conventions de Genève (Genève: Georg & Co., 1943); László Ledermanns, "The organization of the Red Cross," *American Journal of International Law,* XLII (1948), 635; C. Raja Gabaglia, *op. cit.;* Jean S. Pictet, "Les Nouvelles Conventions de Genève et la Croix Rouge," *R. I. Cr. R.*, XXXI (1949), 655–670; Alfred Verdross, *Völkerrecht* (Berlin und Wien: J. Springer, 1950), p. 100. Guggenheim, *op. cit.* n. 1, above), I, 261–262; II, 804–809.

[26] *Conv. I,* Arts. 38–44; *II,* Arts. 41–45.

[27] J. S. Pictet, "Le Signe de la Croix Rouge," *R. I. Cr. R.*, XXXI (1949), 167–201. The exceptions of the "Red Lion" for Persia and of the "Red Crescent" for Turkey were reaffirmed in 1949. But Israel's wish to use a "Red David Star" was rejected. It is interesting to note that Israel made a reservation to the effect that she will respect in others the distinctive emblem, but will use for herself the "Red David Star." Lebanon, at the time of signature, made a declaration to the effect that Israel's reservation, adopting a sign definitively rejected by the conference, has no value vis-à-vis the signatory states. Even in these things, we see not only nationalism, but a tendency away from the symbol of the red cross; many proposals were made in 1949 to adopt a "neutral" sign, such as a red triangle.

[28] See *Conv. I,* Arts. 3, 9, 44, 83; *II,* Arts. 3, 9; *III,* Arts. 3, 9, 123, 124, 125; *IV,* Arts. 3, 10, 140, 142, 143.

[29] Henri Courier, "Les Eléments essentiels du respect de la personne humaine dans la Convention IV du 12 août 1949," *R. I. Cr. R.*, XXXII (1950), 354–369.

[30] Jean S. Pictet, "La Défense de la personne humaine dans le droit futur," *R. I. Cr. R.*, XXIX (1947), 104–126.

[31] *Conv. I,* Arts. 6, 7; *II,* Arts. 6, 7; *III,* Arts. 6, 7; *IV,* Arts. 7, 8.

[32] René J. Wilhelm, "Le Caractère des droit accordés à l'individu dans les Conventions de Genève," *R. I. Cr. R.*, XXXII (1950), 556–590.

[33] *Conv. I,* Arts. 55–64; *II,* Arts. 54–63; *III,* Arts. 133–143; *IV,* Arts. 150–159.

[34] *Conv. I,* Arts. 45–48; *II,* Arts 46–49; *III,* Arts. 126–128; *IV,* Arts. 142–145.

[35] *Conv. I,* Arts. 49–54; *II,* Arts. 50–53; *III,* Arts. 129–132; *IV,* Arts. 146–149.

[36] *Report of the Joint Committee,* p. 11.

[37] P. 13.

[38] The first eleven articles of each convention.

[39] See A. Jauner, *La Puissance protectrice en droit international* (1948). Guggenheim, *op. cit.* (n. 1, above), II, 801–804, 808–809. In World War II Switzerland was sometimes the protecting power for thirty-five states. The institution of the protecting power appeared first in the Geneva Prisoners of War Convention of 1929.

[40] Norms foreseeing special agreements: *Conv. I,* Arts. 3, 6, 9, 10, 15, 23, 28, 31, 36, 37, 52; *II,* Arts. 3, 9, 10, 18, 31, 38, 39, 40, 43, 53; *III,* Arts. 3, 6, 9, 10, 23, 28, 33, 60, 65, 67, 72, 73, 75, 110, 118, 119, 122, 132; *IV, Arts.* 3, 7, 11, 14, 15, 17, 36, 108, 109, 132, 133, 149.

[41] Art. 6 of the first three conventions, Art. 7 of *Conv. IV.*

[42] See Maurice Bourquin, "La Croix Rouge et la protection conventionnelle des civils en temps de guerre," *R. I. Cr. R.*, XXIX (1947), 886–896; Claude Du Pasquier, "Observations générales sur l'elaboration de la Convention relative à la protection des civils à la Conférence Diplomatique de Genève," *R. I. Cr. R.*, XXXI (1949), 631–640.

[43] Text in William M. Malloy, *Treaties* (Washington, 1910), II 1903–1906.

[44] *Ibid.*, pp. 2183–2205.

[45] On the reform of the 1929 conventions see: Helmut Strebel, "Die Anwendung des Art. 30 der Genfer Konvention vom 27, August 1929," *Zeitschrift für ausländisches öffentliches und Völkerrecht,* IX (1939), 411 ff; Åke W. H. Hammarskjöld, "Reforme eventuelle de l'art. 30 de la Convention de Genève de 1929," *ibid.*, VII (1937), 265–294.

[46] Malloy, *op. cit.*, II, 2326–2340. On the reform of this convention sec: Herman Mosler, *Zeitschrift für ausländisches öffentliches Recht und Völkerrecht,* VIII (1938), 282 ff; J. C. Mossop, *British Year Book of International Law* (London: Oxford Univer-

sity Press, 1947), pp. 398–406; Raoul Genet, *Revue Internationale Française du Droit des Gens,* XVIII (1949), 30–34.

[47] On the reform of the 1929 convention see: F. Schuster, *Zur Reform des Kriegsgefangenenrechts* (Würzburg: 1929); Radu Meitani, "Le Régime des prisonniers de guerre," *Revue Internationale Française du Droit des Gens,* VIII (1939), 26–56; Will. E. S. Flory, *Prisoners of War* (Washington: American Council on Public Affairs, 1942); Franz J. Scheidl, *Die Kriegsgefangenschaft* (Berlin: E. Ebering, 1943); R. M. Cramer-Frick, *Le Comité International de la Croix Rouge et les Conventions Internationales pour les prisonniers de guerre et les civils* (1943); M. Tollelsen, "Enemy Prisoners of War," *Iowa Law Review,* XXXII/1, 51–71; Georg Wyss, *Die Rechtsstellung der entwichenen Kriegsgefangenen im neutralen Staat* (Berne: P. Haupt, 1945); Ernst H. Feilchenfeld, *Prisoners of War* (Washington: 1948).

[48] "It is obvious that every wounded, sick or ship-wrecked person, whether a neutral . . . or a national of a belligerent country, is entitled to protection under international law and by virtue of certain humanitarian agreements" *(Report of Committee I,* p. 6).

[49] *Report of Committee I,* pp. 14–15.

[50] *Conv. I,* Art. 27.

[51] *Conv. I,* Art. 32.

[52] *Conv. I,* Art. 43.

[53] *Conv. II,* Art. 15.

[54] *Conv. II,* Art. 17.

[55] *Conv. II,* Art. 21.

[56] *Conv. II,* Art. 25.

[57] *Conv. II,* Art. 32.

[58] *Conv. II,* Art. 38.

[59] *Conv. I,* Art. 37; *Conv. II,* Art. 40.

[60] See Josef L. Kunz, "Neutrality and the European War 1939–1940," *Michigan Law Review,* XXXIX (March, 1941), 719–754.

[61] *Report of Committee II,* pp. 27–28.

[62] *Report of Committee II,* pp. 29–30.

[63] *Report of Committee III,* p. 73.

[64] *Report of Committee I,* Part III, p. 4.

[65] *Ibid.,* p. 13.

[66] *Report of Committee III,* p. 23.

[67] *Ibid.,* p. 24.

[68] *Report of Committee III,* p. 39.

[69] *Conv. I,* Art. 23, Annex I; *Conv. IV,* Arts. 14, 15, Annex I.

[70] See *Report of Committee I,* pp. 7–12, 28–32.

[71] *Conv. I,* Art. 28. See Jean S. Pictet, "La Rétention du personnel sanitaire des armées tombé au pouvoir de la partie adverse," *R. I. Cr. R.,* XXXI (1949), 869–884, 937–976.

[72] *Conv. I,* Art. 29.

[73] *Conv. I,* Art. 32.

[74] *Conv. II,* Art. 36.

[75] *Conv. I,* Art. 33.

[76] *Conv. I,* Art. 35.

[77] *Conv. II,* Art. 38.

[78] No customary or treaty norm existed, forbidding the internment of civilian persons, although the state practice of the nineteenth century shows no case of the older practice of the internment of civilian persons. But this practice of internment was resorted to in World War I and since. See Kunz, *Kriegsrecht und Neutralitätsrecht* (as cited in n. 6, above), pp. 46–48.

[79] Art. 3 of all four conventions. *Conv. I,* Art. 12; *Conv. II,* Art. 12; *Conv. III,* Art. 16; *Conv. IV,* Arts. 13, 27.

[80] *Conv. I,* Art. 12; *Conv. II,* Art. 12; *Conv. III,* Arts. 13, 17, 89; *Conv. IV,* Arts. 32, 100.
[81] *Report of Committee I,* p. 5.
[82] *Conv. IV,* Art. 16.
[83] *Conv. IV,* Art. 24.
[84] *Conv. III,* Art. 12; *Conv. IV,* Art. 29.
[85] *Conv. III,* Art. 12; *Conv. IV,* Art. 45.
[86] *Conv. I,* Art. 12; *Conv. II,* Art. 12; *Conv. III,* Art. 14.
[87] *Conv. III,* Arts. 72, 73; *Conv. IV,* Arts. 108–110.
[88] *Conv. I,* Art. 36; *Conv. II,* Art. 39; *Conv. IV,* Art. 22.
[89] *Conv. I,* Arts. 42, 43; *Conv. II,* Art. 43; *Conv. III,* Art. 23; *Conv. IV,* Art. 83.
[90] *Conv. II,* Art. 12.
[91] *Conv. I,* Art. 19.
[92] *Conv. II,* Art. 34.
[93] See *Report of Committee I,* pp. 23–24.
[94] *Conv. I,* Art. 22; *Conv. II,* Art. 35.
[95] *Conv. IV,* Arts. 18, 19.
[96] *Report of Committee III,* p. 10.
[97] *Conv. I,* Arts. 15–17; *Conv. II,* Arts. 18–20.
[98] *Conv. II,* Art. 22.
[99] *Conv. II,* Art. 27.
[100] *Conv. II,* Art. 29.
[101] *Conv. II,* Art. 33.
[102] On the law of belligerent occupation see: Kunz, *op cit.* (n. 6, above), pp. 88–103; Guggenheim, *op cit.* (n. 1, above), II, 922–952; L. F. L. Oppenheim, ed. by H. Lauterpacht *International Law* (6th ed.; London: Longmans, Green, 1940); II, 336–350; and literature quoted in these works.
[103] See now the detailed study by Oscar Muhler, *Der völkerrechtliche Schutz der Bevölkerung eines besetzten Gebietes gegen Massnahmen der Okkupationsmacht* (Zürich: 1950).
[104] *Report of Committee I,* Part III, p. 5.
[105] Kunz, *op cit.*, p. 82; Oppenheim-Lauterpacht, *op. cit.*, p. 326.
[106] *Report of Committee III,* p. 17.
[107] *Convention III,* Arts. 91–94.
[108] *Report of Committee I,* p. 29.
[109] This construction has been given for the first time in Kunz, *op. cit.*, pp. 68–69, 72.
[110] *Conv. I,* Art. 46; *Conv. II,* Art. 47; *Conv. III,* Art. 13; *Conv. IV,* Art. 33.
[111] "Unfortunately, the terrible events of the years 1940–1945 have compelled Committee I to take account of hard, deplorable facts" *(Report of Committee I,* p. 35).
[112] *Conv. II,* Art. 26; *Report of Committee I,* Part III, p. 7.
[113] See Kunz, *op. cit.*, pp. 95–96 and the literature quoted.
[114] See John H. E. Fried, "Transfer of Civilian Manpower from Occupied Territory," *American Journal of International Law,* XLVI (April 1946), 303–331.
[115] Gutteridge, *op cit.* (n. 1, above), p. 325.
[116] Max Rheinstein is correct, when he states that "the importation of food by the Occupying Powers into Germany is not simply an act of charity or generosity, but the fulfillment of an international duty." "The legal status of Occupied Germany," *Michigan Law Review,* XLVII (November 1948), 23–40.
[117] *Conv. IV,* Art. 34.
[118] Guggenheim, *op. cit.* (n. 1, above), II, 822–833.
[119] For a correct legal analysis see Kunz, *op. cit.*, pp. 77–79 and Oppenheim-Lauterpacht, *op. cit., II,* 459–461.
[120] See Arthur K. Kuhn, "The Execution of Hostages," *American Journal of International Law,* XXXVI (1942), 271–274; Ellen Hammer and Marina Salvin, "The Taking of Hostages in Theory and Practice," *ibid.*, XXXVIII (1944), 20–33; Aleksender C. Melen, "La Question des otages à la lumière du droit," *Revue de Droit International*

Public (January-March 1946); Van Nispetnot Sevenaer, *La Prise d'otages* (The Hague: 1949). Lord Wright, *British Year Book of International Law* (London: Oxford University Press, 1948), p. 296.

[121] In the same sense also the Australian, Dutch, Chinese war crimes laws and the French war crimes ordinance of August 28, 1944.

[122] *U. S. v. Wilhelm List et al.*, in United Nations War Crimes Commission, *Law Reports of Trials of War Criminals* (London: H. M. Stationery Office, 1949), VIII, 34–92.

[123] *Ibid.*, VIII, 12, 83, 85.

[124] Claude Pilloud, "La Question des otages et les Conventions de Genève," *R. I. Cr. R.*, XXXII (1950), 430–447, at 444: "Il n'est pas possible d'affirmer que le droit international prohibe totalement la prise et la mise à mort d'otages."

[125] Close of hostilities means "when the last shot has been fired." *Report of Committee II*, p. 8.

[126] See Helmut Strebel, "Die Genfer Abkommen vom 12. August 1949. Fragen des Anwendungsbereiches," *Zeitschrift für ausländisches öffentliches Recht und Völkerrecht*, XIII (February, 1950), 118–145.

[127] *Report of Joint Committee*, pp. 2–4.

[128] See Fred. Siordet, "Les Conventions de Genève et la guerre civile," *R. I. Cr. R.*, XXXII (1950), 104–122, 187–212.

[129] *Report of Committee III*, pp. 4–7.

[130] *Conv. IV*, Art. 4, par. 3.

[131] *Conv. IV*, Art. 13.

[132] *Report of Committee III*, p. 10.

[133] *Report of Committee III*, p. 5.

[134] *Report of Committee II*, p. 9.

[135] *Report of Committee II*, p. 8.

[136] *Ibid.*, pp. 7–9.

[137] J. P. Trainin, "Questions of Guerilla Warfare in the Law of War," *American Journal of International Law*, XL (July 1946), 534–562.

[138] Gutteridge, *op. cit.* (n. 1, above), p. 313.

[139] Guggenheim, *op. cit.* (n. 1, above), II, 790–792.

[140] Kunz, *op. cit.* (n. 6, above), pp. 65, 66.

[141] *Ibid.*, p. 96.

[142] Oppenheim-Lauterpacht, *op. cit.* (n. 102, above), II, 205.

[143] See Lester Nurick and Roger W. Barbett, "Legality of Guerilla Forces under the Laws of War," *American Journal of International Law*, XL (July 1946), 563–583. To the historical examples given should be added the Belgian franc-tireur war during World War I; see R. P. Oszwall, *Der Streit um den belgischen Franctireurkrieg* (1931).

[144] "Le Franc-tireur capturé a-t-il droit à un jugement régulier?" *Revue Internationale Française du Droit des Gens*, XVII (January-June 1948), 50–20.

[145] Strebel, *op. cit.* (n. 126, above).

[146] Oppenheim-Lauterpacht, *op. cit.*, II, 456.

www.ingramcontent.com/pod-product-compliance
Ingram Content Group UK Ltd.
Pitfield, Milton Keynes, MK11 3LW, UK
UKHW040234290926
15471UKWH00002B/183

9 780520 349551